BEYOND POSTHUMANISM

SPEKTRUM: Publications of the German Studies Association
Series editor: David M. Luebke, University of Oregon

Published under the auspices of the German Studies Association, *Spektrum* offers current perspectives on culture, society, and political life in the German-speaking lands of central Europe—Austria, Switzerland, and the Federal Republic—from the late Middle Ages to the present day. Its titles and themes reflect the composition of the GSA and the work of its members within and across the disciplines to which they belong—literary criticism, history, cultural studies, political science, and anthropology.

Recent volumes:

Volume 22
Beyond Posthumanism
The German Humanist Tradition and the Future of the Humanities
Alexander Mathäs

Volume 21
Feelings Materialized
Emotions, Bodies, and Things in Germany, 1500–1950
Edited by Derek Hillard, Heikki Lempa, and Russell Spinney

Volume 20
Names and Naming in Early Modern Germany
Edited by Marjorie Elizabeth Plummer and Joel F. Harrington

Volume 19
Views of Violence
Representing the Second World War in German and European Museums and Memorials
Edited by Jörg Echternkamp and Stephan Jaeger

Volume 18
Dreams of Germany
Musical Imaginaries from the Concert Hall to the Dance Floor
Edited by Neil Gregor and Thomas Irvine

Volume 17
Money in the German-Speaking Lands
Edited by Mary Lindemann and Jared Poley

Volume 16
Archeologies of Confession
Writing the German Reformation, 1517–2017
Edited by Carina L. Johnson, David M. Luebke, Marjorie Elizabeth Plummer, and Jesse Spohnholz

Volume 15
Ruptures in the Everyday
Views of Modern Germany from the Ground
Andrew Stuart Bergerson, Leonard Schmieding, et al.

Volume 14
Reluctant Skeptic
Siegfried Kracauer and the Crises of Weimar Culture
Harry T. Craver

Volume 13
Migrations in the German Lands, 1500–2000
Edited by Jason Coy, Jared Poley, and Alexander Schunka

For a full volume listing, please see the series page on our website:
http://berghahnbooks.com/series/spektrum

Beyond Posthumanism

The German Humanist Tradition and the Future of the Humanities

ALEXANDER MATHÄS

First published in 2020 by
Berghahn Books
www.berghahnbooks.com

© 2020, 2025 Alexander Mathäs
First paperback edition published in 2025

All rights reserved. Except for the quotation of short passages
for the purposes of criticism and review, no part of this book
may be reproduced in any form or by any means, electronic or
mechanical, including photocopying, recording, or any information
storage and retrieval system now known or to be invented,
without written permission of the publisher.

Library of Congress Cataloging-in-Publication Data

A C.I.P. cataloging record is available from the Library of Congress
Library of Congress Cataloging in Publication Control Number: 2019043816

British Library Cataloguing in Publication Data

A catalogue record for this book is available from the British Library

EU GPSR Authorized Representative

LOGOS EUROPE, 9 rue Nicolas Poussin, 17000, LA ROCHELLE, France
Email: Contact@logoseurope.eu

ISBN 978-1-78920-563-3 hardback
ISBN 978-1-83695-074-5 paperback
ISBN 978-1-83695-209-1 epub
ISBN 978-1-78920-564-0 web pdf

https://doi.org/10.3167/9781789205633

∼: CONTENTS :∼

List of Illustrations	vii
Acknowledgments	viii
List of Abbreviations	ix
Introduction	1
Chapter 1. Signs and Wonders: The Humanist Pedagogy of Eighteenth-Century Universal Histories of Mankind	37
Chapter 2. Religion, Anthropology, and the Mission of Literature in Schiller's *Universalgeschichte*	55
Chapter 3. The Sublime as an Objectivist Strategy	79
Chapter 4. The Importance of Herder's Humanism and the Posthumanist Challenge	93
Chapter 5. Humanist Antinomies: Goethe's *Iphigenie auf Tauris* and *Torquato Tasso*	119
Chapter 6. Incorporating Change: The Role of Science in Goethe's and Carl Gustav Carus's Humanist Aesthetics	138
Chapter 7. Karl Marx's and Ludwig Feuerbach's Materialism in Gottfried Keller's "Kleider Machen Leute"	164
Chapter 8. The End of Pathos and of Humanist Illusions: Schiller and Schnitzler	180
Chapter 9. Blurring the Human/Animal Boundary: Hofmannsthal's *Andreas*	197

Chapter 10. Humanism and Ideology: Thomas Mann's Writings
(1914–30) 216

Chapter 11. Between Humanism and Posthumanism:
Hermann Hesse's *Steppenwolf* 238

Conclusion 261

Works Cited 268

Index 290

~: ILLUSTRATIONS :~

Figure 2.1. Peter Anton von Verschaffelt (1710–93), *Statue des Moses von Michelangelo* (after 1737). 65

Figure 3.1. Caspar David Friedrich (1774–1840), *Wanderer above the Sea of Fog* (1817). 85

Figure 5.1. Scene from *Iphigenie auf Tauris* (1802 version première in Weimar), with Goethe as Orestes in the center (ACT III, Scene 3). Drawing by Angelica Kauffman (1741–1807). 125

Figure 5.2. Carl Ferdinand Sohn (1805–67), *Torquato Tasso and the Two Leonores*. 132

Figure 6.1. Image of the *Urpflanze* (archetypal plant) (1837). Woodcut by Pierre Jean François Turpin according to Goethe's imagination. 149

Figure 6.2. Carl Gustav Carus (1789–1869), *Memory of a Wooded Island in the Baltic Sea (Oak Trees by the Sea)* (1834–35). 151

Figure 6.3. Carl Gustav Carus (1789–1869), *The Goethe Monument* (1832). 152

Figure 8.1. Luise Miller from *Kabale und Liebe*. Steel engraving by Conrad Geyer (1859). 182

Figure 8.2. Gustav Klimt (1862–1918), *Schubert at the Piano* (1899). 189

Figure 9.1. Romanes's 1892 copy of Ernst Haeckel's alleged embryo drawings. 199

Figure 9.2. Ernst Haeckel (1834–1919), *Tree of Life*. 201

ACKNOWLEDGMENTS

While this book is a monograph and bears the name of a single author, it was inspired by the works of others, and it has benefitted from the advice of many colleagues and friends who all deserve to be recognized. Without these transformative influences the volume in its present form never would have seen the light of day. The process of its creation was contingent on the posthumanist assumption that, while human subjects have the freedom to create, their products are shaped by their sources of inspiration.

I am indebted to colleagues at the University of Oregon on whose work I relied in support of my arguments: Mark Johnson, Ian McNeely, Louise Westling, and Jeffrey Librett. Dorothee Ostmeier's collegial encouragement is greatly appreciated. I am particularly grateful to Paal Bjørby, who read an earlier draft of the entire manuscript and made many useful suggestions that benefitted the style, the analysis, and the overall quality of the volume. I owe my colleague Joseph Fracchia many thanks for his advice over countless hours of productive discussions as well as for his insightful editorial feedback during the process of revision. Paul Michael Lützeler's work on the state of *Germanistik* in the United States was also valuable for this study. Kudos to my excellent students for their enthusiasm and inspiring contributions to our class discussions related to the topic of this study.

The editors of the *German Quarterly*, the *Journal of Austrian Studies*, *Humanitas*, and *Konturen* deserve to be acknowledged for giving me permission to include previously published texts in this volume. I am also very much indebted to the anonymous readers and the editorial board of the *Spektrum* series whose constructive suggestions vastly benefited the manuscript. Berghahn Books, senior editor Chris Chappell, Mykelin Higham, and Elizabeth Martinez were wonderful to work with. Special thanks to series editor David Luebke, who encouraged me to submit the manuscript and shepherded it through the production process with great care. I highly esteem his professionalism and support. My lifetime membership in the American Friends of Marbach allowed me to spend several summers of uninterrupted time for writing at the Deutsches Literaturarchiv. The courteous and competent assistance of the archive's staff is also highly appreciated. And lastly I would like to thank Susan Anderson for her unflagging support, patience, wisdom, and guidance during the past ten years of writing this book.

ABBREVIATIONS

BüLM   Carl Gustav Carus. *Briefe über die Landschaftsmalerei.*

CGS   Carl Gustav Carus. *Gesammelte Schriften.* Edited by Olaf Breidbach. 10 vols. Hildesheim: Olms, 2009.

GKFA   Thomas Mann. *Große kommentierte Frankfurter Ausgabe.* Edited by Heinrich Detering et al. 23 vols. Frankfurt am Main: S. Fischer, 2002–2014.

HA   Johann Wolfgang von Goethe. *Werke: Hamburger Ausgabe.* Edited by Erich Trunz. 14 vols. Munich: dtv, 1998.

HoSW   Hugo von Hofmannsthal. *Sämtliche Werke.* Edited by Heinz Otto Burger. 40 vols. Frankfurt am Main: S. Fischer, 1975–2005.

HS   Hermann Hesse. *Steppenwolf.* Translated by Joseph Mileck and Horst Frenz. New York: Picador, 1963.

HSW   Hermann Hesse. *Sämtliche Werke.* Edited by Volker Michels. 21 vols. Frankfurt am Main: Suhrkamp, 2001–2007.

HuW   Wilhelm von Humboldt. *Werke in fünf Bänden.* Edited by Andreas Flitner and Klaus Giel. 5 vols. Darmstadt: Wiss. Buchgesellschaft, 1960.

HuGS   Wilhelm von Humboldt. *Gesammelte Schriften.* Vol. 1, edited by Königlich Preußische Akademie der Wissenschaften. Nachdruck. Berlin: DeGruyter, 1968.

HW   Johann Gottfried Herder. *Werke in zehn Bänden.* Edited by Martin Bollacher et al. 10 vols. Frankfurt am Main: Deutscher Klassiker Verlag, 1985–2000.

KSW   Gottfried Keller. *Sämtliche Werke: Historisch Kritische Ausgabe.* Edited by Walter Morgenthaler et al. 26 vols. Frankfurt am Main: Stroemfeld, 1996–2013.

KU   Immanuel Kant. *Kritik der Urteilskraft.* Edited by Gerhard Lehmann. Stuttgart: Reclam, 1963.

KW   Immanuel Kant. *Werkausgabe.* Edited by Wilhelm Weischedel. 12 vols. Frankfurt am Main: Suhrkamp, 1977.

LeuDe   Carl Gustav Carus. *Lebenserinnerungen und Denkwürdigkeiten.* 2 vols. Weimar: Kiepenheuer, 1966.

LW	Gotthold Ephraim Lessing. *Werke und Briefe in zwölf Bänden*. Edited by Wilfried Barner. 12 vols. Frankfurt am Main: Deutscher Klassiker Verlag, 1985–2003.
MEW	Marx-Engels. *Werke*. Edited by Manfred Kliem et al. 26 vols. Berlin: Dietz, 1966.
PDV	Frank Wedekind. *Prosa, Dramen, Verse*. 2 vols. Munich: Langen, 1964.
SchW	Friedrich von Schiller. *Sämtliche Werke*. Edited by Peter-André Alt et al. 5 vols. Munich: dtv, 2004.
SNA	Friedrich von Schiller. *Werke: Nationalausgabe*. Edited by Julius Petersen and Gerhard Fricke. 42 vols. Weimar: Hermann Böhlaus Nachfolger, 1943–.
SW	Wilhelm Dilthey. *Selected Works*. Vol 1, edited by Rudolf A. Makkreel and Frithjof Rodi. Princeton, NJ: Princeton UP, 1989.

Introduction

Purpose of This Study

A market-driven education has put the humanities under increasing pressure to justify their relevance.[1] Their growing marginalization in a techno-bureaucratic culture has provoked academics to persuade the public of the importance of a universal ethics at a point in time when traditional humanism—in the German context also known as *Neuhumanismus* (neo-humanism)—has come under attack for its narrow Eurocentric point of view and for excluding the voices of women, the LGBTQ community, as well as racial, religious, social, and cultural minorities. Well-known scholars have argued that the interdisciplinary broadening of literary studies to cultural studies—including visual culture, music, gender studies, postcolonial and environmental studies—has led to a fragmentation of the humanities into subdisciplines and contributed to the loss of their common mission (Steiner, Guillory, Eagleton, Nussbaum, Said).[2] These scholars suggest that a reinforcement of humanist values—that is values that coincide with those of the Enlightenment, such as the promotion of human dignity, self-perfection through education, religious and political tolerance, freedom of speech, integrity, and altruism—could provide the humanities with such a common mission and counteract the technocratization of the educational system.[3]

While the humanist model of a broad, general education still determines undergraduate curricula and the premise of academic freedom continues to be favored by the vast majority of educators, socioeconomic factors have infringed upon these principles and made them perhaps less attainable than they were in the last three decades of the twentieth century. The steadily rising cost of a university education, the prospect of future debt and unemployment have prompted significant numbers of students, parents, and even university administrators to question the importance of a liberal arts education.[4] To them, subjects of study that do not have an immediate, measurable, and practical value toward furthering a professional career have become too costly. Dwindling numbers of liberal arts majors and increasing enrollments in the professional schools, such as business and journalism, bear witness to this trend.[5]

Nevertheless, a large contingent of educators, business leaders, and students remain convinced of the importance of a broad education. The humanist objective of educating students to become well-rounded citizens, who can think independently and make informed decisions, is desirable for many constituents inside or outside of academia.[6] This volume addresses the question of whether the humanities and their humanist ideals are still viable in a technobureaucratic society that requires highly specialized knowledge. In view of the countless studies that have lamented the deplorable disinvestment in the liberal arts and emphasized their enduring significance in recent years,[7] it would be redundant to offer yet another theoretical argument for literature and the humanities as a necessary alternative to the corporatization of higher education. What is lacking is a study that shows how humanist ideas are expressed, adapted, undermined, and transformed in literary texts. This study intends to do just that. My critical readings of exemplary philosophical, aesthetic, and literary texts of different periods from the Enlightenment to the twentieth century provide insights into how social transformations and scientific innovations have affected the literary representations of individual lives and how classical eighteenth-century humanist assumptions have been challenged in response to these transformations and innovations. By discussing the ways in which these literary dramatizations and enactments of real-life situations challenge traditional humanist ideas, the study intends to show how literature has contributed to the continuing revision of the humanist discourse until it was eventually labeled *posthumanist* to distinguish it from its predecessor.

The term *posthumanism* became common during the last decade of the twentieth century to separate the traditionalist humanist reception from a more differentiated yet inclusive humanism that recognizes more recent sociopolitical developments—such as an increasingly diverse social fabric that includes the concerns of marginalized groups, gender and ethnicity issues, or scientific innovations, including artificial insemination, genetic manipulation, artificial intelligence, etc.—that challenge traditional ethical norms. The analogy to similar coinages, such as poststructuralism, postmodernism, postcolonialism, or post-Marxism, is no coincidence since all the post-isms share certain common goals, in pursuit of the overcoming of binary oppositions, based on an awareness of the politics of drawing arbitrary disciplinary, ethical, ethnic, and/or social boundaries. The various *posthumanist* positions fluctuate between continuation and radical reformation.[8] While a comprehensive attempt at defining *posthumanism* could be itself the topic of a book-length study and cannot be accomplished here,[9] I will discuss some of the most prevalent assumptions of this relatively new field.[10]

In light of the perversions of and crimes committed against humanity, despite or even in the name of humanist ethics, skepticism toward universal human values is warranted. Feminist, postcolonialist, poststructuralist, and other posthumanist approaches have rejected universalist humanism because it has neglected, if not thwarted, the emancipation of minorities by privileging an essentializing Western ethic (Said, Gilroy). Yet the fundamental values and goals that motivate these emancipation movements are not necessarily incompatible with humanist philosophy. Edward Said, for instance, points out that while humanism has been received with distrust from a postmodernist perspective because of its association with an elitist Western intellectual tradition that ignored minorities and diverging points of view "people all over the world can be and are moved" by humanist ideals in their struggles for justice and equality (Said 10):

> I believed then, and still believe, that it is possible to be critical of humanism in the name of humanism and that, schooled in its abuses by the experience of Eurocentrism and empire, one could fashion a different kind of humanism that was cosmopolitan and text-language-bound in ways that absorbed the great lessons of the past ... (10–11)

Said's call for a self-critical humanism that is aware of its past ideological assumptions could also figure under the label *posthumanism*. As the term implies, "posthumanism occurs as a critical practice *within* humanism" (Hayles, "The Human" 135). Accordingly, a posthumanist approach implies both a continuation and a critical revision of traditional humanist values.[11] While it upholds the inviolability of the rights of all human beings, it does not limit these to a privileged Western elite, but extends them to minorities and marginalized groups that have been ignored in traditional humanist thought. In other words, posthumanist critiques of traditional bourgeois values do not simply reject humanism out of hand but dislodge Idealist concepts of wholeness and replace them with a multiperspectival view of a continuously changing human consciousness. As a literary practice and critique, posthumanist approaches attempt to dismantle humanist master narratives and reveal their ideological underpinnings. For instance, they aspire to debunk the German Idealist assumption of the duality of body and mind as a fiction of the Cartesian tradition—a fiction that attempted to uphold the superiority of the spirit over the flesh. They no longer view the human subject as master of his own destiny but as a historically determined cultural construct that acknowledges larger contexts, such as evolution, technological progress, or ecology (Badmington, Haraway, Hayles, Herbrechter, Landgraf et al.).

In spite of all the criticisms of humanism's historically proven ideological corruptibility and discriminatory practices in its name, there are undeniable reasons for discussing iconic works of the German humanist tradition. Not least of the reasons is that it is impossible to completely evade the grasp of the long-lasting and wide-ranging tradition that thoroughly influenced the entire Western educational system during the past 250 years.[12] Neil Badmington pointed this out, citing Jacques Derrida's call for deconstructive approaches "to repeat what is implicit in the founding concepts and the original problematic" (Badmington, "Theorizing" 15). Of course, this does not mean that repetition is a mere reinforcement of humanism's premises but rather functions as a dislocation by revealing its inadequacies. In Derrida's words, the goal is to "lodg[e] oneself within traditional conceptuality in order to destroy it" (Derrida, "Violence" 111). Rather than "destroying" humanism, however, the goal of this volume is to reveal its inadequate assumptions and to point out aspects that are worth preserving. This implies, of course, that humanism has by no means achieved its emancipatory goals, but the integration of posthumanist critiques will both advance and revitalize its progression. This study will therefore undertake careful and critical readings of canonical texts by eminent German writers in the humanist tradition in order to reveal that the borders between what is deemed humanist and posthumanist are not clear-cut and that the polysemy of many eighteenth-century texts undermines certain foundational humanist premises.

While numerous studies discuss the pros and cons of a humanist universal ethics (Badiou, Eagleton, Guillory, Scholes, Said), few of these studies explore them in the context of the German intellectual heritage of the eighteenth and nineteenth centuries.[13] After all, the humanities and their premise of academic freedom, which is still valued today, are intrinsically tied to the emancipation of the middle classes at the end of the eighteenth century and to the fundamentals of German Idealist philosophy.[14] Education was central to the task of liberating bourgeois individuals from their willing submission to the authoritarian dogmatism of church and the absolutist state. It was seen as a transformative experience that could lead to the enlightenment of middle-class citizens and ultimately of society as a whole. While the Enlightenment idea that all humans, regardless of social and economic standing, are entitled to an education resonated all over Europe, the implementation of a more egalitarian school system that aimed at providing a general education to a broad segment of the population became particularly pronounced in German culture.[15] The development of a standard curriculum for the *Gymnasien* (secondary schools) and the German states' funding of "schools staffed by university graduates" led to "the world's first comprehensive system of universal, public, compulsory education" (McNeely 165). This systematic approach with its humanist agenda, "now imitated from Boston to Beijing" (ibid.), contributed not only to making impoverished Germany one of the most "advanced civilizations" but also to the dissemination of a humanist ethics that included the inviolability of human dignity, individual autonomy, self-tutelage, political and legal equality, and religious and political tolerance. In view of the declining enrollments in the humanities, it is important to stress the significance of these values for Western civilization and its educational system as well as for human rights discussions in general.

By examining the controversy surrounding the development of a humanist ethics against the background of concrete examples from texts advocating a humanist agenda in German philosophy, cultural history, and literature, I will argue that humanism has in recent years not always been given due consideration because of past transgressions allegedly carried out in its name.[16] For instance, writers and intellectuals on the left of the political spectrum reacted to the glorification of the "timeless classics" after World War II by pointing out National Socialism's assimilation of aspects of the humanist tradition, such as its esteem of Greek and Roman antiquity. The implication was that of a common affinity to authoritarianism—an implication that was promoted by the Frankfurter Schule (Frankfurt School) and its neo-Marxist followers of the student rebellion of the 1960s and 1970s. Accordingly, the planned elimination of the Jews was based not only on a populist ideology that appealed to irrational nationalist sentiments with roots in the Romantic tradition but also on a pseudoscientific and rationally justified discrimination of a minority that could be traced as far back as the Enlightenment.[17] In other words, the separation of "subhuman" or "nonhuman" species from the "Nordic" image of "Man" received support from a purposive rationalism that suppressed foreign, non-European characteristics in the name of the advances of an enlightened civilization. According to this critique, the pseudoscientific discrimination of non-Western races was only the beginning of a progressing ostracism of all social groups, nations, races, and ethnicities that did not conform to the German, patriarchal, bourgeois hierarchy.[18]

However, critical readings of literary and theoretical texts that engage with the humanist discourse undermine straightforward designations of cause and effect. Even the following examples, which have been widely regarded as prototypes for a humanist ideology, contain ambiguities that reject humanism's alleged repressive discrimination against deviations from Eurocentric norms. For instance, texts like Lessing's *Nathan der Weise* (*Nathan the Wise*), Goethe's *Iphigenie*, or Schiller's *Don Karlos* did not advocate a repressive rationalism under the guise of a universal humanism. While Lessing's Nathan certainly embodies the ideal of the enlightened bourgeois patriarch and assimilated Jew, one cannot ignore that the play first and foremost promotes tolerance, even respect toward minorities and representatives of other religions or ethnic groups. In addition, Lessing's drama strongly condemns Christian dogmatism and its prejudices and calls for a constant reexamination of ingrained religious and intellectual truisms.[19] In other words, the literary texts under investigation in this volume allow much more differentiated insights into "human nature" than the alleged promotion of a Eurocentric identity politics gives them credit for. While the discrimination against "uncivilized" groups and their sensual instincts has been an implicit or explicit topic in many theoretical texts that promulgate humanist ideas, literary enactments of human behavior often undermine and contest dogmatic forms of humanism.[20] The examples under consideration problematize abstract ethical concepts and ideals by casting them in familiar situations and connecting them to our most intimate self-knowledge as human beings at the sensory and emotional level. Therefore, this study aims at demonstrating how texts that appeal to the imagination can represent life in more tangible and comprehensive ways than abstract theoretical discourses can. What better way of exhibiting the purchase of the humanities than by performing what humanists do in their quests of eliciting meaning from texts? The interpretations in this volume will elucidate how poetic imagery, metaphors, and allegories can subvert normative anthropological, social, and moral assumptions and illustrate, even anticipate scientific concepts, such as human evolution or the unconscious.

Defining Posthumanism

I use *posthumanist* in a broader sense than some theoreticians who claim that humans have adopted characteristics of cyborgs or machines (Hayles, *How We Became Posthuman*; Haraway, "Manifesto"). In contrast to these studies, this volume focuses on humanist and *posthumanist* discourses rather than on the technological innovations that lead these theoreticians to conceptualize contemporary human life as *posthuman*. Posthumanism can perhaps be best described in analogy to the other "post-isms," such as postmodernism, poststructuralism, postcolonialism, etc. As a working definition that by no means claims to do justice to all the possible posthumanist approaches, the following proposition shall suffice: posthumanism contests the premises of humanist ideas that presume the unity and autonomy of the individual and the implications that are connected to these assumptions, such as the privileging and universalizing of the Western male subject, by exposing the Eurocentrism of humanist ideology as historically, geographically, racially, and socially biased (Braidotti, *The Posthuman*, 28–30, 169–85; Haraway, "Manifesto"; Halliwell, 174–75; Herbrechter 149).[21] Yet, posthumanism can be viewed as a continuation of humanism as it aims to extend individual rights to all human beings regardless of race, nationality, ethnicity, gender, sexual orientation, religious belief, or social standing by questioning the presumptions of more traditional, Eurocentric forms of humanism.

In view of the acknowledgment of the sociopolitical, scientific, and ideological factors that have transformed definitions of what is human over the past two hundred years, posthumanist critics would agree with philosopher and feminist theoretician Rosi Braidotti's assertion that the human of humanism is "a historical construct that became a social convention about 'human nature'" (*The Posthuman* 26). Poststructuralist objections to such normative notions of a "unitary subject"—starting with Foucault and postmodernist feminism—targeted the ideal of "Man" precisely because it takes the male European bourgeois citizen as a role model and neglects or even excludes socially, racially, and gender-related divergences from this norm. The generalizing, allegedly objective, and speculative nature of universalist definitions of human subjectivity raises the question of whether one should do away with notions of human agency or selfhood, as some posthumanist approaches have suggested (Braidotti 23–24, 26–29). Braidotti for instance agrees with systems theoreticians and other posthumanist, poststructuralist, and feminist theoreticians that "subjectivity is rather a process of auto-poiesis or self-styling, which involves complex and continuous negotiations with dominant norms and values and hence also multiple forms of culpability" (Braidotti 35, 43; Nayar 36–42). Judith Butler argues in a similar vein by stressing that a subject is conditioned or "given over to a world in which [it] is formed even as it acts or brings something new into being" (*Senses* 6). For Butler the formation of the subject is never complete. It is an ongoing process that involves the subject to some extent but is never fully self-forming (ibid.). This does not mean that one can disregard the human subject as a politically and socially responsible entity. Rather than upholding the unitary, rational, autonomous individual of traditional humanism, posthumanist theories view the subject as "constituted in and by multiplicity, that is to say a subject that works across differences and is also internally differentiated, but still grounded and accountable" (Braidotti 49). As a socially, politically, and economically embedded entity that has to negotiate time and again its continually changing relationship to the outside world, the posthuman subject is much more in flux than its humanist predecessor.[22]

Posthumanism not only borrowed from the neo-Marxist and feminist movements of the 1960s and 1970s, it also integrated the agenda of postcolonialist theory, which confronted humanist norms because "all Humanisms, until now, have been imperial," as John Davies put it (141). As Edward Said stated already in the 1970s, traditional humanist ideas that originated during the Enlightenment neither prevented the domination and exploitation of colonized nations nor of all those who do not have a recognized minority status (*Orientalism*). The Martiniquan activist, poet, and statesman Aimé Césaire was the first to point out that fascism was a form of colonialist racism with eighteenth-century roots in humanist ideology. In his groundbreaking essay "Discours sur le colonialisme," which appeared in 1955 and inspired an entire generation of postcolonialist/-humanist thinkers such as Frantz Fanon (Young, *Postcolonialism* 2), Césaire mentions numerous examples from the Enlightenment tradition that testify to the discrimination, exploitation, and torture of non-European civilizations in the name of Western humanist values. For Césaire, the practice of colonization "works to *decivilize* the colonizer, to *brutalize* him" with the result that the barbaric mistreatment of the indigenous people in non-Western cultures comes home to haunt Western civilization in the form of Nazism (Césaire 35–36).[23] Thus humanism's professed goal of contesting "*the humiliation of man as such*," was not perceived as incompatible with the suppression of "primitive" nonwhite races; to the contrary, the oppression of these "savage cultures" has often been portrayed as a sign of progress on the way to a universally enlightened humanity (Schiller, Kant). Only with "the humiliation of the white man" do the racist underpinnings of the traditional Western "pseudo-humanism" become apparent to "Eurocentric hypocrites" according to Césaire (36–37).[24]

Another aspect of posthumanist thought that criticizes classical humanism's anthropocentrism concerns the human/animal boundary and the maltreatment of animals. Traditional humanism has viewed the human subject as exceptional and insists on a clearly defined human/animal distinction.[25] In contrast, posthumanist thinkers, including Donna Haraway, Cary Wolfe, Cora Diamond, Jacques Derrida, and others, argue in favor of the "decentering of the 'humanist' subject," which means they demand an awareness of trans-individual ecological systems as well as of the discursive networks and information systems, such as the new communication technologies and new media that inform the human consciousness (Soper, "Humanism" 369). Posthumanist thought attempts to take into account the complexities and exigencies of these global megastructures that limit and determine human agency. In light of these limitations, posthumanists no longer grant an exceptional status to the human subject, but view it as a part of the trans-individual context in which it is placed.[26]

Posthumanism, Canonical Texts, and the Neglect of Literary Analysis

How can we explain the contradiction between the call for a humanist education that produces worldly-wise leaders and the tendency to regard a humanist education as elitist and obsolete? While scholars have argued that the continual revision of ideas is part and parcel of the spirit of the Enlightenment from which the German humanist concept of *Bildung* originates (McCarthy, *Crossing Boundaries* 79, Israel, etc.), it is also true that humanism has often been associated with an old-fashioned, elitist education that upholds the somewhat unworldly reverence for Greek antiquity and has ignored more recent scientific, social, political, and cultural phenomena (Israel 22–23). The intransigent reverence for classical antiquity is based on the Enlightenment/humanist notion of an unchanging, essential human nature that is "independent of any particular historical, ethnic or cultural circumstances" (McCarthy, *Crossing Boundaries* 79). This notion is incompatible, however, with the posthumanist assumption of a human nature that depends on its social, historical, and cultural conditioning, and therefore is subject to change.[27] I am arguing that the distinction between humanism and posthumanism is useful in order to differentiate an immutable Eurocentric form of humanism that originated during the Enlightenment from a posthumanism that reflects on the social, economic, and scientific transformations of modern human existence and thus keeps the emancipatory spirit of the humanist agenda alive. In other words, humanism in my usage refers to a set of ideas that was created at a specific time period, ranging roughly from the 1770s to the late nineteenth century, during which the eighteenth-century humanist ideals were conceived and implemented in the German school system. Posthumanism, on the other hand, refers to the open-ended process that attempts to extend the humanist emancipatory agenda of equal opportunity and the right to a comprehensive education to all of those underprivileged groups that had been previously excluded. Therefore posthumanism is a continuing process in pursuit of its ideal of a dignified, just, and self-governing existence for all members of society.

As mentioned above, critical reappraisals of the humanities reflect the fact that scientific, ethical, and social assumptions about the human condition have been deviating from the anthropological or philosophical views of German neo-humanist thinkers, such as Kant, Herder, Schiller, Humboldt, Fichte, and Hegel. These eighteenth- and nineteenth-century philosophers promoted the humanist agenda that shaped the Western educational systems based on "renditions of classical Antiquity and Italian Renaissance ideals" (Braidotti, The Posthuman 13; see also McNeely 165). Their goal was to educate the growing middle class both ethically and intellectually and to create a more democratic and egalitarian society consisting of mature, responsible, and enlightened citizens. Their vision of what it meant to be human was based on the idea of self-perfection and had profound consequences as a civilizational model for the entire Western hemisphere. Yet as Kant's, Fichte's, and Humboldt's anthropological views show, the ability to reason and the right to self-determination were perceived as natural privileges of the male sex.[28]

As we will see later, even early literary representations of and reactions to eighteenth-century humanist ideas challenge, differentiate, and/or subvert various aspects of a programmatic humanism by putting them to the test in specific life-imitating situations. However, these texts do not explicitly question its patriarchal, Eurocentric bias.[29] For that reason and other assumptions, such as individual autonomy, they cannot be called posthumanist in the sense of the critics who introduced the term (Badmington, Hayles, Herbrechter, Wolfe et al.). Yet my study intends to demonstrate how such well-known literary texts from the late eighteenth to the early twentieth century already reveal some posthumanist qualities.

One may rightfully ask why the selection of canonical texts in this volume centers on texts by male authors. This group of educated middle-class men authored the vast majority of eighteenth- and nineteenth-century canonical texts that are still read in schools and universities, performed in theaters, and considered exemplary for the humanist tradition.[30] Idealist thinkers from Kant to Humboldt to Fichte and Hegel, and many others, not only attempted to define the "Bestimmung des Menschen" (vocation of Man) as well as his duties and rights but also to determine whether the sexes have different functions in "nature" and society.[31] In other words, humanist discourses were conceived and shaped by white European men of a privileged elite. Publications by women authors, on the other hand, were relatively rare, received much less critical attention, and often addressed a female audience. In view of the undisputed patriarchal dominance in both the public and the private sphere, which denied women the status of individual autonomy, the discourse about "die Bestimmung des Weibes" (the vocation of Woman) was first and foremost a male discourse, in which women raised their voices only infrequently and with hesitancy (Lange 423).[32] Thus it is not surprising that women make up only a third of the authors in Sigrid Lange's collection of eighteenth- and nineteenth-century philosophical and anthropological essays on the "nature," "vocation," and status of Woman. Lange provides a host of reasons for this gender imbalance. Perhaps the most striking example for the subordination of women is that it was still debated, in the words of Lange, ". . . ob die Weiber Menschen sind" (whether women should be regarded as human beings at all).[33] Not only were women punished, even executed, for their public advocacy of equal rights, such as Olympe de Gouges in 1793, they were not granted property rights or independent legal rights (Lange 416–18). Another major obstacle toward women's emancipation was the "naturalization" of the inequality of the sexes. As many eighteenth-century dramas show, bourgeois ethics, which the middle classes used to justify their struggle against courtly depravity and libertinage, was carried out at the expense of female independence. Women were tied to the home and subject to the "natural" rule of the father.[34] As independent women were often regarded as either unnatural or immoral, many women writers were careful to respect the repressive bourgeois code of honor to avoid tarnishing their reputation (Kontje 235). This may explain why many of the texts authored by women, such as Sophie von La Roche's novel of *Bildungsroman* (novel of education) *Geschichte des Fräuleins Sternheim* (*History of Lady Sternheim*) (1771), echo the masculinist gender norms of the time. While Sophie von La Roche (1730–1807), Susanne von Bandemer (1751–1828), and Betty Gleim (1781–1827) emphasize a woman's right to an education, these women writers tread very carefully to avoid overstepping the boundaries of their traditionally subordinate role.[35] For instance, a woman's education was not intended to make her independent but to enable her "to become a better wife, mother and homemaker" (Fiero 364). Todd Kontje examined a selection of female *Bildungsromane*—a genre that reflects the limitations of the humanist discourse during the Enlightenment—by prominent women authors of this time:

Sophie von La Roche's *Die Geschichte des Fräuleins von Sternheim*, Caroline von Wolzogen's *Agnes von Lilien* (1798), Friederike Helene Unger's *Julchen Grünthal* (1784/98), and Therese Huber's *Die Familie Seldorf (The Seldorf Family)* (1795/96). He summarized his findings with a quote from the *Dialectic of the Enlightenment* that deplores eighteenth-century women's compulsion "'to buy' into an ideology of female subservience" (Kontje, "Socialization" 235). Yet in spite of the women authors' conformity to dominant social expectations out of fear of social ostracism, their narratives "open up a discursive space ... in which their primarily female readers can explore both the possibilities and limitations of the gender roles set forth in the many didactic treatises of the period" (ibid. 236). This last statement is particularly noteworthy in the context of this study because it emphasizes the equivocal polysemy of fictional texts that allows us to examine their ambiguities in innovative interpretations. This is precisely the task of the humanities and their posthumanist mission.

Yet in view of the institutional and social constraints that prevented women writers from advocating a revision of the existing gender norms, it is perhaps just as, if not more, meaningful to examine canonized literary works that do undermine the prevailing sexism and the privileging of the male intellect. Canonical texts like Goethe's *Iphigenie* or Schiller's *Kabale und Liebe* (*Intrigue and Love*) (1784) have had a continuous critical resonance that reveals the gender biases of traditional neo-humanist ideals and the attempts to revise them. The long and extensive reception of such canonized works allows us to trace the modification that foundational humanist values underwent from neo-humanism to anti-humanism to posthumanism, which is the underlying focus of this volume. The critical preservation and continuous refashioning of a set of canonized works through innovative interpretations can show us to which extent this core mission of the humanities has been carried out in the past and what it might look like from a posthumanist perspective. The humanities can survive only if there is a common, albeit always changing, ground for what their core values are and which works best represent these values.

This volume's emphasis on canonical humanist texts arises from concerns about the loss of a common archive as well as "the loss of the knowledge on how to read" (Caruth 1087).[36] In the afterword to the 2010 *PMLA* issue on "Literary Criticism for the Twenty-First Century," Cathy Caruth suggests that "critical language and theoretical language both repeat and differ from the language of literature" and in this sense signal the erasure of the literary work. Thus, she claims, literary works are not only superseded by their criticism but also survive because of the critical attention they receive (Caruth 1091). Caruth refers to an essay by Ankhi Mukherjee in the same issue that emphasizes the ghostly afterlife of classical works. Rather than viewing a classical work as a beacon of timeless essential quality or as a stable pillar of transhistorical values, a canonized literary work deserves the attribute of a classic because it is still alive and capable of capturing conflicts that are of intense interest to posthumanist audiences—or as J. M. Coetze expressed it, a work that "generations of people cannot afford to let go of ... and hold on to at all costs" (cited in Mukherjee 1034).[37] Thus the "postness" of classics that outlive the age of their creation in critical reflections defies widespread denunciations of the humanities as outmoded and irrelevant. In other words, canonical works have become classics not simply because of their timelessness but also because of their timeliness. As the analyses of the selected texts will show, their continuing relevance can be attributed to their engagement with humanist values and to their in-depth explorations of these values that reveal their ambiguities and contradictions. After all, these texts owe much of their critical attention to their polysemous nuances. Moreover, canonical texts can illustrate the changing views and modifications to which traditional eighteenth-century humanism has been subjected over time.

In light of continuous reassessments of literary texts, the humanities are often accused of lacking objective scientific criteria and not producing reliable, applicable research results. Because many humanities research projects have no easily recognizable practical value, outside funding is relatively rare.[38] Given these perceived shortcomings, it is not surprising that university administrators tend to consider the humanities less relevant than the sciences.[39] Although a clear "distinction of a disciplinary dichotomy between nature and culture, matter and spirit" may be neither justifiable nor desirable in light of the coinciding methodologies of the various disciplines, I will maintain this distinction because it continues to exist at the institutional level of higher education. The divide between applicable research with marketable results, generally associated with the natural and social sciences, and interpretive scholarship that is based on historical, social, and cultural variables continues to determine the value attached to specific disciplines and professions. As a response to this customary privileging of the sciences at the institutional and professional levels, many humanities disciplines have attempted to broaden their appeal by making their curricula interdisciplinary. For instance, literary studies have frequently been replaced by cultural studies that focus on more contemporary social, political, and cultural developments. The inclusion of subdisciplines, such as gender and film studies, also contributed to reduced emphasis on literary interpretation. German-American scholar Paul Michael Lützeler is not alone when he expresses his astonishment at "how little is said about the specific qualities of literature in ... volumes that are devoted to German Studies" (Lützeler, "The Role of Literature" 514). As a tireless promoter of German studies for well over four decades, Lützeler has good reasons based on facts and data when he deplores "that we [scholars of literature] have remained silent about the intellectual and emotional joy we derive from reading and discussing literature, and we have failed to mention the imagination and fantasy this sets in motion ..." (ibid.).[40]

In this context it is important to point out that the interpretive and communicative skills commonly practiced and acquired in the humanities are also of practical value. This volume argues that these skills of reading, evaluating, and interpreting literary texts not only sharpen our social sensibilities and our ability to communicate with others successfully but also enable us to question our own prejudices. Literary works of all ages, and especially those of lasting relevance, can teach us these skills. My readings seek to prove that classical literary works survive because they can provide—in Ottmar Ette's terms—"knowledge for living" (Ette 983–93). Ette's plea for reorienting the humanities "*as sciences for living*" supports my intention to demonstrate literature's distinctive qualities in a climate that seems to favor the universal "objectivity" of the sciences over literature's representations of particular and subjective experiences in specific environments. For Ette, the use and "swift dissemination of the term *life sciences*," which has become associated exclusively with the biosciences, illustrates the marginalization of the humanities.[41] Disputing that knowledge of life could be obtained exclusively through scientific exploration, Ette emphasizes the value of literature as transmitting "knowledge for the living gained through concrete experiences in immediate life contexts . . ." (Ette 986).

The textual analyses that follow this introduction will show how literature represents concrete experiences, determined by a multitude of complex situations, contexts, and interactions, and cannot be reduced "to a single logic" (ibid.). In this sense, the literary examples in this volume will also distinguish themselves from the philosophical and aesthetic discourses of the same period. This distinction between aesthetic or philosophical writings, on the one hand, and literary representations that "can translate life knowledge into experiential knowledge . . . , unfettered from the discipline-bound rules of academic discourse," will become clear (ibid.).

On the History of Humanism and Its German Reception

The following condensed history of humanism is meant to provide a brief chronological background to contribute to a better understanding of the roots of the humanist tradition in classical antiquity. It highlights the neo-humanist intentions to liberate the individual from its dependence on religious dogmas and absolutist worldly hierarchies. In addition to providing a historical perspective, this overview of the humanist tradition seeks to reveal the ideological uses and abuses that were carried out in its name. While this volume focuses on neo-humanist concepts from the Enlightenment to the twentieth century, there are certain core principles that the German neo-humanism of the late eighteenth century inherited from Renaissance humanism. The "belief in the power of the human intellect to bring about institutional and moral improvement," the admiration of classical Greek and Roman culture, the "conviction of the importance of the rational faculties of man," the emphasis on "ethics rather than theology" as well as the curiosity about the nature of "Man" are qualities that describe eighteenth- and nineteenth-century humanism as well as its sixteenth-century predecessor (Gilmore 205–6). Back then, the quest for new horizons had led to European expeditions to foreign lands. The discovery of the new world and the encounter with its "savage" population both asserted and questioned the superiority of European civilization before eighteenth-century neo-humanism. While "the travellers' accounts [often] sought in the new lands a confirmation of what the ancient texts had mentioned, fictionally or mythically," such as the Argonaut myth, the encounters with "savages" living together in harmony also challenged the Christian belief in original sin and post-lapsarian corruption: "The image of savages being good, without being compelled to be so by force of law was insulting to the Christian conscience of Western man ..." (Scaglione 66–67). Echoes of this aversion to notions that challenged the belief in the superiority of Christian ethics and Western civilization can still be found in the anthropological views of Enlightenment figures, such as the universal histories of Kant and Schiller. Yet the confrontation with different cultures also inspired self-critical reflections not only on Western values but also on human nature. One could even argue that self-interrogation is always already implicit in the humanist quest for knowledge, as the subject's point of view is challenged in the encounter with the Other.[42] The need to define the role of the human being in an expanding universe on the one hand raised doubts about the "natural" superiority of Western Man, and on the other hand provided an opportunity to export Western civilization to the rest of the world, or in the words of Myron Gilmore, "Europe was in a position to take a view of the world, and this perspective was not to be closed" (31).

While humanism's reliance on Greek and Roman sources and its focus on the individual challenged religious dogmas and metaphysics, it also borrowed ideas from Christian ethics, such as neighborly love and empathy. Christian influences are particularly strong in the German tradition because of the Reformation. For instance, the Lutheran questioning of the church hierarchy and the personalization of the relationship to God can be regarded as both a derivative and substitution of humanist ideas. While Luther deviated from the humanist concept of free will by declaring humans entirely dependent on salvation, the Protestant internalization of religious authority and reliance on introspection can be viewed as a step toward the individual's self-empowerment. The classics and Christian ethics continued to serve as an inspiration for the civilizational model of eighteenth-century neo-humanism. The belief in social progress through education manifested itself in far-reaching educational improvements. The founding fathers of the humanities and of the German educational system, Friedrich Philipp Immanuel Niethammer (1766–1848), and

Wilhelm von Humboldt, sought to defend the study of the classical languages, the *humaniora*, in view of the growing significance of the natural sciences and modern languages, the *realia* (Schauer). Their educational reform for schools and universities advocated a broad rather than specialized education (HuGS 1:282–87). The academic purpose was to educate the middle class in an aesthetic, intellectual, and moral sense. The aesthetic and moral categories of the true, the good, and the beautiful were derived from Greek antiquity of *kalos kai agathos*, the ideal of physical and moral perfection.[43] The humanist curriculum, promoted by Niethammer and Humboldt (1767–1836), comprised ancient Greek, Latin, literature, and history. It was designed to promote and develop all intellectual and emotional faculties in order to achieve perfect harmony of the internal and external capacities of "Man."[44] The neoclassical writings of Winckelmann, Humboldt, Schiller, Goethe, Hölderlin, and others upheld a Hellenic ideal that was not just a matter of the past but also a goal worth striving for. The aim was the formation of a morally supreme, universally educated, autonomous (male) individual, an individual who was independent and in command of his life.[45] These ideals were meant to break down the existing aristocratic class hierarchy by allowing the public to have access to a general education. By teaching individual self-reliance rather than focusing on profession-specific knowledge, this humanist education aimed at avoiding the perpetuation of existing professional hierarchies in a future bourgeois society (Benner 180, 198).

Yet despite the emancipatory trajectory of the neoclassical program that resonated with the ideals of the French Revolution and the American Bill of Rights, the political dimension of the German humanist agenda remained confined to the realm of the private, or spiritual, sphere. It has been argued that the autonomous realm of art promoted by classicist and Romantic aesthetics helped compensate for the lack of the political rights and freedom of the individual (Bürger, Mathäs). The reasons for the so-called German *Sonderweg* are too diverse and complex to be discussed here, ranging from the Lutheran belief in inner freedom and obedience toward authority, German provincialism and lack of a national identity, to the Kantian separation of the spiritual and material world.[46] Both the tendency toward *Innerlichkeit* (introspection) of Pietist autobiographies, the Romantic *Weltabgewandtheit* (detachment from the world), and the elitism of dominant figures of German arts and letters may have contributed to an institutionalized humanist education that was accessible only to the intellectual elite. This intellectual elitism developed regardless of the premises of the Enlightenment that intended to make education available to a broad spectrum of citizens. The empowerment of the individual was stopped short in its tracks, however, by the reinstatement of the old aristocratic order after the Vienna Congress (1815) and by the censorship during the Metternich era. This political development sustained the apolitical if not conservative trajectory of humanist education.

The fact that humanist ideals, such as individual autonomy, became even more illusive during the nineteenth century in the wake of industrialization and urbanization can explain the growing skepticism toward their premises in fin-de-siècle literature. The dire social reality of the majority of working-class people, the alienating conditions of industrialized production, the anonymity of urban life, and the realization that human beings were much more determined by instinctual drives as well as social and economic constraints than their alleged spiritual freedom discredited the humanist ideal of individual autonomy. The dominant late nineteenth-century worldview was no longer compatible with the Romantic and Idealist values of the early nineteenth century. Thus the paradigm shift from the dominance of Idealist to materialist and vitalist perspectives can be attributed to far-reaching socioeconomic, scientific, and demographic developments that had a deep impact on people's prospects, ideals, and attitudes toward life. Under the influence of the Darwinian model of evolution, Nietzsche and Freud initiated attacks against the neo-humanist Idealism in the philosophical realm. Their reflections sought to debunk the false glorification of the intellectual and spiritual capacities of "Man" and demonstrated their dependence on the physical and emotional conditions of the body. The fin-de-siècle "Umwertung aller Werte" (revaluation of values) had deeply rooted causes—causes that were connected to a widespread existential reorientation.

As a reaction to the alienating conditions, many literary works that appeared before and after World War I deal with the precipitous transformations from a nineteenth-century class-based society to a modern mass society with its anonymous bureaucratic networks and lack of binding values. Authors like Arthur Schnitzler, Lou-Andreas Salomé, Stephan Zweig, Frank Wedekind, Franz Kafka, Hermann Hesse, and Thomas Mann, to name just a few, all depicted the impact of these changes on the psyche of bourgeois individuals. In view of the fundamental socioeconomic, demographic, and political changes, the scientific discoveries that radically transformed our understanding of the world and "human nature," it might seem surprising that humanist ideals survived two world wars and are still providing moral and legal guidance when it comes to deciding how one should live ethically. One could certainly argue that these ideals had already been utopian, even at the time of their inception at the end of the eighteenth century, and were far from being realized. The writers who upheld these ideals in their literary works were fully aware that they projected an Idealist foil to which they could compare a less-than-perfect reality. Values like integrity, empathy, tolerance, generosity, truthfulness, loyalty, responsibility, and self-improvement persisted precisely because they are in themselves not subject to historical changes but are meant to be beacons of hope for humanity and a better world. In this sense, humanist values have assumed a quasi-religious status. Classicist works like Goethe's *Iphigenie* or Schiller's *Don Karlos* already foregrounded the idealization of their dramatizations. These plays are not meant to represent the empirical reality of their day and age, although their characters bear universal human traits that let us recognize familiar behavior and empathize with them. Their endurance as canonized classics can be attributed to the distance they create between their audiences and the plays' temporally and socially removed settings and their highly artificial language. Relying on mythical or historical sources of the distant past and representing them in classical meter, they purge the action from all unnecessary empirical detail to direct the focus on the essence of human interaction. Yet, in spite of or because of these distancing formal elements and the universality of their themes, classical works can over time become formulaic, lacking specificity and urgency. For instance, classical plays have very little to say about social problems, such as poverty, unemployment, prostitution, and the abuse of women and children. This is why modern productions of classical plays often try to relate them to contemporary events. Another shortcoming of the generalizing nature of humanist values is their flexibility that makes them vulnerable to ideological (mis)representation, which is particularly obvious in humanism's twentieth-century reception.

The political upheavals after World War I and the disorienting social, economic, and cultural transformations during the first three decades of the twentieth century led to a yearning for the restoration of an autocratic, even authoritarian state. The anxieties of a modern, technological age—an age that resulted in alternative lifestyles and the decline of the traditional patriarchal family, the emancipation of sexual minorities, and the demand for gender equality—and the nostalgic longing for an authoritarian nationalistic state that could compensate for the loss of a binding order were exploited by the National Socialists. Political advocates of the left and the right—conservative monarchists, nationalists, as well as advocates of a modern democracy—appropriated and instrumentalized the humanist legacy for political purposes (Benda, *Die Bildung des Dritten Reiches*; Hesse's and Thomas Mann's speeches). In view of the loss of individual autonomy in an industrialized, technology-driven mass society that supposedly diminished the value of the individual life, humanism was now often invoked to deplore this loss. It could serve as a conservative reactionary ideology that attempted to turn the clock back in search of an unalienated form of existence, an imagined life in tune not only with one's own desires and aspirations but also with a *Volksgemeinschaft* (national or ethnic community) that provided a sense of *Heimat* (home).

However, humanism was also used in opposition to its instrumentalization as a "rein traditionelle, lebensfeindlich-reaktionäre Geisteshaltung" (purely traditional, life-negating reactionary disposition), even before and during the Nazis' rise to power (Maier 3). The term "Der dritte Humanismus" ("the Third Humanism") was coined by philosopher Eduard Spranger and popularized by classical philologist Werner Jaeger. Like eighteenth-century Weimar classicism, the movement modeled the *Bildungsideal* (ideal of education) on the spirit of Hellenic antiquity, yet it also intended to distinguish itself from previous humanist movements by adapting it to modern culture and life (Spranger, *Geisteswissenschaften* 7).[47] In fact, the "Third Humanism" was far from reactionary, and even considered itself as revolutionary (Maier 4). It was open to include Nietzschean and Freudian ideas as well as those of twentieth-century writers, such as Stefan George and Thomas Mann. The movement also viewed itself as part of the European tradition in contrast to conservative and nationalist groups that attempted to claim the humanist legacy for themselves (Maier 4).

The instrumentalization of humanism for the reinterpretation of German history is also obvious after 1945. While the Nazis used aspects of neoclassical aesthetics to show the superiority of the "Aryan" race as represented in Greek sculpture (Breker statues), the restorative humanism of the postwar years attempted to resume the democratic legacy of the Weimar Republic.[48] Humanism was invoked again during the reconstruction after World War II to remind the world that there was an ethical Germany that adhered to the humanist principles of Greek antiquity. After the division of Germany in 1949, both the FRG and the GDR claimed to be the true heirs of the humanist legacy.[49] Since the reception of humanism was more variegated in the Federal Republic, my focus will be on West Germany. The revival of the humanist tradition is understandable because many of its representatives, such as Eduard Spranger (1882–1963), Karl Jaspers (1883–69), Martin Heidegger (1889–1976), Ernst Robert Curtius (1886–1956), Max Rychner (1897–1965), Friedrich Sieburg (1893–1964), and Benno von Wiese (1903–87), had already been active during the Weimar Republic and were well established. They exerted a great deal of influence on postwar cultural politics. While many of these intellectuals had been opposed to the emergence of fascism, there were also some who had collaborated with the Nazis, such as Heidegger, Sieburg, and von Wiese. What all these philosophers and literary critics had in common was the admiration of Goethe and the Hellenistic tradition. Humanism provided a welcome opportunity to improve Germany's badly damaged reputation by pointing out its cultural achievements. After both world wars the adulation of the eighteenth-century classics emphasized the arts' independence from political and economic instability. The privileging of the classics upheld a static high culture with ostensibly universally and eternally binding human values that diverted attention away from Germany's recent national past and toward a common Western culture, of which Germany also wanted to be a part after its "reemergence" from Nazi tyranny.[50]

While the admiration of the classics and their humanist ontology prevailed in both literary and philosophical discourses during the postwar years, there were also differing points of view that advocated either humanism's radical transformation or even its expulsion. Karl Jaspers, for instance, declared "that postwar Germany was permanently separated from all previous traditions" and that it was therefore impossible to simply revive its cultural legacies (Brockmann 127). Nevertheless, he proposed a new type of humanism, one that "can no longer unfold in private" and "is made subject to political conditions" (Jaspers 79). Jaspers condemned as deceptive all forms of "despotism" including Marxism (ibid.) and other ideologies that appeal to the masses, such as psychoanalysis. Instead he promoted a humble devotion to God (73), individual independence (93), and responsibility (77). Despite his call for a "new" humanism, he was very committed to humanism's "Greek sources"—especially the idea of *paideia* (education)—and convinced that Western humanism had "the most venerable tradition" (85). While it was conceivable for Jaspers that "a coming humanism [could be] based on the Western reception of Chinese and Hindu foundations of humanity," he was also concerned about "the end of Western man," which was bound to happen if humanity chose to deny its tradition (87–88). It is not very hard to see why these notions of humanism would be considered inadequate today. The myopic focus on Western Man and the implied marginalization of all other human beings—which was typical of the German postwar discourse—made this brand of humanism untenable by the end of the 1960s.[51]

Growing numbers of the postwar generation had now come of age and were admitted to the universities, although the educational system was still elitist and inaccessible to many underprivileged groups. The call for a more radical democratization of society came from the universities. The students also rebelled against the remnants of fascist authoritarianism, which could still be found in the legal system as well as in the political and educational institutions. For them, post-Marxist ideology of the so-called Frankfurter Schule became a natural ally, because their representatives, such as Theodor W. Adorno (1903–69), Max Horkheimer (1895–1973), Herbert Marcuse (1898–1979), and Walter Benjamin (1892–1940), were decidedly antifascist during the Weimar Republic and suffered from political persecution during the Nazi era. In addition, they also advocated a more socially just society and vociferously opposed late capitalism and its consumerism. The student movement adopted and revived many ideas from their neo-Marxist approach, which had emerged already during the 1920s, such as the criticism of mass culture and the political manipulation of the mass media, as well as the skepticism toward the instrumentalization of reason and technological progress. Because their agenda shares nonetheless many goals with humanism—and adopted Kantian and Hegelian ideas—it might be more appropriate to call the values that emerged during the rebellious 1960s posthumanist rather than anti-humanist, although the term was a later invention. Yet one could argue that the leftwing political movement of the 1960s did not include important aspects of the posthumanist discourse.

For instance, the feminist as well as the gay and lesbian movements emerged precisely because the early student movement displayed a lack of awareness of gender issues (Kraushaar 226–33; Sanders; Koenen 233–56).

During the rebellious decades of the 1960s and 1970s, intellectuals of the postwar generation began to question the values that were espoused by their parents. They accused the established politicians, many of whom had served in political positions during the Nazi era, of using the humanist discourse for opportunistic reasons and for washing themselves clean of their fascist past. They were highly suspicious of a humanist rhetoric, which, under the guise of universal equality, discriminated against all groups that did not conform to the Western European, male, patriarchal norm. In their view, a discourse that had been used to justify authoritarian, nationalist, and antidemocratic politics was indefensible. It only served to justify the status quo and legitimize those who held power. The extraparliamentary opposition on the left as well as the emerging feminist movement identified traditional humanist ideology with a corrupt patriarchal establishment. Like the left-wing activists of the post-1968 generation in the United States, the German student movement attacked "the core of a liberal individualistic view of the subject, which defined perfectibility in terms of autonomy and self-determination" (Braidotti, *The Posthuman* 23) because it did not correspond to the lived reality of the average middle- or working-class individual.[52]

And yet, despite their aversion to the "eternal values" of traditional humanism, which "continued to define the subject of European thought as unitary and hegemonic" (ibid.), the rebellious postwar generation promoted emancipatory ideals, which one might call humanist. For instance, the idea of giving minorities a voice, the criticism of patriarchy, the critical questioning of traditional values and institutions, the contestation of hierarchical power structures, the opposition to fascist and other authoritarian regimes, the fight against the disproportionate distribution of wealth in capitalism, the push for a reform of the elitist education and justice systems, and the fight for world peace and against the resurgence of nationalism, imperialism, and militarism are all part of a humanist agenda, albeit from a socialist point of view. These demands aimed at a more just and equal society that granted more rights to the socially and economically disadvantaged.

The Humanities and the Sciences

While the humanities have a long record of successfully counteracting the fragmentation of human existence by giving meaning to the wealth of seemingly unrelated aspects of scientific knowledge, the increasing specialization of the scientific disciplines during the nineteenth and twentieth centuries raises doubts about their integrative powers. Their waning importance can be attributed to the erosion of universal belief systems that were founded on the privileging of the human mind and the distinction of Man as a thinking animal. While the significance of the sciences has been continually on the rise in view of their practical applicability and immediate benefits to technological, social, medical, and economic progress, they lack the ability to address ethical questions and depict subjective sensations. As mentioned previously, the humanities and their humanist ideals have survived scientific innovations through hundreds of years because they can address these questions from a subjective, internal point of view. Literary imagination enables us to divulge universal human experiences and confronts us with the consequences of complex scientific processes and other historical, external events and constellations in a comprehensible manner. In the following I will discuss how literary imagery and metaphorical language are able to personalize and universalize scientific phenomena, as well as stimulate their exploration.

Already at the end of the eighteenth century, German writers like Herder, Humboldt, Schiller, and Goethe deplored the fragmentation of the sciences. In their view, the specialization of knowledge threatened a holistic worldview, which was the prerequisite for the development of a comprehensively educated, autonomous personality.[53] The neo-humanist curriculum can be considered as an attempt to respond to the specialization of knowledge and the lack of a coherent worldview. The scientific diversification at the time was contrasted to a comprehensive understanding of nature in an idealized ancient Greece that allegedly knew no fragmentation of the self and the world. The goal of the *humaniora* was to overcome the disorienting pace of specialization and the neglect of ethical considerations in scientific advances. With the development of empiricist methods and materialist assumptions during the Enlightenment, German philosophers and writers launched a counterattack against what they perceived as an instrumental reason that neglected the divine, spiritual nature of humankind. Immanuel Kant, his student Johann Gottfried Herder, and Friedrich Schiller, for instance, attempted—with different emphases—to hold on to the spiritual freedom of "Man" *in spite of* or perhaps even *because of* the growing body of empirical scientific research that threatened to undermine human autonomy.[54] Kant's *Idee zu einer Idee einer allgemeinen Geschichte in weltbürgerlicher Absicht* (*Idea for a Universal History with a Cosmopolitan Purpose*) (1784), for instance, deliberately projects an underlying metaphysical intention and chiliastic trajectory onto world history in order to provide a "tröstende Aussicht in die Zukunft" (consoling perspective) and guidance in furthering the progress toward a more enlightened human civilization (KW 11:47–49). During this period, advances in the emerging life sciences boosted the interest in the question of what is human from a scientific point of view and superseded Cartesian assumptions about the "nature of Man."[55] Empirical studies and scientific experimentation contested metaphysical and religious explanations and had the advantage of being verifiable. In the nineteenth century, Darwinism and the emergence of evolutionary biology based on genetics challenged the binary model of Idealist thinking and the claim of the supremacy of the human mind (Whimster 174; Braidotti, *The Posthuman* 146).[56] On a closer look, however, one can see that scientific reasoning was not entirely devoid of metaphysical underpinnings. After all, literary and visual symbols facilitate the communication of scientific knowledge and make it comprehensible to the human imagination.[57]

Charles Darwin's or Ernst Haeckel's genealogical trees present an image of life that reminds us in many ways of Plato's and Aristotle's *scala naturae* or Jean Baptiste Lamarck's Great Chain of Being. Do the scientific uses of the tree metaphor that visually captures evolution and the hierarchical order of the species not suggest that science often relies on anthropomorphic imagery and is frequently informed by figments of the human imagination? In other words, the recurrence of the tree metaphor in scientific discourses seems to imply that knowledge is often based on sensory experiences and ideas. To be sure, it would not be difficult to point out the countless scientific discoveries that have successfully revised human misperceptions or flights of fancy. Yet, the continual revisions of scientific knowledge throughout history suggest that human understanding is tied to its epistemological limitations and their sociocultural contexts. For instance, who could seriously doubt that a human being who lived a few hundred years ago in central Africa had a different understanding of time, distance, and ethical conduct from a contemporary inhabitant of an advanced Western society?[58]

In light of such culturally conditioned sensations, emotions, and perceptions, it is hardly a surprise that scientific knowledge is linked to projections of the human imagination and must be expressed in metaphorical form to be tangible. For instance, human states of emotion, like fear or love, can be rendered in scientific terms. However, their sensory experience may be much more effectively communicated in poetic language. Scientific theories, albeit rationally understandable, often remain obscure to a general audience. Without relating scientific data to phenomena of the human experience through metaphorical representation, science would be incomprehensible to a lay audience, as Goethe's dictum "Gray is all science, and green is the golden tree of life" so vividly expresses (HA 3.1: 2038–39); or in the words of Stephen Toulmin, "Human life does not lend itself to abstract generalizations" (*Cosmopolis* 33). Metaphors are, of course, for the most part represented in language, which leads Edward Said to a broad definition of humanism as "the exertion of one's faculties in language in order to understand, reinterpret, and grapple with the products of language in history, other languages and other histories" (Said 28).

In order to make the increasing body of knowledge accessible to a general audience, Enlightenment writers took advantage of a wide range of literary forms and genres. Fables, essays, dramas, and all kinds of poetry and narrative prose engaged with scientific, philosophical, anthropological, psychological, and ethical concepts and successfully made abstract ideas not only intellectually but also emotionally comprehensible. For instance, Goethe wrote *Die Metamorphose der Pflanzen* first as a botanical essay (1790) and later transformed it into an elegy (1799). Likewise, the pedagogical intention of making abstract moral concepts more tangible can be detected in Lessing's fables or, for instance, his drama *Nathan der Weise*. In opposition to empiricist scientific treatises that generally do not reflect on the subjective perception of the observing subject, poetic renditions of abstract concepts often present the subject in a dialogical situation with nature or another object that renders the dynamic reciprocity of the subject-object relations. The observing subject does not assume an unassailable, "objective" position—taking stock of natural phenomena or pontificating a moral truth—but is presented as part of nature, in a dialogic exchange, and often confronted with a moral dilemma. In other words, *belle letters* are capable of recreating sensory experiences or thought processes from an internal or subjective point of view. This rendition of immediacy allows the author to evoke firsthand impressions by putting the recipients in the protagonists' shoes. In contrast, scientific discourses generally strive to distance the reader from individually distorted perceptions by "objective" descriptions from a neutral, external point of view.

George Lakoff and Mark Johnson's *Metaphors We Live By* (1980) provides a plethora of examples of how our everyday speech is pervaded by metaphors. Accordingly, the metaphorical use of language is derived from anthropologic experiences, such as spatial and temporal orientation, and is deeply embedded in human culture (Lakoff and Johnson 22). Metaphorical expressions and especially "spatialization metaphors are rooted in physical and cultural experience" (ibid. 18). For instance, the idea that "more" often means "up" and "less" is associated with "down" or "happy" is "up" and "good" is "up" and vice versa is an indication that human emotions are surreptitiously associated with universal physical proficiencies, such as the sense of direction, and conceptualized metaphorically according to ingrained ways of perceiving the world. While these metaphorical concepts are culturally determined, they are tangible and easily comprehensible for members of the same culture. Even for members of a different culture, they may be understandable because they can be based on universal physical phenomena, such as gravity. Metaphors are often used because they are able to render abstract concepts in terms of familiar experiences. It is therefore not hard to see why metaphoric language is generally much more captivating than technical jargon. While we associate metaphor with poetic language, we often forget that metaphors are very much part of our everyday speech, even of descriptions of scientific processes. Lakoff and Johnson propose that "[the] intuitive appeal of a scientific theory has to do with how well its metaphors fit one's experience" (19). If this is true, one could even pose the question whether the human imagination, its conceptual orientation, and apperception predetermine our epistemological orientation and therefore our cognitive interest. Consequently, the humanities and the study of language, their verbal illustrations of universally physical and cultural experiences, are able to yield insights into the anthropocentric conditioning of scientific theories. Yet, empiricist and positivist methodologies are deemed to be objective and tend to exclude ancillary, nonmeasurable factors or cultural predispositions that may influence the scientific approach.[59] The hermeneutic examination of empirical and rational methods in the context of their cultural conditioning can reveal the limitations and ideological prejudices of certain scientific inquiries.[60] Interdisciplinary collaborations between scientists in the natural and human sciences can be mutually beneficial as they can elicit connections between sentient and intellectual faculties as well as contextualize empirical processes and make them comprehensible for a broader audience.

Outline of Chapters

The concern with the question of what is human is evident in the great historical narratives that appeared during the late eighteenth century, called *Universalgeschichte* (universal history). Fueled by the growing interest in the evolution of humanity, these accounts link history to genealogy. Chapters 1 and 2 of this study examine examples of such narratives that center on the question of how to educate humanity effectively. The chapters discuss the use of poetic language in theoretical discourses since these histories of humankind transcend disciplinary boundaries and rely heavily on allegories, metaphors, and imagery as pedagogical tools. Chapter 1 focuses on Gottfried Ephraim Lessing's *Die Erziehung des Menschengeschlechts* (*The Education of the Human Race*) (1780); the second chapter examines Friedrich Schiller's "Was heißt und zu welchem Ende studiert man Universalgeschichte?" ("What Is and to What End Do We Study Universal History?") (1789) and "Die Sendung Moses" ("The Legation of Moses") (1789). Chapters 1 and 2 discuss the following questions: Why did these historical accounts become popular during the second half of the eighteenth century? To what extent do these narratives represent and disseminate humanist ideas? Which narrative strategies and rhetorical devices do the authors use to educate their audiences? The chapters problematize Enlightenment teleology by presenting history from subjective points of view that challenge seemingly objective accounts and truth claims.

"The Sublime as an Objectivist Strategy" (chapter 3) suggests that the aesthetic category of the sublime helped objectify an essentially subjectivist aesthetics. The chapter presents the Kantian sublime as an aesthetic category that effectively promotes freedom and individuality. The sublime thus serves to preserve the idea of the human as a spiritual being that is capable of liberating itself from its bodily confinements. While Schiller follows Kant in deriding the sensual aspects of human nature as egotistical and amoral, his dramas also challenge some of the Kantian premises. When Schiller's protagonists sacrifice lives in the service of ethical ideas, the sublime's oppressive spirit reveals itself. The discussion of Schiller's dramas demonstrates how literary fiction, that is the nuanced representation of imagined interactions of fictional characters in hypothetical but concrete situations, can challenge, differentiate, and correct generalizing philosophical and scientific claims.

Chapter 4, "The Importance of Herder's Humanism and the Posthumanist Challenge" examines Johann Gottfried Herder's significance for the humanities. Herder's humanism can serve as a prime example for how the humanities should refocus their central mission of addressing universal, humanist objectives (universalism) without neglecting cultural diversity (particularism). By contrasting Herder's eighteenth-century humanist philosophy with contemporary ideas by German philosopher Thomas Metzinger, the chapter proposes that Herder's humanism preempts some of the posthumanist assumptions about Idealist humanism. A close reading of Herder's essay "Vom Erkennen und Empfinden der menschlichen Seele" ("On Cognition and Sensation of the Human Soul") (1778) reveals how Herder uses poetic descriptions of sensory experiences and emotions to render human states of consciousness more tangible than purely scientific discourses. Moreover, a contrastive analysis of textual passages reveals that contemporary philosophers like Metzinger resort to culturally mediated metaphors of the humanist tradition to illustrate their posthumanist ideas.

Chapter 5 examines Johann Wolfgang von Goethe's dramas *Iphigenie* (1779–86) and *Torquato Tasso* (1790), which have been characterized as canonical literary manifestations of humanism in the German tradition. With reference to philosopher Mark Johnson's *The Meaning of the Body*, the interpretation ties into my underlying argument that literary explorations express the significance of sensory aspects of human nature through metaphoric imagery. Johnson's investigation that is based on recent research in cognitive neuroscience reaffirms Herder's claim that meaning is grounded in our bodily experience. A close reading of select passages demonstrates how both *Iphigenie* and *Tasso* problematize and acknowledge—long before Freud and Nietzsche—the powers of a subconscious human nature. Both texts undermine a humanism that presumes the subject's control over his/her animalistic drives. While

Goethe's plays uphold humanist principles, they also expose their rhetorical invocation to cover up ulterior motives.

Chapter 6, "Incorporating Change: The Role of Science in Goethe's and Carl Gustav Carus's Humanist Aesthetics," focuses on the similarities and differences of Goethe's and Carl Gustav Carus's (1789–1869) aesthetics as examples of a Romantic humanist worldview. Analyses of select passages from Goethe's and Carus's aesthetic, literary, and scientific writings show how these writers promote the concept of *Bildung* (education) by intermingling anthropomorphic image making with theoretical discourses. The chapter situates their amalgamations of scientific, literary, and aesthetic discourses in the context of their indebtedness to Romantic *Naturphilosophie*, which strove to unite the sciences and arts by viewing nature as an all-encompassing monistic system. My reading of Goethe's "Metamorphose der Pflanzen" ("The Metamorphosis of Plants") (1798) and Carus's *Briefe über Landschaftsmalerei* (*Letters on Landscape Painting*) (1831–35) and *Briefe über das Erdenleben* (*Letters on Earthly Life*) (1841) demonstrates how both writers express in these works the philosophical principles that underlie their aesthetics: the tension between the unchanging laws of Nature and its constant *Dauer im Wechsel* (dynamic transformation) as well as *Einheit des Mannigfaltigen* (unity of the manifold). The chapter also reveals how Carus's scientific and philosophical pursuits resulted in taxonomic hierarchies that aimed at preserving the superiority of the "white" race and the Western male scientist.

Chapter 7 interprets Gottfried Keller's novella "Kleider machen Leute" ("Clothes Make People") (1874) against the background of the materialist philosophies of Ludwig Feuerbach and Karl Marx. The chapter presents Keller's engagement with key concepts, such as alienation, objectification, idealization, and nostalgia, in the context of bourgeois society's growing consumerism and depletion of spiritual values. It analyzes Keller's novella in view of the transformative changes that a capitalist economy brought to rural communities and their inhabitants during the second half of the nineteenth century. While Keller's story reveals how socioeconomic conditions influence human behavior, it also portrays fundamental, all-too-human character traits with ironic empathy.

Chapter 8, "The End of Pathos and of Humanist Illusions," reads Arthur Schnitzler's *Liebelei* as a fin-de-siècle response to the Schillerian concept of pathos. More specifically, the chapter discusses how the spiritualization and glorification of romantic love became untenable at the end of the nineteenth century, when sexuality was recognized as an instinctual force and bourgeois morality was unmasked as a smokescreen that served to conceal sexual instincts. While Schnitzler's late nineteenth-century drama is a disillusioning critique of some of Schiller's key assumptions about human nature and the hyperbolic idealization of romantic love, truth, and faithfulness, the play also reveals a melancholy regret over the loss of humanist ideals.

Chapter 9, "Blurring the Human/Animal Boundary: Hofmannsthal's *Andreas*," can be read as a probing critique of the *Bildungsroman* and the Idealist mind-body dualism. The chapter shows how progress in the life sciences influenced the representation of human nature in fiction and thus undermined the mind-body dualism and the humanist concept of *Bildung*. By revealing the protagonist's suppression of animalistic instincts, embodied in the figure of the *Knecht* (groom), Hugo von Hofmannsthal's text exposes the humanist ideal of self-perfection as a self-deluding belief that leads the protagonist on a path to self-alienation. The *Knecht* is presented as a subhuman species between human and animal. The beastly servant can be interpreted as refractions of the protagonist's self-image that expose the gap between his bourgeois aspirations and his animal instincts.

Chapter 10, "Weimar and the Invocation of the Humanist Legacy," focuses on Thomas Mann's political essays with reference to *Tonio Kröger* (1903) and *Der Zauberberg* (*The Magic Mountain*) (1924). The chapter describes Mann's development from his antidemocratic nationalist views before and during World War I to his antifascist humanism during the 1920s. An in-depth examination of biographical, fictional, and essayistic sources seeks to reveal the dialectics between Mann's aesthetics and ideological transformation. The references to *Tonio Kröger* and *Der Zauberberg* show how his probing vacillations between two antagonistic points of view informed both his essayistic and fictional works and allowed him to mobilize his humanist background in defense of the Weimar democracy.

Chapter 11 interprets Hesse's novel *Steppenwolf* (1927) as the precursor of a posthumanist novel. It is posthumanist in a temporal sense because it engages with the nineteenth-century humanist legacy from a twentieth-century perspective. The novel's brazen critique of traditional bourgeois values does not simply reject traditional humanism and its philosophy of individual autonomy. It dislodges Idealist concepts of wholeness and self-perfection and replaces them with a multiperspectival view of a continuously changing human consciousness, an open-ended process toward self-awareness. Hesse's novel depicts the protagonist's gradual disillusionment with this Idealist worldview by giving a detailed account of the deconstruction of his personality—a personality that, as it turns out, does not consist of a spiritual essence but dissolves into an accumulation of acquired conventions, habits, cultural and philosophical traditions, even specific historical events and constellations. Hesse's attempt to go beyond a mere negation of humanist values implies transcending the humanist paradigm in every respect, including its form. Rather than presenting a linear narrative, Hesse chooses three different viewpoints, which contribute to the novel's multiperspectivity.

The conclusion discusses the dialectic between the emergence of the humanist, anti-humanist, and posthumanist constructs of human nature and more recent humanitarian and scientific developments. By referring to posthumanist texts by writer and philosopher J. M. Coetzee (*The Lives of Animals*, 1999) and Peter Sloterdijk (*Regeln für den Menschenpark* [*Rules for the Human Zoo*], 1999), the chapter discusses how these posthumanist texts position themselves in relation to traditional eighteenth- and nineteenth-century anthropological models. Based on this investigation, the chapter reflects on the validity and value of the humanist paradigm—whether it might still have purchase, whether a recovery of the humanities is possible, and, if so, whether it is desirable.

Notes

1. See, for instance, Stanley Fish, "The Crisis of the Humanities Officially Arrives," *New York Times*, October 2010, https://opinionator.blogs.nytimes.com/2010/10/11/the-crisis-of-the-humanities-officially-arrives/ (accessed 14 August 2018).
2. In his "Presidential Address 2004: The Humanities in a Posthumanist World," Robert Scholes refers to George Steiner's "The Muses' Farewell" (2002), Terry Eagleton's *After Theory* (2003), and John Guillory's *Cultural Capital* (1993). The reference to Martha Nussbaum refers to both *Cultivating Humanity* (1999) and *Not for Profit* (2010); the reference to Edward Said refers to *Humanism and Democratic Criticism* (2004).
3. It is easy to see that these values coincide with Enlightenment ideals. John McCarthy, for instance, argues that "enlightenment is the *means* of perfecting humanity (=goal of humanism), and not identical to humanism itself, [as] the ideals of humanism cannot be realized without true enlightenment" (*Crossing Boundaries* 79). Citing Johann Gottfried Herder's *Letters on the Advancement of Humanity* (1793–97), McCarthy asserts that true enlightenment is the "destiny of humanity, [and that] like nature itself, [it] is essentially unchanging and independent of any particular historical, ethnic, or cultural circumstances that might tend to favor or obstruct its fulfillment in the individual." The editors of *Posthumanism in the Age of Humanism* (2019) call "the German cultural sphere, the specifically German Enlightenment classically humanist" (4). Posthumanism deviates from the Enlightenment claim of an unchanging human nature, however. Moreover, Ian Hunter's *Rival Enlightenments: Civil and Metaphysical Philosophy in Early Modern Germany* (2001) contests the thesis of a common monolithic Enlightenment discourse by showing that the early Enlightenment goals and concerns at the end of the seventeenth century were very different from those of the late eighteenth century.
4. Although the liberal arts cannot be equated with a nineteenth-century humanist education since their emphasis is not necessarily on the Greek and Roman classics, they share some common goals with the humanist idea of providing a broad general education that permits their constituents to become well-rounded citizens.
5. For a more detailed analysis of the declining enrollments of humanities majors in American colleges, see Jeffrey Selingo, "As Humanities Majors Decline, Colleges Try to Hype Up Their Programs," *The Atlantic*, 1 November 2018, https://www.theatlantic.com/education/archive/2018/11/colleges-studying-humanities-promotion/574621/ (accessed 4 November 2018).
6. For more information about the popularity and challenges of the Humanities, see *AAC&U News* (August 2017), https://www.aacu.org/aacu-news/newsletter/2017/

august/perspectives; also https://www.aacu.org/aacu-news/newsletter/2017/august/facts-figures; https://www.aacu.org/blog/value-of-and-challenges-for-humanities (all accessed 29 August 2018).
7. Among them are Mark Edmundson, "On the Uses of a Liberal Education" (*Harper's Magazine* [September 1997]: 39–59); National Endowment for the Arts, "Reading at Risk: A Survey of Literary Reading in America" (Washington DC, 2004), https://www.arts.gov/sites/default/files/RaRExec_0.pdf; Don Michael Randel, "The Public Good: Knowledge as the Foundation for a Democratic Society" (*Daedalus* 138, no. 1 [Winter 2009]: 8–12); Michael Bérubé, Hester Blum, Christopher Castiglia, and Julia Spicher Kasdorf, "Community Reading and Social Imagination" (*PMLA* 125, no. 2 [March 2010]: 418–25); Mark W. Roche, *Why Choose the Liberal Arts?* (Notre Dame, IN: Notre Dame UP, 2010); Richard Arum and Josipa Roksa, *Academically Adrift: Limited Learning on College Campuses* (Chicago, IL: U of Chicago P, 2011); Ottmar Ette, "Literature as Knowledge for Living—Literary Studies as Science for Living" (*PMLA* 125, no. 4 [October 2010]: 977–93); Werner Hamacher, "95 Theses on Philology" (excerpt in *PMLA* 125, no. 4 [October 2010]: 1087-95); Paul Jay, *The Humanities in "Crisis" and the Future of Literary Studies* (New York: Palgrave, 2014); William Deresiewicz, "The Neoliberal Arts: How College Sold Its Soul to the Market" (*Harper's Magazine* [September 2015]: 25–32); *Excellent Sheep: The Miseducation of the American Elite and the Way to a Meaningful Life* (New York: Free Press, 2015); Charles Bernstein "95 Theses" (*Profession*, 4 October 2016).
8. The editors of *Posthumanism in the Age of Humanism* (Landgraf, Trop, Weatherby) also point to a "lack of a methodological agreement among posthumanists" (2).
9. See, for instance, Cary Wolfe, *What Is Posthumanism?* (Minneapolis: U of Minnesota P, 2010); Katherine N. Hayles. *How We Became Posthuman: Virtual Bodies in Cybernetics, Literature, and Informatics* (Chicago: U of Chicago P, 1999).
10. Feminist theoretician Rosi Braidotti, for instance, argues that the posthuman condition requires an entirely new concept of human agency that rejects the long-established idea of an implied Eurocentric identity on which humanist ideology rests (*The Posthuman* 37–39, 149). The introduction to *Human, All Too (Post)Human*, a collection of essays that challenges posthumanism from a Marxist perspective, views the prevalent usage of the notion as "'decentering the human in favor of a turn toward the nonhuman'" against "'speciesism' of the 'Anthropocene.'" This characterization is, however, somewhat misleading since the term is not primarily employed to announce "the advent of the nonhuman common," as the authors (Jennifer Cotter et al.) imply, but includes the human, while contesting its dominance over all the other species (1). The authors cite Richard A. Grusin, *The Nonhuman Turn* (U of Minnesota P, 2015) in support of their argument.
11. The editors of *Posthumanism in the Age of Humanism* (Bloomsbury, 2019) emphasize that "the prefix 'post' always implies continuation. Anytime a past is used as a negative foil it continues to shape the 'post' in some way" (2).
12. Landgraf, Trop, and Weatherby even suggest that "any future posthumanism will have to avow a complex relation to the quasi-humanist modernity that arose in the German-speaking countries around 1800" (4).
13. Among the studies that deal with the reception and critique of the German humanist tradition are Theodor Litt, Dietrich Spitta, Max Horkheimer, Theodor Adorno, and Peter Sloterdijk. Their evaluations of German humanism will be discussed later in the book.

14. In this regard I deviate from Jonathan Israel's point of view that rejects the idea that the Enlightenment could be tied socioeconomic shifts. While it is true that "leading representatives of Enlightenment thought came from aristocratic, bourgeois, and artisan backgrounds and the Enlightenment movement itself always remained socially heterogeneous and non-class specific, in terms of its spokesmen, objectives, and socioeconomic consequences" (Israel 33), it is also true that in many works of German literature bourgeois ethical values were contrasted to the immoral courtly society.
15. Wilhelm von Humboldt was appointed head of the section for ecclesiastic affairs and education in the ministry of the interior of Prussia in 1808. Soon after, between 1809 and 1810, he implemented a radical reform of the entire Prussian education system, based on the principle of a free and common education from elementary school through high school. His idea of combining both teaching and research would become the institutional model for research universities throughout Germany and in most Western countries.
16. In this regard, the focus of my study differs from that of *Posthumanism in the Age of Humanism*. While the collection of essays also takes a historical approach and examines the challenges that modern scientific discourses after Kant pose for the philosophical and humanist tradition (4), my study investigates literary, philosophical, and scientific discourses from the Enlightenment to the early twenty-first century in the context of social, ideological, and cultural contexts. By reflecting on the epistemological changes in which period-specific humanist, anti-humanist, and quasi-posthumanist literary texts engage with traditional humanist premises, it reveals the emancipatory trajectory that all humanisms have in common. In addition, it interrogates the distinctions between literary, philosophical, and scientific discourses and makes a case for the humanities and the practice of literary analysis. In spite of their different foci, both volumes complement each other as they are both based on the assumption that the critical responses to traditional humanist thought anticipate aspects of posthumanist thought, and vice-versa that posthumanist discourses must be considered as expansions on humanist ideas.
17. Theodor Adorno and Max Horkheimer's *Dialectic of the Enlightenment* is, of course, the most prominent example of this argument. Numerous scholars, such as John McCarthy, Daniel Wilson, and Robert Holub, reassessed their critique as a somewhat jaundiced yet understandable reaction the fascist appropriation of purposive reason. See Daniel Wilson and Robert Holub, eds. *Impure Reason*, 1993.
18. Richard Gray's monograph *About Face* describes the history of racial discrimination in the German tradition from the earliest attempts to establish physiognomy as a scientific discipline (Lavater) to the chauvinist and racist ideologies of the late nineteenth and early twentieth centuries as a linear development. Paul Gilroy's *Against Race* also points out the connections between eighteenth-century German anthropology and philosophy and twentieth-century racism. I will discuss these connections in chapter 6.
19. Likewise, Goethe's Iphigenie is far too complex a figure to be called a mouthpiece for a monolithic humanist ideology. Her actions to deceive her benefactor not only render her "verteufelt human" (deviously human) according to Goethe's own judgment but also question the assumption of a stable, homogenous subject. Schiller's *Don Karlos* can be read as a critique of purposive reason as well. Marquis Posa, the character who fights for a more humane and enlightened state in an authoritarian system, becomes a manipulative schemer who betrays his best friend, albeit with good intentions, to fulfill his political goals. Thus, the text reflects on the danger of a latent dogmatism in an en-

lightened rationality that supposedly rejects the unquestioned adherence to dogmatic principles.
20. Examples for this dogmatic rationality that privileges the European white educated male and views eighteenth-century Western civilization as superior to all others are numerous and can be found in the anthropological writings of, for instance, Kant, Schiller, Fichte, Lavater, Humboldt, Carus, among many others. I will refer to several of these texts during the ensuing analyses.
21. See Jonathan Israel quoting John Robertson, *The Case for the Enlightenment*: "Postmodernist theorists urge us to forget the Enlightenment's quest for universal moral and political foundations, claiming different cultures should be left 'to determine their own priorities and goals without our discriminating politically or morally between them'" (1–2). Landgraf, Trop, and Weatherby define posthumanism "as an attempt to critically interrogate the status of the human as exceptional, as autonomous, as standing outside of a web of relations, or even as a subject or object of knowledge corresponding to a determinate set of practices" (1).
22. Braidotti, for instance, introduces the term "nomadic subjectivity" to account for the subject's instability and "vulnerability" that does not have to be viewed as frightening, however, but rather as an "interconnection between self and others" that fosters a "global sense of inter-connection between the human and the non-human environment in the face of common threats" (*The Posthuman* 50).
23. Césaire goes even further by claiming that "the very distinguished, very humanistic, very Christian bourgeois of the twentieth century ... has a Hitler inside him" (36).
24. Judith Butler also provides an example of how the postcolonialist discourse permits insights into the parochial universalism of traditional humanism. She shows how Jean-Paul Sartre's preface to the first edition of Fanon's *The Wretched of the Earth* (1963) hands the white reader "dislocation and rejection" by addressing an audience for which the book has not been written. By recommending to the European elite a volume that is not intended for them but for Fanon's black brethren, Sartre attempts to put his white readers in the uncomfortable position of "the socially excluded and effaced" (Butler 174). Thus the white reader is excluded from a discourse among black brethren whose fathers had been humiliated and treated with "that very indifference [that] has been taken up and returned to its sender in new form" (ibid.). By placing his readers in the position of the outsider, Sartre subjects them to social annihilation and forces them to feel the shame and rage of the colonized (Butler 177). Sartre's recreation of this emotional experience makes it difficult for the European liberal to oppose the suffering of the colonized in a noncommittal way and to maintain the aloofness "that outsources its violence to preserve its spuriously humanist self-definition" (ibid. 179). Sartre's direct address to his European readers can also be read as a critique of a universal humanist discourse that maintains the status quo by paying lip service to a nonviolent humanism of Western origin demanding no further involvement. It was this type of ontological discourse that focused on the "Human Condition" in general without making any distinction between oppressors and oppressed, Western and non-Western cultures, etc., that became the target of criticism of the left in the late 1960s.
25. Patrick Fortmann confirms such attempts by German naturalists Herder, Soemmerring, and Gall to defend the distinction between the human and the animal. While these naturalists "cannot help but acknowledge common features in the brains and minds of humans and nonhuman animals," Fortmann shows that their "species-

transcending frameworks [nevertheless attempt] to redeem human exclusivity" (Fortmann 52).

26. Maurice Merleau-Ponty's philosophy—albeit created prior to posthumanist theory—is an example that does not privilege human beings over other living organisms but regards them as codependent on their natural environment. I am only briefly summarizing the main points of his phenomenological approach in view of its posthumanist characteristics. For Merleau-Ponty "there is no essence, no idea, that does not adhere to a domain of history and of geography" (Merleau-Ponty, *Visible* 114–15). Attempting "to define a middle ground between the dualistic extremes of intellectualism (idealism) and empiricism (realism)," Merleau-Ponty's phenomenology "wants to emphasize the particularities of the relations to the world of different kinds of organisms, their specific kinds of embodiment, and their different environments" (Westling 17; see also Moran 417). What makes phenomenology attractive is its consideration of a human perspective that predetermines seemingly objective scientific approaches. Whereas empiricist and positivist methodologies focus on factual details and tend to neglect the ethical, ecological, and spiritual implications of scientific discoveries that affect human well-being, the integrative powers of humanism and the humanities address these questions of meaning. For a more extensive discussion of his philosophy's development and its deviations from Husserl's and Heidegger's phenomenological approaches, see Louise Westling, *The Logos of the Living World: Merleau-Ponty, Animals, and Language* (New York: Fordham UP, 2014).

27. One could even argue that posthumanism takes the Enlightenment/neo-humanist assumption of an unfinished process of enlightenment as the destiny of humanity more seriously than the Enlightenment itself, by declaring human nature subject to perfection as well.

28. See Wilhelm von Humboldt, "Über den Geschlechtsunterschied und dessen Einfluss auf die organische Natur" ("On the Difference of the Sexes and Its Influence on Human Nature"), in "*Ob die Weiber Menschen sind . . . ,*" ed. Sigrid Lange, 284–308; Johann Gottlieb Fichte, "Grundriss des Familienrechts" ("Outline of Family Law") (excerpt), in Lange 362–410; Immanuel Kant, "Der Charakter des Geschlechts" ("The Character of the Sexes"), in Kant, *Schriften zur Anthropologie, Geschichtsphilosophie, Politik und Pädagogik: Werkausgabe,* 12:648–58.

29. Barbara Becker-Cantarino asserts, "Patriarchy is deeply ingrained in German Enlightenment discourse. . . ." Becker-Cantarino, "Patriarchy and German Enlightenment Discourse: From Goethe's *Wilhelm Meister* to Horkkheimer and Adorno's *Dialectic of Enlightenment,*" in Wilson and Holub, *Impure Reason,* 48.

30. See, for instance, Manfred Kluge und Rudolf Radler, eds., *Hauptwerke der deutschen Literatur: Einzeldarstellungen und Interpretationen* (Munich: Kindler, 1995); see also the required readings in German literature of the high school exit exams for 2019–20, http://www.deutsch-unterrichtsmaterialien.de/Deutsch-Landesabitur-Inhaltliche-Schwerpunkte.html (accessed 25 October 2018); see also the book list of the German weekly *Die Zeit,* https://www.fabelhafte-buecher.de/buecher/die-wichtigsten-bucher-der-weltliteratur-aus-westlicher-sicht/die-100-besten-bucher-nur-die-liste/ (accessed 25 October 2018); as an example of required texts for the master's exam in German, see the Literary History Reading List at Washington University in Saint Louis of 2005, https://germanics.washington.edu/sites/germanics/files/documents/grad/lith istmalist.pdf (accessed 25 October 2018).

31. Johann Gottlieb Fichte's (1762–1814) *Die Bestimmung des Menschen* (1800) and Johann Joachim Spalding's (1714–1804) *Betrachtunge über die Bestimmung des Menschen* (*Reflections on the Vocation of Man*) (1748) are the most renowned publications with this title. *Bestimmung* has also been translated as "determination."
32. For instance, women authors like Betty Gleim were influenced by neo-humanist reformers and also advocated the importance of education, yet they "opposed their full integration into the workforce, claiming that to open the public sphere to women would turn the world upside down" (Fiero 364).
33. *Ob die Weiber Menschen sind . . . : Geschlechterdebatten um 1800* is also the title of Sigrid Lange's collection of eighteenth- and nineteenth-century philosophical and anthropological texts that illustrate the most pertinent gender debates at the time.
34. The most striking example is Lessing's *Emilia Galotti* (1772), whose heroine begs her father to kill her because she does not want to violate patriarchal bourgeois ethics.
35. These texts are part of Lange's anthology: Sophie von La Roche, "Über meine Bücher" ("About My Books"), 6–13; Susanne von Bandemer, "Zufällige Gedanken über die Bestimmung des Weibes und einige Vorschläge, dieselbe zu befördern" ("Random Thoughts Concerning the Destiny of Women and Some Suggestions to Promote It"), 14–21; Betty Gleim, "aus: Über die Bildung der Frauen und die Behauptung ihrer Würde in den wichtigsten Verhältnissen des Lebens" ("from: *On the Education of Women and the Defense of their Dignity in the Most Important Relations of Their Lives*"), 86–110. Gleim replicates the male gender discourse by deferring to the presumed natural intellectual superiority of men, warning their female readers not to use their education to contradict their husbands or to show off their erudition in social situations. She also blames women for their husbands' loss of interest in them during marriage (92–93) and for unduly provoking their husbands' anger by contradicting them.
36. A detailed analysis of Cathy Caruth's, Ankhi Mukherjee's, and Ottmar Ette's arguments is not possible within the framework of this investigation. I have chosen to focus only on those points that are relevant for the discussion of my methodology. Their essays are included in *PMLA* 125, no. 4 (2010).
37. In Caruth's opinion, Mukherjee suggests that "the concern with literature's survival in the classic as a thinking humanity . . . at risk of erasing its own traces" engenders literature's subsistence (1090).
38. Fish: "If your criteria are productivity, efficiency and consumer satisfaction, it makes perfect sense to withdraw funds and material support from the humanities—which do not earn their keep and often draw the ire of a public suspicious of what humanities teachers do in the classroom—and leave standing programs that have a more obvious relationship to a state's economic prosperity and produce results the man or woman in the street can recognize and appreciate." "The Crisis of the Humanities Officially Arrives," *New York Times*, October 2010.
39. The divide between science and culture, summarized by C. P. Snow in 1959, has, of course, a history of academic disciplinary practice that goes back much further. The study of literature, philology, linguistics, musicology, art history, and philosophical ethics, commonly associated with the humanities, had existed a long time before the terms were created. Scholars have argued that Snow's concept of two distinct cultures, the *Geisteswissenschaften* and the *Naturwissenschaften*, was artificial since the activities and methods of the scholars on both sides overlapped. See, for instance, Jens Bod and

Julia Kursell, "Introduction: The Humanities and the Sciences," *Isis* 106, no. 2 (2015): 337–40.
40. See also Sarah Colvin, "Leaning In: Why and How Should I Still Study the German," *German Life and Letters* 69, no. 1 (2016): 123–41. Colvin makes a similar argument in favor of reading literature: "In a context where literary studies risks disappearing from some curricula altogether, I make the case for literature as one of our most astonishing resources, not only aesthetically but ethically, because it models the humane and intellectually stimulating practice of 'leaning in' to the lived experience of others."
41. "Literary scholars should know better than to risk relinquishing the term *life* and allowing it to function in such a limited way" (*PMLA* 125, no. 4: 985).
42. Thus the "discovery" of the "noble savage" on the American continent, prevalent in the French intellectual tradition "from Montaigne to Rousseau," may have already anticipated a posthumanist Enlightenment critique by inspiring a subjectivist relativism that threatened to dissolve the boundaries of the Western subject (Scaglione 68).
43. For a more in-depth discussion of these developments, see Buck 376–91.
44. "Studia humanitatis . . . umfassen alles, wodurch rein menschliche Bildung und Erhöhung aller Geistes- und Gemütskräfte zu einer schönen Harmonie des inneren und äußeren Menschen befördert wird." Friedrich August Wolf, *Darstellung der Altertumswissenschaft nach Begriff, Umfang, Zweck und Wert*, Nachdruck der Ausgabe 1807 (Weinheim: Acta Humaniora, 1986): 45. (Studie humanitatis . . . comprise everything that promotes purely human formation and the elevation of all mental and emotional powers for the purpose of achieving the inner and outer human being's beautiful harmony [translation mine].)
45. "Der wahre Zweck des Menschen—‚nicht der, welchen die wechselnde Neigung, sondern welche die ewig unveränderliche Vernunft ihm vorschreibt—ist die höchste und proportionirlichste Bildung seiner Kräfte zu einem Ganzen. Zu dieser Bildung ist Freiheit die erste, und unerlässliche Bedingung" (HuGS 1:106). (The true purpose of Man—not the one that is prescribed by changing inclinations but the one that is determined by unchanging reason—is the highest and most proportional formation of his powers to a whole. Freedom is the first and indispensable condition of this formation [translation mine].)
46. For a discussion of these developments, see Jonathan Israel, *Enlightenment Contested: Philosophy, Modernity, and the Emancipation of Man 1670–1752* (New York: Oxford UP, 2006).
47. "Aber ein Unterschied unseres Humanismus, den man den dritten nennen könnte gegenüber jenem zweiten, liegt in der Weite des Suchens und des Verstehens, das wir Modernen aufzubringen vermögen" (But one distinction between our humanism, which one could call the third one as opposed to the second one, lies in the breadth of the search and the understanding that we modern ones can muster) (Spranger, *Geisteswissenschaften* 7).
48. After all, the name of the young Weimar democracy was a reminder of the humanist tradition.
49. For a detailed investigation of humanism in the GDR, see Horst Groschopp, *Der Ganze Mensch: Die DDR und der Humanismus; Ein Beitrag zur deutschen Kulturgeschichte* (Marburg: Tectum, 2013). Andreas Agocs traces the utilization of the humanist tradition by antifascist circles of émigrés during the 1930s to the GDR's official claims 'to represent the antifascist 'other Germany,'" which lasted until German unification

in 1989: *Antifascist Humanism and the Politics of Cultural Renewal in Germany* (Cambridge: Cambridge UP, 2017).
50. Ernst Robert Curtius's *Europäische Literatur und lateinisches Mittelalter*, for instance, was such an attempt to link Germany's culture to the Western tradition. For Curtius and other literary scholars of this period, such as Reinhard Buchwald, Goethe was a poet of the highest rank and of universal significance, comparable to Homer, Dante, and Shakespeare, poetic geniuses who succeeded in transcending the limits of time and space (Buchwald 289–91; Brockmann 116). Robert Mandelkow confirms the exaggerated elevation of Goethe in the postwar reception that celebrated him as the representative not just of a humanist Germany but of the entire Christian sphere of influence (Brockmann 134). In analogy to Goethe, humanism could be invoked to point out great literature's imperviousness to political instability because it allegedly dealt with eternally valid questions concerning the essence of human nature (ibid. 119). By emphasizing humanism's apolitical universality as a corrective of Germany's fascist degeneracy, it ironically obtained an exculpatory function that belied its alleged time-transcendent neutrality.
51. Antifascist and progressive thinkers on the left (Adorno/Horkheimer, Demetz, Durzak, Hermand, Hinderer, Schonauer, Vormweg) inadvertently furthered the skepticism toward humanism by showing how the Nazis glorified the classics and coopted aspects of the humanist tradition to serve their own ends. In view of such misappropriations, many West German postwar intellectuals shunned humanism's reactionary aura. Some attempted to construe a trajectory from German Idealism to fascism (Sloterdijk, Agamben). Additional examples for the utilization of humanist ideals for political purposes include the GDR's attempt to present itself as the true inheritor of the divided nation's classical humanist legacy.
52. I will refer repeatedly to Rosi Braidotti's *The Posthuman* because her study focuses extensively on posthumanist developments with regard to the German context.
53. "Der Mathematiker, der Naturforscher, der Künstler, ja selbst der Philosoph beginnen nicht nur jetzt gewöhnlich ihr Geschäft, ohne seine eigentliche Natur zu kennen und es in seiner Vollständigkeit zu übersehen, sondern auch nur wenige erheben sich selbst späterhin zu diesem höheren Standpunkt und dieser allgemeinen Übersicht" (HuW 1:234) (The mathematician, the natural scientist, the artist, even the philosopher generally begin their endeavor just without knowing and comprehending it in its entirety now. Only a few of them rise to this higher point of view and general comprehension even later [translation mine]).
54. Kant's, Herder's, and Schiller's assumption of a morally and spiritually free subject that can preserve its freedom over and against all physical and worldly constraints is the foundation of their Idealist philosophies.
55. A more recent collection of essays that deals with the question of what is human in the context of the so-called *Lebenskraft-Debatte* can be found in John A. McCarthy et al., eds., *The Early History of Embodied Cognition, 1740–1920: The Lebenskraft-Debate and Radical Reality in German Science, Music, and Literature* (Leiden: Brill, 2016).
56. Unlike the phenomenological approaches of Husserl and Merleau-Ponty, which attempt to reduce the infinite expansion of the scientific universe to a system that can be understood on a human scale, the open-endedness of newer postmodernist theories attempt to avoid any kind of anthropocentrist utilitarianism. Some scholars are critical of postmodernist influences and their effect on the humanities, however. Terry Eagle-

ton, John Guillory, Masao Miyoshi, and Robert Scholes, for instance, claim that postmodernist approaches have contributed to the waning importance of the humanities. Scholes attributes this decline to attempts "to bring the humanities in alignment with an increasingly technobureaucratic culture" in order to appear "more useful" and regain their lost value "in the cultural marketplace" (Scholes 726).

57. Examples of poetic representations of scientifically informed observations can be found in Brockes's *Irdisches Vergnügen in Gott* (1680–1747); Erasmus Darwin's "The Loves of Plants" (1789); Herder's "Vom Erkennen und Empfinden der menschlichen Seele" (1778), or all the metaphorical depictions of the evolution of humankind in the various chains of being or genealogies in tree form. The use of anthropomorphisms and anthropocentric metaphors is by no means limited to eighteenth- and nineteenth-century science but is still common in neuroscientific research of today (Metzinger). In fact, one of my main contentions is that scientific concepts in the so-called life sciences are often based on bodily and sensory human experiences. For this very reason, popular scientific research that relies on anthropomorphic imagery is able to convey scientific processes more comprehensibly than purely scientific discourses.

58. The first philosopher who linked idiosyncrasies among different cultures, races, and nationalities to anthropological, geographical, and historical distinctions was Johann Gottfried Herder. Although Herder attempted to reject the superiority of his own culture and time over other cultures and ages, he was still indebted to Eurocentric and racial biases. Schiller's universal history, on the other hand, still adheres to an Enlightenment trajectory that privileges eighteenth-century Western civilization over previous ages and more primitive cultures, yet it reveals an awareness of the historicity of human characteristics and its genealogy.

59. For a detailed study on the history of "Objectivity," see Lorraine Daston and Peter Galison, *Objectivity* (New York: Zone Books, 2007).

60. Judith Butler argues in a similar vein by bringing to bear the phenomenology of Maurice Merleau-Ponty (1908–61) on the French philosopher Nicolas Malebranche (1638–1715). Malebranche's "notion that self-understanding is grounded in a necessary obscurity" (60) resonates remarkably well with Merleau-Ponty's inquiry into sentience, which illustrates the chiasmic relationship between touch and being touched. Based on Malebranche's dictum "I can feel only what touches me," Butler problematizes the ontology of the emergence of the "I," which arises from a preconscious state of being touched. This passive sentience of which the "I" is borne through feeling (46) happens "prior to the emergence of the 'I.'" The experience of the touch can be narrated only from hindsight because the "I" has not emerged at the moment of sentience. In the words of Butler, the "'I' can begin to tell its story only after this inauguration has taken place" (ibid.). This is why, for "Merleau-Ponty reading Malebranche, sentience not only preconditions knowing, but gains its certainty of the outside at the very moment that it feels" (47). The postsentient emergence of the "I" also means that the formation of our selves is subject to outside influences. However, such preconscious influences that "pervade the horizon of consciousness" (60) reaffirm Lakoff and Johnson's supposition that metaphorical concepts, especially those based on physical, bodily experiences, may precondition rational thought processes.

CHAPTER 1

Signs and Wonders
The Humanist Pedagogy of Eighteenth-Century Universal Histories of Mankind

> Was Ihr den Geist der Zeiten heißt, –
> Das ist im Grund der Herren eigner Geist,
> In dem die Zeiten sich bespiegeln
> —Johann Wolfgang von Goethe, *Faust*

Introduction

During the last part of the eighteenth century, the European intellectual elites created and promoted an ideal that represented the moral standards and values of the rising middle classes. The self-determined bourgeois individual was male and became the universal norm for humanity. The popular genre of *Universalgeschichte* (universal history) provided a historical and philosophical foundation that supported the bourgeois individual's legitimacy. It offered hypothetical explanations for the phylogeny of humanity from its biblical beginnings to what was now considered the most civilized and accomplished stage of human development. Universal histories lent moral guidance and to some extent took on the function of theodicy by conjuring up a past that suggested a trajectory toward salvation.

A literary examination of universal histories can yield insights into the humanist paradigm because the narratives of this genre make exemplary assumptions about what a human being is, where it came from, and what it should strive for. While these histories reveal a new historical awareness of human evolution by giving accounts of the species' behavioral transformations during the course of civilization, their trans-historical claims about human nature go beyond the representation of historical events. The texts under discussion here—Lessing's *Erziehung des Menschengeschlechts* (*Education of the Human Race*) (1780) and Schiller's "Was heißt und zu welchem Ende studiert man Universalgeschichte?" ("What Is and to What End Do We Study Universal History?") (1789)—exhibit a high degree of self-reflection, fueled by the scientific thinking of the Age of Reason. Their main focus lies on education in a broader sense than its contemporary meaning suggests. Their concept of

Bildung (literally: formation) is not limited to an education toward a specific professional goal but is rather perceived as an education that comprises the cultivation of the entire personality approaching the ideal of the well-rounded autonomous individual. In addition, *Bildung* in the life sciences refers to the development of biological organisms. With the advances in the life sciences—that is what later became the disciplines of biology, zootomy, anatomy, botany, and genetics—the dynamic and holistic dimensions of living organisms began to be recognized and started to supersede prevailing mechanistic views (Zammito, *Gestation* 223–39, 245–85). Ironically, the scientific acknowledgment of the physiological and emotional aspects of life began to challenge the unmitigated belief in reason. The authors of *Universalgeschichten* utilized this heightened awareness of subconscious, nonrational sensory processes in their texts by appealing to their recipients' emotional and sensory sensibilities. Although the emphasis on the faculties of perception ostensibly serves a rational goal—the education of the individual—these histories do not lecture or impart factual knowledge in discipline-specific jargon. Instead, they perform their literary pedagogy by stimulating their recipients' participation through literary devices such as allegories, parables, and metaphors that are often inspired by biblical sources. The literary polysemy of these texts encourages their readers to think for themselves and search for meaning: the prerequisite of a humanist education.[1]

While the authors of these historical narratives are influenced by the discourse of reason, they also question seemingly objective factual accounts and contradict rationalist or empiricist truth claims, as the analyses of the texts under consideration will show. The critical examination of "correct," "objective," or authorized readings regardless of their religious, historical, or scientific nature is central for my argument, which regards *Universal-Historie* as a fusion of history and philosophy. This hybrid genre not only challenges existing dogmas but also demonstrates how literary imagination can complement both historical and philosophical discourses. By transcending fixed disciplinary boundaries and imbuing theoretical texts with poetic imagery, these narratives make history more vivid and comprehensible. They also include poetological reflections on why fiction can communicate abstract problems more effectively than putatively theoretical philosophies and factual historical accounts. Ultimately the communicative inadequacy of abstract, rational discourse provides the motivation for the poetic imagery that saturates these universal histories.[2]

The fusion of history, philosophy, and literature was fairly common until the end of the eighteenth century and attempted to provide some practical orientation and moral guidance for the general public. However, the emerging discipline of history as science, which separates history from literature, attempted to purge the new academic discipline from all ideological, philosophical, and political concerns during the course of the nineteenth century. Historian Hayden

White deplores the increasing specialization of the discipline, which focused exclusively on "the historical past" without taking into account the past's relevance for the present:

> The historical past is a theoretically motivated construction, existing only in the books and articles published by professional historians; it is constructed as an end in itself, possesses little or no value for understanding or explaining the present, and provides no guidelines for acting in the present or foreseeing the future. (White, *Practical* 9)

Unlike the specialized academic "historical past," the "practical past"—a term that White took from political philosopher Michael Oakeshott—concerns itself with notions "which all of us carry around with us in our daily lives and which we draw upon ... for information, ideals, models, formulas, and strategies for solving all the practical problems" (ibid.) In other words, the "practical past" would look at history in terms of its effect on the present and possibly on the future. For instance, Hegelian or Marxist representations of history belong to this category, and so do the universal histories by Lessing, Herder, and Schiller.

The authors of universal histories were aware that their accounts were to some degree hypothetical and subjective. Nevertheless, they questioned accepted mythical or religious narratives and examined them through rational inquiry. After all, inductive reasoning became prevalent during the eighteenth century with the emergence of hermeneutics, allowing enlightened philosophers, historians, and literati to challenge unsustainable biblical and mythological claims of the genesis of humankind by supporting their assertions with historical evidence.[3] Despite their scientifically motivated skepticism toward religious myths, the authors relied to various degrees on biblical events to support their arguments. In short, many universal histories attempted to reconcile traditional religious beliefs and modern secular views based on scientific knowledge by rationalizing accepted biblical truths. These histories included speculations about early stages of the human species, which had remained in the dark for lack of scientific explanation and written documentation. The absence of scientific evidence, however, stimulated imaginative hypotheses about early human history. Moreover, the authors' awareness of their narratives' hypothetical nature resulted in philosophical reflections on historiography.

In the following I will examine Lessing's *Erziehung des Menschengeschlechts* in the context of the debate on *Vernunftreligion*—that is, religion that complies with the laws of reason—and the role of divine revelation through miracles in biblical accounts. This contextualization is necessary because it sheds light on the connection of Lessing's didactic intentions and his aesthetics: *Erziehung durch Offenbarung* (education through revelation). The allegorical function of miracles is central in light of the growing importance of subjective sensory perception and the communicative efficiency of poetic discourse. An in-depth analysis of selected textual metaphors and allegories will demonstrate the didactic efficacy of Lessing's aesthetics. My interpretation will also show how the formal structure of the text supports its educational intention. Chapter 2 will discuss Schiller's universal histories, especially his programmatic "Was heißt und zu welchem Ende studiert man Universalgeschichte?" ("What Is and to What End Do We Study Universal History?") and, more briefly, "Die Sendung Moses" ("The Legation of Moses") (1790). Read together, chapters 1 and 2 will provide a comparative analysis of the many literary commonalities and differing aspects of Lessing's and Schiller's historical narratives. The chapters will conclude with some reflections on Enlightenment anthropology from a posthumanist perspective.

Lessing's *Erziehung des Menschengeschlechts*

Lessing's *Die Erziehung des Menschengeschlechts*[4] is less concerned with historical facts than with the adaptation of biblical accounts of the early history of mankind for a contemporary audience.[5] Like many universal histories, Lessing's *Erziehung* equates the history of the human race with the development of an individual.[6] It concentrates on biblical sources, such as the Egyptian captivity and Legation of Moses, as well as the appearance of Christ. These biblical stories are called upon to illustrate the relationship between God and humankind, the distinctions between divine revelation and human education through rational inquiry, as well as between sensory experience and intellectual understanding. While the narrative deviates from traditional histories of salvation because of its hypothetical nature and open-ended structure, it nevertheless follows the conventional trajectory from life in sin toward redemption (LW 10:690).[7]

The text has a three-part structure. Beginning with the Old Testament, the narrative focuses on the education of the Hebrew people. It stands for the education of mankind, and their unification under an almighty single God who punishes the Hebrew people for their sins and rewards them for their good deeds (§1–53). In part 2, which captures the period of the New Testament, God no longer rewards or punishes humans during their lifetime because Christ has taught them that they will be rewarded in the afterlife (§54–76). In the third part, humans would be enlightened enough to lead virtuous lives without the promise of a reward. The third part extends into the future because humankind has not achieved this state of perfection (§77–100). This part ends with speculations and questions about the possibility of an afterlife or metempsychosis (§97–100). Lessing's text is particularly concerned with the fundamental question: how is divine revelation related to reason? As an example of *Vernunftreligion*, *Die Erziehung des Menschengeschlechts* applies rational argumentation to explain a deistic world order. It addresses the question why God created imperfect human beings and allowed them to lead immoral lives without being punished in this life (§28–29). The answer to that question is embedded in Enlightenment pedagogy, namely that humans can only become autonomous individuals if they are permitted to discover their own errors.

The friction between traditional religious dogma that demanded the unconditional belief in biblical miracles and a deist position of a rationally organized universe is reflected in the so-called *Fragmentenstreit* (1777–79), which surrounded the creation of the *Erziehung*. This tension is apparent on several levels and throughout the text.[8] Therefore it is important to provide some necessary background information. The *Fragmentenstreit* followed Lessing's publication of excerpts of Samuel Reimarus's "Apologie oder Schutzschrift für die vernünftigen Verehrer Gottes" (1774–78), a polemic against the fundamental dogmas of orthodox Christianity and their insistence on the verbatim veracity of the Bible.[9] Lessing criticized, above all, that Reimarus did not take into consideration that perceptions of reality keep changing through the ages.[10] In other words, Lessing objected to Reimarus's ahistorical point of view, which disputed the credibility of miraculous revelations in general. For Lessing, these biblical revelations have a different function other than showing God's omnipotence and ability to make miracles happen. He suggests that enlightened recipients could interpret the depiction of miracles in multiple ways if they take into account the continuously changing epistemological horizon.[11]

Lessing originally figured only as editor but not as author of *Die Erziehung des Menschengeschlechts*.[12] The editor alerts the reader to the author's limited and provisional point of view. In his "Vorbericht" (preface) he presents the author as someone who addresses his audience from an elevated position on a hill with a commanding view that allows him to *believe* (italics mine) to see "beyond his projected path" (LW 10:74).[13] By separating editor from author and creating a fictitious narrator, Lessing emphasizes the text's fictional tenor, which undermines any claim to objectivity.[14] Thus he lets the text speak for itself with the modest hope that readers may recognize the illuminating aspect of religion. Many of the author's crucial suppositions are expressed in the form of questions or obvious speculations, adding to the text's polysemy (Eibl 247).[15] By exhibiting inconsistencies, contradictions, poetic imagery, and equivocal open-endedness, Lessing stresses the text's pedagogical function over and against its historical truth claims. In other words, he creates an evidently fictitious story of the development of humanity in analogy to its biblical accounts (Eibl 249) in order to shift the attention from the focus of the veracity of historical events to readings that ask for the "inner truths" of metaphors, allegories, and images. By encouraging the readers to find answers for themselves, Lessing stimulates the recipients to become self-reliant.

Lessing's endorsement of divine revelation in the *Erziehung* seems paradoxical in view of his refusal to accept the historical veracity of biblical miracles. His defense of divine intervention becomes understandable, however, if one considers that he supports the depiction of miracles as poetic expressions of universal truths and not as actual events that happened at a specific time and place. For Lessing, the use of biblical miracles is meaningful only if it teaches the readers to become autonomous human beings who act according to a humanist ethics. Biblical miracles can be compatible with reason because of their pedagogical effectiveness.[16] In short, Lessing's aesthetics takes advantage of the correspondences between the literary and religious imagination and their common evocation of allegorical and metaphorical imagery for educational purposes.

The text's numerous ambiguities also should be seen as a deliberate authorial strategy. The citation from Augustinus's soliloquies that prefaces Lessing's text supports this assumption and can be regarded as its motto: "Haec omnia inde esse in quibusdam vera, unde in quibusdam falsa sunt" (This is all true in a certain respect, from which it is also wrong in a certain respect) (LW 10:73). The oxymoron addresses a problem that pertains to all artistic depictions, namely that representations are generally based on dissimulation. Norbert Altenhofer reveals many references to Augustinus's *Soliloquia* throughout Lessing's text and demonstrates that they were an influential source with regard to both content and dialogical form. Whereas Augustinus stresses art's dissimulating disguise in order to proclaim the unique integrity of Christian faith, Lessing employs his poetic depictions to show that poetic "disguises" in the form of analogies, images, metaphors, etc., are able to reveal an "inner truth" that cannot be expressed literally (LW 10:864–65, Schilson). He defends the depiction of biblical revelations as long as we recognize their parabolic or symbolic qualities (Hayden-Roy 400–401). Thus, Lessing acknowledges biblical revelations in the "Vorbericht des Herausgebers" (editor's foreword) to *Die Erziehung des Menschengeschlechts* because they can enhance human understanding.

This brings us back to the frequently discussed question of why Lessing introduces an editor to preface the *Erziehung*.[17] Both the editor and the author of the treatise remain anonymous, which caused some confusion among the first recipients about the actual author's identity, especially since Lessing never identified himself as the author and even tried to divert the attention away from himself by suggesting other possible authors (Schilson, LW 10:795–900; Nisbet, *Lessing* 572–73).[18] Altenhofer and other reviewers point out that the persona of the editor enables the author to distance himself from the contents of the treatise (Altenhofer 29; Schilson, LW 10:860).[19] According to this argument, the editorial introduction suggests that the treatise lays no claim to universality. This suggestion seems plausible if one considers the conspicuous hesitation with which the editor expresses his introductory remarks:

Der Verfasser hat sich [in seinem Aufsatz] auf einen Hügel gestellt, von welchem er etwas mehr, als den vorgeschriebenen Weg seines heutigen Tages zu übersehen glaubt.... Er verlangt nicht, daß die Aussicht, die ihn entzücket, auch jedes andere Auge entzücken müsse.

Wenn er aus der unermeßlichen Ferne, die ein sanftes Abendrot seinem Blicke weder ganz verhüllt noch ganz entdeckt, nun gar einen Fingerzeig mitbrächte, um den ich oft verlegen gewesen!

Ich meine diesen.—Warum wollen wir in allen positiven Religionen nicht lieber weiter nichts, als den Gang erblicken, nach welchem sich der menschliche Verstand jedes Orts einzig und allein entwickeln können, und noch ferner entwickeln soll; als über eine derselben entweder lächeln, oder zürnen? Diesen Hohn, diesen unsern Unwillen verdiente in der besten Welt nichts: und nur die Religionen sollten ihn verdienen? (LW 10:74)

(The author of the essay has taken an elevated position on a hill, from which he believes to see somewhat farther than today's prescribed route. ... He does not demand that the view, which delights him, has to delight all other eyes.

If only he were to provide a hint from the immeasurable distance, which to his eye is neither entirely veiled nor entirely disclosed by a soft afterglow—a hint, which has often eluded me!

I mean this one.—Why don't we want to simply see in all positive religions the mere course according to which the human mind of each place can develop all by itself and shall continue to develop, rather than to ridicule or deride them? Nothing in the best world shall deserve our mockery or scorn: and yet only religions are supposed to deserve it?)[20]

The editor's equation of the author with a wanderer who assumes an elevated position emphasizes the subjectivity and the uncertainty of his point of view. The editor leaves it up to the readers to form their own opinion. This technique allows him to express his hopes that the author will perhaps provide a "Fingerzeig" (pointer), which calls our attention to the allegorical meaning of religions and their function of providing a sense of direction.[21] Significantly, the "Vorbericht des Herausgebers" ("Foreword of the Editor") ends with the rhetorical question: "Gott hätte seine Hand bei allem im Spiele: nur bei unseren Irrtümern nicht?" (God had allegedly his hand in everything except in our errors?) (LW 10:74), which resonates with the text's underlying tenor that error is intrinsic to learning and self-improvement.

The abundance of poetic images is striking and calls attention to the text's metaphors in general, which sets the tone for the following discussion of the differences between revelation and reason (Althaus 171). The pointing finger is a sign of revelation and marker of orientation in an immeasurable distance that is neither completely veiled nor unveiled by a faint afterglow of the sunset. While the hint embodied by the finger cannot adequately represent the infinite distance to which it refers, it serves nevertheless as a palpable visual image that points to the transcendence of infinity. Infinity itself can only be detected because the faint glow of the sunset illuminates it, but cannot unveil it. The image of the pointing finger induces an analogy to the ensuing history of mankind. In this narrative the recipients have to detect their own signs of revelation, which serve as markers of orientation and will point them to the transcendent truth that is partially hidden and partially unveiled during the process of civilization. Altenhofer demonstrates that Lessing follows Augustinus also with regard to the latter's doubts about the truth-value of the sciences. Accordingly, the sciences can express the truth only through signs that mediate the truth. In fact, the mediating discourse of seemingly objective signs prevents the insight into the truth because the signs themselves become fetishes that overshadow the hidden inner truth that they are supposed to reveal (Altenhofer 29). In contrast, Lessing wants to engage the readers in a dialectical process of self-interrogation that resonates with the textual ambiguities of both revealing and concealing a truth that can only be depicted indirectly (Schilson, LW 10:855, 860). As this truth is incommensurable and goes beyond the recipients' intellectual comprehension, the author has to convey the divine inner truth metaphorically in analogy to biblical revelation.

The dialectic between secrecy and revelation was influenced by Lessing's interest and expertise in *Freimaurerei* (Freemasonry).[22] The poetic disguise of an inner truth was part of the rituals at the secret societies of the *Freimaurer*, which became very popular among German intellectual circles during the 1770s and 1780s (Assmann, *Moses* 140). The Freemasons were a product of the European Enlightenment. In Germany they mainly consisted of members of the educated bourgeoisie. They rejected the hierarchical structures of absolutism and sought ways to implement a republican state, based on the laws of reason (Dülmen 15–20). They promoted the democratization of society according to humanist ideals. Their goal was to establish a free and equal cosmopolitan society consisting of emancipated, responsible individuals. Formation and self-cultivation were necessary to achieve this goal. The group's members disagreed with traditional Christian dogmas and favored pantheist ideas. While Lessing's humanist points of view influenced this group, he was not initiated and did not become a member (Schilson, LW 10:705).[23] However, he remained a loyal supporter of Freemasonry and agreed in principle with the secret society's philosophical orientation. Lessing's attempts to become a member, his admitted fondness of Spinoza's pantheism (Assmann, *Moses* 139), his "dialogues for freemasons" titled *Ernst und Falk* (1779), as well as his reference to the Anglican theologian William Warburton (1698–1779) (§24), suggest that he was familiar with the latter's *The Divine Legation of Moses Demonstrated on the Principles of a Religious Deist*—a foundational text of Freemasonry that had already been translated into German in 1751–53.

In order to explain the Masonic influence on Lessing's aesthetics, I will have to briefly sketch out Warburton's dialectic of concealment and revelation. Warburton contributed to the dissemination of the widespread legend that monotheism originated in Egypt, evoking parallels between an absolute truth in Freemasonry and in the Egyptian religion from which the Israelites, as a less-educated people, copied monotheism. Warburton's text also led to the common assumption that "the 'Symbolic' script ... was developed for the purpose of secrecy" (Assmann, *Moses* 107).[24] According to this belief, the esoteric symbolism was necessary to protect the "truth" from misunderstanding and abuse by the uneducated masses. Likewise, the secret society of the Freemasons claimed that the Egyptian caste of priests had to conceal the esoteric concept of monotheism from the uninitiated and uneducated because they were unable to understand such abstract concepts or were likely to misinterpret them (Assmann, *Moses* 102). To avoid the premature initiation of the unenlightened public, Warburton distinguished between "lesser" and "greater mysteries" (ibid. 97). The lesser mysteries were represented "through symbolic icons, sensual rituals, and sacred animals." Although they addressed a larger audience, only those who proved able to understand the symbolism became aware of their secret meaning (97). The "greater mysteries" were reserved for those who had been initiated or those who were deemed to withstand the disillusioning realization that polytheism was a lie.[25]

In this context, it is important to bring into play the author's assertion that education, which is tantamount to revelation (*Erziehung* §2), can teach human beings nothing that they could not detect by themselves through reason, except that revelation accelerates the process of learning.[26] This assertion seemingly undermines the alleged importance of revelations or depictions of miraculous events. Why would an enlightened individual give up his autonomy to blindly trust such stories if he could discover the truth by relying on his own intellectual capabilities? The author explains, however, that miracles are suitable for a certain age in the development of a human being, and likewise in the development of an entire people. Similarly, the initiated cast of priests in Egypt, described above, had to resort to symbolic and allegorical depictions that were comprehensible to people who were not educated enough to comprehend the underlying abstract truth of an omnipotent single God (§23, §34). Only after the Jewish people had been introduced to monotheism "by the wise Persians" during the Babylonian captivity were they ready to grasp intellectually what the concept of monotheism means (*Erziehung* §35). This radical change from a people that idolizes the concrete pictorial representations of a multiplicity of local gods to one that worships an omnipotent universal deity who cannot and must not be visually represented constitutes an intellectual leap that reverses the dialectics of revelation and reason according to Lessing's text. Whereas at an earlier stage of human development revelation informed reason, from now on reason guides revelation (*Erziehung* §36). The fact that reason becomes more dominant and former revelations become seemingly superfluous in the progression toward self-perfection does not mean, however, that revelations in general have become insignificant. After all, the process of self-perfection is by no means accomplished, as the text's open-ended structure demonstrates.

Likewise, in his preface the editor is still hoping that he might detect a visible sign of orientation and that the wanderer on the hill "aus der unermesslichen Ferne ... gar einen Fingerzeig mitbrächte" (would convey a signal from the infinite distance) (LW 10:74). The image places the expectant wanderer in the realm of an inexplicable infinity, whose tender afterglow evokes expectations because of its partial concealment. This seductive image exemplifies the message of §77, in which the narrator suggests that religion might be able to provide more adequate notions "of the divine being, of our own nature, of our relations with God, than human reason." It also implies the perpetual need of revelations or poetic allusions. This passage apparently contradicts §4, cited above, which claims that revelations could not teach anything that human reason could not discover on its own. While there have been numerous scholarly contributions that attempted to solve this problem,[27] I would argue that the contradiction is deliberate and emphasizes the existential uncertainty—an uncertainty that continues into the future as long as humankind has not achieved the utopian goal of being completely enlightened (see also Altenhofer 32). Moreover, the passage underlines the distinction between poetic and theoretical discourse, which is crucial to Lessing's aesthetics and its representation in the *Erziehung*. While theoretical representations of abstract concepts speak to the intellect, their poetic enactments appeal to the senses and emotions and thus are more palpable. This is precisely the point that Lessing pursues in his essay, and this is also why the unbridgeable distinction between revelation and reason manifests itself in the poetic evocation of images, contradictions, allegories, and Socratic questions throughout the text. It may well be true that revelations cannot teach us anything that human reason cannot discover on its own; however, the assumption does not deny that these poetic representations might provide a more tangible and comprehensible perspective. Moreover, the ambiguity leaves it open for the recipient to decide, which is in keeping with Lessing's pedagogy.[28]

Lessing's *Erziehung* applies this Socratic technique to the entire human race: "Was die Erziehung bei dem einzeln Menschen ist, ist die Offenbarung bei dem ganzen Menschengeschlechte" (That which enlightenment is to the individual, revelation is to the entire human species) (*Erziehung* §1). The author uses the people of Israel as an example to demonstrate their progressive enlightenment from ignorance to civilization because God chose them as the "roheste" (crudest) and "verwildertste" (most savaged) people in order to start from the very beginning: "... um mit ihm ganz von vorne anfangen zu können" (*Erziehung* §8). The *Erziehung* follows the premises laid out in the editor's foreword by presenting an open-ended development in analogy to the wanderer who has not reached his goal. While the author is able to observe the past of the human race from his vantage point, he can only guess what the future has in store (see also Thielicke 44).[29] The "Fingerzeig" that the editor hopes to glean from the author's depiction of human history corresponds to God's revelations for the cultivation of the Israelites. Because of their inability to comprehend abstract concepts like monotheism, God teaches the uncivilized Israeli people his omnipotence through miracles (*Erziehung* §12). Yet, God applies the dialectic of revelation and disguise and lets the human race discover for themselves the meaning of these miracles (*Erziehung* §28, 44–47). This discovery, which is also a self-discovery, is essential for God's education of the Israelites as he intends them to become the future teachers of other peoples. After all, only a people taught in this fashion of self-discovery can truly understand what enlightenment means. Another example for this dialectic of disguise and revelation can be detected in God's refusal to reward virtue and punish vice in this life. Only because God veils his eternal justice does the Israeli people discover the idea of a beyond where justice will be eventually served (*Erziehung* §28). In other words, the deficiencies of this life stimulate the idea of transcendence.

The discovery of transcendence is portrayed as a defining moment in the development of the chosen people, when revelation no longer guides reason, but reason guides revelation (*Erziehung* §36).[30] This turning point both constitutes the internalization of authority and enables a people to take responsibility for its own conduct. For instance, when confronted with more civilized people, the Israelites no longer blame *Offenbarung* (divine revelation) but themselves for their shortcomings (*Erziehung* §38).

The role of literature in this formation of the individual is analogous to that of biblical revelation, namely to provide a *Fingerzeig* or sensory stimulus pointing to a truth that the recipient has not been able to deduce by means of reason. This sensory stimulus in form of an image, analogy, or parable is supposed to inspire the recipient to fill in the gaps of the partially concealed object of cognition and thus construe an inner truth or *Vernunftwahrheit* by means of reasonable inference. The narrator also mentions specific examples of allegorical representation or "Einkleidung" in the Old Testament, such as "creation in the image of the dawn of day; the source of evil in the narration of the forbidden tree; the origin of multiple languages in the story of the tower Babel, etc." (*Erziehung* §48). The polysemy or ambiguity of such "Einkleidungen" that can be "einfältig" (simplistic), poetic, or even full of tautologies provoke the intellect ("den Scharfsinn üben") "by seemingly saying something different, but actually saying the same or, vice versa, claiming to say the same but meaning something else" (*Erziehung* §49). Poetic or metaphoric language inspires the desire to comprehend because it is equivocal, even confusing, and opens up a variety of possible meanings. In analogy to the divine clues of biblical miracles that prompt revelations, Nathan the Wise replaces the divine authority by creating hypothetical situations or clues that stimulate empathy and self-reflection, and responsible action. Although these situations are fictional, perhaps even miraculous, their clues must be concrete, be easily comprehensible, and appeal to human emotions or senses. For Lessing, revelation provides the intuition and trajectory toward the goal of self-perfection.

The temporal aspect in comparing revelation and reason is of significance insofar that it allows insights into the author's ideas of what it means to be human:

> Erziehung giebt dem Menschen nichts, was er nicht auch aus sich selbst haben könnte: *sie giebt ihm das, was er aus sich selber haben könnte, nur geschwinder und leichter.* Also giebt auch die Offenbarung dem Menschengeschlechte nichts, worauf die menschliche Vernunft, sich selbst überlassen, nicht kommen würde: *sondern sie gab und giebt ihm die wichtigsten dieser Dinge, nur früher.* (LW 10:75; italics mine)

> (Education does not offer a human being anything that he could not figure out for himself: it provides what he could figure out for himself, only faster and more easily. Thus revelation does not offer humankind anything, which human reason left to itself could not fathom: but it has been offering the most important of these things, only earlier.)

Sensory comprehension generally precedes intellectual understanding. Images, metaphors, and analogies affect emotions and can convey phenomena with much greater immediacy than rational discourse. Poetic imagery is particularly compelling if it conveys bodily experiences or emotions that are physically comprehensible.[31] While the immediacy of emotions and their artistic expression gain momentum during this period, reason is equally important for the formation for the self-empowerment of the bourgeois individual. The narrator mentions explicitly the interdependence of reason and revelation or their "mutual service" (*Erziehung* §37), or, as Nisbet succinctly puts it, "Revelation is the historical vehicle of reason, and reason is the necessary content of revelation" (*Lessing* 575). Without reason, an individual would not be able to link a physical experience like suffering to a moral imperative in order to avoid future suffering in others and oneself. The subject would thus not be able to grow beyond a state of awe, joy, admiration, sadness, etc. Likewise, as the *Education of the Human Race* demonstrates by example of the biblical history of the Israeli people, if it were not for reason, the human species would not progress from its ignorance to self-awareness and would not be able to comprehend abstract concepts, such as the eternal life of the soul or the notion of the Holy Trinity (*Erziehung* §71–73).[32]

Although the development toward a higher intellectual awareness suggests that reason is superior to the sensory faculties, the latter are often indispensable stimuli of the intellect. For instance, the emotion of empathy is crucial for an ethical awareness. While the narrator claims that metaphoric or allegoric depictions are no longer necessary once the revelations have become rationally grounded "Vernunftwahrheiten" (rational truths), he also emphasizes that the "Fingerzeige," "Anspielungen" (allusions), or "Vorübungen" (preparatory exercises) can lead to a greater awareness in hindsight.[33] Despite all these revelations, God leaves it to humans to discover the truth for themselves because the discovery belongs to the transformative process of self-tutelage (§76).

Finally, the author's speculations about the future remain open-ended because the human species has not achieved the state of perfection (see also Thielicke 44). The fact that the last nine paragraphs end with a question underlines the author's seemingly superior, but ultimately humble and limited perspective, a perspective that can only attempt to discover a *Fingerzeig*. After all, the text begins with a reflection on the author's search for a clue in the infinite vastness of nature, and it returns to the concept of infinity, this time temporal infinity: eternal life.[34] The narrator's speculations about metempsychosis have to be seen in this context. While Lessing's ideas about metempsychosis are purely speculative, for the narrator speculations are "die *schicklichsten* Übungen des Verstandes überhaupt" (the most appropriate exercises of the intellect) (*Erziehung* §79). Speculations are "Vorübungen" that eventually lead to rational comprehension. Metempsychosis itself could be seen as a kind of revelation that points to an afterlife, albeit in a different form.[35]

The dialectic of revelation and reason implicitly acknowledges the increased significance of sensate representations or the "untere Wahrnehmungskräfte" (lower capacities of cognition) during the late Enlightenment. Lessing's *Erziehung* no longer considers sensory representations as inferior to rational analysis but as addressing a separate cognitive capacity. Consequently the sensory faculties are capable of providing a different perspective that "makes a perception lively" and has a "'painterly' form of clarity ['*eine malende*'] . . . that consists in richness of imagery rather than analytical clarity" (Baumgarten §393, p. 119). The second aspect that gives sensory representations an advantage over rational discourse is their ability to mediate various sensory perceptions simultaneously. Although the *Erziehung* asserts that all revelations or sensate representations are simply "Vorübungen" (*Erziehung* §43) that comply with the laws of reason and can eventually be formulated as *Vernunftwahrheiten*, the parallel existence of sensate and rational cognition seem at times incompatible and may well constitute the reason for the text's abundance of unsolved ambiguities. Lessing's pedagogical aesthetics of disguising abstract concepts with metaphoric polysemies and unveiling different aspects of these concepts intend to empower the recipient and to evoke speculations about the future. Lessing's hermeneutic model has left a legacy that laid the groundwork for phenomenological as well as reader-response approaches reaching into the twentieth and twenty-first centuries.

Notes

1. On the literariness of such forms as essay, sermon, dialogue, and other short prose forms, see McCarthy, *Crossing Boundaries* (1989).
2. Lessing's *Die Erziehung des Menschengeschlechts* (*The Education of the Human Species*) (1780), Kant's *Idee zu einer Geschichte in weltbürgerlicher Absicht* (*Idea for a Universal History from a Cosmopolitan Point of View*) and *Mutmasslicher Anfang der Menschheitsgeschichte* (*Speculative Beginning of Human History*) (1786), Schiller's "Was heißt und zu welchem Ende studiert man Universalgeschichte" ("What Is, and to What End do We Study Universal History") (1789) and *Etwas über die erste Menschengesellschaft nach dem Leitfaden der Mosaischen Urkunde* (*Some Thoughts on the First Human Society Following the Guiding Thread of the Mosaic Documents*) (1790), Herder's *Ideen zur Philosophie der Geschichte der Menschheit* (*Reflections on the Philosophie of the History of Mankind*) (1784–91) are only a few examples of this genre that attracted eighteenth-century historians, philosophers, and authors of belles lettres. At the time when the examples mentioned above appeared, *Universalgeschichte* had already been an established term, as Herder indicates in the title of his essay *Auch eine Philosophie der Geschichte zur Bildung der Menschheit* (*This Too a Philosophy of History for the Formation of Humanity*) (1774).
3. While the term "hermeneutics" has already "been part of common language from the beginning of the 17th century" and has been practiced in the form of biblical exegesis since the Middle Ages, the awareness that the understanding of texts cannot be separated from their historical horizons and the subjects who read them was new (http://plato.stanford.edu/entries/hermeneutics, publ. 9 November 2005).
4. On the sources of this text, see Arno Schilson's commentary to *Die Erziehung des Menschengeschlechts* in Arno Schilson and Axel Schmitt, eds., *Gotthold Ephraim Lessing Werke 1778–1781* (Frankfurt am Main: Deutscher Klassiker Verlag, 2001): 10:794–816. All future references to this volume will be cited parenthetically in the text as LW. *Die Erziehung des Menschengeschlechts* will henceforth be cited as *Erziehung*. References to the body of this text will simply be quoted as § numbers. Among the most influential sources, Schilson mentions Spinoza and Leibniz, as well as, according to Lessing's own words, the "Kirchenväter der ersten vier Jahrhunderte" (the church's elders of the first four centuries). With regard to the text's triadic structure—Old Testament, New Testament, and a new age of an "Ewigen Evangelium" (eternal gospel)—Schilson mentions a direct influence of Joachim Fiore, a medieval monk and scholar (LW 10:803). In addition to these older sources, Schilson names more recent works, such as John Locke's *The Reasonableness of Christianity* (1695), John Toland's *Christianity Not Mysterious* (1696), and Adam Ferguson's *An Essay on the History of Civil Society* (1767), as well as the so-called *Neologen*—a group of Lutheran theologians who attempted to do justice to the Enlightenment spirit during the second half of the eighteenth century. Among the works that represent the phylogeny of the human race, Schilson cites Herder's *Auch eine Philosophie der Geschichte zur Bildung der Menschheit* (1774), and Charles Bonnet's

(1720–93) *La palingénésie philosophique, ou idées sur l'état passé et sur l'état future des êtres vivans* (1769).
5. Several critics (Althaus, Michel, Eibl) emphasize the hypothetical character of his *Erziehung des Menschengeschlechts*. In a letter to Johann Albert Heinrich Reimarus of April 6, 1778, Lessing himself called his text a "Hypothese" (hypothesis) (LW 10:810, 841, 848).
6. Remarkably, this perspective of comparing the development of an individual to that of the entire race comes almost one hundred years before Ernst Haeckel's (1834–1919) discovery that the growth of an individual organism (ontogeny) recapitulates the evolutionary history (phylogeny) of its species. For a better understanding of Lessing's sources, see also Klaus Bohnen's short contribution on "Lessings 'Erziehung des Menschengeschlechts' und Charles Bonnets 'Palingenesie,'" *Germanisch-Romanische Monatsschrift* 62 (1981): 362–65. British literary scholar H. B. Nisbet points out that "the analogy between the development of mankind and the education of the individual has a long history . . ." He mentions Clement of Alexandria, Justin Martyr, Irenaeus, Tertullian, and Origen as possible forerunners (Nisbet, *Lessing* 573).
7. All references to Lessing's *Erziehung des Menschengeschlechts* are taken from G. E. Lessing, *Werke und Briefe*, vol. 10, ed. Arno Schilson und Axel Schmitt (Frankfurt am Main: Deutscher Klassiker Verlag, 2001). Subsequent references will be documented parenthetically in the text as LW including volume and page numbers.
8. For a thorough and informative discussion of the *Fragmentenstreit*, see Arno Schilson's enlightening commentary in LW 9:913–86 and LW 10:710–803. The concern with religious questions was of particular interest to Lessing in view of his involvement in this debate, which I will not discuss in detail since Priscilla Hayden-Roy has provided a comprehensive account of the *Erziehung*'s publishing history in regard to the *Fragmentenstreit* (Hayden-Roy 393–95). Hayden-Roy contrasts Samuel Reimarus's *Fragmente* to Lessing's position in the *Erziehung*, which he wrote in response to the fourth *Fragment*. Her remarks connected to Lessing's criticism of Reimarus's lack of a historical perspective are significant for this interpretation because Lessing bases his aesthetics on the assumption of a historically conditioned reception or what Hegel later called the *Zeitgeist* (ibid. 395–99).
9. Reimarus argued from a deist point of view, interpreting the biblical message according to the premises of reason. While Lessing concurred with Reimarus in doubting the literal veracity of miraculous biblical revelations, he disapproved of Reimarus's ahistorical perspective. As a response, Lessing offered his critical comments to each of the five *Fragmente* in his five *Gegensätze zu Reimarus*. The first fifty-three paragraphs of the *Erziehung* appeared as an appendix to the fourth *Gegensatz*. Thus one could argue that Lessing's universal history is the result of his attempt to clarify his own position in response to that of Reimarus.
10. For instance, Reimarus argued that the Old Testament could not be regarded as a "seligmachende Religion" (beatifying religion) because it lacked three concepts that were a condition for this type of religion: the immortality of the soul, the reward or punishment in the afterlife, and the eventual union with God (Hayden-Roy 396). Lessing, on the other hand, argued that these concepts might not have been comprehensible to the Israelite people at the point of their revelation because humans of biblical times were unlikely to think in abstractions (ibid.).
11. I agree with Priscilla Hayden-Roy that the dynamic hermeneutics laid out in the *Erziehung* have far-ranging implications that go beyond differences in the representation of history (396–97). However, my analysis will not examine the *Erziehung* in the

context of the influences of its aesthetic predecessors (Christian Wolff and Alexander Baumgarten).

12. Future references to Lessing's *Erziehung des Menschengeschlechts* will be abbreviated in the text as *Erziehung*. Specific passages (excluding the "Vorbericht des Herausgebers") will be quoted as § and number.
13. For Karl Eibl, for instance, the separation of author and editor is "ein eindeutiger Akt der Fiktionalisierung des ganzen Texts" (an obvious fictionalization of the entire text) ("Lauter Bilder" 250).
14. In the *Fragmentenstreit*, Lessing was held accountable for the publication of Reimarus's polemic and banned from publishing further writings on religion, although his position as editor deviated in significant aspects from that of Reimarus. The editor's gestures of humility and feigned ignorance in the *Erziehung* are perhaps intended to distance him from the content of the published materials making him thus unassailable.
15. The text's ambiguities can be read as an authorial strategy, shifting the emphasis from the opinionated prose of Lessing's earlier debate with the theologian Melchior Goeze (1717–86) to a more ambiguous treatment of the topic that leaves it to the recipient to take a stand.
16. After all, Lessing had already justified the use of miraculous elements, such as speaking animals, for educational purposes in his *Abhandlungen über die Fabel* (1759).
17. Schilson and several other critics have pointed out the significance of this "Vorbericht des Herausgebers" for the understanding of the entire text (Schilson, LW 10:852). Schilson also mentions Inge Strohschneider-Kohrs, *Vernunft als Weisheit*, and Thomas Althaus, *Das Uneigentliche ist das Eigentliche*.
18. In a letter to the younger Reimarus of 6 April 1778, Lessing describes it as the work of "a good friend." See also Nisbet, *Lessing* 572.
19. Altenhofer makes the compelling argument that the separation between editor and author constitutes a dramatic monologue or conversation with the self that reflects on its own discourse. Consequently, Lessing works in the tradition of Augustinus for whom the splitting of the self allows the author to reflect openly without the reservations that a dialogue with a different interlocutor may cause (Altenhofer 26–27).
20. If not indicated otherwise, all translations from the German are mine.
21. A positive religion is a religion that has an identifiable founder.
22. For more information on Lessing's connection to the Freemasons, also in the context of his "Gespräche für Freimäurer," titled "Ernst and Falk," see Nisbet, *Lessing* 585–99 passim.
23. For more details on Lessing's failed attempts to join the Freemasons, see Nisbet's biography of Lessing (*Lessing* 586–87).
24. Warburton's *Devine Legation of Moses* actually refuted the commonly accepted legend "that Egyptians invented their hieroglyphs solely 'to express the mysteries of their religion and theology, so that they might be concealed from the prophane vulgar'" (Assmann, *Moses* 104).
25. It is not surprising that Lessing's *Erziehung* was informed by these ideas, especially since Warburton was—like Lessing—also focusing on the distinction of revelation and reason (Assmann, *Moses* 102). The pedagogical strategy of addressing the audience at an appropriate level involves an awareness of the effect that the teachings might have. As a dramatist who introduced *Wirkungsästhetik* to the German stage and established a theory on affecting spectators through "Mitleidstheorie" (empathy) in the *Hamburger Dramaturgie*, Lessing was, of course, an expert in the hermeneutics of representation.

Yet his late writings, like *Nathan the Wise* and *Erziehung*, add a new dimension that probes into the mediation of truth and the significance that the distinction between fiction and nonfiction has for his aesthetics.
26. "Also giebt auch die Offenbarung dem Menschengeschlechte nichts, worauf die menschliche Vernunft, sich selbst überlassen, nicht auch kommen würde: sondern sie gab und giebt ihm die wichtigsten dieser Dinge nur früher" (§4).
27. I agree with Nisbet that "it makes little difference whether the contradiction (between §4 and §77) are resolved or not" (*Lessing* 575), in fact I would even go further and claim that trying to solve this incongruity would contradict Lessing's point because both statements are not mutually exclusive. While the first statement makes a general claim, the second statement describes a more nuanced distinction of quality within the first statement.
28. In this respect, Lessing's aesthetics parallels Merleau-Ponty's interpretation of Malebranche's anthropological assumptions, according to which conscious human acts are predisposed by unconscious sensory stimuli "that form the basis for sentience" (Butler 41). Butler's reading of Merleau-Ponty goes even further in stating that these unconscious sensory impressions constitute "a certain passivity as the condition of freedom" (ibid. 61). In other words, our openness to sensory stimuli provides an impetus for a subjective free agency. Lessing's plea to recognize the pedagogical value of religion in the "Vorbericht des Herausgebers" is a classical example of instructing the reader in the form of rhetorical questioning. His Socratic technique bears resemblance to a scene in *Nathan der Weise* (1779) where Nathan teaches his stepdaughter Recha by persistently questioning her with the intent to make her realize that recourse to a miraculous intervention deprives humans of their ability to act ethically (LW 9:491–97). While Nathan instructs Recha about the dangers of indulging in *Schwärmerei* (religious phantasies), the introduction to the *Erziehung* emphasizes the didactic efficacy of religious revelation. Yet both texts emphasize that the belief in miracles is both frivolous and harmful, unless it serves an educational purpose. For instance, Nathan carefully instructs his stepdaughter that, contrary to her belief, she was not rescued by a "real" angel but by an angelic human being who risked his life to safe her from the fire. Nathan does not reject the existence of miraculous deeds. In his opinion, the rescuer's action of saving Recha's life can be called a "miracle" (LW 9:492). This miracle has a moral purpose as it reinforces the belief in the goodness of human beings who help strangers out of empathy. In his capacity as an educator who figures as a spokesperson for the author, Nathan assumes the role of author himself by reiterating the significance of the metaphorical depictions that can enlighten those who cannot comprehend abstract concepts. Nathan also takes advantage of the powers of allegorical fiction as he uses the parable of the three rings to convince the Sultan that the three major religions each deserve respect and the right to coexist. Like in the other examples above, Nathan never addresses his audience directly and tells them what to do but always lets them discover the "truth" for themselves.
29. "Zwar befindet er [Lessing] sich—wie der 'Vorbericht des Herausgebers' . . . meldet—auf einem 'Hügel,' von welchem er etwas mehr als den vorgeschriebenen Weg seines heutigen Tages zu übersehen glaubt.' Aber damit steht er noch keineswegs am Ende der Entwicklung. . . . Auch für ihn liegt das Ziel noch in 'undendlicher Ferne,' wohl im Ahnen erfaßbar, aber nicht deutlich zu sehen" (Thielicke 44).
30. "Die Offenbarung hatte seine [des Volkes Israel] Vernunft geleitet, und nun erhellte die Vernunft auf einmal seine Offenbarung" (Revelation had guided its [the Israelites'] reason, and now reason suddenly enlightened its revelation).

31. Nisbet points out that revelation evokes "obscure feelings" and that these "obscure perceptions (*perceptions insensibles*) and confused feelings" are "precursors of rational knowledge." These "obscure impressions" are indebted to Leibniz's epistemology as outlined in his *Nouveaux Essais* (Lessing 576). This reading corresponds to Maurice Merleau-Ponty's reading of Malebranche, according to which sentience preconditions knowing (Butler 47). Hayden-Roy makes a similar claim in tracing the trajectory of the *Erziehung* and demonstrating its indebtedness to the Wolffian model that progresses from sensuous (*sinnlich*) and "below the threshold of rational . . . cognition" to "distinct" (*deutlich*) representations (401–2). What these obscure sentiments and sensate impressions gain in clarity and distinctness during the process of rationalization they lose in richness of meaning or polysemy. Hayden-Roy argues that the "polysemic richness of [Lessing's] metaphorical, sensate language' allows him to assume the role of 'one of the privileged souls' who by means of a more highly developed faculty of reason, are able to see 'the greater light' more clearly than their contemporaries" (404). Yet neither the author nor the editor speak from a superior position, given their hesitation and careful probing stance in this admittedly hypothetical sketch of human history.
32. The narrative shows the entire trajectory from a primitive to a highly civilized human state of development and divides this progression into several phases: the state of ignorance or infancy, which requires both divine intervention to make the omnipotence of monotheism known and an education that punishes the morally bad and rewards the morally good in this life (§1–53); the internalization of moral categories that no longer require God's intervention and the assumption of divine justice in the afterlife; the arrival of Jesus and the concept of eternal life (§54–72); the use of human reason, which allows mature human beings to recognize the affinities of revelations and rational truths (§75–77) as well as to speculate about the future and metempsychosis (§79–100).
33. For instance, in the process of reviewing former *Elementarbücher* (primers), a people may have to acknowledge that the reception rather than the representation of miracles has led to stagnation. In other words, the blame for a belated comprehension of such metaphoric insinuations or "Fingerzeige" lies not with the text but with the initially limited understanding of the recipient (§38). The author also explicitly warns the reader not to feel self-satisfied once he has mastered an *Elementarbuch* and advises him to check whether he has overlooked hidden messages (§68–69).
34. Nisbet quotes Jacobi, who reports, "Lessing could not come to terms with the idea of a personal and absolutely infinite being in the unchanging enjoyment of its supreme perfection. He associated it with such an impression of *infinite boredom* that it caused him pain and anxiety."
35. Jeffrey Librett points out that Lessing "turns, as the *Education of the Human Race* nears its conclusion, toward an affirmation of a synthesis of Jewish and Christian—which he [Lessing] understands as a synthesis of sensuous and spiritual ways of being and of time and eternity . . . in the form of transmigration" (247). Transmigration promises, on the one hand, liberation from the body and, on the other hand, reincarnation in a transcendent eternal realm. Once the goal of enlightenment has been achieved, the process of education is still not completed, however, but extends into an endless repetition. The paradox of a spiritual physicality in eternity finds expression in the form of a circle.

CHAPTER 2

Religion, Anthropology, and the Mission of Literature in Schiller's *Universalgeschichte*

"Was heißt und zu welchem Ende studiert man Universalgeschichte?" (1789)

Schiller's and Lessing's historical methodologies are similar in many respects. Both writers follow the conventional model of *Universalgeschichte*, which attempts to detect an underlying teleology in world history based on contextual inferences by studying the cause and effects of events (SNA 17:373).[1] This method is particularly advantageous for examining the early history of humankind, for which no written sources exist (SNA 17:371). According to Schiller, world history is full of gaps, and the historian has to fill in the blank spaces by creating a coherent narrative that bridges them (SNA 17:372).[2] Schiller explicitly states in his inaugural public lecture as a professor of history at the University of Jena, titled "Was heißt und zu welchem Ende studiert man Universalgeschichte?" ("What Is and to What End Do We Study Universal History?") (1789), that the historian's task is to impose order on what appears to be an overwhelming amount of fragmented historical data ("ein Aggregat von Bruchstücken") (SNA 17:373).[3] Schiller's universal historian brings order into the seemingly chaotic accumulation of facts by selecting those events "... welche auf die *heutige* Gestalt der Welt und den Zustand der jetzt lebenden Generation einen wesentlichen und leicht zu verfolgenden Einfluß gehabt haben" (... that have had a relevant, significant, and easily traceable influence on the current state of affairs and the contemporary generation) (SNA 17:371; Alt, "Natur" 534–35). Surprisingly, this order is the creation of the historian's imagination (SNA 17:373; see also Alt, "Natur" 536). The historian takes the harmonious order, which he finds within himself, and projects it onto the outside and arranges it into a meaningful order of things: "Er nimmt also diese

Harmonie aus sich selbst heraus, und verpflanzt sie ausser sich in die Ordnung der Dinge d.i. er bringt einen vernünftigen Zweck in den Gang der Welt und ein teleologisches Prinzip in die Weltgeschichte" (SNA 17:374). It is easy to see that Schiller's historian is very closely affiliated to a writer of fiction (Hofmann, *Epoche* 79–83; see also Alt, "Natur" 541). The implication that narrative texts in general are fictitious did not become fully accepted by many historians for a long time to come:

> Wo der Brotgelehrte trennt, vereinigt der philosophische Geist. Frühe hat er sich überzeugt, daß im Gebiet des Verstandes, wie in der Sinnenwelt, alles ineinander greife, und sein reger Trieb nach Übereinstimmung kann sich mit Bruchstücken nicht begnügen. Alle seine Bestrebungen sind auf Vollendung seines Wissens gerichtet; seine edle Ungeduld kann nicht ruhen, bis alle Begriffe zu einem harmonischen Ganzen sich geordnet haben, bis er im Mittelpunkt seiner Kunst, seiner Wissenschaft steht und von hier aus ihr Gebiet mit befriedigtem Blick überschauet. (SNA 17:362)
>
> (Whereas the *Brotgelehrte* [scholar whose professional goal is primarily to make a living] dissects, the philosophical mind unites. He has convinced himself early on that everything is connected in both the intellectual realm and the realm of the senses, and his lively ambition to achieve harmonious agreement cannot be satisfied with fragments of knowledge. All his motivations are directed toward the completion of his knowledge; his dignified impatience cannot rest until all terms have formed a harmonious whole, until he is in the center of his art and his science and overlooks its realm from this vantage point with satisfaction.[4])

The distinctly subjective perspective of Schiller's universal historian resembles that of Lessing's wanderer, who orients himself by standing on a hill from which he can overlook his path. Lessing and Schiller also concur in their attempt to bridge the gap between the senses and the intellect. The universal historian is capable of creating a totality that speaks to the entire human being by appealing equally to the intellectual and sensory faculties. The historian's fictitious totality corresponds to the recipient's desire for coherence and order. This harmonious totality is based on the assumption that human nature is in essence universal despite the cultural differences that have evolved during the long process of human civilization, which Schiller depicts in graphic language. While the assumption of a universal human nature is biased and modeled on the archetype of the Western male philosophical mind, Schiller's and Lessing's implied notion that universal history is tantamount to the historian's subjective interpretation seems astonishingly modern considering the dominance of empiricist scholarship during the nineteenth century. Schiller's reasons for rejecting claims of objectivity appear also quite progressive by taking into account the unreliability of historical sources and the personal biases of their interpreters.[5]

However, these historical projections—which Schiller also calls "Gemälde" (paintings)—are not arbitrary. They must follow the laws of reason, be coherent and meaningful. Schiller's historian has to connect the events in a methodical way. In order to establish a cause-and-effect relationship, the historian must slowly go back in history from the present to the origin of things, always looking for the preceding causes of later events. Once he has established a cause-and-effect relationship, he can then develop a continuous historical narrative (SNA 17:371–74). In short, world history according to Schiller is the historian's freedom to give meaning to an arbitrary and chaotic reality. Yet, how can one call truth what is in fact the historian's poetic illusion? Schiller's vision could not claim to be true were it not for an assumed inner correspondence that links the historian to his recipient. They share a common belief in "Wahrheit, Sittlichkeit und Freiheit" (truth, morality, and freedom), which governs the meaningful order that underlies Schiller's claim to universalism. Schiller sees the justification for his belief in a "reasonable totality" and in the continuous and unchangeable unity of human nature that constitutes the basis for the similarities between ancient and modern-day events (SNA 17:375). In other words, understanding human nature is for Schiller the key to understanding human history. And history is only relevant as long as it sheds light on the dark recesses of the human soul.

Although these universal histories are speculative rather than empirical in nature, they concur with significant Enlightenment premises. For one thing, they stress the value of a comprehensive education; they encourage the individual historian to question historical events and recreate history according to his own rational abilities rather than accepting factual truth claims. Yet, as we have already seen in Lessing's case, they intend to educate their audiences by conveying ethical, inner truths that affect the recipients' moral convictions and behavior. While the emphasis on the historian's subjective point of view seems self-deprecating and possibly harmful to his scientific credibility, these universal histories encourage the creation of alternative accounts. They exemplify the different missions of "die schönen Wissenschaften" (the arts) and the empirical sciences by viewing history in allegorical or metaphorical instead of factual terms. This does not mean, however, that universal history should ignore empirical knowledge but rather use this knowledge to shed light on the purpose and destiny of human nature. Instead of separating the sciences and the "schönen Wissenschaften," Schiller envisions a synthesis or totality of both. By emphasizing the need for an interdisciplinary approach to history, Schiller's lecture speaks to the overspecialization of academic disciplines. Thus it can be interpreted as a plea for the mission of the humanities to provide a broad general education that prepares students to become well-rounded cosmopolitan citizens.[6] In this respect Schiller's philosophy of history influenced Humboldt's humanist ideal of a university education (Hofmann, *Epoche* 79).[7]

At first glance, Schiller's introductory lecture reveals all the typical biases of Enlightenment historicism. By depicting almost every narrated event in the starkest, most vivid colors, the author applies his hyperbolic pathos to his theoretical and historical texts. His proclivity for portraying every constellation in antagonistic dualisms, such as the distinction between the so-called *Brotgelehrte* (pragmatic scholar) and *philosophische Kopf* (philosophical mind), his contrastive comparison between the less-developed societies of ancient times and other continents, and the "edlere Freyheit" (gentler freedom) of human beings in civilized societies is meant to justify the superiority of European civilization and to celebrate the enlightened autonomous individual (SNA 17:366). Schiller calls these depictions of human development "vom ungeselligen Höhlenbewohner – zum geistreichen Denker" (from antisocial cave dweller to ingenious thinker) "entgegengesetzte Gemälde" (contrasting pictures), which exhibit in graphic detail how far humanity has evolved.

Like Lessing, Schiller makes extensive use of visual metaphors. Schiller's inaugural lecture portrays history as continuous progression toward Enlightenment, extolling his own era as the pinnacle of human civilization. The author not only looks back with pity on the less enlightened eras from the vantage point of the late eighteenth century, he also looks down on the "primitive civilizations" of his own time. He regards them as remnants of the dark days of a violent, barbaric age, and he disdains the "bondage," "stupidity," and "superstition" that plague the so-called savage tribes of Africa (SNA 17:365). He demonstratively compares what he views as a miserable life in the primitive societies to life in a free, prosperous, enlightened Europe in order to let his audience know how infinitely more refined and civilized humankind has become over the course of history.

In order to describe human nature, Schiller goes back in history to preliterary times when he believes the animalistic side of man was still dominant and easy to detect (SNA 17:364). The more barbarous and violent "Man's" ancestors are depicted, the more moral strength is necessary to civilize them and the more heroic humanity's victory over its animal nature would appear. In Schiller's words, civilized Man "has sacrificed the freedom of the predator to preserve the gentler freedom of the human being" (SNA 17:366). Yet in spite of his moralistic tone, Schiller is fascinated with the depiction of uncontrollable outbursts of the senses because it highlights the intensity of humans' inner struggle for control over the instincts. This is why for Schiller moral freedom can only be represented "through the most vivid representation of suffering" (SNA 20:196). The tension between divine history, which starts with Edenic perfection, on the one hand, and human history, which starts with a state of uncontrolled barbarity and progresses during the process of civilization toward perfection, is endemic to Schiller's literary works and can be traced to his early anthropological writings as well as to his indebtedness to Kantian historiography (Alt, "Kommentar," SchW 4:1057).

Kant's essays "Idee zu einer allgemeinen Geschichte in weltbürgerlicher Absicht" ("Idea for a Universal History with a Cosmopolitan Aim") (1784) and "Mutmaßlicher Anfang der Menschengeschichte" ("Presumed Beginning of the History of Humans") (1786) resonate with Schiller's philosophy of history.[8] While both Kant's and Schiller's narratives are indebted to the continuum of a progressive improvement of civilization, they also acknowledge Rousseau's critique of civilization's degenerate influences (KW 11:93). They reconcile these seemingly contradictory views by portraying human imperfection as preferable to the paradisiac state of innocence. Both justify their preference of human imperfection and its progressing civilization by making freedom the decisive quality of human existence. "Man's" freedom to trade that paradisiacal state of blissful ignorance for knowledge is what makes us human (KW 11:88–92; SNA 17:398). If "Man" had not dared to challenge the divine order to eat from the tree of knowledge, he would never have transcended the limited consciousness of an animal: "... aus der Vormundschaft des Naturtriebs wäre er niemals getreten, frey und also moralisch wären seine Handlungen niemals geworden, über die Gränze der Tierheit wäre er niemals gestiegen (SNA 17:398–99). In other words, the expulsion from paradise, or what Peter-André Alt has termed the "Sturz ins Bewußtsein" (fall into consciousness), distinguishes humans from other species (Alt, "Kommentar," SchW 4:1057). Another analogy between Kant's and Schiller's philosophies of history is the aim to regain the unity with nature at a higher, conscious level through culture and reason (SNA 17:399). In both narratives the struggle of culture versus nature can be overcome when art and human culture are perfected to the extent that they become identical with nature: "... bis vollkommene Kunst wieder Natur wird: als welches das letzte Ziel der sittlichen Bestimmung der Menschengattung ist" (... until perfect art reverts to nature, which is the telos of humankind's moral destiny) (KW 11:95).

What Kant calls the telos and moral destiny of the human species finds expression in neoclassical art: the conformity of nature and civilization. While Schiller's tendency to present world history in extreme dramatic tensions seems to contradict the category of the neoclassical ideal of beauty as natural harmony, the dramatic conflicts can be overcome through a seemingly unrestrained, and therefore graceful, self-control in the face of adversity. By showing the tension between human desire and moral duty leading to the eventual overcoming of the instinctual forces, Schiller's dramatic conflicts illustrate the civilizational progress of human nature from its animal origins to its sublime renunciation of its selfish drives.[9]

Schiller's anthropological views, especially his emphasis on the dramatic representation of the emotional and instinctual powers as well as his awareness of the mind-body dialectic, are informed by the concept of the *ganze Mensch* (entire human being). Medical advances and the discovery of the nervous system induced this holistic philosophy that was disseminated by the *philosophische Ärzte*, a group of physicians that rejected the separation of physiology and philosophy (Riedel, *Anthropologie* 14–16). Their scientific interest, the interrelations between body and soul, coincides with Ernst Platner's assumption that "the human being is neither body nor soul by itself; it is its harmonious unity" (Riedel, *Anthropologie* 16) and demanded an interdisciplinary approach (Zelle, "Sinnlichkeit" 5–8). As has already been suggested, the anthropological assumptions of late eighteenth-century *Popularphilosophie* (empirical philosophy) prepared the fertile ground for the humanist concept of *Bildung* (formation, education) that requires the cultivation of *all* human faculties, including physical and emotional capacities. Lessing's and Schiller's universal histories can be regarded as exemplary in showing why these two authors resorted to biblical accounts and favored poetic narratives, parables, and metaphors over summaries of events and empirical facts.

Schiller's aesthetic philosophy presumes that the striving for individual autonomy is an essential human quality and carries trans-historical validity, although it is said to have evolved and progressed over time. Yet, the tension between humanity's destiny of self-determination and its instinctual animal nature is very much part of the human psyche in all his works. Schiller's anthropological views date back to his education at the *"Hohe Karlsschule."* His teacher Jakob Friedrich Abel (1751–1821) introduced him to current medical and philosophical trends, with particular attention to the mutual influence of body and mind (Riedel, *Anthropologie* 18, 27, 91–93, 173–75). Schiller's anthropological views on the dialectic relationship between the sensual and spiritual faculties, depicted in his medical-philosophical dissertations (1779–80), resonate with his aesthetic theory. For instance, the overcoming of the mind-body dualism in the ideal of the *"ganze Mensch"* comprises both the *sittliche* (moral) and *sinnliche* (sensory) nature of the human being and constitutes the utopian background of his entire dramatic oeuvre (ibid. 112–13).

Rousseau's and Herder's skepticism toward the dominance of civilizing reason are also noticeable in Schiller's historiography. In their view the exigencies of modern existence restrict the formation of well-rounded personalities by putting too much emphasis on the intellectual faculties at the expense of the so-called "untere Erkenntnisvermögen" (lower cognitive faculties) and emotions (Baumgarten, Zelle). For Schiller, art is a means to restore the lost equilibrium because it appeals to both intellect and emotions. Already Schiller's early essay "Was kann eine gute stehende Schaubühnge eigentlich wirken?" ("What Can a Good Permanent Stage Really Achieve?") (1784) lauds drama as a genre that engages "alle Kräfte der Seele, des Geistes und des Herzens" (all faculties of the soul, the mind, and the heart) (SNA 20:89). As a synaesthetic form of art, it has the capacity of restoring the spectator's "mittleren Zustand" (inner equilibrium) by harmonizing the tension between his exhausted physical and mental powers (SNA 20:90). Like Lessing, Schiller finds poetic inspiration in the evocative imagery of biblical stories as they incorporate tropes and metaphors that appeal to the senses rather than the intellect. The stage takes on the legacy of religion and captivates the human mind with greater power than secular laws because of its "Gemählde der Phantasie, Räzel ohne Auflösung, Schreckbilder und Lockungen aus der Ferne" (fantasy imagery, its riddles without solution, its horror visions, and allures from afar) (SNA 20:91).

In analogy to the narrator of Lessing's *Erziehung des Menschengeschlechts*, Schiller interprets the Bible in terms of a *Vernunftreligion*—religion based on reason—that can be read on two levels. I would call these two perspectives (a) the allegorical level and (b) the philosophical level. While the allegorical point of view provides moral guidance by illustrating Man's fall from innocence, the philosophical perspective recognizes the enormous significance of freedom and the opportunities that the fall from innocence creates for the human destiny. Although the human being has become what Hegel later called "ein unglückliches Bewußtsein" (an unhappy consciousness) in view of its alienation from its original identity with divine nature, the prospect that Man can accomplish this desired reunification on his own makes his present state as an imperfect but autonomous individual preferable to his previous state of happy ignorance. Schiller's dual perspective can also be linked to his aesthetic theory. While he did not articulate the connection between the aesthetic, spiritual, and moral categories in his *Universalgeschichte*, a connection that became the center of his aesthetic theory, the associations are latently present. When he describes the fall from grace that transforms the human being "from a happy tool [of nature] to an unhappy artist" (SNA 17:400), he implies that artistic impulses originate in the recognition of moral imperfections.

"Die Sendung Moses" (1789)

Schiller's second lecture that he presented as a newly appointed professor of history at the University of Jena has the very same focus as Lessing's *Erziehung*. "Die Sendung Moses" ("The Legation of Moses"), published in 1790, deals with the origin of monotheism and the civilization of the "Hebrew people." Both texts share some of the same sources, especially William Warburton's (1698–1779) *The Divine Legation of Moses* (1737), which was widely known among German literati and "came to substantiate the views of the free-thinkers and Freemasons ..." (Assmann, *Moses* 102).[10] Schiller became familiar with Warburton through philosopher Karl Leonhard Reinhold (1757–1825), who published a masonic treatise under the pseudonym Bruder Decius titled *Die*

Hebräischen Mysterien oder die älteste religiöse Freymaurerey (*The Hebrew Mysteries, or the Oldest Religious Freemasonry*) (ibid. 115–16).[11] Both texts were based on the assumption that monotheism originated in Egypt and that Moses had the privilege of being educated among an elitist group of priests who were privy to the secrets of their religious practices. In Warburton's account, Moses adopted the secretive rituals of the Egyptians and their strategy of building religion around a "nucleus of original wisdom" for his mission to unite the Hebrew people after their exit from Egypt (ibid. 102). Thus Moses translated "the Egyptian premises of monotheism into revealed truth" (ibid.). Lessing and Schiller depict God and his representative Moses as teachers who must convince their uneducated audience to believe in abstract ideas that they are not prepared to comprehend, such as monotheism or the Holy Spirit. For them, God and Moses serve as exemplary vehicles for the authors' reflections on their mission as writers. As we have seen in Lessing's *Erziehung*, God figures as the author's alter ego in his role of pedagogue who reveals incommensurable truths by providing clues in the form of images, metaphors, and analogies. Likewise, Schiller's Moses resorts to the creation of miracles/revelations and stories to unite the Hebrews under monotheism (SNA 17:394–95). One could argue that Schiller expands on Lessing's *Wirkungsästhetik* (aesthetics of effect) by using similar literary strategies that appeal to the recipient's senses.

Schiller calls Moses a "Volkslehrer" (teacher of the people) who provides moral instruction (SNA 17:400). He uses the book of Moses as an example for universal history. As the first people with a monotheist religion, the Jews became a people of universal importance according to Schiller. He concurs with Lessing that the Bible is capable of teaching universal truth because it makes the truth fascinating to a general audience. How was Moses able to convince his people to believe in one God instead of in the many natural gods that they worshiped? Schiller attributes Moses's success in founding a new religion to the deceptive demagoguery that he had learned from the Egyptians. His Egyptian teachers, the so-called *Epoptoi*, had invented various techniques to conceal the truth from the broad masses of the uninitiated who would not be able to comprehend it in its pure and abstract form. In order to effectively convert and convince nonbelievers, they used signification techniques to make the "truth" sensually attractive (SNA 17:384). Schiller mentions the hieroglyphs as an example of a pictorial language that concealed the naked truth from the uninitiated and yet stimulated their curiosity (ibid.).[12] The priests also aroused their disciples' passions during their initiation rites to prepare them for facing the truth. According to Schiller, these seductive rituals taught Moses how to convert his own people. In order to win them over to monotheism, he invents a personalized God with supernatural powers who is able to protect the Hebrew people from its enemies. This is Schiller's explanation of how religion became "die stärkste und unenbehrlichste Stütze aller Verfassung" (the most powerful and indispensable buttress of any constitution) (SNA 17:396).

Moses, of course, bears many similarities to Schiller. In analogy to Moses who learned from his Egyptian teachers how to convince his people of the truth by appealing to their senses, Schiller learned from Lessing's *Education of the Human Race*. Lessing had already viewed the Bible as an allegorical revelation of the truth that can be grasped before reason can explain it. Just as Moses uses illusion to convert his people to monotheism, so does Schiller use theatrical deception in the service of "truth." The question, however, of what exactly "truth" is remains open for both Schiller as well as for Lessing. For them, "truth" is a totality that still exceeds human comprehension. This is why "truth" cannot be represented in rational discourse. The author, embodied by Moses, has to resort to symbolism in order to express his prophetic vision, a vision whose realization is incommensurable and which eludes human understanding. Man's fall from grace necessitated a perpetual quest for salvation through incremental apprehensions of the "truth." While metaphorical or poetic representations are inadequate to depict "truth" in its entirety, they provide partial insights and inspire the search for it by stimulating the rational faculties. This explains why art is at home in both the physical and spiritual domains. The artifact thus points to the restoration of the lost unity of self and world by mediating between body and mind. As in Lessing's text, sensual perception precedes and inspires human understanding. Likewise, revelation is given as a manifestation of nature, which then inspires human motivation to overcome the mind-body schism and thus restore the lost identity of self and world:

> ... so thut man ganz recht, das Schöne, *objektiv*, auf lauter Naturbedingungen einzuschränken und es für einen bloßen Effekt der Sinnenwelt zu erklären. Weil aber doch—auf der andern Seite—die Vernunft von diesem Effekt der bloßen Sinnenwelt einen transzendenten Gebrauch macht und ihm dadurch, daß sie ihm eine höhere Bedeutung leiht, gleichsam ihren Stempel aufdrückt, so hat man ebenfalls recht, das Schöne, *subjektiv*, in die intelligible Welt zu versetzen. Die Schönheit ist daher als die Bürgerin zweier Welten anzusehen, deren einer sie durch *Geburt*, der andern durch *Adoption* angehört; sie empfängt ihre Existenz in der sinnlichen Natur und erlangt in der Vernunftwelt das Bürgerrecht. (SNA 20:260)

> (... and we are absolutely correct to limit Beauty *objectively* to mere natural conditions and to explain it as a mere effect of the world of the senses. But since—on the other hand—Reason makes a transcendental use of this effect of the mere world of the senses and presses its stamp on it by endowing it with a higher significance, we are also correct to place Beauty *subjectively* into the intelligible world. Beauty is therefore to be viewed as a citizen of two worlds, belonging to the one by *birth*, and to the other by *adoption*; she receives her existence in sensuous nature and attains the right of citizenship in the world of reason.)

The literary dimension of Friedrich Schiller's portrayal of Moses has not received much scholarly attention. This seemingly ancillary text is nonetheless key to central aspects of its author's philosophical and aesthetic positions because it encapsulates his views on both the relationship between religion and aesthetics and—perhaps even more pertinent—on human nature in general. In fact, Schiller's text is less about the historical figure of Moses than about what it means to be human.

Most of the scholarship on this particular lecture examines its significance in the context of either eighteenth-century historiography or Schiller's use of literary sources (Wübben 125–26).[13] Schiller's reference to Karl Leonhard Reinhold's *Die hebräischen Mysterien* (*The Hebrew Mysteries*) contributed to the scholarly preoccupation with the complex history of Schiller's sources (SNA 17:397).[14] This somewhat narrow research focus has resulted in the assumption that Schiller mainly paraphrases Reinhold's essay (Hartwich 30).[15] While my analysis builds on this research in order to provide necessary background information on the intellectual climate in which Schiller's "Die Sendung Moses" was written, I will read the text in light of the author's anthropological and poetological assumptions.[16] Of particular interest is the question of whether it is possible to preserve the rights of the individual in a society that is guided by abstract principles of truth. This question ties into the larger debate about the dialectic of the Enlightenment that—as some would argue—already began during Schiller's time and continues to this day: namely, whether the pursuit of Enlightenment ideas could lead to a tyranny of reason and the perversion of ethical principles, such as freedom, truth, and honor (Borchmeyer, "Marquis Posa" 130).[17] Adherence to universal ethical concepts often prohibits or restrains individual human needs, which have generally been associated with the biological nature of the human species. Schiller, in accordance with Kant, considered egotistical instincts subordinate to the higher moral values that would lead to the perfection of the human species. "Die Sendung Moses" is one of the author's numerous attempts at defining a human nature that, on the one hand, justifies his artistic utilization of the senses and, on the other, devalues them in the name of a higher universal truth. In Schiller's reinterpretation of Moses's life, Moses becomes the archetypical poet/writer who, like Schiller himself, was committed to converting his audience to "truth" by appealing to their base instincts and ingrained habits. Schiller relies on a widely known biblical source to reinterpret the beginnings of monotheist religion in a way that supports his Enlightenment anthropology. The question is whether Schiller's elevation of reason to the status of a *Vernunftreligion* prepares the path for the tyranny of reason, and whether his concomitant devaluation of "bare life" (Agamben 15–16)—that is, of a creaturely, instinctual life without higher meaning—paves the way for a political theology that legitimates the manipulation of a people in the name of ethical ideals.

Figure 2.1. Peter Anton von Verschaffelt (1710–93), *Statue des Moses von Michelangelo* (after 1737). Wikiedia Commons, public domain.

Beginning in the 1780s there is an intense debate among different factions of the Freemasons about whether Moses's monotheism originated from Egyptian mythology and to what extent Moses deliberately embellished this mysticism to further his political and theological goals (Wübben 127).[18] Some deist thinkers doubted the miraculous stories of the Bible and contrasted the scientific methods of the Enlightenment to what they considered to be the obscurantist political strategies of the Mosaic religion (Hartwich 22–23).[19] Yet not all Enlightenment thinkers concurred with such indiscriminate condemnation of the Old Testament. Others like Lessing and Schiller recognized the sensuous appeal of biblical stories and used them in the service of reason as a vehicle to further Enlightenment goals. While Schiller gives the story of Moses his own spin, his text still echoes the debate.

Schiller's "Die Sendung Moses" reflects a certain ambiguity about the debate's central issue of whether Moses was a divine messenger or an impostor by presenting Moses as both a shrewd ideologue and yet a person with moral integrity. The question of whether Moses's creation of a poetic illusion in the name of truth by telling stories of miracles is legitimate, even morally desirable, or whether it results in political demagoguery is also significant in the context of the so-called *Illuminatendebatte*. My analysis, which highlights the resemblance between Schiller's Moses and some of his most well-known dramatic heroes and Machiavellian villains, such as Franz Moor, Fiesco, Don Carlos, and Wallenstein, will, however, show that Schiller addressed the despotic abuse of Enlightenment ideals even before the *Illuminatendebatte*.[20]

According to Hans Jürgen Schings, the debate over whether the Illuminati's clandestine pursuit of Enlightenment ideals has to be viewed as a deceptive manipulation marks a new level of awareness as its participants discover the dialectic of the Enlightenment for themselves (*Brüder* 164). Schings and others[21] generally examine Schiller's connections to the *Freimaurer Logen* and to the Illuminati in the context of *Don Karlos* (1787) and his *Briefe über den Don Karlos* (*Letters on Don Karlos*) (1788). At the beginning of the tenth letter Schiller explicitly states that he is "weder Illuminat noch Maurer" (neither a member of the Illuminati nor a Freemason) (SNA 22:168) and distances himself from the pursuit of political schemes in the name of universal ideals in his eleventh letter (SNA 22:170–71). In light of these letters and passages taken from *Don Karlos* and *Die Geschichte des Abfalls der Vereinigten Niederlande von der spanischen Regierung* (*The History of the Revolt of the United Netherlands against Spanish Rule*) (1788), Schings concludes that Schiller was without doubt directing his criticism against the despotism of the Enlightenment whose universalist ideals tended to disregard human nature and the rights of the individual (Schings, *Posa* 163–65; Borchmeyer, "Marquis Posa" 130).

The principles that Schiller laid out in his lecture on universal history, however—one year after his letters on *Don Karlos*—reveal the historian's/

dramatist's fundamental and deliberate dependence on universal abstractions. Without the ability to generalize individual human characteristics and project them onto the larger canvas of world history, history would remain limited to recording empirical data. Schiller's universal historian is not nearly as interested in what happened as in how and why it happened. The uncertainty of how Moses was able to convert and unite an entire people under monotheism provides Schiller with the opportunity to fill in the gaps and to create a meaningful totality from a compilation of historical fragments (SNA 17:373).[22] Just as writers like Lessing, Gellert, and others took advantage of the genre of the fable to teach the uneducated, so did Schiller, Herder, and others exploit the allure of biblical myths to convey abstract moral concepts in the form of illustrious examples that would captivate the imagination of an unenlightened audience. Schiller's distinction between an illusory surface appearance and an inner truthful core in "Die Sendung Moses" shows his commitment to search for meaning beneath empirical reality.[23]

Schiller's elevation of reason to the status of a *Vernunftreligion* is accompanied by his contempt of creaturely life, such as the diseased, degenerate, and utterly pitiful existence of the "pre-monotheistic" Hebrew people who were "durch eine solange anhaltende Dummheit endlich fast bis zum Thier herunter gestoßen" (eventually pushed down, almost to the state of the animal by such an enduring stupidity) (SNA 17:380).[24] In his essay on the *Schaubühne*, his lecture on universal history, and "Die Sendung Moses," Schiller stresses the beneficial powers of the Enlightenment by contrasting it to the "uncivilized" societies in the distant past and in distant locations (SNA 17:364–67) or by equating "der Pöbel" (the rabble) of his own time to animals (SNA 20:100). Schiller excludes all those groups or aspects of life from humanity because in his view they lack a spiritual dimension that would enable them to recognize truth. Not only does he degrade uncivilized societies but also human needs that are essential to bare survival. A corollary to this idea would be his admiration for the "heroic" decision to sacrifice one's material existence in order to uphold a universal ideal, which one can find throughout his work.[25]

The exclusion and sacrifice of all those particular aspects of life that cannot be controlled by reason is, of course, where enlightenment becomes its tyrannical other. Is Schiller's conspicuous distinction between a human Moses and animalistic Hebrews a rhetorical exaggeration that intends to extend the power of reason to all civilizations? Does his exclusionary definition of the human contradict such intentions? Does the author attempt to impose his ideological view onto what he considers a barbaric group under the guise of brotherly love? By depicting the Hebrew people as uncivilized, he coerces his audience to identify with Moses, the exception, rather than with the Hebrews.

Schiller portrays Moses as a leader who transformed the highly philosophical and abstract mysticism of an elitist Egyptian circle of priests into a national religion. Establishing an inner correspondence with Moses allows the author to understand and rationalize his protagonist's actions from his own, personal point of view. Schiller literally follows the premise laid out in his lecture on universal history: namely to take the harmony that he finds within himself and project it onto the external order of things (SNA 17:374). He projects his own points of view onto historical figures like Moses to make them more understandable to his eighteenth-century audience.

Schiller psychologically motivates Moses's extraordinary accomplishment of liberating and uniting the Hebrew people under an entirely new religion. Accordingly, Moses was predestined to unite his people under the banner of monotheism because he was neither a born Egyptian nor a "mere Hebrew": "Einem gebohrnen Egypter fehlte es ... an dem Nationalinteresse für die Ebräer, um sich zu ihrem Erretter aufzuwerfen. Einem bloßen Ebräer mußte es an Kraft und Geist zu dieser Unternehmung gebrechen" (A born Egyptian lacked ... the passion for the Hebrew people in order to emerge as their savior. A mere Hebrew had to lack the power and spirit for this undertaking) (SNA 17:381). Schiller stresses that Moses's Hebrew mother managed to raise him under a false identity as his "nurse," and that she probably did not forget "ein recht rührendes Bild des allgemeinen Elends [seiner Nation] in seine zarte Seele zu pflanzen" (to instill in her son's tender soul a thoroughly moving impression of the general misery [of his nation]) (SNA 17:382). The mother's visual depiction of the mistreatment of the Hebrew people at the hand of the Egyptians conditions young Moses to always remember his Hebrew descent.[26] His "tender soul" is receptive to sensory impressions that have a lasting effect on his moral disposition and affect his personality more deeply than his Egyptian education, so much that he identifies with the Hebrew people and harbors feelings of revenge against the Egyptian oppressors (SNA 17:388). His anger against the Egyptians is reinforced whenever he remembers the injustice of slavery. The continuous discrimination of his people fosters his hatred and finally provokes him to murder an Egyptian whom he witnesses abuse a fellow Hebrew. Moses becomes an outlaw and flees into the Arabian Desert, and his political instincts are awakened by the humiliation he has to experience.

Schiller puts himself in Moses's shoes to depict the emotional turmoil of an aspiring political leader whose tragic fall and deep disappointment over the loss of all his hopes fuse his personal fate with the fate of his oppressed fellow Hebrews: "Seine Phantasie, durch Einsamkeit und Stille entzündet, ergreift was ihr am nächsten liegt, die Partey der Unterdrückten. Gleiche Empfindungen suchen einander, und der Unglückliche wird sich am liebsten auf des Unglücklichen Seite schlagen" (Inflamed by loneliness and silence, his fantasy takes sides for those who are dearest to him: the oppressed. Similar emotions attract each other and the unfortunate one will preferably side with the unfortunate) (SNA 17:389). Once again, the inner emotional correspondence gives Moses the ability to connect with his fellow Hebrews, despite their different cultural backgrounds of education. Compassion forms an invisible bond among all humans regardless of their different social standing.[27]

Moses would not have been able to convert his uncivilized, pagan people to monotheism without his ability to think in abstract terms, an ability he owes to his Egyptian education. Neither Hebrew nor Egyptian, only an exception like Moses is capable of transcending the limits of his assumed identity and of forming a unifying bond. In "Die Sendung Moses" Schiller presents Moses as an innovator who is capable of preserving and promoting the ideal through the power of reason. While Schiller's Moses, like the elitist priests who taught him, uses his intellectual superiority to manipulate the Hebrew people, he differs from the Egyptian elite because he has actually suffered the hardship of his people and therefore is able to identify with them. Moses is not simply privy to a universal truth, he has also developed a particular identity as a Hebrew. The fate of the outcast in the Arabian desert makes him aware of the common bond that he shares with his people. Moses has the advantage of understanding the full impact of social discrimination against his fellow Hebrews because he can see the difference between his former privileged existence as a "Menschenherrscher" (ruler of the people) and his later existence in the desert as a "Lohnknecht eines Nomaden" (slave to a nomad) (SNA 17:389).

Nevertheless his intellectual superiority as well as his ability to adapt his vision to the imagination of his uneducated fellow Hebrews endows him with an instinct for power that is more fully fleshed out in the political leaders of Schiller's dramas, such as Fiesco, Posa, and Wallenstein (Alt, *Schiller* 1:455). Moses shares with these larger-than-life figures the potential to exploit his leadership skills for opportunistic goals. And Schiller himself presents the precarious proximity of idealist altruism and opportunist despotism as an inherently human trait by emphasizing in his eleventh letter on Don Karlos

> daß der uneigennützigste, reinste und edelste Mensch aus enthusiastischer Anhänglichkeit an seine Vorstellung von Tugend und hervorzubringendem Glück sehr oft ausgesetzt ist, ebenso willkürlich mit den Individuen zu schalten, als nur immer der selbstsüchtigste Despot, weil der Gegenstand von beider Bestrebungen in ihnen nicht außer ihnen wohnt, und weil jener, der seine Handlungen nach seinem innern Geistesbilde model, mit der Freiheit anderer beinahe ebenso im Streit liegt als dieser, dessen letztes Ziel sein eigenes Ich ist. (SNA 22:170)

> (that the most selfless, purest, and noblest human being is just as prone to manipulate individuals out of his enthusiastic commitment to his idea of virtue and the creation of happiness as the most selfish despot because the object of their ambitions does not reside outside [but within] them, and because the former who models his actions according to his inner ideal is just as much in disagreement with the liberty of others as the one whose goal is his own ego.)

While Schiller's tragic heroes often fail because of their personal ambitions, Moses successfully manages to reconcile his personal aspirations with a universal ethics.[28] For him, religion promises to recover his lost national identity as well as guarantee the human dignity of his entire people by letting them be part of a universal ethics. Moses's calling "humanizes" his people as Schiller wishes his writings would do for his society. Moses's growing awareness of his own "true" identity as a Hebrew goes hand in hand with his calling to instill national sentiments in his fellow Hebrews. Religion helps Moses transform his people's negative self-image as outcasts of Egyptian society into a positive identity. In a sense, Moses makes up for his disregard of the Hebrews' right to individual self-determination by providing them with a specific national pride that they had lacked.

Ironically, Moses not only brings about the unity of his people but also entices them into believing in a national myth and miraculous stories of an omnipotent God. Yet for Schiller the creation of myth is not plain deception because it works in the service of a higher ideal and ultimately in the service of "truth." Schiller's emphasis on Moses's need for "Einsamkeit" (solitude) and "Stille" (tranquility) in order to be inspired underlines the parallels between himself, the writer, and Moses who, like himself, needs an aesthetic strategy to win over his audience. Moses's idea, "seinen wahren Gott auf eine fabelhafte Art zu verkünden" (to announce his true God in a miraculous fashion) (SNA 17:392), is designed to convince his unenlightened audience of a God who is neither comprehensible nor attractive nor useful to them (SNA 17:390–91). Moses is well aware that his "true" God is unable to fight for the Hebrews and help them in a miraculous way (SNA 17:391); nevertheless, he feels justified to present him as omnipotent. In other words, Schiller/Moses creates a poetic illusion that advances the "truth" and calls his theology a "Vernunftreligion," a religion in the service of reason.

How was Moses able to convince his people to believe in one God instead of in the many natural gods that they worshiped? Schiller attributes Moses's success in founding a new religion to the mythmaking technique that he learned from the Egyptians. He mentions the hieroglyphs as an example of a pictorial language that concealed the naked truth from the uninitiated and yet stimulated their curiosity (SNA 17:384). Paradoxically, the hieroglyphs and ceremonies assumed the opposite function, as their mystique began to appeal to increasing numbers of nonbelievers and were eventually taken as symbols for truth itself. This dual function of the sign as veil and revelation is at the heart of Moses's/Schiller's pedagogical genius (SNA 17:384). The priests aroused their disciples' passions during initiation rites to prepare them for facing the truth. Yet Moses cannot copy the hieroglyphs and ceremonies because his people would not have been able to understand them. His goals are also different from those of the Egyptians. While the elitist order of priests that trained him originally intended to protect the "truth" from the uninitiated, Moses aims at attracting a following and therefore has to adapt his stories to the intellectual abilities of his audience. Moses learned from the Egyptians to take advantage of the contradiction between "essential truth" and "surface appearance" and the tendency of the uneducated to mistake the latter for the former.

Ironically, Moses benefits from a technique that resulted in the profanization of religion while Moses's aesthetic utilization of the senses has the opposite effect and serves the reclamation of the spiritual with the establishment of monotheism. In Schiller's text—which was written before the hieroglyphs had been deciphered—the hieroglyphs are represented as a secret code that has no other function than to protect the truth from the uneducated and prepare uninitiated members for "the truth." Yet as more inapt members pushed themselves into the circle of the initiated because they felt attracted by the cultural rites, the religious leaders saw themselves compelled to make the truth less accessible by inventing more theatrical gimmicks (SNA 17:387). As a consequence, the rituals gradually lost their original meaning of purifying religion from superstition. Eventually these hieroglyphs—with the help of the priesthood who felt they had to mislead the people for opportunistic reasons—assumed the powers of divine truth (SNA 17:382). Thus the attraction of the obscure caused the unenlightened people to take signs for wonders. Their idolatry makes Moses aware of the psychology of the "uncivilized" state of mind, which is enticed by the sensual presence of the mysterious. By fusing monotheism with the foundational myth of the Hebrew nation and embellishing it with miraculous stories, Moses manipulates his fellow Hebrews and makes them receptive to monotheism, which, according to Schiller, brings them closer to the truth (SNA 17:383–84; 392; 396).

Monotheism opens the door to freedom because in monotheism it is up to the individuals to decide whether they want to live according to God's commandments, and—needless to say—it is freedom that matters to Schiller. Only through the freedom of choosing a moral life over and against nature can the individual live a godly life. This is Schiller's explanation of how religion became "die stärkste und unenbehrlichste Stütze aller Verfassung" (the strongest and most indispensable support of the constitution) (SNA 17:396). Schiller explains this in his lecture, "Etwas über die erste Menschengesellschaft nach dem Leitfaden der mosaischen Urkunde" ("Some Thoughts about the First Human Society According to the Mosaic Document"), which appeared in November 1790 in the journal *Thalia*, two months after "Die Sendung Moses." Here he depicts human development from prehistoric paradisiac innocence to the beginnings of an ethical existence. Accordingly, the fall from paradise is an advantage because it grants humans the freedom to become masters of their own fate. Humans have emancipated themselves from animal-like blissful ignorance, and reason allows them to regain a state of innocence without divine control. Schiller argues just as Lessing in *Erziehung des Menschengeschlechts* in claiming that individual autonomy is only possible if human beings can decide for themselves between Good and Evil.

While reason enables human beings freedom of choice to live a moral life, it also permits the simulation of so-called natural signs, signs whose subject matter is grounded in the very properties of what is designated. Tears, for instance, are generally considered a natural sign of sadness. In primitive societies nature is often understood as the language of the gods. In contrast to these natural signs, which render the truth apparent, the Egyptian *Epoptoi* invented the hieroglyphs as a hermetic system of symbols in their attempt to protect the sacred truth of their religion from the uninitiated. Just as Moses invents miraculous stories to wean his people from their polytheistic superstitions and prepare them for the abstract truth of monotheism, so does Schiller create a counter illusion in his dramas that unveils surface reality as false and conveys an inner, universal truth. Yet Schiller goes one step further than Moses by making the deceptive use of signs transparent.[29] Schiller's use of biblical imagery to reveal deception is apparent in his first drama *Die Räuber (The Robbers)* (1782). Franz Moor fabricates the story of his brother's death to distort the truth. Like the dramatist himself, Franz creates a dramatic illusion by producing a forged letter and reenacting his brother's last words. However, Old Moor uncovers the deception by having Amalia read the analogous biblical story of the fraudulent production of Joseph's bloodstained cloak (SNA 3:51–52). In these scenes Schiller uses dramatic enactment to reveal a fraud just as Moses repeats the technique of deception to convert his fellow Hebrews to monotheism, which brings the Hebrews closer to the "truth" or "einzige höchste Ursache aller Dinge" (singular highest origin of all things) (SNA 17:385). Significantly, he repeats the *Epoptoi's* illusive signification practices to correct the deception caused by their artificial production of *hieroglyphs, ceremonies, and rituals*.

Although there are obvious parallels between Moses and the playwright who both use fiction in the service of the truth, there is still a certain ambiguity as to whether Moses's actions are ethically commendable according to neo-humanist standards. While Schiller clearly presents Egyptian civilization as superior to Hebrew culture and therefore tends to favor reason over faith, the final sentences of "Die Sendung Moses" leave open whether Moses uses his superior intellectual abilities to impose a premature way of thinking on the Hebrew people: "Die Epopten erkannten die Wahrheit durch ihre Vernunft, die Hebräer konnten höchstens nur blind daran glauben" (The Epoptoi knew the Truth by force of reason, the Hebrews could only believe blindly in it) (SNA 17:397). On the one hand, Moses's political theology unites the Hebrew people and thus preserves their national identity, yet his calculated manipulation is reminiscent of Schiller's Machiavellian protagonists. The ambiguity of these tragic leaders is an expression of Schiller's dialogue with the dialectic of the Enlightenment. Schiller's texts illustrate inconsistencies in Enlightenment thought that are still relevant for present-day skepticism about the compatibility of the optimistic belief in reason, progress, and human perfection on the one hand and human nature on the other. For one thing, "Die Sendung Moses" makes clear that reason can take on the function that religion once had as a tool to exert power over others. Although reason can bring humanity closer to the "truth," Schiller often connects it to exceptional figures who, like Moses's "despotic brothers" Franz Moor, Fiesco, Posa, and Wallenstein, use it for opportunistic reasons. To be sure, Schiller's fascination with such larger-than-life figures is partially motivated by the search for suitable biographies for his tragedies. Yet one could also ask whether the admiration of human superiority is a necessary precondition of enlightenment, as Schiller's text suggests indeed that progress depends on an intellectual elite or superior mentor figures.

Although Schiller's narrator claims that Moses's fictitious account is not based on "Betrug" (deception) (SNA 17:391), the narrative perspective emphasizes that Moses considers his fictitious account as a legitimate means "seinen wahren Gott auf eine fabelhafte Art zu verkünden" (to announce his God in a miraculous fashion) (SNA 17:392). For Moses, the truth simply needs to be mediated in such a fashion that the Hebrew people will accept it. Moses accomplishes this by inventing a national myth and making his God the *Nationalgott* of the Hebrew people (ibid.).

Schiller's plea for *Vernunftreligion* can be associated with the "tyranny of Reason" because it excuses demagoguery for the purpose of starting a nationalist movement. Moses's masterful use of propaganda is based on mass manipulation. After all, the text presents the Hebrew people as blind followers of Moses's ideology. The fact that Schiller's psychological insights justify Moses's actions by emphasizing the commonalities between Moses and the author suggests that Schiller admires Moses's political skills because in his opinion "[er] läßt eine ganze Nation an einer Wahrheit Theil nehmen, die bis jetzt nur das Eigenthum weniger Weisen war" (he lets an entire nation participate in a truth that has been the exclusive property of a few until now) (SNA 17:397). The birth of the Hebrew nation thus can be seen as both emancipation and submission. While the Hebrew people are liberated from their status of a discriminated minority under Egyptian rule, they submit to their new leader and his political theology. For them, the conversion to monotheism means liberation for the nation but not necessarily for the individual. Schiller's promotion of national unification over the emancipation of the individual points to Schiller's own struggle with rationalism's coercive potential.

"Die Sendung Moses" exposes the psychological processes that underlie the formation of national and cultural identities and shows how these processes can be exploited for political purposes. Yet the text undermines Schiller's positive depiction of Moses by revealing how the author degrades and distances himself from the animal aspects within man and projects them onto "the slave, the barbarian, the foreigner as figures of an animal in human form" in order to construe the Western human being as a superior, spiritual, civilized, and reasonable being (Agamben 37). This kind of reading would be in keeping with Giorgio Agamben's suggestion that "man must recognize himself in a non-man in order to be human" (ibid. 27). One could infer that shame about their sensual nature may have caused eighteenth-century German elitist thinkers like the Illuminati to distance themselves from the masses in order to confirm their human superiority. It could also explain Schiller's ambivalent attitude toward the senses: of both detesting them and at the same time having enormous respect for their power, a power that he tried to take advantage of in his theatrical mission. "Die Sendung Moses" not only reveals how artful manipulation can be applied toward progress but also how it can be used to create a hierarchy of human beings based on reason in order to assert a more privileged position.

The text's similarities to Lessing's *Erziehung des Menschengeschlechts*, discussed in chapter 1, are striking. Both texts refer to the education of the "uncivilized" Hebrews to depict the development of humankind from "superstitious polytheism" to a more enlightened monotheism. The ability of thinking in abstractions allows the enlightened reader not only to discover the inner truths of literary signs, images, or metaphors but also to grapple with the ethical justification of literary fantasies, which is at the core of both Lessing's and Schiller's aesthetics. While both writers use biblical stories as sources of inspiration that can convey an inner truth that lies beneath the surface of allegorical and metaphorical signification, they differ in the degree of endorsing the production of literary imagery for the purpose of advancing the civilization of the human race. Although both writers are aware that sensory stimuli often precede and shape intellectual reflection—this is why Lessing called revelations or sensate representation *Vorübungen* (preliminary exercises)—Schiller puts more emphasis on the danger of the manipulative abuse of others in the service of an ideology. Both Lessing's *Die Erziehung des Menschengeschlechts* and Schiller's "Die Sendung Moses" stress the ambiguities and polysemy of literary texts, which give the recipients the freedom of thought that is necessary for their progress toward individual autonomy. Whereas in Lessing's text God or Christ acts as the ultimate authority that produces revelations to guide the people of Israel toward enlightenment, Schiller chooses Moses, a human being, to represent the divine idea of monotheism. Although Moses acts in God's interest, he carries the stigma of being fallible, and Schiller's text emphasizes this human trait by narrating Moses's rage-filled murder of an Egyptian. Yet, there is no doubt that Schiller presents Moses as one of the great role models who successfully worked for the advancement of a more humane society. Perhaps one could say that Schiller's text problematizes the conflict between the Kantian categorical imperative, which prohibits the manipulative use of other human beings for another purpose, and his idea that there will always be a few people, even among the institutional "guardians," who think for themselves.

Notes

Parts of this chapter were published previously as "Faith and Reason: Schiller's 'Die Sendung Moses,'" in *German Quarterly* 81, no. 3 (2008): 283–301.
1. Future references to Schiller's texts are taken from *Friedrich Schiller: Werke; Nationalausgabe*, ed. Julius Petersen and Gerhard Fricke (Weimar: Böhlaus Nachfolger, 1943–). The references are cited parenthetically as SNA followed by volume and page number.
2. The chapter focuses on what Hayden White has termed the "practical past by addressing ethical and aesthetic questions." As mentioned in the introduction, *Universalgeschichte* is less concerned with the veracity of facts than with their consequences for the present and possibly the future of humanity.
3. Peter-André Alt notes that Schiller points out that August Ludwig Schlözer had used the terms "Aggregat" and "System" to distinguish "Spezial- und Universalhistorie." Accordingly, Schlözer used the latter for *Universalhistorie* that had been integrated into an overarching system of causal relationships, whereas "Aggregat" was used for a mere accumulation of empirical facts without assigning them a specific place in an overarching historical point of view (Alt, "Natur" 534; see also August Ludwig Schlözer, *Vorstellung seiner Universal-Historie* (1772/1773), edited and introduced by Horst Walter Blank (Hagen, 1990), 46–50. Alt also points out that, contrary to Schlözer, Schiller is not interested in the empirical relationship between "Spezial- und Universalhistorie" but in the methodological distinction between the historiographic perspective of the accumulation of events and a universal point of view, which reveals the teleology of historical processes through causal and consequential evidence (Alt, "Natur' 535).
4. If not indicated otherwise, all translations from the German are mine.
5. "Das Mistrauen erwacht bey dem ältesten historischen Denkmal, und es verläßt uns nicht einmal bey einer Chronik des heutigen Tages" (Suspicion arises regarding the oldest historical monument, and it does not even leave us when we consider the chronicle of today's events) (SNA 17:371).
6. Schiller's disregard for factual knowledge also has a personal motivation. As an untrained historian who had received his academic appointment through Goethe's intervention, Schiller was most likely lacking the knowledge of historical details. The preparation of his lectures took more time than expected.
7. See also Peter Hanns Reill, "Science and the Construction of the Cultural Sciences in Late Enlightenment Germany: The Case of Wilhelm von Humboldt," *History and Theory* 33, no. 3 (1994): 345–66. Reill shows how Wilhelm von Humboldt attempted to overcome the mind-body dualism under the influence of current anthropological vitalist ideas by Blumenbach, Schiller, and Bouffon (353, 357).
8. Both texts pursue a very similar goal: namely to reveal a *Leitfaden* (red thread) in world history that is analogous to the natural laws in the sciences (KW 11:33–34).
9. Many of Schiller's heroes or heroines are willing to renounce their egotistical ambitions at the plays' cathartic climaxes (see, for instance, Karl Moor, Marquis Posa, Mary Stuart, among others).

10. "The deists and Spinozists of the eighteenth century looked to Egypt as the origin and homeland of their concept of God and they drew their evidence from Warburton" (Assmann, *Moses* 100). Assmann provides an in-depth study of Warburton's sources as well as of the reception of his widely known book in *Moses the Egyptian* (96–143).
11. Not all of Lessing's sources, other than Warburton, are known. Assmann suggests that Lessing's study of Spinoza and William Cudworth's *True Intellectual System of the Universe* (1678) was Lessing's original inspiration. After all, Lessing adopted the Greek formula of *Hen Kai Pan* (one and all), the very same expression that "Cudworth chose to characterize Egypt's arcane theology," which triggered the so-called pantheism debate (Assmann, *Moses* 80–81; 140). "On August 15, 1780, Gotthold Ephraim Lessing wrote the words *Hen kai pan* ("One-and-All") in Greek characters on the wall paper of Gleim's garden house . . ." (Assmann, ibid. 139). ". . . *Hen kai pan* . . . immediately became a motto, appearing in the writings of Herder, Hölderlin, Goethe, Schelling, and others (many of them, Freemasons)" (ibid. 140).
12. Another example is animal symbols like the sphinx that represent divinity by embodying the combined powers of the mightiest animals and humans (SNA 17:386).
13. A fairly extensive body of research covers this aspect of Schiller's essay. See, for instance, Janßen; Buchwald 288; Schieder, "Schiller als Historiker"; KH Jahn; Engelberg; Sharpe; Hahn; Weimer; Malter; Süßmann 41.
14. See, for instance, Assmann, "Nachwort"; Hartwich 20–49; Wübben.
15. Scholars have suggested that he simply emphasizes those aspects of Reinhold's treatise that appear particularly important to him without adding any new arguments (Assmann, "Nachwort" 184). Yvonne Wübben also pointed this out in her investigation of Schiller's use of sources (125–26).
16. Unless Schiller contradicts his own premises laid out in his well-known lecture on universal history "Was heißt und zu welchem Ende studiert man Universalgeschichte?" (1789), one can assume that the author is not interested in summarizing his sources but in recreating history according to his own point of view (SNA 17:377–97).
17. Dieter Borchmeyer uses Schiller's friend Körner as a source to substantiate his claim that Schiller's letters on *Don Carlos* "explizieren eine 'Dialektik der Aufklärung' (vom 'Despotismus der Aufklärung' redet schon Körner in seinem Brief an Schiller vom 18. September 1787), die sich aus dem Drama selber, aus der Handlungsweise des Marquis Posa ableiten läßt" (explain a 'dialectic of the Enlightenment' [Körner already speaks of the 'despotism of the Enlightenment' in his letter to Schiller of 18 September 1787], which can be deduced from the drama itself and from Marquis Posa's behavior) (130).
18. Schiller must have been aware of this debate (Wübben; Schings). Several radical atheist Enlightenment thinkers regarded the founding of the Jewish religion as a deceptive invention by religious leaders for political purposes. For them, Mosaic monotheism became a symbol of religious fanaticism, which contradicted Enlightenment ideas.
19. The idea of religious imposture was not new, however. Wiep van Bunge traces "some of the ways in which the idea of religious imposture was passed down from the early sixteenth to the early eighteenth century. . . ." For instance, Paul Thiery d'Holbach claimed that Moses led the Jewish people into the desert in order to brainwash them and make them blindly obedient (Hartwich 22).
20. See also, Kurt Wölfel, "Machiavellische Spuren in Schillers Dramatik"; Peter Michelsen, "Schiller's Fiesko: Freiheitsheld und Tyrann"; Wolfgang Wittkowski, "Höfische Intrige für die gute Sache: Marquis Posa und Octavio Piccolomini."

21. See also Walter Müller-Seidel's introduction to *Die Weimarer Klassik und ihre Geheimbünde* (21–26) and Wolfgang Riedel's essay on "Aufklärung und Macht" (107–25) in the same volume.
22. Schiller in particular mentions in his lecture that the origin of Christianity, albeit most important for the history of the world, has never found a satisfying explanation (SNA 17:372–73).
23. According to Schings, Schiller followed his friend Körner in regarding the *Illuminaten* as responsible for the "despotism" of the Enlightenment (164–65).
24. Schiller uses the animal metaphor in a variety of contexts. In his dramas *Die Räuber* and *Kabale und Liebe*, villains like Franz Moor or Sekretär Wurm are compared to low and often dirty forms of creaturely life (SNA 3:21, NA 5:114). The conspiring, dishonest Sekretär Wurm is characterized as the spineless, despicable character that his name suggests.
25. Most of Schiller's tragic heroes and heroines, such as Karl Moor, Luise Miller, Marquis Posa, Wallenstein, and Maria Stuart, share this willingness to sacrifice their lives for their ideals.
26. Schiller already formulated this idea of enhancing pedagogical instruction by sensory stimulation in his essay "Was kann eine gute stehende Schaubühne eigentlich wirken?" (1784), probably referring to Johann Georg Sulzer's *Betrachtungen über die Nützlichkeit der dramatischen Dichtkunst* (1760) (Alt, *Schiller* 1:380).
27. The common bond that supposedly unites all individuals in humanity informs Schiller's anthropological and ideological views. Schiller learned about the idea of a chain of beings from Abel, who taught the doctrines of French biologist and philosopher Charles Bonnet (1720–93) at the Hohe Karlsschule. Although Schiller sharply criticizes Bonnet's hypothesis on how mechanical stimuli are transformed into sensory perceptions in his first doctoral dissertation, "Philosophie der Physiologie" (SNA 20:22), he was influenced by Bonnet's emphasis of the body's impact on the mind as well as by his theory of attention (Safranski 81; Riedel, "Introduction" 438–39; see also McCarthy, *The Early History of Embodied Cognition*).
28. Fiesco and Posa illustrate that progressive and Macchiavellist politics are far from separate but can be interrelated in the most precarious ways (Alt, *Schiller* 1:465). In Fiesco and Posa, the well-intended striving for a better society is overshadowed by personal ambition and hunger for power. Fiesco, whose conspiracy initially aims at the liberation of the Republic of Genova from the despotic Andreas Doria, turns into a despotic leader himself. Similar to Moses, who invents miraculous stories, Fiesco wins the support of the representatives of the people by telling them a fable. Yet while Moses intends to convince his audience of "the Truth," Fiesco convinces his credulous audience of the need for a strong leader, like himself, by equating human society with the animal kingdom (SNA 4:49–50). He implies that the inequality of the animal kingdom is natural and therefore must also be accepted in human society. The strong leader—embodied in the figure of the lion—is of course no one but himself. Fiesco shares with Moses the opinion that the masses are intellectually inferior and in need of guidance. Just as in "Die Sendung Moses," the people appear simply as the mob (Michelsen 343; SNA 4:46). Schiller created a whole string of Machiavellian figures, whose abilities in manipulating others can make them devious, and it is difficult to overlook their affinities to certain aspects of Schiller's Moses. Wallenstein, for example, shares with Schiller's earlier tragic heroes, such as Fiesco and Posa, an enigmatic, mysterious quality that leads to both an air of charisma and inscrutability (Alt, *Schiller* 2:438). Wallen-

stein promotes this image of deceitfulness as part of his political strategy (Alt, *Schiller* 2:442). Like Moses, Posa, and Fiesco, he disregards the opinions of his fellow humans by using them for his political objectives. For instance, he intends to marry his daughter against her wishes to one of the European rulers in order to increase his own status and power (SNA 9:242–43).

29. See "On the Main Principles of the Fine Arts and Sciences" in Mendelssohn, *Philosophical Writings*, trans. Danliel O. Dahlstrom, 177–78.

CHAPTER 3

The Sublime as an Objectivist Strategy

Introduction

Carsten Zelle attributes the emergence of the sublime to what he calls "Emotionalisierung der Kunsttheorie" (the infusion of art theory with emotions) (*Angenehmes Grauen*, 58). Accordingly, the sublime is not so much an object but rather an experience that takes place in an observer/recipient in view of an object that exceeds the observer's comprehension. The shift from a normative aesthetics that concentrated on the adherence to classicist form—such as structural uniformity, order, harmony of proportion—to one that focused on the artifact's emotional effect on the recipient took hold at the beginning of the eighteenth century in France (Zelle, *Angenehmes Grauen* 58–59). An increasing number of scientific studies that dealt with the human subject's emotional sensibilities examined and articulated the interest in the recipient's affective reactions.[1]

Yet what does this infusion of art theory with emotions have to do with the emerging distinction between "objective," scientific approaches and creative subjectivity that has been attributed to the liberal arts or humanities?[2] In fact, the preoccupation with the self and the awareness of literature as metaphorical representation of subjective experiences and impressions—particularly obvious during the *Sturm und Drang* and *Empfindsamkeit*[3]—went hand in hand with the emergence of hermeneutics.[4] This literary methodology defines itself in opposition to the positivist approaches that prevailed in the sciences. While the latter sought to establish factual knowledge and universal natural laws, hermeneutics tried to account for the changing historical, social, and cultural conditions that affected both the production and the reception of a work of art. In other words, hermeneutic methods distinguished themselves from the sciences by forgoing claims of objectivity in favor of contextualization.[5] In contrast to the natural sciences that explain phenomena in isolation, the human sciences describe and investigate human experiences or phenomena in the context of their historical, ethical, and psychological effects on human life. This does not mean, however, that hermeneutic analyses abandon all rationalist principles, as they are still based on scientific reasoning. Yet with the emergence of the bourgeois individual as both the creator and recipient of art, it became necessary to consider this heightened self-awareness in a scientific methodology.

While the preoccupation with the self is present in all facets of late eighteenth-century literary production, it was at the same time frowned upon and often criticized as vanity.[6] Many literary works of all genres drew on writers' personal experiences in portraying characters that aspired to live according to bourgeois ethical standards and ideals. These ideals were incompatible with lingering antiquated values and traditions that prevented the emancipation of the individual.[7] Such obstacles arose both from social pressures and from ingrained residues of autocratic power structures. For instance, the paradoxical demand that proper self-examination had to be exercised without vanity or self-centeredness can be viewed as a remnant of Christian morals. Neoplatonism helped foster the idea of a selfless self-contemplation by promising a spiritual progress or inner transformation of the self as an ascent "from matter to Soul to Spirit to the One" (Hadot 2). A self-indulging complacency, however, would allow the soul to be fascinated by its corporeal reflection (ibid. 10). Narcissists remain preoccupied with their particular individual existence and therefore are unable to partake in the spiritual universe, which requires distance from the self.

The sublime, on the other hand—according to German philosophers Immanuel Kant (1722–1802) and Friedrich Schiller (1759–1805)—is a state of mind that accomplishes what narcissism prevents: the independence from forces that threaten to obstruct a human being's spiritual autonomy (KU 161).[8] Although narcissism denotes *dependence on* the body and the sublime *independence from* the body, both concepts have in common a deep reverence for the self. While Kant and Schiller claim that the subject with a sublime disposition is devoid of individual self-interest and acts solely at the behest of universal moral laws, one could still argue that the freedom from egotistical desires is in the interest of individual autonomy. In fact, the merging of the self with higher universal principles could be regarded as objectivist idealization of the self in order to avoid the allegation of narcissism, commonly understood as excessive preoccupation with the self.

This chapter will explore how Kant and Schiller used the sublime to aestheticize narcissistic impulses by creating a male inner self and protecting it from the stigma of vanity. I propose that their use of this aesthetic category helped objectify an essentially subjectivist aesthetics. Yet while Schiller follows Kant in degrading the sensual aspects of human nature as egotistical and amoral, Schiller's dramas also challenge some of the Kantian premises. When

Schiller's protagonists sacrifice lives in the service of ethical ideas, the sublime's repressive spirit reveals itself. Moreover, the protagonists' "unselfish" identification with moral principles or ideologies is problematic because what appears to be a pursuit of justice can inadvertently become a matter of personal ambition, as shown in the previous chapter. Schiller's tragedies not only present the sublime as otherworldly, they also question the Kantian gender dualism that attributes moral strength exclusively to male characters. In the larger context of this volume, the analysis of Schiller's dramas exemplifies how the polysemy of literary texts can aptly challenge broad aesthetic and philosophical claims by exposing their ideological biases. My analysis will focus on the correlation between narcissism and the sublime in the context of Schiller's aesthetic essays "Vom Erhabenen" ("Of the Sublime") (1793) and "Über das Erhabene" ("On the Sublime") (1794–96) with reference to his dramas *Die Räuber* (*The Robbers*) (1782), and *Don Karlos* (1787/1805).

The Sublime

The emergence of the sublime marks an aesthetic shift favoring emotion over beauty (Zelle, *Angenehmes Grauen* 58–59). A new experience of nature was responsible for this shift. John Dennis (1657–1734) described this experience when crossing the Alps as "a delightful Horrour, a terrible Joy, and at the same time, that I was infinitely pleas'd, I trembled" (Dennis 2:380). Apparently the sublime involves a mixed emotion, a delightful shock in view of an unexpected, unsettling experience that either exceeds human comprehension or imagination (KU 144).[9] The mountain peaks of the Alps, the immense force of breakers in the stormy sea, the infinite and bleak vastness of the desert, and other objects that instill a sense of awe in the spectator are considered suitable for evoking the sublime. The object's unprecedented vastness, its irregular, often threatening features that defy classicist norms of beauty cause an emotional disturbance that can be overcome once the observer recoils from the overwhelming sensory impression and manages to gain some distance from nature's imminent threat.

The sublime emerges precisely at this point when, as a result of the growing awareness of the self's sensibilities, aesthetic experience is endowed with emotions. "Zwischen Grenzerfahrung und Größenwahn" ("Between Liminal Experience and Megalomania") is the subtitle of a noteworthy collection of essays that analyze the sublime's impact on aesthetic theory during the past two hundred years (Pries). This characterization of the sublime as an experience that is both self-limiting and self-enhancing could, however, just as well describe narcissism. Both concepts refer to a subjective engagement with an Other, and both concepts involve an intense if not illusory perception of the self. While the object that evokes the sublime is obviously different from the object of narcissistic self-reflection, both the sublime and the narcissistic experience make the subject aware of its limitations and, at the same time, provoke a desire to transcend them.[10] For instance, Kant's idea that the sublime is an inner capacity that allows the subject to withstand the allure of the senses is reminiscent of the Protestant tendency to defy all worldly desires. In contrast to beauty in nature, which appears harmonious and meaningful, the sublime is both terrifying and liberating. The infinite power of nature confronts the subject with its mortality and in the moment of terror, as in a revelation, makes the subject aware of its own internal infinite powers. Feminist philosopher Bonnie Mann reminds us of the narcissistic nature of the sublime by claiming that "the Kantian subject uses what most approximates the sublime in nature as a mirror, which allows him to experience his own might and magnitude as sublime" (B. Mann 46). One must add here, however, that the mirror is not a mimetic representation of the sublime. The sublime can by definition not be represented adequately. For the representation of nature's overwhelming powers is in itself not sublime, but only evokes the spirit of the sublime in the observing subject:

> Das Erhabene kann in keiner sinnlichen Form enthalten sein, sondern trifft nur Ideen der Vernunft: welche, obgleich keine ihnen angemessene Darstellung möglich ist, eben durch diese Unangemessenheit, welche sich sinnlich darstellen läßt rege gemacht und ins Gemüt gerufen werden. (KU 136)
>
> (The sublime cannot be contained in a perceptible form, but only meets ideas of reason: which, even though they cannot be adequately represented, can be evoked and called to mind precisely through this presentable inadequacy.)

Because the sublime transcends the capacity of our senses, it cannot be depicted. Images of threatening thunderclouds, majestic mountaintops, or fear-instilling breakers conjure up the inner faculty of reason that surpasses the power of imagination. We recall that reason is, according to Kant, completely separate from the realm of the senses. This separation, reminiscent of the Lutheran separation of flesh and spirit, is the basis for the freedom of the individual. Consequently, the individual is free only if it overcomes the dependence on the senses. Nevertheless, the Kantian subject relies on sensory impressions of nature's powers by mentally internalizing them and withstanding them. Reason rejects the dependence on nature as the sublime induces a sense of superiority over nature. In other words, the subject recognizes an ideal version of himself through the appropriation and subjection of nature.[11]

Mann succinctly summarizes Kant's clandestine appropriation of individual autonomy, also called "subreption": "Kant cuts the subject loose from the natural world and reverses the order of dependence so that the world is dependent on the autonomous subject" (B. Mann 47). In contrast to the sublime that permits the subject to become aware of its spiritual capacity as a human being, narcissism leaves the subject fixated on surface appearances that create its sensual desire to merge with an idealized self. While narcissism's "immoral selfishness" is fixated on surface appearance, the sublime's foremost ethical quality is its selflessness, or overcoming of the physical self. It serves therefore as a suitable antidote to a vain preoccupation with the self. In other words, the sublime has been used as a tool that allows the subject to transcend the limitations of the empirical subject by pointing to its infinite inner potential. The creation of this inner potential promotes the empowerment of the subject in the name of individual autonomy. Contrary to narcissism, which entails the creation of an idealized self and failure to merge with this ideal, the sublime is a triumphant overcoming of human limitations. And yet both the sublime and narcissism share the common trajectory toward self-expansion by merging with an ideal that is greater than the empirical self. Even though the experience of the sublime claims to be selfless, the question remains who experiences the sublime if not an expanded self. In short, one could view the sublime as a spiritualized form of narcissism in that it allows the subject to recognize its physical limitations and yet intuit its infinite spiritual capacity.

Kant's juxtaposition of the sublime and the beautiful can be read as an attempt to endow art with a deeper meaning—a meaning that addresses the ethical dimension of human nature (KU 168–69). The Kantian sublime underlines human independence from nature by showing that the subject possesses a superior inner capacity capable of withstanding the adverse conditions of nature, no matter how powerful they are (KU 161–62). This empowerment, however, is preceded by a feeling of self-annihilation in view of the overwhelming power of nature. The independence from nature has to be acquired at the price of a willingness to sacrifice one's life in order to partake of the higher ideals of humanity. Both Cornelia Klinger and Bonnie Mann emphasize that the independence from and dominion over nature inherent in the sublime is a privilege of the male subject (Klinger 198, B. Mann 45). As a gendered concept advocating male individual autonomy, the Kantian sublime is indeed more closely related to male narcissism than to an objective universal truth. The sublime seems to be motivated by a desire for power over nature, or perhaps even a desire for an idealized, divine self. For Kant, even war has sublime qualities because it can only be waged if a nation is willing to sacrifice lives for an idea:

> Selbst der Krieg, wenn er mit Ordnung und Heiligachtung der bürgerlichen Rechte geführt wird, hat etwas Erhabenes an sich, und macht zugleich die Denkungsart des Volks, welches ihn auf diese Art führt, nur um desto erhabener, je mehreren Gefahren es ausgesetzt war, und sich mutig darunter hat behaupten können: da hingegen ein langer Frieden den bloßen Handelsgeist, mit ihm aber den niedrigen Eigennutz, Feigheit und Weichlichkeit herrschend zu machen, und die Denkungsart des Volks zu erniedrigen pflegt. (KU 153)

(Even war, if waged in an orderly fashion and with observation of all civil rights, harbors something of the sublime, and makes the way of thinking of the people who is waging it all the more sublime the more it is exposed to danger and was able to prove its courage; whereas a long peace usually leads to mere mercantilism, which reinstates base egotism, cowardice, and effeminacy and degrades the spirit of the people.)

In the following, I will use examples from Schiller's literary works to show how Schiller follows Kant in degrading the sensual aspects of human nature in his attempt to uphold the autonomy of the spirit of "Man." According to Kant and Schiller after him, this sublime victory over the body distinguishes "Man" as a reasonable being and liberates him from the constraints of the senses. Art has a humanizing function in that it advances the transition from the sensual to the spiritual realm and thus promotes mankind's spiritual independence from nature (SNA 20:175). Yet, as we will see later, the enactment of the sublime in Schiller's dramas also reveals its despotic nature. As the sublime has to be achieved at such high cost, it can undermine the very humanist aims that it is supposed to serve.

Schiller's Dramas

The following examples from Schiller's *Die Räuber* and *Don Karlos* suggest that the literary enactment of the sublime is more complex than the Kantian premises suggest. Schiller is enough of a Kantian, even in his pre-Kantian phase, that his characters inhabit both an ideal and a real sphere and fail in their attempts of reconciling them. The sublime is most apparent when the hero/heroine keeps his/her composure in the face of death. It is therefore presented as spiritual victory in view of a tragic failure. Yet the heroic sacrifice that the sublime exacts seems so excessive that one may ask whether the relentless pursuit of moral principles over and against personal inclinations may cause greater suffering than a less self-castigating disposition. While Schiller's dramas on the one hand uphold the moral ideal in view of a corrupt nature/reality in order to improve and civilize human nature, they at the same time expose repressive aspects of these moral principles. Moreover, Schiller's enactments of the sublime reveal that the boundaries between selfish and unselfish ethical motivations become easily blurred as the achievements of the moral good are taken over by narcissistic ambition.

Although Schiller's *Die Räuber* was written long before the author studied Kant, the play seems to build up to a conflict that dramatizes Karl Moor's ascent from a horrific, albeit noble-minded, *Räuberhauptmann* (leader of a band of robbers) to a sublime hero. Moor sacrifices his one-and-only love, Amalia, to

Figure 3.1. Caspar David Friedrich (1774–1840), *Wanderer above the Sea of Fog* (1817). Wikimedia Commons, public domain.

keep an oath that he has sworn to his fellow robbers (SNA 3:160). In Kantian terms, this action would characterize Moor as a sublime hero as he decides in favor of the moral principle of keeping his promise over and against his inclination to make his beloved Amalia happy. In a scene of unrestrained pathos, Moor takes fate into his own hands and kills Amalia before his fellow robbers can kill her (SNA 3:232–34). What seems to be motivated also as mercy killing raises questions about whether Karl's emotional reaction to preempt his fellow robbers should be interpreted as an act that shows his sublime strength. For instance, Karl's emotional agitation and egotistical desire to have control over Amalia's life strongly discredit his "sublime" action. Traditional readings, however, accept Schiller's efforts to present Karl as a man who honors his moral obligations toward his fellow robbers and who liberates himself from all earthly commitments by bringing the ultimate sacrifice through this mercy killing of Amalia (Hofmann, *Epoche* 48).[12] The play's ending, which shows Karl as an autonomous human being who turns himself in to be judged by a higher judge, seems to support such a reading. After all, Schiller compares Moor to Plutarch's "erhabene Verbrecher" (sublime criminals) in his anonymous review of *Die Räuber* (SNA 22:118).

Yet the author also emphasizes Karl's monstrous character traits (SNA 22:120). Karl's impulsive behavior certainly does not suggest that he has sublime control over his emotions (SNA 3:158–61; 217–19; 233). Schiller created such an ambiguous figure to depict the full range of human emotions and to intensify the play's dramatic effect (SNA 22:118). Nevertheless, he feels compelled to explain Karl's shocking and unexpected killing of Amalia because it appears utterly unnecessary (SNA 22:127).[13] This killing, on which Karl comments with the words "Ich habe Euch einen Engel geschlachtet. Banditen! Wir sind quitt—Über dieser Leiche liegt meine Handschrift zerrissen—Euch schenk ich die eurige" (I have slaughtered an angel for you. Bandits! We are even—my signature lies torn over this corpse—I spare you yours) (SNA 3:234), initiates his inner sublimation that makes him a free man. Moor's pronouncement, according to which he must be free in order to be great, could also be taken as the play's message: "Frei muss Moor sein, wenn er groß sein will" (Free must Moor be, if he wants to be great) (SNA 3:234). Moor becomes autonomous by killing Amalia because he is no longer bound by any "worldly" commitment, neither by the oath he had sworn to the robbers, nor by the vow of love to Amalia. The sublime depends in the end on the exclusion of everything that does not correspond to an idealized image of the autonomous male individual. Schiller acknowledges that Amalia may be underrepresented as "die einzige Repräsentantin ihres ganzen Geschlechts" (the only representative of her gender) (SNA 22:124). She serves exclusively to confirm Karl's ascent to a sublime human being.[14] Schiller leaves it open as to whether Moor is able to redeem himself by sacrificing the person he loved. While the play excuses Moor's lack of respect for Amalia's life by stressing his male protagonist's struggle for individual autonomy, it also reveals the tyranny that ideals, however noble, can exert over individual lives. Karl's brother Franz Moor, as the extreme case of someone who subordinates all human emotions to reason, exemplifies Schiller's awareness of the potential dangers of abstract principles. Even though Karl is not a cold-hearted, inhumane schemer like Franz, he nevertheless shares with his counterpart a willingness to sacrifice his fellow humans for what he deems "grander" rationales.

The problem of whether the end justifies the means becomes even more central in *Don Karlos*. Here the dubiousness of the sublime is personified in the character of Marquis von Posa. Schiller clearly shows Posa as an idealist who is not afraid to risk his life for the idea of individual freedom. By contrasting him to Don Karlos, who at the beginning of the play has abandoned his political aspirations for his personal love interests, Schiller underlines Posa's seemingly unselfish struggle for the liberation of his country from absolutism that culminates in his bold admonition to the king to grant his people *Gedankenfreiheit* (freedom of thought) (SNA 7.1:301). Yet, despite his sublime willingness to sacrifice his life for the noble cause of freedom, Posa reveals a lack of consideration for those who are not prepared—like his best friend Karlos—to forfeit their personal interests for his political cause. Ironically, it is Posa's determination to put his ideals above all personal inclinations that raises questions about the "unselfishness" of the sublime. When Posa, in an act of betrayal, risks Karlos's life to accomplish his political goals, he makes decisions for his friend and thus violates the premise of individual autonomy for which he supposedly fights. Posa resembles Karl Moor in his disregard for the lives of others. Although Posa seems sublime because his struggle for freedom serves his country and not his self-interest, his intrigue, which plays off the king against Don Karlos, exposes a manipulative streak that makes his altruism questionable. In this regard Posa resembles Schiller's other deceitful yet heroic protagonists, such as Karl Moor, Fiesco, Wallenstein, Elizabeth, and Maria Stuart. In view of reviewers' strong reactions to Posa's duplicitous actions, Schiller felt compelled to defend his character in his *Briefe über Don Karlos* (1787), where he points to the affinity of narcissism and idealism in great leaders. He also explains how enthusiasm and inner conviction can lead the most virtuous and unselfish person to despotic, selfish behavior (SNA 22:170).

Schiller makes the general claim that in order to defend a moral principle with conviction, one must identify with this principle. Once the subject internalizes his idea of virtue it becomes his personal ambition, and his inner conviction becomes so compelling that it is no longer possible for him to respect the freedom of others. Schiller's claim seems to differ from the Kantian assumption of an "objective" moral law because in his opinion all ethical principles become part of subjective human actions and as such are far from impartial. What appears to be Posa's selfless pursuit of noble political ideals becomes a narcissistic striving for power, albeit in the name of a higher moral principle. Posa's action loses its sublime quality as soon as the pursuit of his moral principles is tied to his personal ambition. Schiller considers motivations that are derived from ideals of moral perfection "nicht natürlich im Menschenherzen" (not natural in the human heart) (SNA 22:171). In his view these motivations are "äußerst gefährlich in [menschlichen] Händen" (extremely dangerous in human hands) because individuals with a limited perspective tend to treat them as if they were universally true (ibid.). It is even more dangerous if certain passions, such as hunger for power, egotism, and pride, play a role in the pursuit of these ideals of moral perfection, which seems almost inevitable according to Schiller (ibid.).

This is why the effect of the sublime has to be represented as a purely spiritual conquest of one's egotistical desire to live in the presence of an existential defeat. Posa's taking responsibility for his intrigue by sacrificing himself for the idea of freedom would be an example that reveals a sublime frame of mind: "... um für sein ... Ideal alles zu tun und zu geben, was ein Mensch für etwas tun und geben kann, das ihm das Teuerste ist" (... to do anything for his ideal, and to offer everything what a human being can possibly offer for what is dearest to him) (SNA 22:174).[15] By portraying Posa's actions as the result of his less-than-perfect personality, Schiller makes him appear more human but less sublime. The more Schiller fleshes out Posa's character, the more his actions appear selfish. In contrast to maintaining a measured and reasonable attitude in the face of danger, which the sublime requires, Posa follows his spontaneous inclination "sich durch eine außerordentliche Tat, durch eine augenblickliche Erhöhung seines Wesens bei sich selbst wieder in Achtung zu setzen" (to regain his self-respect through an exceptional deed or an instantaneous aggrandizement of his very being) (SNA 22:176). Consequently Posa's actions are motivated less by the "selfless" sacrifice for his political ideals than by his desire to preserve his self-image. Posa's like-minded brothers, Karl Moor and Fiesco, whose sublime character traits also become overshadowed by their political ambitions, illustrate the difficulty—if not impossibility—of separating self-interest from abstract moral principles. As soon as these protagonists identify with their political causes, they no longer act only in the interest of mankind but also in the interest of their own personal aspirations. This is when lofty ideals suddenly become political instruments that serve the narcissistic goals of their purveyors.

Schiller, who, on the one hand, follows in Kant's footsteps by maintaining a moral distinction between selfish and unselfish actions, exposes, on the other hand, this distinction between narcissistic and sublime motivations as a construct that is unsustainable in life. The tragedy in Schiller's dramas is that the effort to realize the ideal is bound to fail. Some of Schiller's heroes and heroines, such as Karl Moor, Marquis Posa, Maria Stuart, and Joan of Arc, accept their tragic fate, however, with great dignity, which leaves the audience with the impression of a sublime inner strength that does not falter in the face of death (SNA 3:235; SNA 6:297–99; SNA 9:153; SNA 9:314–15). Neither the sublime nor narcissism is represented as gender specific in Schiller's dramas. Just as it would be inaccurate to consider the sublime as limited to Schiller's male heroes, it would be just as inaccurate to associate narcissism with his women figures. However, one could argue that Schiller represents Kant's essentially male Idealism by enacting the desired sublimation of emotions in his dramas.

Yet Schiller's presentations of the sublime reveal both its potentially repressive nature as well as its affinity to personal ambition. Schiller's art depends on the sublime because it is capable of expressing the tension between the two antagonistic spheres of human existence: the existential fear of death and the spiritual ability to overcome it. Schiller's explorations of the sublime then reveal that even the noblest ideals are in danger of being compromised by selfish motivations. The disclosure of the sublime's susceptibility to these motivations necessitates a widening of the gap between art and life to a point where art exposes its own artificiality, an artificiality that threatens to transform the sublime into irony.

In the overall context of this study, the Kantian sublime can be seen as an aesthetic concept that extends the lasting impact of the Idealist legacy well into the nineteenth century. The internal capacity to reason allowed the human subject to transcend empirical reality and partake in universally valid, "objective" laws that extended to the realms of ethics and aesthetics. The Kantian assumption of an "objective," universal "science of the mind" degraded empiricist scientific knowledge because it was subject to fallible human perception (Daston and Galison 262). While ethical and aesthetic norms are no longer considered "objective" or universal, the privileging of a philosophy and science based on reason over a philosophy and science based on experience resonates with later positivist attempts to exclude the fallibility of human perception in scientific experiments. The division between "objective" science that focuses on universally valid laws and principles of select external phenomena and "subjective" literature that explores human sensations and perceptions of particular experiences from an internal point of view informed Dilthey's distinction of *Naturwissenschaft* (science) and *Geisteswissenschaft* (human sciences). This distinction does not fully coincide with the Kantian premises. In contrast to Dilthey, "[f]or Kant the line between the objective and the subjective generally runs between universal and particular, not between world and mind" (Daston and Galison 30). Kant's neo-platonic assumption that ideas, beliefs, and thoughts can be "objective," as long as they are universally valid, conflicted with the commonplace notion of the subjective as individual and the objective as factual and therefore universally true. In the course of the nineteenth century, empiricist methods became more predominant, and the Kantian distinction of subjective and objective depended now on "whether the will could change a perception or not" (ibid. 214). Nevertheless, Kant's influence persists in the continuing attempts to minimize or eliminate subjective interferences from scientific experimentation (ibid. 253–73).

The attempts to eliminate the researchers' own sensations and ideas in favor of universally recognizable formal structures resulted in a formulaic language that "abandoned representations altogether" (ibid. 259). While the abstraction from empirical processes through numbers and symbols lent the research greater generality and objectivity, it also made it less concrete and communicable (ibid. 266–73). The growing abstraction of scientific language as well as the concentration on small segments of empirical reality confirm Dilthey's claim that the natural sciences succeeded in discovering causal laws of nature because they focus on processes in isolation from their natural environment: "*The conditions* sought by the *mechanistic explanation* of nature explain only *part of the contents of external reality*" (SW 203; italics in original). For Dilthey, the human sciences, on the other hand, deal with more complex human interactions and lived experiences in the historical world. Understanding (*Verstehen*) the real world differs from mere intellectual understanding by involving all human faculties, including sensations, emotions, and perceptions. The human sciences and literature in particular aim to comprehend, interpret, and evaluate representations of lived experiences. Dilthey believes that human beings can empathize with others only if they have similar or the same experiences. Imitating (*Nachbildung*) or reliving (*Nacherleben*) enables us to connect our own experiences to those of others. For Dilthey, this dialogue with the represented world of the text and the self is open-ended and follows a hermeneutic process that deduces the understanding of the whole from the particular and vice versa.

Schiller's *Die Räuber* and *Don Karlos* preceded Kant's theoretical explanation of the sublime and Dilthey's definition of *Geisteswissenschaften* (the human sciences). His plays exemplify these aesthetic theories *avant la lettre*. For one thing, Schiller's dramas illustrate the protagonists' sublime overcoming of sensual desires and at the same time problematize the willful suppression of emotions in the service of an abstract ideal. The enactments of insoluble dilemmas of true-to-life conflicts also epitomize Dilthey's description of the human sciences as discourses that focus on human interactions engaging all human faculties.

Notes

Parts of this chapter were previously published as "Keeping Narcissism at Bay: Kant and Schiller on the Sublime," *Konturen* 3 (2010): http://konturen.uoregon.edu/vol3_Mathas.html/.

1. In the German context, one could mention the writings of Kant, Herder, Moses Mendelssohn, Ernst Platner, Karl-Philip Moritz, and Schiller, among others, all of which betray an intense interest in human psychology and anthropology. Zelle points out that the exploration of the self had already been announced in René Descartes's study of the human passions (Traité des passions de l'âme).

2. Kant's usage of "objective" and "subjective" differed considerably from post-Kantian use after the first half of the nineteenth century. "Kant's 'objective validity' (*objektive Gültigkeit*) referred not to external objects (*Gegenstände*) but to the 'forms of sensibility' (time, space, causality) that are the preconditions of experience" (Daston, Galison 30). Mere empirical sensations, like anger, fear, and pleasure, on the other hand, are subjective. The sublime is not just a subjective feeling because the mixed sensation of beauty and terror shocks the observer and induces him to distance himself and reflect on his subjective emotions. This self-distance objectifies the aesthetic category because it involves both sensation and reason.
3. The late eighteenth-century convention that relied on exaggerated emotions was also called the "cult of sensibility."
4. While the origins of textual analysis or hermeneutics reach as far back as antiquity, Johann Conrad Dannhauer coined the term "hermeneutics" in the seventeenth century. Kant's *Kritik der reinen Vernunft*, which pointed to the limitations of the human capacity of understanding, contributed to the awareness of the interpreter's subjective point of view. Friedrich Ast (1778–1841), a student of Schelling, introduced the hermeneutic circle. As in Schelling's philosophical writings, the whole is also contained in each part of an organism or work of art. The work of art is an expression of the spirit of the era of its production. Friedrich Schleiermacher (1768–1834) developed hermeneutics as a methodology, turning it into an *Allgemeine Kunstlehre* (general science of the arts) or aesthetics. Here the interpreter attempts to empathize with the spirit of the time of the artifact's creation as well as with its author. The interpreter recreates the work of art by what has been called *einleben*, or by experiencing it from an internal point of view.
5. In fact, the methodological separation between the *Geisteswissenschaften* (humanities) and *Naturwissenschaften* was not fully expressed until Dilthey formulated the distinction. Rudolf Makkreel summarizes Dilthey's distinction between *Geisteswissenschaften* and *Naturwissenschaften* in his entry of the *Stanford Encyclopedia of Philosophy*: "Whereas the main task of the natural sciences is to arrive at law-based causal explanations, the core task of the human sciences is the understanding of the organizational structures of human and historical life." Rudolf Makkreel, "Wilhelm Dilthey," *The Stanford Encyclopedia of Philosophy* (Fall 2016 Edition), Edward N. Zalta (ed.), https://plato.stanford.edu/archives/fall2016/entries/dilthey/. The human sciences (*Geisteswissenschaften*) encompass both the humanities and the social sciences. They range from disciplines like philology, literary and cultural studies, religion and psychology, to political science and economics. The *Geisteswissenschaften* according to Dilthey "consist of three classes of statements: "facts, theorems, value judgments and rules" (SW 78). Dilthey implies that mechanistic explanations of nature have been successful because of their "precision of quantitative determinations" of sense impressions and their ability to predict "future impressions" (SW 203). Yet, he also points out that such causal explanations abstract from the full scope of the external world and therefore can explain only *part of the contents of external reality* (ibid 203).
6. Karl Philipp Moritz's novel *Anton Reiser* depicts the protagonist's difficulty to distinguish serious preoccupation with the self from mere self-indulgence.
7. Here are just a few examples among many others: Karl Philipp Moritz's *Anton Reiser* (1785–90), Johann Heinrich Jung-Stilling's *Lebensgeschichte (Story of His Life)* (1777–1817), Ulrich Bräker's *Lebensgeschichte und Ebenteuer des armen Mannes im Tockenburg (Life Story and Adventures of the Poor Man in Tockenburg)* (1789), Jacob Michael Rein-

hold Lenz's *Der Hofmeister oder Vorteile der Privaterziehung* (*The Tutor or Advantages of Private Education*) (1774), and Goethe's *Torquato Tasso* (1790) and his early poetry of the 1770s.

8. See Kant, "Analytik des Erhabenen," *Kritik der Urteilskraft*, ed. Gerhard Lehmann (Stuttgart: Reclam, 1986), 161. Future references to this source will be cited parenthetically in the text as KU; see also Schiller, "Vom Erhabenen," *Schillers Werke: Nationalausgabe* (Weimar: Hermann Böhlaus Nachfolger, 1962), 20:184–85. Future references to this source will be cited parenthetically in the text as SNA 20.

9. "Erhaben ist, was auch nur denken zu können ein Vermögen des Gemüts beweiset, das jeden Maßstab der Sinne übertrifft" (The sublime proves the human soul's ability to think beyond any capacity of the senses). If not indicated otherwise, all translations from the German are mine.

10. Narcissus wants to merge with an idealized image of himself that is never quite attainable. See Mathäs 13.

11. Although Kant makes every effort to distinguish the sublime from any self-serving interest, his description of the sublime comes close to admitting to the sublime's underlying narcissism: "Also ist das Gefühl des Erhabenen in der Natur Achtung für unsere eigene Bestimmung, die wir einem Objekte der Natur durch eine gewisse Subreption (Verwechslung einer Achtung für das Objekt statt der für die Idee der Menschheit in unserm Subjekte) beweisen, welches uns die Überlegenheit der Vernunftbestimmung unserer Erkenntnisvermögen über das größte Vermögen der Sinnlichkeit gleichsam anschaulich macht" (Therefore the feeling of the sublime in nature is respect for our own vocation, which we attribute to an object of nature through a certain subreption [substitution of respect for the object of nature instead for the idea of humanity in our own self—the subject]; and this feeling renders, as it were, apparent the supremacy of our rational faculties over the greatest faculty of sensibility) (KU 154).

12. Walter Hinderer offers a deviating interpretation by analyzing the characters' citation of literary sources. Accordingly, Schiller's figures identify with illustrious characters from the Bible or Greek and Roman myths while the action of the play contradicts their wishful thinking (Hinderer 57). In Hinderer's opinion, Schiller's multifaceted representation of the characters also shows their illusory perception of the world and themselves. One could read Karl's murder of Amalia as the deed of an idealist who has lost touch with reality and no longer feels bound by secular justice.

13. Schiller cites technical reasons in justifying Karl's murder of Amalia. He stresses that if Amalia had simply acquiesced to a life without Karl, "dann hätte sie *nie* geliebt" (she would have *never* loved) (SNA 22:127). Yet the author also characterizes the "zweideutige Katastrophe" (the ambiguous catastrophe) as the pinnacle of the entire play: "Offenbar krönt diese Wendung das ganze Stück" (obviously this turning point crowns the entire play) (SNA 22:128).

14. Schiller's concession that he did not know "was das Mädchen will, oder was der Dichter mit dem Mädchen gewollt hat" (what the girl wants, or what the poet intended with her) (SNA 22:125) highlights the author's identification with the male characters.

15. This action cannot be considered entirely selfless, however, because it is motivated by the intention to leave a lasting impression on others, as Schiller explains, citing the example of Lykurgus and the Spartans (SNA 22:174). Schiller de-emphasizes Posa's sublimity by attributing his self-sacrifice to his emotional disposition. He cites Posa's impetuous decision to rid himself of the guilt feelings over jeopardizing his best friend's life (SNA 22:176–77).

CHAPTER 4

The Importance of Herder's Humanism and the Posthumanist Challenge

Introduction

This chapter will highlight Johann Gottfried Herder's (1744–1803) significance for the humanist cause and the humanities in general. Herder's contributions are momentous because he recognized early on that the mind-body dualism of traditional Enlightenment philosophy had erected an arbitrary boundary between the faculties of feeling and thinking, between imagining and reasoning. For Herder, such a dissection of the human organism ignored the interrelatedness of all the sensory and intellectual faculties that support and constitute a human being. In short, the mind-body duality failed to view the human being in its entirety. Although Herder had enormous influence on the literary, aesthetic, historicist, and philosophical discourses of German Idealism, his philosophical contributions are often overlooked and overshadowed by his teacher Kant. The lack of attention toward Herder's philosophy can be partially attributed to the fact that many of his works rely on empirical, anthropological, as well as historical knowledge and are conceptually less stringent than Kant's critiques.

Philosopher Mark Johnson addresses this issue of the Enlightenment philosophy's adherence to the qualitative distinction between the mind and body. Not surprisingly, this mind-body dualism favored thought over sensory perception and thus explains the disciplinary contempt of *Popularphilosophie* or positivist empiricism. Johnson refers to Kant's *Critique of Judgment* as a main source that contributed to the "derogation of the aesthetic" in philosophical discourse. Kant complied with the prevailing mind-body dualism that resulted in his differentiation between the "higher," intellectual cognitive faculties and the "lower," or sensory, faculties (Johnson, *Meaning* 211). The Kantian legacy of devaluing the practical, ethical, and political engagements with art "persisted most forcefully into the twentieth century" (ibid. 212). As Johnson lucidly argues, Kant's preferential treatment of form over content resonates with his attempt to develop a universally valid norm for judgments of taste that do not depend on private sensations and feelings. According to Kantian aesthetics, formal concepts are decisive in the aesthetic experience because they initiate a dialectic between our imagination and understanding that allows us to perceive the harmony of form and content as aesthetically pleasing (ibid. 217). Art becomes a stylized expression that idealizes nature/reality by depicting or insinuating a harmonious ideal as if it were natural. Notwithstanding this attempt to objectify aesthetic experience, Johnson argues, Kant persisted in distinguishing "the aesthetic" as a partially sensory experience and as such "subjective and nonconceptual" (ibid. 218). Precisely because of the assumption that the aesthetic experience involves a noncognitive, albeit "refined, intellectual kind of feeling," aesthetics could never "be the basis for universal concepts, propositions, or knowledge" (ibid.). This is also why, according to Johnson, the mainstream view of philosophy has privileged epistemology, logic, and metaphysics over and against "value fields" such as "ethics, social and political philosophy, and aesthetics" (ibid. 213).

Johnson argues against the conventional exemption of aesthetics from the process of generating "cognitive" meaning by claiming that "all meaning is embodied" (ibid. 222). His interpretation of literary passages illustrates this point and demonstrates that embodied meaning is inherent in both aesthetic experiences as well as philosophical universalisms. Yet one did not have to wait until recently to find opposition to Kant's dualist thinking. Kant's student Herder already emphasized the importance of the sensory faculties and the unity of mind and body.

While his approach included a wealth of empirical facts, he was acutely aware that empirical science alone was inadequate for capturing the totality of the human experience. Rather than imitating the sciences, Herder and after him many other writers, philosophers, and scientists of his time—such as Goethe, Alexander von Humboldt, Lorenz Oken, Novalis, Friedrich Wilhelm Joseph Schelling, Johann Friedrich Blumenbach, and Carl Gustav Carus—conceived nature as an organic totality with an inner purpose or life force and attempted to integrate scientific knowledge into a universal human ethics.[1]

Herder's philosophical legacy distinguishes him as a central figure in German and European arts and letters who strove to define what it means to be human in a physiological, intellectual, and ethical sense.[2] With his attempts to resist the separation of human knowledge into more narrowly defined disciplines, Herder could indeed be regarded as an early proponent of interdisciplinary studies.[3] Herder's goal was to work against social fragmentation and contribute to restoring the human being to its "original unity," which comprised more than the sum of its individual parts. The universal ideals he helped to promote, such as freedom, equality, moral justice, and compassion, influence today's moral values. Whether these universal values can still have a justification in a racially, culturally, ethnically, and socially diverse society with a pluralist mix of lifestyles ties into the more fundamental question of whether these values are compatible with present attempts to define human nature. In light of discoveries in neuroscientific research and recent debates about the moral implications of genetic manipulation, the question of what it means to be human has gained new relevance.[4] This analysis discusses to what extent Herder's eighteenth-century humanism provides justifications for linking specialized scientific discourses to today's questions of human ethics and by extension for revitalizing the humanities.

After all, eighteenth-century philosophers like Herder attempted to defend the rights of the individual against the threat of an instrumental reason that viewed the human subject only as a means to an end, a threat that continues to this day. Progress in the natural sciences resulted in more specialized research areas and thus had consequences for a redefinition of disciplinary boundaries. Herder—albeit open to new empiricist approaches—was concerned about the increasing specialization as it, in his view, contributed to the human subject's fragmentation. As this analysis will show, he attempted to maintain human sovereignty by subordinating scientific progress to a humanist ethics, without neglecting the particular discoveries in the emerging fields of empirical philosophy, psychology, anthropology, and medicine.

As mentioned in the introduction to this volume, both humanism's diminished credibility and new findings in neurobiological research have caused contemporary philosophers to question some of the most fundamental assumptions of what a human being is and consequently some humanist prerogatives. The German philosopher Peter Sloterdijk, for instance, argues in his 1999 essay "Regeln für den Menschenpark" ("Rules for the Human Zoo") that humanism is based on repression. He even insinuates that the unsuccessful domestication of human instincts may have culminated in fascism (Sloterdijk, *Regeln*). Sloterdijk implies that the biogenetic revolution of our time could provide an opportunity to liberate mankind from its self-imposed repression and offer an alternative to humanism (ibid. 17, 30–31, 39, 46–47). Sloterdijk's essay came in the wake of humanists' growing preoccupation with the consequences of the Human Genome Project. Far from welcoming its promise of unlocking the human genetic makeup, some scholars have expressed reservations regarding the project. Catherine Waldby, for instance, warns us of the project's ideological assumption that humans are a "stable, knowable 'species,' an organic integrity whose limits can be positively specified."[5] Yet other theorists—who could be described as posthumanist feminist thinkers, such as Donna Haraway, Teresa de Lauretis, and Sadie Plant—perceive biogenetics as an opportunity to challenge the myth of biological humanism and liberate women from their traditional role as "a deficient version of humanity which is already male" (Plant 266).

Recent discoveries in the cognitive neurosciences and consciousness research have led German philosopher Thomas Metzinger to claim that there "is a new image of man emerging, an image that will dramatically contradict almost all traditional images man has made of himself in the course of his cultural history" (Metzinger, "Introduction" 6). Metzinger bases this claim of "a radically new understanding of what it means to be human" on recent scientific research, "since about 1990," that supposedly has enabled scientists "to learn more about the human brain than in the three preceding centuries" (ibid.). Metzinger, a philosophy professor at Johannes Gutenberg University in Mainz, claims "that no such things as selves exist in the world."[6] According to his theory, subjects perceive themselves as subjects due to misrepresentations or simulations of brain signals. These simulations appear as real due to an inherent blind spot that does not allow humans to grasp the constructed character of phenomenal reality. Subjects experience themselves as being someone because the system mistakes the internal model of itself for an actual conscious self or, in Metzinger's words, "The phenomenal property of selfhood as such is a representational construct; it truly is *phenomenal* property in terms of being an appearance only" (563).

I am introducing Metzinger's self-model here because it stands in opposition to Herder's idea of the human self. Contrary to Herder, who takes the self for granted and describes sensations from the perspective of the perceiving subject, Metzinger approaches the self from an external position that aims at avoiding the fallacies of a distorted, subjective point of view. And yet, while Metzinger uses an abundance of empirical data to substantiate his claims, his theory cannot explain how a subject with an independent self-awareness appears, or "how the body that sits presently in front of my computer, gives rise to *me* as a subject with a first-person point of view that is unique" (Himma).[7] Even though Herder's philosophy cannot explain the mind-body problem—and it is questionable whether any philosophy will be able to establish how brain activities constitute a unique self—his approach of depicting subjective sensory experiences from a first-person point of view is in many ways more tangible than Metzinger's phenomenological account.

This chapter will show how Herder uses poetic descriptions of sensory experiences and emotions, which render human states of consciousness more vividly and clearly than Metzinger's scientific discourse on electrochemical processes of our brain. Since this analysis, however, is not based on neuroscientific expertise, its focus will be limited to the ethical implications and possible ramifications of these discoveries for understanding Herder's humanist views. After all, Herder addresses ethical problems connected to freedom, individual autonomy, and subjectivity that over two hundred years later have arisen again in connection with such bioethical issues as cloning. While Herder's views about human nature contain metaphysical assumptions regarding the autonomy of the human self that would not be acceptable to many contemporary neuroscientists and posthumanists, one can still justifiably ask whether his interdisciplinary method of synthesizing scientific and poetic discourses could serve as a model for conveying human experiences that purely scientific discourses are unable to convey. Related to this issue is the question whether scientific standards can adequately judge Herder's poetic and emotionally charged discourse and whether the knowledge we gain from it transcends the scientific purview.

In light of the challenges to universally acceptable humanist core values that are often associated with Western culture, such as reason, freedom, virtue, the pursuit of happiness, tolerance, religion, education, culture, truth, and beauty, the proposition of a reinvigoration of the humanities through humanism seems daunting.[8] Yet while one has to refrain from overstating analogies between current and late eighteenth-century notions of humanism, one could speculate that current trepidations about the fragmentation of the humanities are still symptomatic of more deep-seated concerns about the loss of the value of the human. The widespread use of humanist ideals for diverse political agendas suggests their broad significance, for it addresses not only ethical and spiritual standards of human existence but also its physical and emotional dimensions. Herder's philosophical writings attempt to appeal to the envisioned totality of human existence by employing a language rich in metaphors and imagery that replicates human emotions and feelings from an internal point of view. Naturally this type of poetic language differs from the distanced or seemingly objective description of conventional scientific discourses. In contrast to such seemingly objective scientific discourses that examine natural phenomena in isolation, Herder's descriptions aim at rendering a totality of sensual impressions from a first-person perspective by integrating emotional, physiological, and spiritual experiences.[9] My analysis of excerpts from Herder's "Auch eine Philosophie der Geschichte zur Bildung der Menschheit" ("This Too a Philosophy of History on the Formation of Humanity") (1774), "Über den Ursprung der Sprache" ("Treatise on the Origin of Language") (1772), and "Über das Erkennen und Empfinden der menschlichen Seele" ("On Cognition and Sensation of the Human Soul") (1778) seeks to demonstrate how Herder rises to the challenge of investing a growing body of scientific discoveries with universal meaning. By showing how Herder integrates scientific knowledge into his literary descriptions of concrete sensual and physical experiences, this investigation will point out techniques that allowed him to traverse disciplinary boundaries and thus open the doors for viewing the human in a new light.

In contrast to those philosophers who reject the benefits of a humanist education or who dispute the notion of individual autonomy or the subject's agency altogether in view of the latest biogenetic research, German philosopher Manfred Frank has defended the subjective position of philosophical and literary discourses against the threat of privileging the seeming objectivity of brain research.[10] In an interview with the German weekly *Die Zeit*, Frank argued that brain research is unable to account for the fact that humans have an emotional understanding or feeling for themselves before they can express it. Subjective self-knowledge and the ability to have empathy for other human beings permit individuals to make ethical decisions and remain the domain of the humanities (Frank). For Herder, the freedom to decide liberates humans from the reign of instinctual forces and allows them to act according to moral principles (HW 6:144).[11] In contrast, philosophies like Metzinger's attribute human actions to biological processes and reject the subject's freedom to make decisions.

Yet there are epistemic analogies between eighteenth-century goals of humanist thought and current efforts at revitalizing the humanities. After all, today's calls for a renewal of the humanities can be linked to trepidations about the loss of universal human values. Such fears were also germane for Herder's philosophy, which can be interpreted as an attempt to give meaning to a growing body of scientific knowledge and empirical facts. After an introduction to Herder's unique philosophical ideas within the context of eighteenth-century Enlightenment discourse, I will analyze a passage from "Über das Erkennen und Empfinden der menschlichen Seele" to illustrate how Herder uses poetic language to integrate the latest empirical knowledge of his day and age in his humanist philosophy. The third part of this chapter will contrast Metzinger's philosophical model to that of Herder in order to underline the significance of the humanities in today's academic environment.

Herder's Anthropological Views

Herder distinguished himself from the rationalist metaphysics of the Wolff-Leibniz tradition as well as from the newly emerging empiricist approaches, the so-called *Popularphilosphie*.[12] The fact that Herder's approach stands in contrast to a number of established scholarly discourses has a historical explanation. During the late Enlightenment, dogmatic metaphysical philosophies prevailed because empiricist scientific approaches were unable to provide all-inclusive explanations of the universe and its development.[13] Herder's philosophy of history can be understood as a response to the inadequacy of conventional metaphysical models of explanation in light of a growing body of empirical knowledge. His unique position comes to the fore in his philosophy of history, especially in his essay "Auch eine Philosophie der Geschichte zur Bildung der Menschheit." Emphasizing how specific geographical, climatic, and social differences account for physical and cultural characteristics, he rejects both the Idealist standpoint that bases human knowledge on innate ideas (Descartes, Leibniz) and mechanistic concepts of human life (La Mettrie, Ernst Platner). Yet in the very first sentence of his essay, Herder subordinates the study of historical and cultural particularities to the discovery of the human species' common origin: "Je weiter hin es sich in Untersuchung der ältesten Weltgeschichte, ihrer Völkerwanderungen, Sprachen, Sitten, Erfindungen und Traditionen aufklärt: desto wahrscheinlicher wird mit jeder neuen Entdeckung auch *der Ursprung des ganzen Geschlechts von Einem*" (HW 4:11) ("The further illumination advances in the investigation of the ancient world history, its migrations of peoples, its languages, ethics, inventions, and traditions, the more probable becomes, with each new discovery, the origination of the whole species from a single man as well" [Forster 272]).[14] In spite of his awareness of the empirical differences that shape cultural diversity, Herder adheres to a pantheistic idea of nature that unfolds its divine destiny in history. He attempts to integrate cultural, social, and geophysical particularities by claiming an underlying correspondence between the spirit of history and a divine inner human nature.[15]

Herder's seemingly paradoxical attempt at combining empiricist and pantheistic views reflects the desire to reconcile the increasingly disparate body of knowledge with a philosophy that was still indebted to an overall purpose. As the ushering in of the modern scientific age undermined the divine cosmic order, in which each living creature had its place and meaning, the philosophers of the Enlightenment attempted to compensate for the uncertainty of a purely secular perspective by investing the new scientific outlook with meaning. Establishing analogies between human existence and the cosmic order, understanding nature in allegorical, mathematical, or geometrical correspondence expressing a universal harmony, or reading the universe as a book are just a few examples of such anthropocentric projections that aimed at providing existential comfort in a rapidly changing outlook on the world. Hans Dietrich Irmscher pointed out that the analogies in Herder's thought establish relationships between totalities and structures. In his *Ideen zur Philosophie der Geschichte der Menschheit* (*Ideas on the Philosophy of the History of Mankind*) (1784–91), Herder attempts to capture the essence of what is human by drawing analogies to plant and animal life (Irmscher, "Beobachtungen" 68). In "Auch eine Philosophie der Geschichte zur Bildung der Menschheit," Herder confronts the great philosophers of the age of Enlightenment by telling them that human understanding has not been able to make sense of the enormous changes of world history (HW 4:57). Even though he concludes that everything in history is "Schicksal! von Menschen *unüberdacht, ungehofft, unbewürkt*" (fate! unreflected, undesired, unaffected by man) (HW 4:58) and that human beings are just like little ants crawling on the big wheels of fate, he is absolutely convinced that history has a divine purpose. Instead of imposing a rational system on historical events, Herder respects the increasing body of empirical facts about seemingly unrelated cultural developments and incidents. His method trusts in the observation of individual developments that in his view are part of a cosmic order and divine nature, as they belong to "dem großen Buche Gottes" (to the great book of God) (HW 4:106).

In spite of its rejection of the metaphysical rationalism of the Wolff-Leibniz school, Herder's own discourse is replete with associative analogies and relies on metaphors that suggest a different kind of metaphysics.[16] In book fifteen of the *Ideas*, Herder still clings to a notion of reason that is capable of uniting the incongruities of natural phenomena, thus permitting humans to create order out of chaos (HW 6:649). In light of such claims about an inexplicable presence of an underlying ordering principle, Kant's criticism of Herder's unscientific methodology, which accuses the *Ideas on the Philosophy of the History Mankind* of falling prey to the very metaphysical speculations that he is claiming to avoid, is well taken, indeed (Menges 53). However, if one were to judge Herder's philosophy according to Kantian principles, one would hardly do justice to the inner logic of Herder's philosophical thinking. Herder's philosophy is based on assumptions that are radically different from those of Kant "concerning the very idea of science, its purpose and status within culture as a whole, its standards of rationality, methods of inquiry and verification, and—last but not least—its proper use of language" (Knodt 1). Katherine Arens exposes the Kantian attack on Herder's scientific method as an attempt to present philosophy as "the queen of the sciences . . . , while essentially rejecting the humanities as anything but arts, as tradition or critique instead of scientific interpretation" (109). In contrast to Herder, who bases his philosophy of history on empirical evidence, Kant rejects all knowledge obtained through human experience as nonphilosophical. Consequently, "Kant designates historical (or perhaps, practical) knowledge as second rate, as knowledge *ex datis*, not *ex principiis*" (ibid. 108). Kantian philosophy "privileges the mind over empirical data" and focuses on "the relation of all knowledge to the essential ends of human reason" (ibid.). Likewise, one could argue, as Arens does, that the Kantian privileging of conceptual reasoning anticipates the later denigration of the humanities as second-class faculties.[17] While Herder has been in the shadow of Kant, one often neglects his immense legacy for the humanities and the arts—a legacy that addresses a wide range of historical, anthropological, linguistic, ethical, and aesthetic questions that Kant ignored. It would therefore be unsuitable to judge Herder's philosophy according to Kant's standard, as he deliberately considered the adherence to abstract principles as an obstruction to the realization of a human being's fullest potential.

Herder's awareness of the heterogeneity of cultural and historical developments is counterbalanced by his all-pervasive attempt to make sense of a rapidly growing body of knowledge. By comparing the course of world history to different ages of an individual human life, he imposes an organic, anthropocentric order on an otherwise disjointed accumulation of events that allows him to discover meaning in world history.[18] While this anthropocentrism gives the historian a superior point of view that overlooks the entire course of history, Herder de-emphasizes the claim to universality by stressing that his philosophy is only one among many other possible accounts—as the title of his essay "Auch eine Philosophie der Geschichte zur Bildung der Menschheit" suggests. The title of his more comprehensive *Ideen zur Philosophie der Geschichte der Menschheit* (1782–91) also refers to the open-ended sketchiness of his system.[19] This duality between Herder's belief in an underlying universal order and reliance on empirical knowledge pervades his entire philosophy.

For Herder, humans constitute themselves as human by creating their individual image of the world through the production of language.[20] This assumption makes Herder's philosophy unique and provides another opportunity to bridge the gap between the empirical and the spiritual world, between body and mind, between the particular and the universal.[21] Herder's theory of language anticipates poststructuralist theories as it views human existence embedded in preexisting language structures (Menges 59). For Herder, it is language and not consciousness that constitutes human existence. As the first sentence of Herder's *Abhandlung über den Ursprung der Sprache* indicates—"*Schon als Tier, hat der Mensch Sprache*" (italics in original) (HW 1:697) ("Already as an animal, the human being has language" [Forster 65])—language is embodied in the human being's physical or animal existence. It transcends the limits of human consciousness as an *a priori* structure and at the same time constitutes the individual human being in a dialogic process of interaction. Herder emphasizes the reciprocity of reception and production in the creation of speech, which allows humans to define and recognize themselves as individuals. Jürgen Trabant made this clear by pointing to Herder's privileging of the spoken sound over the written word. Accordingly, Herder favors the spoken word because it lets the subject experience its own production of sound through the medium of the ear: "Hearing guarantees the reflexivity of the sound movements and hence their production.... Through the ear wo/man experiences her/himself as a maker, as a poet ..." (Trabant 16). As an all-pervasive medium that connects the human to the nonhuman and the body to the mind, language also transcends all disciplinary boundaries. What constitutes human beings is their ability to create themselves through the production of language (Irmscher, HW 7:817–19).

Every human being is an artist because of the ability to express individual sensory impressions of nature. The individualized representation of sensory impressions is key to human existence. Without this creative activity, humans would not distinguish themselves from other living beings. Artistic representation is the calling and purpose of human nature. The senses play a very important role because they allow the subject to see, feel, and hear in an original fashion, making the subject aware of his/her unique individuality. By representing their own particular nature in relation to nature at large, human beings become godlike as they recreate their image in the image of nature. Similarly, language as medium of this artistic self-representation aims at expressing an utterance that is both characteristic and at the same time universal as it can communicate a subjective experience to the human community at large.

Herder's proclaimed coexistence of the universal and the particular permits him to define the human according to what it lacks versus an all-encompassing meaningful totality. In his essay "On Cognition and Sensation of the Human Soul," Herder characterizes humans as composed of an outer and inner sensorium that are intertwined, and recognition always builds on sensation. In this essay Herder develops the fundamental principles of his theory of cognition, which affects all aspects of his cultural historicism. Accordingly, we can recognize only what we first grasp with our senses.[22] Humans create the universe in analogy to the unity of the human body. Herder's poetic imagery illustrates how particular stimuli become synthesized into sensations and how language can reflect the totality of the sensual and spiritual convergence of the human faculties. The subjective and poetic quality of his language aims at synthesizing the complex diversity of sensory experience into a meaningful totality.[23] Scientific language, on the other hand, is analytical and therefore concerned with the particular.[24] The following citation is an example of Herder's poetic depiction of the dialectic interaction between the physical and spiritual, between automatic stimulus and conscious sensation:

> Die Natur hat tausend kleine lebendige Stricke in tausendfachem Kampf, in ein so vielfaches Berühren und Widerstreben verflochten: sie kürzen und längen sich mit innerer Kraft, nehmen am Spiele des Muskels, jeder auf seine Weise, Teil, dadurch trägt und ziehet jener. Hat man je etwas Wunderbareres gesehen als ein schlagendes Herz mit seinem unerschöpflichen Reize? Ein Abgrund innerer dunkeln Kräfte, das wahre Bild der organischen Allmacht, die vielleicht inniger ist, als der Schwung der Sonnen und Erden.—Und nun breitet sich aus diesem unerschöpflichen Brunnen und Abgrunde der Reiz durch unser ganzes Ich aus, belebt jede kleine spielende Fiber—alles nach Einartigem einfachen Gesetze. Wenn wir uns wohl befinden, ist unsere Brust weit, das Herz schlägt gesund, jede Fiber verrichtet ihr Amt im Spiele. Da fährt Schrecken auf uns zu; und siehe als erste Bewegung, noch ohne Gedanken von Furcht und Widerstände, tritt unser reizbares Ich auf seinen Mittelpunkt zurück, das Blut zum Herzen, die Fiber, selbst das Haar, starrt empor, gleichsam ein organischer Bote zur Gegenwehr, die Wache steht fertig. (HW 4:332)

> (Nature has woven together a thousand little living strings into a thousand fold fight, into such a manifold touching and resisting; they make themselves shorter and longer with inner force, participate in the play of the muscle, each one in its own way—that is what makes the muscle carry and pull. Has anything more wonderful ever been seen than a beating heart with its inexhaustible irritation?

An abyss of inner obscure forces, the true image of the organic almighty, which is perhaps deeper than the motion of suns and earths.—And now irritation spreads out from this inexhaustible fount and abyss through our whole I, enlivens each little playing fiber—all according to a single-formed simple law. If we are in good health, our chest is broad, the heart beats healthily, each fiber performs its duty in the play. Then fright storms upon us, and behold, as our first movement, without yet any thought of fear or resistance, our irritable I retreats to its center, our blood to our heart, our fiber, even our hair, stands on end—so to speak, an organic messenger ready for counterattack, the guard stands ready. [Forster 189–90])

For Herder, the human heart serves as a microcosm that mirrors the spirit of nature. The human body exemplifies nature's universal laws as each part of the human organism follows the same unanimous principle. The metaphor of "verflechten" (weaving) stresses the intricate diversity and complexity of the human organism, which had become apparent with the discovery of the nerve system as a mediator between body and mind.[25] Herder emphasizes organic nature's dynamism, which is driven by an all-pervasive inner force or energy that is reminiscent of pantheist and vitalist philosophies.[26] Empirical observations of biological processes, such as the interrelatedness of physical and mental sensations, made it necessary to explain the mutual stimulations of body and mind or the continuity of matter and spirit (Zammito, *Kant* 317). Herder's metaphorical, emotionally charged language effectively recalls the totality of the human body's psychophysical processes.

The first part of "Vom Erkennen und Empfinden der menschlichen Seele," from which the passage above is taken, is titled "Vom Reiz" ("Of Irritation"). Here Herder refers to Albrecht von Haller's (1708–77) physiological experiments with nerve tissues. Simon Richter has shown how Herder deliberately misinterpreted the Swiss physiologist's usage of "Reiz" for his own purposes: "Wo der Physiologe [Haller] strikt zwischen 'reizbar' und 'empfindlich' unterschied, erzwang Herder eine Verbindung" (where the physiologist [Haller] distinguished between excitable and sensitive, Herder forged a connection) (S. Richter 89). In the passage above, Herder uses "Reiz" not only in a medical sense as "Reizbarkeit" (irritability) but also in an aesthetic sense as "reizend" (appealing or attractive). "Hat man je etwas Wunderbareres gesehen als ein schlagendes Herz mit seinem unerschöpflichen Reize?" denotes also the aesthetically appealing effect that this heart has on its observer, a meaning of "Reiz" that became part of the eighteenth-century aesthetic discourse (Richter 84–86). While "unerschöpflichen Reize" is a direct translation of Haller's "perpetua irritatio" (HW 4:1130), Herder does not limit it to the medical sense in which Haller uses it but consciously applies it to the semantic field of sensibility and affect (HW 4:1085). Herder's broader usage of "Reiz" connects the physiological with the emotional and aesthetic dimension of the term and thus supports his underlying argument that life is permeated by an energy that links all organic processes to a meaningful totality. In other words, Herder implicitly criticizes Haller's strictly empiricist method that separates organic parts from living organisms and bases its scientific conclusions on what Herder must view as artificial mutilations of organic entities: "Wer ist nun, der den Gang der Analogie, den großen Gang der Schöpfung mit seinem Federmesserchen hier plötzlich abschneide?" (HW 4:337) ("Who would suddenly here cut off the course of analogy, the great course of creation, with his pocket knife?" [Forster 194]). In fact, Haller derived his insight that nerve tissue itself was not excitable from countless experiments with living animals.[27] Since excitability occurs in organs that have been separated from their link to the brain, for instance in decapitated chickens, Haller concluded that "Reiz" was not connected to the soul and therefore had nothing to do with life. In contrast to Haller, Herder views "Reiz" as "die Triebfeder unseres Daseins" (the origin of life) (HW 4:360). He uses "Reiz" as a focal point for his inquiry into the human soul as he regards it as an expression of the life force that no philosophy has been able to explain (HW 4:337). Although Herder believes that this force is ultimately inexplicable and simply has to be *geglaubt* (believed), all human beings can nevertheless feel this life-giving energy both within themselves and through their affinity to all other living organisms (HW 4:335).

For Herder, the life-giving force can be perceived in the living organism's interaction with its environment. This is why Herder, unlike Haller and the French materialists, is not interested in the analysis of isolated body parts but rather in the effect of outside influences on the entire human organism. In the passage above, Herder's narrator does not give a distanced scientific description but an emotionally charged eyewitness account of an oncoming panic attack. Herder's reenactment of this emotional reaction blends the "objective" scientific terminology of empiricist observation with "subjective" expressions of amazement. By directly addressing his audience through a rhetorical question and shifting the point of view from that of scientific observer to that of a personally stimulated spectator, the narrator imparts the intensity of the emotional effect on the reader. The sudden interruption of the descriptive mode conveys the abruptness of an overwhelming thrust of fear and puts the readers in the shoes of the experiencing *I*, having his readers live through the panic attack in the present from the inside perspective of the affected body. He resorts to this technique in order to stress the common bond between the narrative voice and its audience and to illustrate the mutual relationship between body and mind. Significantly, the body's effect on the mind happens in a pre-conscious state. The fact that sensual perception is guided by nature's divine spirit *before* the I can reflect resonates with Herder's idea that life progresses from simple organic plant life to more complex processes in animals to the human organism as the highest form of existence. Accordingly, human consciousness is always a reaction to a previously existing "life energy" or "Reiz."

Herder's intermixing of different discourses is a deliberate choice of style that serves to support his claims about the dialectic interrelations of life and its environment (HW 4:1085). Herder's fusion of poetic and scientific discourse was by no means always considered successful. In his review of the *Ideen zur Philosophie der Geschichte der Menschheit*, Kant questioned the validity of Herder's "Gewebe von kühnen Metaphern, poetischen Bildern, mythologischen Anspielungen" (canvas of bold metaphors, poetic images, mythological insinuations) because he felt it veiled his ideas rather than revealing them (Kant, *Geschichtsphilosophie* 60). Kant criticizes the lack of "logical accuracy" and "precise definitions" in what he calls Herder's idiosyncratic method, which reveals sweeping analogies and bold imagination rather than cool judgment (ibid. 40–41).[28]

While Kant separates the spiritual from the material world and aims at establishing an absolute *a priori* truth that transcends worldly experience, Herder integrates the spiritual with the material world in his attempt to account for the totality of human experience. Ironically Herder, expresses his thoughts in more concrete terms than Kant who resorts to philosophical abstractions. Herder clearly stated already in 1775—nine years before Kant's critical review of Herder's *Ideen zur Philosophie der Geschichte der Menschheit*—that he is hardly concerned about "the superterrestrial abstraction which places itself beyond everything that is called 'circle of our thinking and sensing' onto I know not what throne of divinity, creates there words of worlds, and passes judgment on everything possible and actual" (Forster 188).

Herder's invectives were directed against the discourse of Wolffian *Schulphilosophie* (dogmatism), with its rationalist generalizations and tautological explanations.[29] Kant, albeit also opposed to the assumptions of *Schulphilosophie*, nevertheless follows this tradition insofar as he attempts to establish a universal truth that he can formulate in abstract, general terms.[30] While both make human experience the mother of all knowledge, Herder also believes in a divine, rational order of the universe that can be discovered through the senses. This divine order reveals itself in the analogies between human nature and nature in general (HW 4:338). Although the human subject has a certain freedom from nature, it is also part of nature and generates its meaning and purpose from within by force of an inner power. This inner power or life force permeates all of nature and cannot be comprehended by reason alone.[31] It must first be perceived by the senses, and only then can the human subject try to understand it by using reason. This is why, for Herder, reason is a secondary human faculty that attempts to rationalize the sensory impressions, with which the inner power or "Reiz" of nature makes itself known to all living beings. Contrary to animals, humans have the ability of understanding nature's inner power by reflecting on it.

Language illustrates this process of reflection, a process that also marks the beginning of human self-awareness. For Herder, humans distinguish themselves from all other living organisms through their freedom to be creative and reflect this freedom from nature in human language. In other words, language is the self-reflection of the human soul (HW 1:715–22):

> Der empfindende Mensch fühlt sich in Alles, fühlt Alles aus sich heraus und druckt darauf sein Bild, sein Gepräge. . . . Wie unsere ganze Psychologie aus Bildwörtern bestehet, so wars meistens *Ein* neues Bild, *Eine* Analogie, *Ein* auffallendes Gleichnis, das die größten Theorien geboren. (HW 4:330)
>
> (The sensing human being feels his way into everything, feels everything from out of himself, and imprints it with his image, his impress. . . . Just as our whole psychology consists of figurative terms, for the most part it was a single new image, a single analogy, a single striking metaphor that gave birth to the greatest and boldest theories. [Forster 188])

Language is the mirror in which the human subject can define itself over and against the rest of nature. Yet before humans can express themselves, they have to feel nature's "Reiz" or power through their senses. In contrast to animals, which respond to nature's call instinctively, humans define themselves in opposition to nature by translating the imprint of nature's call into their own idiom (HW 1:716). While animals react to pain, hunger, and other physical emotions by making undifferentiated sounds characteristic of their species, humans have the ability of responding to sensory impressions by impregnating their reactions with their own individual mark. This is why language is essentially different from animal sounds. Although human language is a less direct answer to the calls of nature than the sound of an animal, it gives humans the freedom of defining themselves in relation to nature by recreating nature on a human scale in the medium of language. Abstract language expresses the distance to nature to the extent that it loses sight of the human element. Metaphorical or poetic language is capable of portraying the human in relation to nature by building bridges between the self and nature. Whereas traditional philosophy and science are interested in analyzing objects by taking them apart, Herder's goal is to provide an account of how human life is connected to natural phenomena. For Herder, all human knowledge is based on subjective experience and therefore on a comparison of the self with the outside world: "Was wir wissen, wissen wir nur aus Analogie, von der Kreatur zu uns und von uns zum Schöpfer" (HW 4:330) ("What we know we know only through analogy, from the creation to us and from us to the Creator" [Forster 188]). Consequently the predominant rhetorical feature that allows humans to develop self-consciousness is analogy.[32] Poetic images, metaphors, anthropomorphisms, and onomatopoeias, for instance, permit Herder to illustrate the relationship between nature's powers and the human. The truth is guaranteed by the subject's candid self-examination in light of personal experiences:

> Die stille Ähnlichkeit, die ich im Ganzen meiner Schöpfung, meiner Seele und meines Lebens empfinde und ahnde: der große Geist, der mich anwehet und mir im Kleinen und Großen, in der sichtbaren und unsichtbaren Welt Einen Gang, Einerlei Gesetze zeiget: der ist mein Siegel der Wahrheit. (HW 4:330–31)

> (This quiet similarity which I sense and intuit in the whole of my creation, my soul, and my life; the great spirit [Geist] that breathes upon me and shows me a single course, a single sort of laws, in what is small and what is large, in the visible world and the invisible world—this is my seal of truth. [Forster 188–89])

Herder emphasizes the mutual dependence of body and mind and the interrelatedness of all organisms in order to render human experience in its totality. His language intends to render aspects of human experience that lie beyond the scope of scientific discourse. By reenacting from an inside perspective sensory experiences that are also subject to new scientific discoveries, such as the transmission of nervous impulses, through literary descriptions of the affects that accompany these bodily phenomena, Herder makes sensory experience come alive. His synthesis of anthropological, religious, philosophical, and poetic discourses depicts a broader horizon and, in many instances, more concrete rendition of human sensory experience than Kantian philosophy or Haller's scientific writings. In this regard, Herder's humanism points to the humanities' broader mission of connecting the outside world to human life and looking at the impact of the sciences from a human perspective.

Herder vs. Metzinger

From a posthumanist point of view, Herder's philosophy includes metaphysical conjectures about the human subject that are unverifiable. For instance, his assumption that human reason permits human beings to participate in divine reason and presupposes an essential human nature distinct from all other living creatures is, of course, incompatible with anti- and posthumanist perspectives. These philosophies from Nietzsche to Heidegger to the deconstructionists and the contemporary posthumanist approaches informed by recent biotechnological and neuroscientific developments view human beings in terms of a process rather than an essence.[33] Yet, as Hans Adler pointed out, Herder also "moves away from the traditional type of concept [of *Humanität*] defined by its 'substance' and conceives of his new type of concept in terms of function and relationship" (Adler, "Herder's Concept" 106). While Herder still upholds the notion of individual autonomy (HW 6:630), he also envisions human beings as part of a nature that changes through history (HW 6:627). In this respect Herder's philosophy resembles posthumanist approaches that imagine the human determined by historical, social, and cultural phenomena (HW 6:671). Herder's tautological definition of what is human suggests that human nature is continuously evolving according to divine laws: "Humanität ist der Zweck des Menschen—Natur und Gott hat unserem Geschlecht mit diesem Zweck sein eigenes Schicksal in die Hände gegeben" (Humanity is the purpose of the human being—with this purpose Nature and God put our own fate into our hands) (HW 6:630; translation mine). This seeming contradiction allows Herder to view the development of the human species as a process while the underlying laws of nature, including human nature, remain essentially the same: "Die Natur des Menschen bleibt immer dieselbe" (Human nature always remains the same) (HW 6:628; translation mine).

Philosopher Thomas Metzinger's *Being No One* could serve as an example of a contemporary posthumanist discourse that in some respects follows Herder's spirit. However, there are fundamental differences between Metzinger's and Herder's approach. While Herder attempts to preserve the unity of the human subject as a metaphysical entity, Metzinger aims at exposing this very unit as a construct that prevents higher levels of self-knowledge. Although Metzinger's differentiated model of human consciousness that draws heavily on neuroscientific research makes no mention of Herder, his study does make an effort to build "a better bridge between the humanities and cognitive neuroscience" to achieve "a philosophically interesting growth of knowledge" (Metzinger, *Being* 3). Like Herder, Metzinger resorts to metaphorical descriptions, albeit more technical, to depict his self-model theory of subjectivity (SMT), which aims at providing "a general outline for a theory of consciousness, the phenomenal self, and the first-person perspective" (ibid. 547). This phenomenal self is an inner representation. In this respect it resembles Herder's assumption of an inner stable self. While Herder's inner self is a "true" self because it corresponds to the underlying divine and essential laws of nature, Metzinger's phenomenal self model (PSM) is a virtual apparition that represents not only the external world but also the phenomenal body's interactions with it with a deceptive consistency so that the self-model is mistaken for an actual autonomous subject. Metzinger uses Plato's famous parable of the cave dwellers to illustrate the internal makeup of human consciousness. In contrast to Plato, Metzinger equates the entire cave to "the physical organism as a whole, in particular its brain" (ibid. 548). The shadows on the cave's walls are "phenomenal mental models" or "low-dimensional projections of internal or external objects in the conscious state" (ibid.). The fire that causes the flickering shadows of consciousness "is the incessant, self-regulating flow of neural information processing, constantly perturbed by sensory and cognitive input" (ibid. 549). Metzinger's cave model is another attempt to depict how physiological stimuli become transformed into subjective perceptions. Like Herder, whose poetic analogies served to emphasize the interconnectedness of mind and body, Metzinger also stresses that "the wall and the fire are not separate entities: they are two aspects of one and the same process" (549). In other words, the brain and its neurological activities constitute human consciousness, which are an ongoing activity and not a thing or image of the self. In fact, in Metzinger's model "the cave itself is empty," which means that the projection of the self does not exist as a thing but only as a process.

In contrast to Herder, who attempts to find the "true" self by moving inward to the deep recesses of the soul—as expressed in his poem "Selbst" (HW 3:830–34)—Metzinger compares the inner self to a dungeon that keeps human beings in a state of deception tied to the mistaken belief in such an autonomous inner self. Metzinger's model negates Herder's metaphysics by claiming that the inner self is an illusion. This illusion is created by a complex system of neurological processes in the brain that provide a first-person perspective. Metzinger introduces a "representational metaphor" that equates the mind to a virtual city map to illustrate how the self is situated in the world.[34] The phenomenal self does not recognize the system as such because the data that create the first-person perspective are constantly updated and surreptitiously change the perspective of the phenomenal self in accordance to the changes of its position in the outside world. In other words, whereas an external city map leaves the traveler with a choice to identify with the position of the arrow, the virtual city map conceals the fact that the phenomenal self is the product of a system and not an autonomous self (Metzinger, *Being* 552).

Metzinger likens this fully immersed state of mind to the first-person experience created by a flight simulator. Just as these complex devices let student pilots experience a virtual reality as close as possible to actual real-life situations, the brain creates through this all-encompassing subjective experience a subjective reality (ibid. 557). Metzinger concedes, however, that the human brain has creative and introspective capabilities that a flight simulator lacks. In addition, human subjectivity has the capacity of not only experiencing the world from a first-person point of view but also "of mentally 'ascribing' this act of reference *to* oneself while it is taking place" (ibid. 574). These additional resources make his model come close to the idea of self-determination that he denies (ibid. 556–57). In contrast to traditional Neoplatonic models, Metzinger emphasizes that there "is no homunculus in the system" but that the subject's ability to control itself grew over time with the process of both ontogenetic and phylogenetic evolution. Thus, it is the brain and its neurological processes that activate the pilot or subject in charge and not vice versa.

This idea of neurological stimuli that always precede human agency is, however, not very different from Herder's notion of "Reiz." In his illustration of an oncoming panic attack, Herder also emphasizes that the subject only reacts to sensory stimuli and that sensual perception necessarily happens *before* the I can reflect. Metzinger's claim that the subject is born into a virtual reality from the beginning and only gradually develops both phylogenetically and ontogenetically into a more complex system that is capable of self-reflection resonates with Herder's idea that life evolves from simple organic plant life to more complex processes in animals to the human organism as the highest form of existence.

Metzinger's assertion that "[subjectivity] is not a *thing*, but a property of complex representational processes" finds a parallel in Herder's description of the oncoming panic attack that also presents the human organism as a dynamic, constantly changing system that responds to its ceaseless exposure to sensual stimuli. As mentioned earlier, the historical and developmental dynamics in Herder's historical and anthropological writings are counterbalanced by an underlying ideal human nature that is in agreement with the eternal laws of nature (HW 6:628–36). As Herder states in book fifteen of his *Ideen*, human beings have access to these laws through their God-given, natural predisposition to be reasonable and fair. It is against the metaphysics of such universal laws that Metzinger launches his posthumanist theory.

Metzinger attributes the attraction of "the integrity and stability of the self-model" to the fact that humans like to view themselves as independent of their physical bodies and can overcome death (*Being* 597). Herder certainly suggests the possibility of a continuing existence after death, or so-called palingenesis, in his religiously informed *Ideen*, which was one of Kant's major criticisms in his review (Kant, *Geschichtsphilosophie* 50). Metzinger concedes that the belief in a stable inner self is most likely beneficial for an individual's mental health. He attributes the human awareness of mortality to a relatively recent transformation in human evolution, awareness that he considers responsible for the continuing dependence on "essentialist fantasies" (*Being* 597). However, Metzinger's goal is to minimize the "*lack* of introspective self-knowledge" by destroying such fantasies (italics in original) (ibid. 564). He expects that the realization about the self's fictitious nature will liberate human beings from their Neoplatonic dungeon and open the path to higher forms of consciousness and to a new ethics.[35] This new type of ethics would be bold enough to make use of neuroscience in order to transcend the limitations biological evolution has prescribed for us.

The ethical problem arises when the quest for self-knowledge is in conflict with the drive for self-preservation; for instance, if scientific investigation would threaten the very existence of the human being as we know it. Metzinger's call on the human subject to emancipate itself from the false assumption that the phenomenal self as such is a knowable entity—or in Metzinger's words, "an epistemically justified form of mental content"—culminates in an emphatic plea to mankind to "wake up from biological history" in order "to define its own goals, and become autonomous" (ibid. 634). Here Metzinger positions himself squarely in the Enlightenment tradition by attempting to achieve domination over nature and transform both the self and eventually the entire universe according to the laws of reason. He could not deviate further from Herder in this regard, who wants to restore the lost connection to nature by integrating the rational faculties with the irrational nature of man. One may wonder, however, whether Metzinger reintroduces a transcendentalist aspect to his model by assuming that it is possible to overcome the human dependence on biological nature? After all, Metzinger's reliance on neuroscientific research, which serves to refute the human acceptance of selfhood as a natural given, resembles Herder's integration of empirical scientific knowledge to minimize the dependence on transcendental assumptions promoted by the so-called *Schulphilosophie*.

Although Herder's model is less differentiated than that of Metzinger, one could argue that it is both sensuously more comprehensible and human(e) than Metzinger's. While Herder's model reveals the fundamental contradiction of a human being that is both whole and yet divided, both spiritually stable and yet subject to constant transformation, it respects biological history of the human species as an integral part of human progress toward humanism. Metzinger, on the other hand, rejects Herder's belief in a sensory-cognitive continuum or in knowledge that can be immediately obtained through the senses. Yet his denial of any "epistemically immediate contact to reality" (ibid. 599) comes at the price of suppressing the rationally unknowable, sensual side of human nature. Metzinger is aware of this and concedes "that there may be *phenomenal immediacy*" at particular moments, such as when two individuals are "catching each other in the act of falling in love" (italics in original) (ibid. 603). Yet his explanation seems to evade the problem that there are sensual experiences that cannot be adequately represented by a scientific discourse (ibid. 603). Metzinger declares sensory perceptions as invalid because the unconsciously selective processes that render them provide an incomplete picture of the complex nature of human consciousness. In other words, the very idea of a first-person perspective or personhood is in Metzinger's view a construct that prevents self-knowledge. Metzinger's suggestion "that there are no such things as selves" poses a phenomenological dilemma: it cannot account for the fact that someone must act as agent and someone as recipient (ibid. 627–28). Who is coming up with Metzinger's idea and who is its recipient if it is not a particular human subject? Although Metzinger is aware of this problem, he still defends the radical dismantling of human subjectivity in the service of a "*higher* degree of consciousness," which humans will in his view inevitably arrive at if they pursue the path of reason (ibid. 630). This categorical appeal in favor of progress poses the ethical question whether the striving for such an allegedly "higher degree of consciousness" could result in a new hierarchical taxonomy of knowledge that would devalue all forms of experience that are considered inferior—a possibility that Metzinger neglects to discuss. Even though Metzinger bases his research on concrete physiological evidence, the trajectory of his philosophy aims at overcoming bodily constraints. His model therefore seems to replicate the "erasure of embodiment" that is typical of Enlightenment constructions of subjectivity that Katherine Hayles has also detected in the "cybernetic construction of the posthuman" (Hayles 4). Herder, on the other hand, did not view the body simply as an object for control and mastery but integrated it very effectively in his holistic philosophy and aesthetics, as the discussion of the textual passage "Vom Erkennen und Empfinden der menschlichen Seele" has shown. In this respect, Herder's philosophy can serve as a model that provides an "opportunity to put back into the picture the flesh that continues to be erased in contemporary discussions about cybernetic subjects" (ibid. 5).

Undoubtedly, posthumanist approaches like Metzinger's are useful in accounting for recent scientific and epistemic developments that address the question of what it means to be human today. These approaches are invaluable for revealing the ideological biases and historicity of normative premises, such as individual autonomy and the metaphysics of subjectivity with its universalization of an inner, essential spiritual self, modeled in accordance with the core values of male Western Enlightenment thinkers. Even though Herder's philosophy still follows the eighteenth-century premise of individual autonomy, it anticipates the significance of historical, local, and social factors as well as the significance of language for the constitution of identity.

Is it fair to say that Herder's depictions of sensory experience from a first-person, inside perspective do not yield any valid insights into human nature and possibly even prevent self-knowledge? Should one consider the possibility that poetic and literary depictions of human nature may yield knowledge about certain aspects of human consciousness that scientific discourse is unable to render adequately?

For philosopher Manfred Frank, scientific discourses are unable to explain how conscious mental states of mind are connected to physical processes. According to Frank, they will never be able to explain the mind or soul "weil die Lebenswelt zu vielgestaltig und das neuronale Geschehen zu komplex ist" (because the lived world is too diverse and neural processes are too complex) (Frank, interview; translation mine). Scientific discourses are only capable of treating human conditions "objectively," that is from an external perspective. The description of emotional states requires a different vocabulary, however. As my analysis has shown, it is one of Herder's major accomplishments to translate scientific processes into a vocabulary that is capable of describing the subjective effects of these processes on a human being's mental and emotional states. Herder's language is ripe with images and metaphors that can evoke and recall universal human experiences and human emotions as well as illustrate inner processes. Such appeals to the senses are inspirational because the subjective experience of mental and emotional states is of a different quality from "objective" observations. Love, fear, and joy, for instance, can be expressed and perceived in more diverse and meaningful manners in poetic language than in scientific descriptions. A philosophy that tries to render the subjective experience in purely scientific discourse would be reductive and ignore the evocative qualities of the human imagination. The fact that the language of Herder, Goethe and other late eighteenth-century writers had such a long-lasting and profound impact on the development of German literature can be attributed to their ability to mediate subjective experiences.

Humanism and its focus on the human subject have remained of such importance over the past two hundred years because they deal with ethical issues and discuss how individuals can contribute to a better humanity. Such ethical questions would not be addressed in a philosophy that explains all humans in terms of genetic dispositions or neuronal processes. Just as the emerging empirical sciences were inadequate for providing ethical guidance in Herder's age, so is today's neurobiology unfit to answer questions that deal with moral issues. By connecting poetic imagery with the anthropological discourse of his day and age, Herder went beyond particularist approaches in the sciences that contributed to establishing disciplinary boundaries. His essay "Vom Erkennen und Empfinden der menschlichen Seele" provides an example of how the humanities could capitalize on the question about the meaning of human existence by relating all scientific queries to subjective human experience. By trying to integrate the particularities of scientific discoveries with his anthropocentric philosophy, he builds the case for a humanist mission in its own right. Herder's emphatic endorsement of human unity—a unity that nevertheless does not deny its contradictions and utopian outlook—could serve as a reminder to us humanists not to lose sight of the forest for the trees by refocusing the humanities on their original mission of exploring the self from a human point of view that is both aware of its limited purview and open to new discoveries about human nature and capable of engaging in the negotiation of a common ground.

Notes

Parts of this chapter have been previously published as "Building Bridges: The Importance of Herder's Humanism for the Humanities," in *Humanitas* 26, nos. 1–2 (2013): 94–128. Web 4 November 2014, http://www.nhinet.org/hum.htm.
1. A detailed discussion of the differences of the individual philosophies of these thinkers would go beyond the framework of this study. However, they all share the common philosophical assumption that nature is an organic totality with an inner purpose or life force that is at work in all of its elements and organisms. See, for instance, Goethe's "Studie nach Spinoza" and "Morphologie," *Hamburger Ausgabe* (Munich: Deutscher Taschenbuch Verlag, 1994), 13:7–8, 55; on Goethe's pantheism and his opinion on the ability to recognize "Inner" nature, see Alfred Schmidt, *Goethes herrlich leuchtende Na-*

tur (Munich: Hanser, 1984), 47–54, 134; Friedrich Wilhelm, Joseph von Schelling, "System des transzendentalen Idealismus," *Sämmtliche Werke*, ed. K.F.A. Schelling (Stuttgart: Cotta, 1858), 3.1:629; Novalis, *Schriften in vier Bänden* (Stuttgart: Kohlhammer, 1960), 3:468; Alexander von Humboldt, *Kosmos: Entwurf einer physischen Weltbeschreibung*, 5 vols. (Stuttgart: Cotta, 1845–58), 1:65; Johann Friedrich Blumenbach, *Über den Bildungstrieb und das Zeugungsgeschäfte* (Stuttgart: Fischer, 1971); Carl Gustav Carus, *Lebenserinnerungen und Denkwürdigkeiten*, 4 vols. (Leipzig: Brockhaus, 1865), 1:70; on Carus's philosophy of nature, see; Jutta Müller-Tamm, *Kunst als Gipfel der Wissenschaft* (Berlin: De Gruyter, 1995), 1–50.
2. For a concise assessment of research on Herder up to 2003, see Hans Adler, "Einführung: Denker der Mitte: Johann Gottfried Herder 1744–1803," *Monatshefte* 95, no. 2 (2003): 161–70.
3. In his introduction to an anthology that investigates Herder's significance for the "academic disciplines and the pursuit of knowledge," Wulf Koepke has already addressed Herder's unconventional universalist approach that advocated a "holistic" view of the human being. Koepke, "Introduction," *Johann Gottfried Herder: Academic Disciplines and the Pursuit of Knowledge*, ed. Wulf Koepke, ix–xii (Columbia, SC: Camden House, 1996), x.
4. James Rachels lists the following principles, among others, as relevant to today's bioethics: "that people are moral equals—that no one's welfare is more important that anyone else's; that personal autonomy, the freedom of each individual to control his or her own life, is especially important; that people should always be treated as ends in themselves, and never as mere means; . . . that what is 'natural' is good and what is 'unnatural' is bad." James Rachels, "Ethical Theory and Bioethics," *A Companion to Bioethics*, ed. Helga Kuhse and Peter Singer (Oxford: Blackwell, 2001), 19. Herder contributed to promoting all of these principles. His philosophy can be regarded as an attempt to protect human life from technological advances that threatened to subordinate human life to reason.
5. Catherine Waldby, *The Visible Human Project: Informatic Bodies and Posthuman Medicine* (London: Routledge, 2000), 7. For another skeptical perspective, see Michael J. Sandel, *The Case against Perfection Ethics in the Age of Genetic Engineering* (Cambridge, MA: Belknap, 2007).
6. Thomas Metzinger, *Being No One: The Self-Model Theory of Subjectivity* (Cambridge, MA: MIT Press, 2003): 563.
7. Kenneth Einar Himma argues that "Metzinger's framework does little more than change the terms of the question [of how brain activities constitute the appearance of a self]. . . . While it might be that conceiving of selves this way makes it easier to explain how particular selves arise from particular bodies . . ., much more is needed to resolve the problem: merely equating selves with self-models says nothing about why particular self-models arise from particular organisms. . . ." *Metapsychology Online Reviews* 7, no. 21 (2003): http://metapsychology.mentalhelp.net/poc/view_doc.php?type=book&id=1720&cn=394.
8. Herder's understanding of *Humanität* is complex and cannot be defined in one word. In letter 27 of *Briefe an die Humanität*, he associates *Humanität* with *Menschheit, Menschlichkeit, Menschenrechte, Menschenpflichten, Menschenwürde*, and *Menschenliebe* (HW 7:147); for the values associated with humanism, see Löchte 48 and Hans Erich Bödeker, "Menscheit, Humanität, Humanismus," in *Geschichtliche Grundbegriffe: His-*

torisches Lexikon zur politisch-sozialen Sprache in Deutschland, ed. Otto Brunner, Wilhelm Conze, and Reinhart Kosellek (Stuttgart: Klett, 1982): 1090–93.
9. See Hans Dietrich Irmscher, "Beobachtungen zur Funktion der Analogie im Denken Herders," *Deutsche Vierteljahrsschrift* 55 (1981): 64–97. Irmscher emphasizes that Herder's deviation of the scientific discourses of his time serves the purpose to inspire creativity through his use of poetic language and analogy. According to Irmscher, Herder attempts through his deliberate use of analogy to describe historical or natural phenomena from the subjective perspective of the individual because human comprehension of reality depends on personal bodily experience: "Verstehen also kann der Mensch die Wirklichkeit nur, wenn er seinen eigenen Leib von innen her kennt" (86).
10. Manfred Frank, "Der Mensch bleibt sich ein Rätsel," interview, *Die Zeit*, 27 August 2009.
11. All references to Herder's essays will be taken from Johann Gottfried Herder, *Werke in zehn Bänden*, ed. Martin Bollacher et. al. (Frankfurt am Main: Deutscher Klassiker Verlag: 1985–2000). Future references to this source will be documented parenthetically including volume and page number.
12. Even though Herder became "one of the earliest and most radical advocates of supplanting philosophy with anthropology" in order to break free from the metaphysical tradition, as John Zammito points out, he also distinguished himself from a materialist empiricism. See Zammito, *Kant, Herder and the Birth of Anthropology* (Chicago: U of Chicago P, 2002), 3.
13. See Karl Menges, "Erkenntnis und Sprache: Herder und die Krise der Philosophie im späten achtzehnten Jahrhundert," in *Johann Gottfried Herder: Language, History, and the Enlightenment*, ed. Wulf Koepke (Columbia, SC: Camden House, 1990), 48. Menges refers to Hegel when he explains the crisis of philosophy at the end of the eighteenth century: "In dieser Phase dominiert ein Interesse an der Empirie, auch an der Nützlichkeit 'als dem Wesen der Dinge'. Doch es ist gerade das unmittelbare, empirische Bewußtsein, das in seinen Deutungsversuchen der Realität ... an seine Grenzen stößt.... Dem Zuwachs an Wissen fehlt ein Erklärungsmodell, ein transzendentales Paradigma, wie es erst die Bewußtseinsphilosophie des deutschen Idealismus ... bereitstellen wird. Da dieses Konzept der Aufklärung inzwischen noch abgeht, erscheint die Ordnung der Dinge vorderhand nicht anders erklärbar, als im Rückgriff auf eine dogmatische Metaphysik." (During this phase the interest in empiricism and utilitarianism as the "essence of things" dominates. Yet it is precisely the immediate, empiricist state of mind that has its limitations in its attempts to interpret reality. The increase in knowledge lacks an adequate model of explanation, a transcendental paradigm that only the German Idealist philosophy of consciousness will provide. Since this concept of Enlightenment at this point is still lacking, for the time being only a recourse to a dogmatic metaphysics seems to provide an explanation for the order of things) (translation mine).
14. The translated passages of Herder's essays are taken from Michael N. Forster, ed., *Johann Gottfried von Herder: Philosophical Writings*, trans. Michael N. Forster (Cambridge: Cambridge UP, 2002): 272. Future references to this source will be cited parenthetically.
15. This is particularly obvious in "This Too a Philosophy of History for the Formation of Humanity," where Herder compares the history of humankind to the different ages of one human being. While he depicts a multifaceted, panoramic view of the cultural,

climatic, geographical diversity of humankind throughout the ages, he acknowledges history's divine purpose (HW 4:48).
16. In "This Too a Philosophy of History for the Formation of Humanity," he compares world history to a whole series of natural and cultural phenomena, such as the different phases in the life of a human being, a tree, a river, and drama. While Herder's analogies are sometimes contradictory and were far from conforming to the discursive conventions of his day, they produce an aesthetic experience that renders the subject matter from an individual's subjective perspective.
17. Arens stresses that "Kant's 1798 *Conflict of faculties* echoes this point: the humanities are listed among only the second tier of sciences essential to the university."
18. E.g., the so-called patriarchal age of the Orient is portrayed as the childhood of humankind (HW 4:17); the Egyptian era is likened to boyhood as a phase of learning; ancient Greece is associated with early manhood with its awakening individual freedom and the blossoming of the arts; the Roman empire is equated to male maturity.
19. See Zammito, *Kant, Herder and the Birth of Anthropology* (Chicago: U of Chicago P, 2002): 331. Zammito points out that the "ontogeny/phylogeny parallelism is central to [Herder's] whole way of thinking."
20. While Herder refers to language as the distinctive feature between humans and animals in his early "Treatise on the Origin of Language" (HW 1:708–17), he also implies that the human race has evolved from animals. Although Herder points out the communicative similarities between the utterances of early humans and animals, he rejects the idea that animal sounds developed into human language as Condillac and Rousseau had suggested. For humans have the ability to reflect on themselves in language, according to Herder (HW 1:717). Whereas animals produce their sounds instinctively, humans create language as free expressions of an individual self-awareness. In this respect, Herder's anthropological views certainly comply with eighteenth-century attempts to define the human in opposition to the nonhuman.
21. Herder is certainly indebted to the Western tradition of privileging the human species as the crowning glory of creation. His claim that humans are not related to apes could suggest a paranoid attempt to set humans apart from other anthropoid species. According to Giorgio Agamben, such efforts to distinguish the human from the nonhuman can be attributed to the fact that eighteenth-century scientists were at a loss to find generic differences between humans and apes (26). Carolus Linnaeus, the founder of modern taxonomy, admitted, however, to hardly knowing "a single distinguishing mark which separates man from apes" (Agamben 24). Herder's philosophy reveals an ambiguity that is typical of the Idealist exemption of the human from nature. Accordingly, human beings distinguish themselves from all other creatures by having the freedom to control and suppress their animal nature (HW 6:138–39). This ability to resist instinctual forces sets humans free and allows them to act according to a "higher" moral justice. Yet while Herder grants humans independence from nature, he attributes the privilege of human reason to the species' developmental characteristics within nature. Since humans are born helpless and remain physically weak for a much longer period than other species, their cognitive and cerebral abilities are more differentiated (HW 6:110–46).
22. In this respect, Herder is still indebted to his teacher Kant, for whom knowledge is shaped by the categories of human understanding.
23. Kant already noticed Herder's "poetic spirit" in his well-known review of Herder's *Ideen*. Although Kant acknowledges some well-phrased passages, he criticizes Herd-

er's alleged tendency to hide unsubstantiated truth claims behind his abundant use of allegories, bold metaphors, poetic imagery, and mythological references: Imanuel Kant, "Rezensionen von J. G. Herder's 'Ideen zur Philosophie der Geschichte der Menschheit' Teil 1.2," *Schriften zur Geschichtsphilosophie*, ed. Manfred Riedel (Stuttgart: Reclam, 1974): 59–60.
24. In recalling Aristotle's comparison between poetry and history, one could sum up this distinction more succinctly: "For poetry tends to express the universal, history the particular." Eva Knodt has pointed this out with regard to Herder's philosophy of history and its affinity to Arestotelian poetics.
25. As Wolfgang Riedel points out, Albrecht von Haller was instrumental in endorsing the central nerve system's significance as a mediator between body and mind. Wolfgang Riedel, *Die Anthropologie des jungen Schiller* (Würzburg, Königshausen & Neumann, 1984): 97.
26. John Zammito, *Kant, Herder and the Birth of Anthropology* (Chicago: U of Chicago P, 2002). Zammito points out that these vitalist influences stem from Herder's occupation with Spinoza and Leibniz: "In short, Herder sought to revise Leibnizian dynamism from a transcendent to an immanent monadology." In order to accomplish this, Herder "read Leibniz through Spinoza and Spinoza through Leibniz to find a philosophical mode for articulating his consistently naturalist insight" (316). Another source for Herder's occupation with "the problems of 'vitalist materialism'" was Diderot (317).
27. Richter also provides an explanation for the ideological spin that underlies Haller's conclusions (86–87). The claim that nerve tissue itself is not "reizbar" (irritable) permits Haller, whose "religious and philosophical orientation remained very traditional," to refute materialist theories that claimed the nervous system was purely mechanical (Zammito 232). Haller's other claim that irritability cannot be connected to life can also be attributed to his religious convictions. It is based on the assumption that any life-giving force must be connected to the soul.
28. See Michael Maurer, "Geschichte zwischen Theodizee und Anthropologie: Zur Wissenschaftlichkeit der historischen Schriften Herders, in *Johann Gottfried Herder: Academic Disciplines and the Pursuit of Knowledge*, ed. Wulf Koepke (Columbia, SC: Camden House, 1996): 120–36. Herder's prose was attacked not only by philosophers like Kant but also by eminent historians, such as August Wilhelm Schlözer, professor of history at the Universität Göttingen. Maurer argues that Herder published his philosophy of history at a time when "disciplines such as academic historiography were defining themselves as separate and autonomous fields of knowledge" (Maurer 136). Like Kant, who is disturbed by Herder's loquacious imprecision (61), Schlözer also disapproves of Herder's inappropriately allegorical language (Maurer 123). Schlözer condemns his imprecise imagery (ibid. 129). And they both have objections to Herder's method of rendering the interconnectedness of natural developments and human history (Kant 51; Maurer 136).
29. For a detailed historical analysis of the crisis of Wolffian *Schulphilosophie*, see Zammito. Zammito identifies three impulses that "conjoined to spawn an opposition to Wolff even before his death. First, there were the immanent philosophical objections to his system, especially to the idea of the mathematical method in philosophy. Second, there was the massive incursion of foreign thought, both French and British. Third, there was the retrieval of Thomasius's idea of 'eclecticism' precisely as a resource to bring the philosopher, the university scholar in general, 'down to earth' or back into the 'world'" (10).

118 ~: *Beyond Humanism*

30. The pre-critical Kant was influenced by all three factors mentioned above that contributed to the crisis of Wolffian philosophy, and he was an outspoken critic of Wolffian philosophy. He was also opposed to the mathematical dominance in *Schulphilosphie*: "Kant aimed for a universal, necessary transcendental grounding of human experience; he remained in the established disciplinary order of philosophy" (Zammito 214).
31. For a discussion of Herder's understanding of reason, see Hans Adler, "Herder's Concept of Humanität," *A Companion to the Works of Johann Gottfried Herder*, ed. Hans Adler and Wulf Köpke (Rochester, NY: Camden House): 105–11. Accordingly, human *Vernunft* "is the faculty that makes human beings godlike because it enables them to participate in God's reason, which is accessible to the human beings via recognition of the order that regulates the universe" (106). And "it is through reason that the human being can understand the word of God and read the 'book of nature'" (ibid.). Yet Herder also stresses that *Vernunft* is "an acquired faculty that changes with the changing world of experiences" (111). For Herder, *Vernunft* corresponds to its original meaning derived from *vernehmen* (to hear, learn, perceive), which makes it dependent on the sensory perception.
32. For an in-depth discussion of Herder's use of analogy, see Irmscher, "Beobachtungen zur Funktion der Analogie im Denken Herders," *Deutsche Vierteljahrsschriften* 55 (1981): 64–97.
33. For a concise overview of current posthumanist approaches, see Stefan Herbrechter, *Posthumanismus* (2009); also Landgraf, Trap and Weatherby, 2019).
34. Like an external city map, the virtual city map created by the brain has "a little red arrow and the indexical sentence YOU ARE HERE" (ibid. 551). However, in the virtual city map this arrow is neither fixed nor "recognizable as variable" (ibid. 552). In contrast to an external city map, "the conscious self-model in the caveman's brain . . . is in large portions transparent" (ibid. 552).
35. This new ethics will "dissolve any form of autoepistemic closure" and not shrink "from violating the adaptivity constraint that Mother Nature has so cruelly imposed on our biological ancestors" (ibid. 632).

CHAPTER 5

Humanist Antinomies
Goethe's Iphigenie auf Tauris *and* Torquato Tasso

Goethe's Plays and the Legacy of the *Sturm und Drang*

Herder's anthropological and aesthetic views as well as his philosophy of history and language had a profound influence on the young Goethe and the entire generation of *Sturm und Drang* (storm and stress) writers. While Herder's influence is perhaps not very obvious in Goethe's *Iphigenie auf Tauris* (1787) and *Torquato Tasso* (1789) due to the neoclassical aspiration of achieving a universal timelessness, certain anthropological assumptions that inform the characterizations of the plays' protagonists can be traced back to Goethe's exposure to Herder's philosophy of history. For instance, in *Iphigenie* the Greek characters that in eighteenth-century classicist representations serve as cultural ideal are not portrayed in a more favorable light than the archaic and "barbaric" Scythians. The Greek rhetorical (Iphigenie) and strategic (Pylades) superiority is counterbalanced by the Scythian ruler's integrity and generosity, which makes the Greek figures in the play appear less trustworthy and thus detracts from the model civilization that traditional humanism upheld. In contrast, the Scythian lack of sophistication is presented as more authentic than the glib eloquence and scheming superiority of the more civilized Greek figures. The portrayal of civilizational refinement as a source of moral corruption, which can already be detected in Goethe's early *Sturm und Drang* dramas such as *Götz von Berlichingen* and the first part of *Faust*, echoes Herder's assumption that cultural sophistication is acquired at the expense of intimacy with nature. Likewise, the protagonist of *Torquato Tasso* also suffers from the alienating refinement of courtly society that comes across in the characters' highly stylized language that harnesses their emotional spontaneity. Tasso's passionate outbursts, which can be understood as a reaction to the deceptive courtly conventions of communicating, present him as emotionally volatile, a quality that he shares with other *Sturm und Drang* figures.

The conceptions of both plays date back to 1776 (*Iphigenie*) and 1780 (*Torquato Tasso*), a time when Herder's influence on the *Sturm und Drang* was still acute. *Torquato Tasso*'s central conflict between two middle-class parvenus who compete for recognition in courtly society bears similarity to the motif of *die feindlichen Brüder* (the inimical twins), a dramatic configuration that was popular during the *Sturm und Drang* period. Goethe consulted Herder repeatedly while he was working on *Iphigenie* (HA 5:406–7; 420–21) and was pleased to receive his appreciation of *Torquato Tasso* (HA 5:501). One may recall that Herder and Goethe rejected the strict obedience to Aristotelian rules as practiced in French neoclassical drama and favored an emphasis on intricacies of character in the Shakespearean spirit. The goal was to bring to life the full spectrum of human nature by casting light on its emotive, instinctual impulses, rather than representing a moralistic rationalism that privileged the intellect. As is well known, the histrionic language of these plays made verbal expression too demonstratively theatrical to be considered natural after the 1770s. In contrast, the neoclassical dramas' measured versification moderated verbal excesses and lent the language a more natural flow (see also Adorno 503). Yet regardless of the significant changes, the dramatization of the characters' complex, conflicted personalities may not have been possible without Herder's early influence on Goethe.[1]

Considering the background of their creation, one can conclude that *Iphigenie* and *Torquato Tasso* undermine a humanism that simply presumes the subject's control over his/her animalistic drives. This is why the plays problematize humanist ideas rather than promoting them. In spite of their "graezisierend" (antiquated) patina, they have to be seen as engagements with the challenges that a humanist point of view poses for eighteenth-century individuals. Not surprisingly, Schiller called *Iphigenie* "so erstaunlich modern und ungriechisch" (so astonishingly modern and un-Greek) (HA 5:415), not least because the nuanced portrayal of the characters' inner emotional disturbances renders the one-sided privileging of the rational faculties dubious.

The Mind-Body Dualism

I am briefly reviewing some philosophical underpinnings of the Neoplatonic mind-body dualism recalling some foundational assumptions of earlier chapters and clarifying my position with regard to future considerations. My goal is to show how dualist models that attempt to draw qualitative distinctions among species, races, intellectual and emotional faculties were becoming increasingly questionable after the Enlightenment. Surprisingly these qualitative classifications and ethical distinctions persisted throughout the nineteenth century and were ultimately to proof the mental and ethical superiority of the

Caucasian male. Ironically, species, subspecies, and gender distinctions according to qualitative norms persisted,[2] even as progress in the life sciences challenged these distinctions.[3]

Human epigenesis, which was discovered in the eighteenth century (Lehleiter 16–19), presupposes that education starts at the motor-sensory level with explorations and replications of body movements and gestures, etc.[4] The development of the mind and its capacity for abstract reasoning evolve gradually over time and are dependent on subjective experiences. This means that reason and emotion are inextricably intertwined and that there is no *a priori* metaphysical realm of ideas that distinguishes humans from other organisms, as traditional humanism and its dualist mind-body relationship presumed. Embodied forms of learning through gestures, facial expressions, body movements, etc., precede abstract forms of learning as they already can take place prior to reflection and before the development of language, according to philosopher Mark Johnson. This may explain why visual or acoustic enactments of human behavior were part of an aesthetic practice and well recognized in the eighteenth century,[5] long before the embodiment of reason and spiritual faculties was widely acknowledged.

Emotions like fear, anger, and desire are indispensable tools for the preservation of the human species and often experienced beneath the level of conscious awareness (Johnson 57). Emotions help assess social situations and act appropriately. Feelings are intrinsically interwoven with mental and social capacities. They enable us to interpret meaning and communicate effectively. Nevertheless the dualist model often stigmatizes emotions, feelings, and instinctual desires as morally reprehensible, deceptive, egotistical, and self-indulgent. This is why in literature of the humanist tradition, such as eighteenth-century dramas by Lessing, Schiller, and Goethe, the protagonists are often represented with the choice of either overcoming their instinctual desires through *Entsagung* (abstinence) and other forms of self-control that prove the superiority of reason over bodily instincts, or cultivating their instincts until these obey the dominant moral norms.[6] The latter alternative would be preferable to neoclassical aesthetics because the agreement of the emotional inclinations and the moral imperatives of reason would bridge the mind-body separation and restore the subject's unity.

The mind-body dualism became an assumption that prevailed, regardless of the many emerging literary, philosophical, and scientific discourses that contested it (Johnson 61, 112, 222).[7] The persistence of metaphysical "truths," such as life after death, absolute freedom and self-determination, objective reason, and universal moral values, can be explained by people's reluctance to part with ingrained intellectual and cultural assumptions that they hold dear (ibid. 15).[8] Yet, modern developments in cognitive neuroscience offer strong evidence that categorical distinctions, such as the mind-body separation, are unsustainable.[9]

Goethe's Neoclassical Plays in Historical Context

But what do Goethe's neoclassical plays have to do with the philosophical, scientific, and aesthetic challenges of an Idealist metaphysics that promulgates the mind-body dualism and all its implications, such as a spiritual realm of universal truths, to which humans have access by means of their mental capacity? Goethe's philosophy of nature no longer viewed human reason as independent from and superior to an outside nature (*res extensa*). Herder's assumption that human beings were only part of a larger, single, universal, organic whole, rather than the sovereigns of the natural world by force of their intellectual capacity, reduced the confidence in human reason considerably (Beiser 361–68). This loss of control contested the role of human sovereignty vis-à-vis the external world and the privileged status of the intellect over the emotions and drives. The realization that preexisting physical and emotional dispositions, called animal nature, restricted human freedom to a greater extent than previously assumed provided the writers of the era with a fertile ground for experimentation, as they could stage in various constellations the struggles between drives and rational faculties, the conflicts between external cultural influences and internal desires as well as socially conditioned aspirations.

I will interpret Goethe's classical plays in the context of this tension between the humanist ideals and the increasing awareness of their limitations caused by changing anthropological, philosophical, and social beliefs concerning human nature at the turn from the eighteenth to the nineteenth century. The following readings of Goethe's *Iphigenie auf Tauris* and *Torquato Tasso* will focus predominantly on the ideological implications of their often-touted humanist outlook and classicist form. My analysis will examine these plays not as attempts to establish an aesthetic norm that can withstand the test of time but rather as historically conditioned confrontations with Enlightenment rationality that became particularly problematic in the aftermath of the French Revolution. The incongruence between classicist formal perfection and the display of the characters' less-than-perfect behavior bears witness to the uncertainties of modern individuality and reveals both the limitations and "repressive" aspects of Enlightenment premises. Likewise, the discrepancies between the polite, measured discourse of courtly society and its manipulative intentionality (HA 5:99; 966–69) disclose the pretentiousness of conventions that attempt to disguise surfacing personal desires. The plays' classicist formal perfection, including their highly stylized language, is exposed as artificial and constraining in view of the characters' insecurities, deceptions, and self-deceptions. The tension between the characters' calculated eloquence and their surfacing selfish motivations challenges the one-sided privileging of a *Zweckrationalität* (instrumental reason), over and against basic human emotional needs.

The characters of Goethe's *Iphigenie* and *Torquato Tasso* reveal both the traits of the mind-body duality and the desire to overcome their inner schism. However, the tension between the plays' formal unity and the characters' inability to achieve the closure of perfection reveals a subtle criticism of the repressive nature of an Enlightenment pedagogy that requires either adaptability to the point of self-denial (Tasso, Antonio, Iphigenie) or abstinence for the sake of moral imperatives (Thoas, Princess Leonore d'Este).

The dramatizations of the contradictions of the characters' inner conflicts undermine the dichotomy of rational ethical behavior and emotional self-indulgence. For instance, Tasso's object of infatuation, Princess Leonore d'Este, is both self-indulgent and capable of *Entsagung* for propriety's sake. To make matters more complicated, it is impossible to know with certainty whether her abstention from accepting a romantic relationship with Tasso arises from passivity, her acute sense of propriety, or self-control. There are indications in the text that could support each of these alternatives (HA 1022; 1118–24; 1955–59).[10] Likewise, it is difficult to determine to what extent Iphigenie takes advantage of Thoas's romantic feelings for her and to what extent she uses her privileged position as a priestess to advance her personal desire to escape. Because of her inner conflicts, it is impossible to either affirm or negate the question of whether her decisions can be regarded as acts of self-determination or mere opportunism. A definitive moral judgment of the characters' actions is problematic not only because of the characters' intricacies but also because the Enlightenment values per se become ambiguous in social interactions. For instance, rational behavior can be selfish and inconsiderate. Likewise, emotional malleability can reveal empathy. While these imponderables of human behavior may all seem obvious, they are worthy of mention as they can explain why the dramatic enactment of human behavior can convey its complexities in a more nuanced and tangible way than rational scientific discourses.

Another dimension that one must consider when interpreting neoclassical dramas is their formal elements, which, of course, also contribute to the production of meaning. The number of characters is reduced to a minimum, and the action is focused on a central conflict in a linear time continuum. The language of these neoclassical dramas is highly stylized and uniform. The dramas aim at homogenizing sociohistorical differentiation and focus on universal human traits that are assumed to be independent of sociohistorical constellations. Of course, this purging of art from its empirical contexts is, despite its intended universality, itself motivated by specific historical conditions that surreptitiously or deliberately influence the dramas' aesthetic and semantic aspects. One could also argue that some neoclassical dramas, such as Schiller's *Don Karlos, Maria Stuart,* or *Wallenstein,* are set in specific historical situations. Yet, while historical events form the framework of the dramatic plot, the characters' actions are not primarily motivated by these events. Certainly, Marquis Posa's and Wallenstein's ambitions are brought about by their extraordinary social standing and the highly volatile political situation that contribute to their ascent to power. However, the focus is on the characters' inner struggles, and their emotional constitution. Goethe's protagonists reveal a degree of self-reflection, an individuality that could hardly be found in antiquity or even in the sixteenth century (HA 5:436). Yet they are idealized and presumed capable of liberating themselves from social constraints in order to take their fate into their own hands. To be sure, neoclassical aesthetics strove to separate *reine Menschlichkeit* (pure humaneness) from ideological influences by transposing the dramatic action into the distant past, which only seemingly severed the connection to the present empirical reality. Nonetheless, the promotion of individual autonomy was motivated by political issues, such as bourgeois emancipation during the second half of the eighteenth century. The nonaristocratic citizenry's desire for freedom of thought was responsible for the institution of self-determination as a fundamental human right. In turn, this right to self-determination is grounded in an idealized human nature that presumes the existential autonomy of the individual, the foundation of bourgeois ideology.[11]

Regardless of all the efforts to universalize the human condition, eighteenth-century scientific and philosophical assumptions about human nature inevitably affect and in certain aspects overshadow the neoclassical idea of a timeless classical aesthetics. In Goethe's *Torquato Tasso*, for instance, the sociopolitical analogies between the play's fictitious setting in an Italian Renaissance court and the Weimar court of Goethe's time are deliberately foregrounded. The economic and artistic autonomy of the bourgeois artist was as limited in eighteenth-century Weimar as it was in the fictitious court of Ferrara, and scholarship justifiably points to this historical analogy (Wagner 138; Adorno 496–99).[12] In view of the critical depiction of the artist's predicament in courtly patronage, the play does not advocate the often-presumed classicist separation between art and life, as has been argued by the play's left-leaning critics of the postwar generation (Wagner 78–79).[13] Instead the play probes the ideal of aesthetic and individual autonomy. This is why *Iphigenie* cannot be regarded as an uncontested plea for "reine Menschlichkeit" (pure humaneness) but must be seen as a polysemous problematization of this ideal.[14] The critics' inconclusive controversy in the play's long history of reception of whether one should regard the character of Iphigenie as a role model of the humanist ideal points to the play's multifaceted ambiguity, which Goethe himself characterized in an 1802 letter to Schiller as "verteufelt human" (diabolically human) (HA 5:408). The waning interest in Schiller's and Goethe's Weimar classicist productions after the 1960s can be attributed to their alleged apolitical aestheticism. Perhaps the time has come to reexamine those classical works with respect to their ambiguous undertones.

Figure 5.1. Scene from *Iphigenie auf Tauris* (1802 version première in Weimar), with Goethe as Orestes in the center (ACT III, Scene 3). Drawing by Angelica Kauffman (1741–1807). Wikimedia Commons, public domain.

Irmgard Wagner has documented a significant shift in the German *Iphigenie* reception that was initiated in reaction to a polemic by aspiring German writer Martin Walser at a *Germanistentag* (Germanists' conference) in Essen in 1964. Walser's criticism was directed at the postwar instrumentalization of *Iphigenie*, this "Paradestück für Humanität" (exemplary model for the humane) that, in his opinion, was used to "to teach the Germans 'how to deal with the burdening echo [lastender Nachhall] of the Third Reich'" (Wagner 78; Walser 122). Accordingly, German audiences were instructed to identify with Iphigenie's and Orest's ordeal in order to liberate themselves from the gods' curse— or in the postwar context the national disgrace—which haunted them because of their forebears' sins. In Walser's opinion, the Germans were supposed to feel like Tantalids, who could be reeducated (Walser 122). Walser supplemented his criticism of such a simplistic analogy between the Greek myth and contemporary Germany with a demand for the recipients' critical distance, a distance that must not deprive the play of its historical context. According to Wagner, "Walser's sample of critical distancing and historical relativization was to become a battle cry for the rising generation of German scholars in their war against the classics" (ibid.). Walser's criticism did not stop at the alleged instrumentalization of Goethe's play for contemporary purposes. Lamenting Goethe's and Schiller's apolitical elitism that ignored sociohistorical reality, Walser's anticlassicist rhetoric was, however, also influenced by the historical burden of the Nazi past. The postwar era's denunciation of Weimar classicism as reactionary became widespread, and opened the door to interpretations that no longer viewed the humanist message as a timeless truth but examined its ideological implications in the historical context of their enunciation. This led to innovative readings by critics on the left, such as "Thoas representing the Third World wronged by civilization; the failure of Enlightenment reason and ideals; beautiful language hiding and harmonizing a contradictory substance" (Wagner 80). While such criticism from the point of view of *Ideologiekritik* is acutely aware of the sociopolitical context, it can fall victim to generalizations if it neglects to consider the ambiguities of literary texts. The tendency of the "New Left" to denounce Weimar classicism as elitist, conformist, and apolitical was most likely one of the major reasons for the sparse resonance that these texts had during the 1970s, a tendency that ignored the drama's self-reflective equivocality (ibid. 79).[15]

"*Verteufelt human*"? *Zum Humanitätsideal der Weimarer Klassik* is the title of an anthology that approaches Weimaranian neo-humanism from a postcolonial and gender-conscious point of view that previous methodologies lacked according to the editors (Dörr and Hofmann 10). Their intention to recognize the Weimar authors' critical attitude toward a dogmatic form of humanism, to which Goethe's dictum refers, is also significant. Michael Hofmann in particular emphasizes the distinction between previous attempts to discover "zeitentrückte, ewige Wahrheiten" (timeless, eternal truths) in the literature of the neoclassical period and the intention to show the ambiguities of neo-humanist texts. Goethe and Schiller staged problematic constellations with all their contradictions and dilemmas rather than offering specific solutions (Hofmann, "Wege" 144). As already addressed in previous chapters, the literary enactments of these predicaments are far more complex than programmatic statements about the humanist agenda may suggest. Hofmann's claim that the late works of Schiller and Goethe no longer attempt to realize humanist ideals but foreground the absence of the human in the process of modernization can be attributed in equal measure to the polysemy of literature in general and to the authors' alleged disillusionment with the political fulfillment of the Enlightenment ideals after the French reign of terror.[16]

Thus, the despotic Skythian ruler of Goethe's *Iphigenie auf Tauris* shares several traits with King Philipp of Schiller's *Don Karlos*. Both rulers are introduced as uncompromising and tyrannical, which predisposes the reader to sympathize with their enlightened opponents. Yet, their gradual deviation from their original dogmatic rigidity shows a learning process that outshines the unblemished justness of their opponents, Iphigenie and Posa. Although Thoas owes his initial tolerance of foreigners to Iphigenie's influence, his eventual kindness is the result of an inner struggle that characterizes him as an empathetic human being. The Greek's treatment of Thoas in Goethe's *Iphigenie* reveals the repressive potential of Enlightenment values, such as the lack of respect toward those who, like the Skythian ruler, are considered uncivilized from an "enlightened" point of view. Thoas's remarkable development from tyrannical to empathetic and magnanimous sovereign is neither rewarded nor even acknowledged. After all, he pardons Iphigenie, her brother Orestes, and Pylades, even after he learns about their conspiracy to deceive him and escape with the sacred image of Diana. Regardless of Thoas's humanist generosity, many critics considered Iphigenie's decision to confess the truth of their conspiracy as the play's central humanist message. These critics focused on Iphigenie's determination that allows her to liberate herself from both religious and secular authorities. However, the drama also shows that her liberation is only possible because of Thoas's generosity.

Hofmann's reading points out the marginalization of the Skythian ruler with reference to Adorno. According to him, Thoas's conduct is more dignified than that of his Greek guests. Adorno also emphasizes the continuing relevance of Goethe's play by adding that the discrimination of "uncivilized" societies continues after these societies have long left their alleged barbarity behind:

> Die Opfer des zivilisatorischen Prozesses, die welche er herabdrückt und welche die Zeche der Zivilisation zu bezahlen haben, sind um deren Früchte geprellt worden, gefangen im vorzivilisatorischen Stande. Zivilisation, die historisch über Barbarei hinausführt, hat diese bis zum gegenwärtigen Tag vermöge der Repression, die ihr Prinzip, das naturbeherrschende, ausübt, auch befördert. (Adorno 507)
>
> (The victims of the process of civilization, who are suppressed by it and have to pay its cost, are bereft of its fruits, imprisoned in a pre-civilizational state. Civilization, which historically transcends barbarity, has also promoted it to the present day due to the repression, which its nature-dominating principle exerts.)

The despotic undertones of neo-humanism also come to the fore in Goethe's other classical play: *Torquato Tasso*. The perfectly polished language and the hermetically closed setting of the court create a seemingly timeless realm of ideas that is contrasted to a less-than-ideal courtly reality. Beneath the discourse of courtesy, the play is fraught with intrigue (HA 5:517). The drama's elevated language is replete with courtly mannerisms, exposing its own sterility. Benjamin Bennett, for example, calls *Torquato Tasso* the play that "offers no escape from its 'prison-house of language'" (*Goethe's Theory* 209). The metaphor of spatial confinement, emphasized by Tasso's punitive incarceration, illustrates his social and spiritual captivity within the confines of the court. While the play's stringent form, with its homogenous and stylized language and its setting in the distant past—Renaissance court of Ferrara—contribute to the construction of an idealized human condition, there are many references that connect the play to the Weimar court of Goethe's time. The play's reception history abounds with identifications of actual people from Goethe's biography (Wagner, esp. 92–94, 97). Apart from such biographical allusions that subvert the intended abstraction from historical contexts, the dramatization of the characters' specific sociohistorically anchored sensibilities justifies a historical approach. Whether it is Iphigenie's emancipation from divine predetermination or Tasso's process of maturation (*Bildung*), the eighteenth-century construction of bourgeois individuality permeates both dramas. Parallels between Goethe's outsider role as a bourgeois artist at the Weimar court and Tasso's dependence on the benevolence of Duke Alfons have captured scholarly attention (Bürger, Girschner, Mathäs). Goethe's unannounced escape to Italy was triggered by his loneliness in the very hermetic setting of the Weimar court—a loneliness that bears resemblance to Tasso's feelings of alienation in courtly society (Schulz 186, Safranski 48).

Tasso, the artist, and Antonio, the politician, represent the divided responsibilities that Goethe had to fulfill at the Weimar court, including time-consuming administrative duties that distracted him from his intellectual and literary pursuits. In the drama, this division of obligations finds expression in the antagonistic relationship between Tasso, the artist, and Antonio Montecatino, the statesman. Goethe's socially problematic relationship to a married woman, Charlotte von Stein, may have contributed to his role as an outsider as well as motivated the dramatization of the distrustful Renaissance artist's life (HA 5:506, *Nachwort*). While the drama's classicist form was certainly inspired by Goethe's encounter with antiquity during his Italian journey, the formal stringency assumes a self-reflective distance that lends the classicist style an affected touch. The characters' perceptive comments about each other's conduct and personal qualities underline the drama's introspective quality.

The central conflict between the poet Tasso and the statesman Antonio represents not only two opposing characters with different philosophies—self-indulgent dreamer versus pragmatic politician—but also two different phases in Goethe's development. Whereas Tasso embodies the impetuousness, exaggerated sensitivity and psychological instability of the *Sturm und Drang* hero, Antonio represents the mature yet compromising opportunist who gladly serves his aristocratic rulers. While Tasso feels like an awkward outsider in a deceptive environment, Antonio embraces courtly life even though he is, like Tasso, of bourgeois descent. In addition to their antagonistic characterization, Tasso and Antonio also comment ironically, derisively, angrily, and condescendingly on each other's qualities and shortcomings. This opposition is matched—although in a much less hostile way—by the two aristocratic women figures:

Princess Eleonore d'Este, sister of Duke Alfons, and Eleonore Sanvitale, Duchess of Scandiano. Their characterization parallels those of Tasso and Antonio. While Eleonore d'Este's passivity and self-centeredness bear a certain affinity to Tasso, Eleonore Sanvitale's political scheming bears some resemblance to Antonio's statesman-like activity. The drama's abundance of introspective monologues and dialogues, as well as its symmetrical configuration, enhance the play's mirror effect, which allows insights into the characters from various points of view. The play's focus on emotions, psychological tensions, and secret thoughts characterizes it as true *Seelendrama* (drama of the soul). All of the characters, with the exception of Duke Alfons, reveal certain character flaws in their verbal interactions. Their flawless eloquence contrasts and underlines their ethical inadequacies.

The clash between a traditional courtly aesthetics that serves the rulers' glorification through formal perfection on the one hand and Tasso's introspective self-expression on the other is the focus of the disagreement between Antonio and Tasso over their poetic role models: the contemporary Renaissance poet Ariosto (1474–1533) and the legendary Roman poet Virgil (70 BCE–19 BCE). Tasso's subversion of traditional courtly aesthetics is highlighted by his inability to finish his poem in honor of the duke. As a result of the bourgeoisie's increasing cultural influence during Goethe's life, late eighteenth-century art now reflected the self-awareness of the bourgeois artist instead of displaying the splendor of his patrons. Consequently, Tasso's artistic goals are in conflict with the courtly art that serves only the glorification of the ruler. Tasso's growing awareness of his artistic integrity leads him to demand his poem back that he presented to Duke Alfons as a gift (HA 5:83, 380–89; HA 5:155; 3026–27).

Tasso's dilemma arises from his duty of loyalty to his patron, Duke Alfons, and his envisioned ideal to become an autonomous bourgeois artist. Alfons urges him to complete his poem because he is eager to have the finished product that will augment his prestige as an art-loving ruler (HA 5:84; 392–96). Tasso is unable to consider his poem finished because, with its completion, he would compromise his artistic integrity and forfeit his potential for the perfection of his art (HA 5:83; 380–85).

The discrepancy between the closure of perfection and continuous striving toward perfection reflects the paradox of bourgeois ideology. On the one hand, the ideal of individual autonomy implies the subject's self-confidence and stability that guarantees its independence from sociohistorical influences. On the other hand, both Tasso and Antonio are social climbers and strive not only to perfect themselves but also to find recognition in the eyes of their patron, the duke (HA 5:85; 444–46). In other words, they are far from autonomous in their dependence on the duke's approval. Although Antonio represents the self-certainty that Tasso both admires and dreads, he has achieved this apparent steadfastness at the expense of his personal integrity, by internalizing the ethics of the dominant hierarchical order to the point of identifying with it (HA 5:90; 638–43).

Antonio's self-assurance is the result of his identification with the ruler's views. The trust in oneself is acquired at the price of willful obedience. Whereas Antonio has the appearance of a stable identity, Tasso's continuous striving toward artistic perfection represents the dynamic aspect of bourgeois ideology. Ironically, it is Tasso who wants to preserve his integrity as an artist, whereas Antonio has compromised his bourgeois identity to ingratiate himself with the aristocrats. As Eleonore Sanvitale mentions, both men are at odds with each other "weil die Natur nicht *einen* Mann aus ihnen beiden formte" (because "nature" did not unite their complementary abilities into one) (HA 5:119; 1704–10). The dramatic constellation of separating the protagonists into two complementary halves points to the bourgeois paradox of trying to combine both the striving for perfection (Tasso) and stability (Antonio). The play's final tableau, in which Tasso clings to Antonio like a stranded seafarer in distress grips a rock, illustrates that the union between these two adversaries is not a voluntary choice but rather a matter of necessity:

> Verschwunden ist der Glanz, entflohn die Ruhe.
> Ich kenne mich in der Gefahr nicht mehr,
> Und schäme mich nicht mehr es zu bekennen.
> Zerbrochen ist das Steuer und es kracht
> Das Schiff an allen Seiten. Berstend reißt
> Der Boden unter meinen Füßen auf!
> Ich fasse dich mit beiden Armen an!
> So klammert sich der Schiffer endlich noch
> Am Felsen fest, an dem er scheitern sollte. (HA 5:167; 3445–53)

> (Gone is the splendor, vanished the peace.
> I no longer know myself in the danger,
> And no longer feel embarrassed to confess it.
> Broken is the rudder, and the ship
> Is breaking on all sides. Bursting asunder
> The floor under my feet!
> I take hold of you with both my arms!
> Thus clings the mariner at last
> To the rock, which made him almost strand.)

Significantly, the union comes to pass only when the two adversaries are left to their own devices after the courtly society's departure. The absence of the aristocratic patrons results in Tasso's disorientation because he has lost Duke Alfonse's paternal guidance and protection. The idealist dreamer cannot survive without the help of his alter ego, the pragmatic citizen and statesman, Antonio. As this final tableau suggests, the artist's union with his worldly-wise adversary is not a matter of equal consent. It forces the artist to admit his lack of orientation. Tasso's confession can also be seen as a call for a new aesthetic that depicts the artist's own plight. Tasso's embrace of Antonio illustrates his need to redirect his focus away from courtly society and toward his bourgeois alter ego. Yet Tasso's newly gained freedom is achieved at the expense of his self-assurance and results in an existential crisis that remains unsolved. Tasso, who initially thinks that he can see through the other characters' secret motivations and recognize their true face behind the mask of polite pretense, must eventually realize the unreliability of his knowledge (HA 5:108–9; 1317–19; 3446).

Goethe's leitmotif of *kennen, verkennen, erkennen, bekennen* (to know, to misconceive, to recognize, to confess) emphasizes the difficulty to know something for certain in this polite society that requires diplomacy. It also underlines Tasso's loss of self-confidence and the need to confess his inner conflicts without inhibition (HA 5:3447). Knowledge, invariably at risk of being misconstrued or misleading, is always related to knowledge of other human beings. The challenge of knowing the true intentions of other people is particularly daunting in the hermetic setting of the court because the social etiquette prescribes politeness regardless of one's true opinion. The first dialogue between Eleonore Sanvitale and the princess, which sets the tone for the entire play, illustrates the uncertainties connected to courteous flattery. Eleonore Sanvitale praises the princess's taste and aesthetic judgment, yet the princess takes her compliment as flattery:

> Leonore: Dein Urteil grad, stets ist dein Anteil groß
> Am Großen, das du wie dich selbst erkennst.
> Prinzessin: Du solltest dieser höchsten Schmeichelei
> Nicht das Gewand vertrauter Freundschaft leihen.
> Leonore: Die Freundschaft ist gerecht, sie kann allein
> Den ganzen Umfang deines Werts erkennen. (HA 5:76; 93–98)

> (Leonore: Your judgment is plain, and always great your part
> In great things, which you recognize like yourself.
> Princess: You should not lend this highest flattery
> The guise of friendship.
> Leonore: Friendship is just. It alone can
> Recognize the full extent of your value.)

The princess's response is striking because it reveals her guarded skepticism, which she shares with Tasso. While the tone of this polite exchange is light and does not imply any sincere criticism, Goethe's metaphorical wording presents their friendship as a borrowed dress, thus characterizing it as a disguise. The duplicity of politeness in courtly society provokes Tasso's suspicion to the point of an obsession.

Figure 5.2. Carl Ferdinand Sohn (1805–67), *Torquato Tasso and the Two Leonores*. Wikimedia Commons, public domain.

The central conflict of this *Seelendrama* is based on the improbability of knowing the "true" intentions of others, not even one's own. As the male individual is expected to assume full responsibility for his decisions and actions, the striving for personal autonomy has to be acquired through a higher degree of introspection. Thus the gain in personal freedom also meant a higher moral standard and stricter self-control. By continuously analyzing the relations between the self and the world, bourgeois ideology was gradually demystifying its objective: the autonomous individual. Self-reflection contributed to the gradual dissolving of clearly defined subject-object relations. In the wake of the disappointment over the improbable realization of bourgeois emancipation, the subject can be best understood in terms of a trajectory or process, and not as a fixed entity, regardless of the protagonists' endeavor to uphold the emancipated individual's unwavering moral integrity.[17] In other words, the ideal of the aspiring achiever requires a flexibility that challenges the notion of the subject's stable identity.

Another factor that destabilizes the male "autonomous" self is the duty of civility. Good manners distinguish human beings from their instinctual others. Goethe's classicist plays subvert courteous restraint by revealing the deceptive potential of social gallantry. The loss of trust among humans due to this potentially hypocritical courtesy provokes the search for a "true," genuine identity that is capable of uniting civility with moral integrity in opposition to superficial courtly etiquette. Yet, as the example of both Goethe's and Schiller's classical dramas show, pretentious civility had already become an integral part of a civic code of conduct that feigned both courteous conformity and authenticity. The contradiction between a well-defined stable identity and the pledge of self-perfection induced the bourgeois individual to fake the authenticity of an idealized self. Ironically, Tasso can preserve his artistic integrity and individuality only by clinging to the parvenu, Antonio, who has forfeited his integrity in exchange for an ostensible autonomy that borders on self-denial, as it is based on compliance with courtly values. In view of these dilemmas, the drama's open-endedness also undermines the humanist ideal of a stable and coherent self.

On the one hand, Tasso can be read as an example of Schiller's notion of the idealist artist who reproduces "the absolute unchangeable of his being" in his art (SNA 20.1:333; HA 5:166; 3426–33).[18] On the other hand, Goethe deviates from Schiller by emphasizing in the play's final tableau that art is part of an infinite dynamic process.[19] Just as the shipwrecked mariner, Tasso, needs to cling to the rock to survive, art depends on the realities of life (HA 5:167; 3451–53). Yet what seems to be a final reunion between art and life turns out to be a last helpless effort to hold on to the subject's unity, which has been lost forever: "So klammert sich der Schiffer endlich noch / Am Felsen fest, an dem er scheitern sollte" (HA 5:3452–53) ("So in the end will the mariner cling / To the rock on which he was to founder" [3444–45]). Goethe's *Tasso* marks the transition from a presumed stable symbolic order to a dynamic process that discredits the desire for individual autonomy as illusory. This shift can be detected in Tasso's final words. Here he compares himself to the mariner who no longer can rely on the guidance of the stars and the sun, after his ship has been destroyed by the rock to which he now clings. The mariner has lost the transcendental points of reference. But what is more, he is no longer ashamed to confess his mishap.

The absence of a reliable metaphysical order and the uncertainty of truth are also central to the dramatic conflict in *Iphigenie*. In contrast to classical Greek drama, the divine reveals itself only indirectly through human mediation. In other words, the divine has become internalized (HA 5:60, 1949). The image of the gods changes with the changing situation of the characters. While the gods seem to disregard the individual human fate when they punish Iphigenie for the transgressions of her ancestors, Iphigenie gratefully accepts their "weise zubereiteten Geschenken" (wisely chosen gifts) after Orest has arrived on Tauris to save her and take her home with him (HA 5:37; 1102–4). Yet, Iphigenie herself seems to have doubts about divine justice and serves them as a priestess "mit stillem Widerwillen" (with reluctance) (HA 5:8, 36). After all, she uses her privileged position as priestess to interpret the divine law not only to humanize Skythian society but also to her own advantage. While her emancipation from religious dogma allows her to take personal responsibility for her fate, it also reveals her imperfection. Iphigenie's concealment of her conspiracy to escape to Greece finds an excuse in her claim that her individual desire is compatible with the will of the gods. Yet, she cannot be considered self-determined as long as she justifies her actions by invoking them. Only after Thoas presses her on her relationship to her co-conspirators, Orestes and Pylades (HA 5:59; 1837–39; 1886–87; 1890–91), does she confess her knowledge of the conspiracy to steal Diana's sacred image (HA 5:60; 1919–36). While her eventual confession shows her integrity and loyalty toward Thoas, it also puts her brother's life at risk. In view of Thoas's history as an uncivilized barbarian who used to kill foreign intruders of his island indiscriminately, his clemency toward Iphigenie and her co-conspirators shows him to be a true proponent of "der Wahrheit und der Menschlichkeit" (truth and humanitarian compassion) (HA 5:60; 1938). While his astonishing development seems to lend itself to a didactic message, namely that even the most barbaric rulers can be moved to become civilized, caring human beings—a message that was particularly expedient and offered an opportunity of exculpation in guilt-ridden postwar Germany[20]—Thoas's magnanimity is only part of the play's message. The optimism suggested by his successful development for the better is offset by the all-too-human fragility of Iphigenie's self-emancipation, which cannot be accomplished without Thoas's relinquishment of his desire to be loved. Her inclination to evade Thoas's unwanted advances by taking advantage of her protected position and presenting her own needs as the will of the gods, or by using this excuse to escape his scorn and retribution, reveal her dilemma as a vulnerable human being. While Iphigenie's state of double dependence on the grace of Thoas, on the one hand, and the mercy of the gods, on the other, is undeserved, her taking refuge in her privileged position as a high priestess not only keeps her in a state of dependence but also shows her susceptibility to opportunist political manipulation. In that regard she is not all that different from Schiller's Marquis Posa or Goethe's Leonore Sanvitale. Yet it is precisely Iphigenie's frailty, her vulnerability to human weakness that affirms humanist ideals by questioning them. In this sense, Goethe's and Schiller's neoclassical plays challenge the Idealist optimism that has often been ascribed to them and criticized in their reception.

The protagonists' ambiguous, inconsistent personalities, the dramas' indeterminate endings, and the discrepancies between the stylistic idealization of the dramatic action and morally imperfect interactions that point to a less-than-ideal eighteenth-century reality undermine any clear-cut boundaries between the ideal and the real. These ambiguities also challenge the notion of a stable individual unity and autonomy almost at the same time as these humanist ideals were created. This raises the question of whether the posthumanist challenge—a challenge that is aware of humanism's potentially deceptive idealist dualism—has always already been implicit in the literary enactments of humanist ideas.

As for this volume's underlying task of providing answers as to why the humanities matter, this chapter intended to illustrate how literary enactments can reveal the ambiguities and imponderables of human behavior in a much more palpable fashion than abstract theoretical discourses. Although the belief in the True, Good, and Beautiful still persisted in neoclassical literature, Goethe's *Iphigenie* and *Tasso* challenge the underlying Idealist dualism of these values by problematizing them. In contrast to theoretical discourses on humanist aesthetics or ethics, the dramas offer multiperspectival views of human conduct that cannot and must not be pigeonholed if the goal is to show a broad spectrum of mind-body interrelations. The purpose of a humanist education is precisely to do justice to the polysemy of literary texts and go beyond the dogmatic reiteration of humanist premises. From this perspective, humanism should not be regarded as a fixed, clearly definable ideology but rather as an overarching collective term that needs to be tested in concrete historical situations. A humanist education will allow the readers to educate themselves by discovering the dilemmas and ambiguities in literary texts. Such a nondogmatic approach will not take humanism for granted but will always attempt to probe according to ever-changing cultural contexts. In this sense, posthumanism can be regarded as inherently humanist.

Notes

1. Adorno interprets the mythical dimension of Goethe's drama as a "Verstricktheit in Natur" (entanglement in nature) and underlines the play's "geschichtsphilosophische Akzent" (historical self-awareness) (496). As mentioned earlier, the dialectic of nature and history are intrinsic elements of Herder's pantheist philosophy.
2. See, for instance, Richard T. Gray, *About Face* (Detroit: Wayne State UP, 2004).
3. For instance, Johann Friedrich Blumenbach (1752–1840) and his predecessors, George-Louis Leclerc, Comte de Buffon (1707–88), Caspar Friedrich Wolff (1734–94), Albrecht von Haller (1708–77), and Charles Bonnet (1720–93) all contributed to the gradual dissolution of a static mind-body separation by viewing organisms in terms of a dynamic evolutionary process. Especially Blumenbach's *Bildungstrieb* or formative vital power influenced Herder's anthropological views, which resonated with those of Goethe.
4. Philosopher Mark Johnson cites numerous sources of recent research in cognitive neuroscience, as well as pragmatists John Dewey (1859–1952) and William James (1842–1910), in support of his thesis that meaning is grounded in our bodily experience, a claim that Herder already introduced in the German context in the 1770s. Johnson uses the epigenesis of a human being as an example to illustrate how meaning "is prepared and developed in our non-conscious bodily perceptions and movements" (*Meaning* 25). Obviously, infants do not have the intellectual abilities to understand

abstract language, and yet they are able to learn through bodily gestures, postures, and expressions and to experience emotions.
5. This is particularly obvious in the drama and poetry of the *Sturm und Drang*. Notable examples are Schiller's *Die Räuber, Kabale und Liebe*, and Goethe's early poetry, such as "Willkommen und Abschied" and "Maifest." See also, Wellbery, *The Specular Moment* (1996).
6. See, for instance, Schiller's *Kabale und Liebe* and *Don Karlos*, Lessing's *Miss Sara Sampson* and *Emilia Galotti*, and Goethe's *Iphigenie* and *Torquato Tasso*.
7. Johnson criticizes the reluctance of philosophers of language "to grant any cognitive function to emotions," and also their rejection of the idea "that emotions are part of cognitive meaning" (*Meaning* 61). He cites Searle, Davidson, Rorty, and Fodor as prominent examples for language theories that do not fully acknowledge the significance of metaphorical language (196–205). He also deplores that some philosophers "are captivated by the dream of a pristine language—a language of carefully defined literal concepts free from the alleged bodily processes" (*Meaning* 222). To support his claim, Johnson refers to C. K. Ogden and I. A. Richards, *The Meaning of Meaning* (1923). Johnson reasons that "even today, some proponents of nondualistic views nevertheless allow a dualistic ontology to creep back into their theory..." (*Meaning* 112).
8. Herder was one of the first philosophers in German culture who opposed the mechanistic mind-body division. While he pleaded for a holistic anthropology and a panentheist philosophy, he still held on to a spiritual realm, a divine nature according to which the history of the world unfolds.
9. Johnson's references to second-generation (embodied) cognitive neuroscience argue for a mind-body continuum and lend support to his hypothesis that meaning is always embodied (157–75). Johnson refers to Damasio, Fogassi, Gallese, Lakoff, Rizzolatti, Tomasello, and Tucker, among others.
10. Leonore believes that the princess lacks the energy to be passionate when she describes her inclination for Tasso as follows: "Denn ihre Neigung zu dem werten Manne / Ist Ihren andern Leidenschaften gleich. / Sie leuchten wie der stille Schein des Monds / Dem Wandrer spärlich auf dem Pfad zu Nacht; / Sie wärmen nicht und gießen keine Lust / Noch Lebensfreud umher" (For her attraction to this honorable man / Is like her other passions. / They shine as does the silent moon / shine sparingly upon the wanderer's path at night; / They do not warm and do not pour out pleasure / or joy of life; if not indicated otherwise, all translations from the German are mine) (HA 5:126; 1954–59). While the princess confides in Leonore that she loves Tasso (HA 5:124; 1888–93), she often tells him to moderate his passion (HA 5:103; 1120–22) and eventually rejects him (HA 5:108; 1283–84).
11. In the German tradition, Immanuel Kant famously laid the philosophical foundations for the discourse on individual autonomy by claiming that the faculty of human reason could liberate the human being from its subjection to the constraints of empirical reality.
12. "For Christa Bürger, the drama creates an illusion of court and poet united by bourgeois family bonds and the Enlightenment ideology of *Humanität*, in order to draw attention to the hidden reality of absolutism, whose political interests use and functionalize the poet" (Wagner 138). Adorno regards Goethe's classical dramas *Iphigenie* and *Tasso* even more representative of the sociopolitical conditions of late eighteenth-century reality than his *Sturm und Drang* plays, which are usually associated with Goethe's social criticism (Adorno 499).

13. Irmgard Wagner's reception history of Goethe's *Iphigenie auf Tauris* and *Torquato Tasso* documents the shift from the *Iphigenie* adulation of the immediate postwar years to a much more critical attitude that condemned Goethe's and Schiller's apolitical elitism: "During the coming decades *Weimarer Klassik* ... would be the denigrating name chosen by the Left of what used to be called (*Deutsche*) *Klassik*" (Wagner 79).
14. In the words of Theodor Adorno: "So eindeutig indessen die Iphigenie fürs Humane optiert, so wenig erschöpft sich ihr Gehalt im Plädoyer; eher ist Humanität der Inhalt des Stücks als der Gehalt" (Adorno 499) ("As unequivocably as *Iphigenie* opts for the humane, however, its substance is not exhausted in that *plaidoyer*; humanity is the content of the play rather than its substance"; translation borrowed from *Notes to Literature*, edited by Ralf Tiedemann, translated by Shierry Weber Nicholsen [New York: Columbia UP, 1992], 157).
15. There were, however, exceptions, such as Adorno's "Zum Klassizismus von Goethe's *Iphigenie*." Like Walser, Adorno does not read *Iphigenie* as the timeless classical work that prevailed in the 1950s but historicizes it, albeit from a different point of view.
16. Adorno argues in a similar vein. By stating that the mythological aspects of Goethe's play have to be understood as "leibhaftige Verstricktheit in Natur" (physical entanglement in nature) (496), he also points to Goethe's skepticism toward Enlightenment ideology. Adorno underlines Goethe's adversity to unequivocal messages by contrasting him to Schiller, who in Adorno's opinion celebrates the "Kantische Ideenwelt" (Kantian world of ideas) in his art (ibid.).
17. Schiller conceptualizes this contradiction between being and becoming in his essay "Über die ästhetische Erziehung des Menschen" as follows: "Nur indem er [der Mensch] sich verändert, e x i s t i r t er [emphasis in original]; nur indem er unveränderlich bleibt existirt er. Der Mensch vorgestellt in seiner Vollendung wäre demnach die beharrliche Einheit, die in den Fluthen der Veränderung ewig dieselbe bleibt" (Only in that he [the human being] changes, he exists; only in that he remains unchanged, he exists. Man, presented in his perfection, would consist of the stable unity that remains eternally constant in the ebb and flow of change) (SNA 20.1:343).
18. In the original, the passage reads: "Den Stoff zwar wird er von der Gegenwart nehmen, aber die Form von einer edleren Zeit, da jenseits aller Zeit, von der absoluten unwandelbaren Einheit seines Wesens entlehnen" (SNA 20.1: 333).
19. Whereas for Goethe experience lends stability to a character, Schiller believes that abstraction guarantees a character's solidity (SNA 20.1:343).
20. As Martin Walser's speech claimed at the *Germanistentag* in Essen in 1964.

CHAPTER 6

Incorporating Change
The Role of Science in Goethe's and Carl Gustav Carus's Humanist Aesthetics

Carus and Goethe in the Context of Romantic Philosophies of Nature

Carl Gustav Carus (1789–1869) took it upon himself to carry on the humanist legacy of bridging the gap between the sciences and the arts, between empiricist and speculative explorations, between factual and philosophical knowledge. At a time when progress in the life sciences—especially anthropology, zoology, and botany[1]—made it harder to believe in the Idealist concept of individual self-determination, Carus attempted to resist the diversification of academic disciplines by emphasizing the integrative powers of a unifying, subjective point of view. Inspired by the Romantic nature philosophies of Friedrich Wilhelm Joseph Schelling (1775–1854) and Lorenz Oken (1779–1851), he strove to unite the arts, especially the visual arts and landscape painting in particular, and contemporary scientific research, such as geology, anthropology, botany, zoology, and physiology (Müller-Tamm 3). Just as Herder and Goethe before him, Carus had a panentheist view of the world, one that presumed the interrelatedness of all organic and inorganic life and yet maintained the distinction between the "sinnliche" (sensual) and "übersinnliche" (spiritual) spheres (Müller-Tamm 15).[2]

Jutta Müller-Tamm has devoted a monograph to Carus's endeavors to reunite the arts and the sciences in the context of his time, titled *Kunst als Gipfel der Wissenschaft* (*Art as the Apex of Science*). The following chapter will expand on Müller-Tamm's scholarship by demonstrating how Goethe's and Carus's scientific studies intersect and, further, how some of their aesthetic creations represent the dialectical interrelations of scientific, literary, and aesthetic discourses. Reading Goethe's and Carus's amalgamations of scientific and artistic discourses as attempts to preserve the integrity of the human subject in view of its dreaded scientific fragmentation will permit me to discuss the philosophical underpinnings of the anthropomorphization of scientific discourses and their significance for a humanist education or the concept of *Bildung*. I will resort to a reading of Goethe's *Metamorphose der Pflanzen* (*Metamorphosis of Plants*) to show how the abundance of anthropomorphic metaphors both aims at educating a growing literate audience and foregrounds the role of aesthetics in the making of meaning. In other words, I argue with Goethe and Carus that literary and visual imagery not only enhances the understanding of natural phenomena but also that anthropomorphic metaphors precede and constitute the foundational assumptions of scientific discourses.

Goethe expressed the far-reaching nature of anthropocentric image making for the conceptualization of human understanding in his novel *Die Wahlverwandschaften* (*Elective Affinities*) (1809), where several protagonists emphasize the human subject's narcissistic habit of reflecting itself in nature: "[D]er Mensch ist ein wahrer Narziß; er bespiegelt sich überall gern selbst, er legt sich als Folie der ganzen Welt unter" (HA 6:270) (Man is a true Narcissus; he likes to reflect himself everywhere; he spreads himself under the whole world like a foil of a mirror[3]). This anthropomorphic image making is central to my argument because it emphasizes the significance of metaphorical conceptualization and expression of human thinking in general. The assumption that human beings recognize in natural phenomena first and foremost their affinities to these is pivotal for the humanities because it implies that scientific conceptualizations are often based on anthropocentric metaphors.[4] While we have already discussed the anthropocentric nature of metaphors in previous chapters, we have not answered the question how these metaphors change over time and reflect the epistemic horizon of a specific age. The analyses of Carus's and Goethe's nature philosophies and their aesthetic manifestations will show these fundamental transformations that situate the human intellect no longer above nature but rather as part of it. Consequently, the human being is no longer viewed as the master of a well-regulated and transparent natural order but rather as a living organism among an unknowable, constantly evolving, dynamic natural system. This also implies that the human subject is constantly changing and not entirely transparent to itself. The discovery of the subconscious is closely related to this development. The dwindling domination of the human over nature, however, is compensated by a spiritualization of natural organisms and by the attempt to integrate science into a larger organic unison. Prior to my textual analyses, I will present Carus's and Goethe's aesthetics in the context of the philosophical and scientific discourses of their times.

As a broadly educated scholar and scientist, Carl Gustav Carus was well positioned to promote an "interdisciplinary" point of view. The literary mediation and popularization of scientific knowledge can be seen as a prime motivation for Carus's aesthetic and artistic productivity (Müller-Tamm 138).

As discussed in the chapter on Herder, many scholars of different fields deplored the specialization of scientific discourses that had already begun in the eighteenth century. Like Lessing, Herder, Schiller, and Humboldt before him, Carus attempted to make scientific knowledge more accessible and meaningful for a broader, literate but nonacademic audience. In line with his neo-humanist predecessors, Carus viewed the arts as a medium to communicate natural phenomena and their underlying philosophical foundations to the growing circles of educated readers. The humanist agenda of popularizing scientific knowledge in an increasingly complex world became more urgent and difficult during the nineteenth century. Carus relied on the Idealist legacy, and especially Goethe, as a role model to transmit a rapidly growing body of scientific knowledge to an educated audience by aestheticizing it:

> Der Bau eines kunstgemäß und schön gegliederten wissenschaftlichen Werkes muß notwendig auch dem Gebildeten, der nicht selbst Forscher ist, auf eine klare und übersichtliche Weise dargelegt werden können, ja man darf behaupten, daß die durchgreifendere und allgemeinere Bildung einer Nation erst dann als möglich erscheint, wenn durch solches Zugänglichwerden der verschiedenen Wissenschaften jedem Gebildeten und jedem in irgendeiner Sphäre Selbstthätigen auch der gesunde und klare Überblick der übrigen Reiche menschlichen Wissens und Könnens zugänglich geworden. (CGS 10:5–6)

> (The construction of an aesthetically and beautifully structured scientific work must necessarily be representable in a clear and transparent fashion to an educated individual who is not a scholar. Yes, one may claim that the more effective and general education of a nation seems possible only if the sound and clear command of the other areas of human knowledge and capacity have become available to every educated and self-reliant person of any domain.)[5]

Carus's programmatic statement about the close relationship between art, education, and aesthetics is key for his interdisciplinary approach. His pedagogy seeks to mediate between different scientific disciplines in order to produce well-rounded individuals with a broad general education, thus providing the tools that enable them to conduct independent research on their own. The ultimate goal is to contribute to the advancement of the entire nation. It is noteworthy that in spite of his awareness of the rapidly expanding scientific disciplines Carus is still convinced that individuals can obtain a sound and clear overview over all the other domains of human knowledge.

Carus published medical textbooks on gynecology, zoology, comparative anatomy and physiology, psychology, several works on the philosophy of nature, aesthetic treatises on landscape painting, and a volume on Goethe's works, as well as autobiographical writings.[6] While his artistic achievements were overshadowed by those of his famous friend and mentor Caspar David Friedrich (1774–1840), his paintings have nevertheless received some recognition.[7]

Yet his rediscovery in the 1920s by psychologist Ludwig Klages was based on his reputation as a forerunner of *Tiefenpsychologie* (depth psychology) and not on his accomplishments as a painter (Müller-Tamm 51). Carus also became known as an admirer of Goethe with whom he shared many views on concepts of science and the philosophy of nature (Müller-Tamm 27–34). After all, he wrote two volumes that express his admiration for Goethe's literary and scientific accomplishments.[8] Goethe in turn used his young admirer's scientific insights as confirmation of his own scientific suppositions (Grosche 11). Carus's aesthetic and philosophical views reflect the tensions between his dedication to his scientific pursuits, on the one hand, and his belief in the holistic concept of nature of late eighteenth-century *Naturphilosophie* on the other. His humanist Idealism was tarnished by a Eurocentric, racist physiognomics that postulated "the superiority of particular races over other races" (Gray 120) and thus anticipated "the perverse attitudes of the German anthropologists whose hierarchical theories of racial value will not emerge until half a century later" (ibid. 118).[9]

To today's reader, Carus's humanism seems at odds with his racist physiognomic and cranioscopic writings. Yet his chauvinistic taxonomy can be explained as an attempt to preserve a Eurocentric universalism in view of a growing body of empirical knowledge that challenged his holistic worldview. In the context of the emerging discourse of *Naturphilosophie*, Carus's physiognomic and cranioscopic classifications—as prejudiced as they are—appear less as the chauvinistic eccentricities of a racist than as pseudoscientific evidence that offers reassurance to a philosophy designed to explain the meaning of life in a secular and spiritually depleted world (CGS 4:57).[10] Yet, as I will show in the last part of this analysis, Carus's empiricist classifications helped establish a hierarchical taxonomy of organic evolution that not only contradicts the dynamic openness of an egalitarian humanism but also served to justify racist speculations and prejudices.

Rather than focusing on the ill-fated political consequences of Carus's anthropological views, this chapter will examine his efforts to reconcile the tensions between his scientific concerns and the Romantic *Naturphilosophie*, which he espoused in his aesthetic and philosophical writings, such as his *Briefe über die Landschaftsmalerei* (*Letters on Landscape Painting*) (1831–35) and his *Briefe über das Erdenleben* (*Letters on Earthly Life*) (1841). After historically situating Carus's basic philosophical views, I will examine his efforts to mediate between the desire for a meaningful, comprehensive natural order and the rapid expansion of scientific knowledge. In his *Briefe über die Landschaftsmalerei* (BüLM), for instance, Carus develops a comprehensive aesthetics that goes beyond his interest in painting.

Carus's philosophical and scientific roots reach back to the end of the eighteenth century, with its diverse reactions to the wide-ranging impact of Enlightenment science and its rationalist view of the world. While he attempted to overcome the rigidity of the Linnaean taxonomy by viewing nature as a dynamic organism, his morphological and anthropological classifications still adhere to a hierarchical order that privileges the "Caucasian race." His classifications are based on physiognomic analogies between natural organisms and phenomena, analogies that are speculative and at times far-fetched. As already shown in previous chapters, analogical deduction was an established scientific method. While it attempts to mitigate the dehumanizing effects of empirical science, it also prevents the dynamic openness of an egalitarian humanism.

Carus's belief in an underlying kinship of mind and matter, of human consciousness and objective reality inspired his attempts to reconcile the discrepancies between empirical facts and a meaningful natural order. And in this respect Carus coincides with Goethe's and Schelling's holistic philosophies of nature.[11] As nature is constantly changing, human thinking had to be flexible and cohere with the changes of empirical reality. The aim of his exploration of an ever-changing nature, however, was the identification of archetypal, essential forms of life that point to underlying eternal laws of nature.[12] In this context Carus apodictically cites Schiller at the very beginning of the first letter of his *Briefe über das Erdenleben*: "'Wie wohltätig ist uns doch die Identität, dieses gleichförmige Beharren der Natur!—Wenn uns Leidenschaft, innerer und äußerer Tumult lange genug hin und her geworfen, wenn wir uns selbst verloren haben, so finden wir sie immer als die nämliche wieder und uns in ihr'" (How beneficial for our well-being identity is this steady persistence of nature!—When passion, internal and external uproar have thrown us about for a long enough time, when we have lost ourselves, we can always find nature as the self-same in us and us in her!) (CGS 10:1). The more dynamic and complex nature appeared in view of scientific discoveries, the greater was the need to identify the unchanging laws of nature's transformations. Art complemented the scientific identification of these laws by illustrating them and thus making them palpable:

> Die Naturschönheit ist göttlicher, die Kunstschönheit ist menschlicher, und so wird es erklärlich, warum eben erst durch die Kunst der Sinn für die Natur wahrhaft aufgeschlossen wird. Es ist, als wäre der unendliche Raum der Natur in einer Sprache geschrieben, welche der Mensch erst erlernen müsste, und welche er allein dadurch erlernen könnte, dass er mittelst Eingebung eines höhern, oder durch den Vorgang eines verwandten Geistes einen Teil dieser Worte in seine Muttersprache übersetzt erhält; ja es wird auf diese Weise die eigentliche Naturerkenntnis, die Naturwissenschaft, durch die Kunst vorbereitet und gefördert. (CGS 4:62–63)

> (Natural beauty is divine, artistic beauty is human, and this is why the appreciation of nature in its true sense is disclosed only in art. It is as if the infinite space of nature were written in a language that the human subject still had to learn, and which he could only learn through inspiration of a higher or the mediation of a kindred spirit who translates part of these words into his recipient's own language; yes, in this manner art prepares and enhances actual cognizance of nature, natural science.)

Like Schelling and Goethe, Carus also postulated an original unity of the poetic and the scientific (Müller-Tamm 21–23). While he distanced himself from Romantic subjectivism by incorporating factual findings of the empiricist sciences, he nonetheless attempted to integrate the emotional sensibilities of the perceiving subject into an art that conveys the totality and universality of the human experience of nature. As one of the last *Universalgelehrte* (polymaths) who attempted to bridge the growing schism between the humanities and the natural sciences, he deplored the dehumanizing effects of purely empiricist approaches. His expertise in the emerging natural sciences (botany, zoology, psychology, medicine) made him aware that the diversification of academic disciplines with their growing bodies of empirical facts fragmented, and thus ultimately degraded, human existence and became a threat to a holistic worldview that regarded nature as an interconnected totality. Carus was a proponent of Schelling's idea of the *Weltseele*, "der Gedanke von der innern nothwendigen und unerlässlichen Verbindung des Weltgebäudes zu einem einzigen unendlichen organischen Ganzen" (idea of the inner necessary and indispensable cohesion of the world order that forms a singular infinite organic whole) (CGS 5:70). Carus's reception of Schelling's holistic system was enthusiastic especially since it also resonated with the sciences (ibid.). Carus shared his criticism of the specialized and utilitarian approaches to the study of nature with his role model Goethe, who looked back on the empiricist spirit of the Enlightenment era in his own contribution to science, "Zur Morphologie" (1817):

> Vereinzelt behandelte man sämtliche Tätigkeiten; Wissenschaft und Künste, Geschäftsführung, Handwerk und was man sich denken mag, bewegte sich in abgeschlossenem Kreise. ... Indem sich nun jeder einzelne Wirkungskreis absonderte, so vereinzelte, zersplitterte sich auch in jedem Kreise die Behandlung. (Goethe, "Zur Morphologie"; HA 13:117)

> (One treated all activities in isolation; science and the arts, business management, craftsmanship and whatever one can imagine was confined to a closed sphere. ... The secession of each sphere of influence resulted in the isolation and fragmentation of their individual methods.)

Goethe's criticism of scientific diversification was by no means an exception. As mentioned in previous chapters, during the second half of the eighteenth century a group of prominent physicians, also known as *philosophische Ärzte*—among them Albrecht von Haller (1708–77), Johann Georg Zimmermann (1728–95), Johann August Unzer (1729–99), and Ernst Platner (1744–1818)—favored a holistic approach to medicine and advocated that physicians should also have a philosophical education. They opposed the dominant medical discourse because it neglected the mental and emotional dimensions of human health and their effect on the body (Riedel, *Anthropologie* 11–12). This group had a lasting influence on many writers, philosophers, and scientists, such as Herder, Schiller, Goethe, Moritz, Schelling, and Carus.[13] According to

Goethe, scientists were dissatisfied with the empiricist specialization because, like all human beings, they have a *Trieb* (desire) "die lebendigen Bildungen als solche zu erkennen, ihre äußeren sichtbaren, greiflichen Teile im Zusammenhange zu erfassen, sie als Andeutungen des Innern aufzunehmen und so das Ganze in der Anschauung gewissermaßen zu beherrschen" (to recognize the living formations as such, to comprehend their outer, visible, palpable parts in their interrelatedness, to perceive them as signs of the interior, and thus to intuitively master the entirety) (HA 13:55).

The passage from Goethe's introduction to *Die Metamorphose der Pflanze* can be read as a prime example of Romantic *Naturphilosophie*. The holistic approach of observing living forms in their interactions with other organisms is driven by the desire to understand their function and comprehend nature through sensual perception rather than intellectual deduction. The idea that nature is dynamic and that all natural phenomena are a reflection of an inner spiritual force could be inferred from Schelling's or Oken's philosophies of nature. Carus presumed that the natural sciences would not have captured his interest had he not been inspired by Schelling and Oken, who both viewed nature as an organic totality and as manifestation of an omnipresent force (CGS 3:70–73). Oken, on his part, closely followed Schelling's Idealist system of the "all-in-all" and "all-in-every-part," which means that each microorganism is a small-scale repetition of the macroorganism of the universe.[14] The significance of the human element in Schelling's and Oken's philosophies of nature stimulated Carus to discern morphological and developmental similarities between different forms of life (LeuDe 67–68). Oken's analogical approach established a developmental hierarchy and was readily adapted by Carus's hierarchical taxonomy, which also progresses from the simplest forms of life to the most complex living beings, culminating in the human (LeuDe 69). One could interpret the adherence to such hierarchical taxonomies as expression of the need for stability in an infinitely evolving nature that can no longer be known in its entirety. Recalling Carus's programmatic Schiller citation in the *Briefe über das Erdenleben*, which expresses the human yearning for the "gleichförmige Beharren" (monotonous persistence) that we humans can find in nature in view of its analogical formations can explain his desire to establish essential laws that underlie the complexity and dynamism of nature. Yet the scientific impetus to discover and identify the essential laws of nature through taxonomic classifications and abstractions must be counterbalanced in the classicist work of art by the depiction of natural phenomena as "lebendige Bildungen" (living formations). The dialectic of movement and stillness has been aptly expressed in the title of Goethe's poem "Dauer im Wechsel" ("Permanence in Transformation"). Here Goethe underlines the affinity of art and science. He emphasizes that the scientific motivation to discover the inner laws of nature is closely related to the human desire to create art by imitating the transformations of organisms (*natura naturans*). According to this line of reasoning, the creation of art and scientific pursuits are inspired by the same impetus to fully comprehend and imitate nature's creative process. Close observation of nature and its external formations in their functional context leads to the recognition intuition of its underlying inner laws (HA 13:55).[15]

According to Schelling's theory of dynamic evolution, expressed in *Von der Weltseele* (1798), there is "a continuity between inorganic and organic matter as well as between organic life and human consciousness" (Rigby 31). The formative processes of this constantly evolving nature permeate and affect human states of mind inadvertently *before* the surreptitious transformations enter consciousness. Goethe's sonnet, titled "Natur und Kunst," which he composed around 1800 during a time when he regularly met with Schelling and his circle of young nature philosophers, expresses the idea that nature and art share a common bond prior to reflection: "Natur und Kunst, sie scheinen sich zu fliehen / Und haben sich, eh' man es denkt, gefunden" (Nature and art seem to avoid each other / and yet have found each other sooner than one thinks) (HA 1:245). Goethe's positive reaction to Schelling's *System des transzendentalen Idealismus* (*System of Transcendental Idealism*) (1800) underlines his attraction to *Naturphilosophie*, which emphasizes the affinities between philosophical, aesthetic, scientific, and creative discourses. These affinities were assumed to point to nature's underlying eternal laws and considered responsible for the developmental metamorphoses of living organisms. The realization that nature had always preexisted and influenced but not predetermined the human perception and consciousness expanded the meaning of *Bildung*. In this sense, *Bildung* is not simply an education that can be acquired and disposed of by an autonomous, freely acting subject, but denotes a much more universal concept that describes the forming principle of all natural and material things. It is always already at work *before* the subject becomes aware of it. *Bildung* is analogous to the transformative principle that Blumenbach called the *Bildungstrieb* (formation drive). In contrast to the latter, it is, however, not a physical force that is confined to biological organisms but rather a spiritual principle that organizes and shapes the universe. This underlying principle of an all-permeating vital force, reminiscent of pantheist ideas as well as of Herder's pre-Romantic philosophy, was suitable for correlating current aesthetic, religious, and philosophical concepts and the latest scientific theories.[16]

Goethe's "Die Metamorphose der Pflanzen"

In his poem "Die Metamorphose der Pflanzen," Goethe poeticizes his *Naturphilosophie* by focusing on the relationship between human nature, nature, and art. Goethe wrote his poem in 1798 in reference to Schelling's philosophy of nature, which postulated that "Die Natur soll der sichtbare Geist, der Geist die unsichtbare Natur sein" (Nature should be the visible spirit and Spirit the invisible nature) (HA 1:648).

In view of its title, it is surprising that the poem begins with an address to the narrator's beloved (HA 1:199). The narrator voices his frustration over the confusing botanical nomenclature, which presumably puzzles his listener. While the dialogic situation of the poem's beginning is that of a mentor and his student, it deviates from the conventional authoritative role of the teacher who simply instills his superior knowledge in his pupil. Considering his admitted lack of the proper word that would provide a deeper insight into the "sacred" law of botanical life, the narrator takes it upon himself to observe step by step the various stages of a plant's growth to unlock the underlying eternal principle of organic life:

Dich verwirrt, Geliebte, die tausendfältige Mischung
Dieses Blumengewühls über dem Garten umher;
Viele Namen hörest du an, und immer verdränget
Mit barbarischem Klang einer den andern im Ohr.
Alle Gestalten sind ähnlich, und keine gleichet der andern;
Und so deutet das Chor auf ein geheimes Gesetz,
Auf ein heiliges Rätsel. O, könnt' ich dir, liebliche Freundin,
Überliefern sogleich glücklich das lösende Wort! (HA 13:107)

(The rich profusion confounds thee, my love,
Of flowers, spread around the garden.
Name upon name assails your ears, and each
More barbarous-sounding than the one before—
All shapes are similar, yet none alike;
And so their choir points to a secret law,
A sacred mystery. Oh, could I only, sweet friend,
Provide you right now happily with the proper word.)[17]

The poem is composed in distiches—pairs of metrical lines, predominantly a dactylic hexameter followed by a pentameter—and has the form of an elegy. It begins with the narrator's lament of lacking "das lösende Wort" (the proper word) that would solve the riddle of "ein geheimes Gesetz, ... ein heiliges Rätsel" (a secret law, a sacred mystery) that the multiplicity of "Blumengewühl" (flowers) in the garden share. The narrating voice tells his beloved that the "barbarischem Klang" (barbaric sound) of the plants' names hinders the discovery of their commonality because, spoken in sequence, they override each other in the listener's ear. In other words, the scientific naming and appraising as in empiricist approaches will not reveal the plants' underlying kinship. Rather than naming the plants in succession, perceiving them simultaneously, like the polyphonic voices of a choir of plants that are all different but similar, can allude to their common secret: "Alle Gestalten sind ähnlich, und keine gleichet der andern; / Und so deutet das Chor auf ein geheimes Gesetz, / Auf ein heiliges Rätsel" (All shapes resemble each other, and none are exactly the same; / And thus the choir points to a secret law,/ To a sacred enigma). The "choir" of plants is contrasted to the barbaric sound of the plants' names and indicates that the key to the inner secret of a plant's life can be found in similarities, rather than differences. Whereas scientific discourses categorize plants according to their distinctions, Goethe's poem aims at conveying the underlying commonalities, which point to the "secret" laws of nature.

The narrator's concession of lacking the proper word to mediate the plants' "inner secret of life" places him in the position of a learner, who sets an example to his beloved by following his own advice. He detects the hidden law of life by studying the generic qualities of a plant. The description of the various parts of the plant—such as blossoms, fruit, and seed—does not portray them in isolation but depicts their transformative function. All the organs are presented as living agents that further the evolving organisms. Even the seed is shown as a living organism in a dormant stage of life: "Einfach schlief in dem Samen die Kraft; ein beginnendes Vorbild / lag, verschlossen in sich, unter die Hülle gebeugt . . ." (Simply the power slept in the seed; an incipient model / lay, closed in itself, bent under the cover . . .). The enjambment "ein beginnendes Vorbild lag . . ." underlines the fluidity of the growing process in which each stage evolves from the previous one without interruption, and yet the final position of "Vorbild" stresses its significance as a template that harbors the blueprint of the plant's development. Everything is in flux. Even the template is evolving and is therefore described as "beginnend" (beginning). The *Vorbild* unites the plants' unchanging archetypal form and its transitional temporality that links its past to its future.[18]

The poem's elegiac form, with its intimate address to a beloved and its abundant anthropomorphic imagery, is intended to render the scientific content more palpable and comprehensible to the non-scientist.[19] Beyond the communicative purpose of representing the biological process in vivid imagery, the personal address also conveys the process of *Bildung* not only with regard to the plant but also with regard to the recipient. It humanizes science by anthropomorphizing it and involves the recipients by having them participate in the process of contemplation of living organisms. The anthropomorphization and worship of nature, the elicitation of emotional immediacy are reminiscent of Herder's pantheistic philosophy, which also seeks to evoke the dynamic forces of living nature and the underlying correspondences of all living organisms, or "ein geheimes Gesetz, / . . . ein heiliges Rätsel" (a secret law, / a sacred enigma) (HA 13:107). This secret law is then verbally illustrated in the description of the process of growth and procreation of a primordial plant: the *Urpflanze*.

Goethe's morphological studies suggest that all plants evolve according to the same internal law. This law manifests itself visibly in the metamorphosis of plants and their changing *Gestalt* (shape). The *Urpflanze* is the visual manifestation of the idea of a primordial plant. It comprises the characteristics that all plants have in common and embodies two core ideas of neoclassical art: *Dauer im Wechsel* and *Einheit des Mannigfaltigen* (Permanence in Change and Unity of the Manifold). The poetic depiction of the metamorphosis of plants renders the idea of the elemental plant in concrete and tangible terms.

Yet the metaphorical rendering of a plant's growth also deifies and mystifies the ontogenesis of the plant and thus overcomes the Cartesian dualism of the spiritual and empirical realms, as divinity is immanent in all of nature. Living nature is comprehensible through empathy because empathy permeates all living beings and forms a common bond among them as well as with the human subject. For instance, the continuous expansion and contraction is an essential movement all organisms have in common. The abundance of anthropomorphisms underlines the empathetic kinship between the human observer and the developing plant: "schlief ... die Kraft" (slept ... the power), "sich milder Feuchte vertrauend" (trusting to the gentle dew) (HA 13:108). The analogy between a young plant and a child not only emphasizes the kinship between humans and plants but also treats the plant as an autonomous creature with self-awareness: "Aber einfach bleibt die Gestalt der ersten Erscheinung; / Und so bezeichnet sich auch unter Pflanzen das Kind." The reflexive verb "bezeichnet sich" has a double entendre that in German can either be synonymous with impersonal "bezeichnet man" (one calls) or can mean "calls itself," which underlines the plant's individual autonomy:

> Einfach schlief in dem Samen die Kraft; ein beginnendes Vorbild
> Lag, verschlossen in sich, unter die Hülle gebeugt,
> Blatt und Wurzel und Keim, nur halb geformet und farblos;
> Trocken erhält so der Kern ruhiges Leben bewahrt,
> Quillet strebend empor, sich milder Feuchte vertrauend,
> Und erhebt sich sogleich aus der umgebenden Nacht.
> Aber einfach bleibt die Gestalt, der ersten Erscheinung,
> Und so bezeichnet sich auch unter den Pflanzen das Kind.
> Gleich darauf ein folgender Trieb, sich erhebend, erneuet,
> Knoten auf Knoten getürmt, immer das erste Gebild.
> Zwar nicht immer das gleiche; denn mannigfaltig erzeugt sich,
> Ausgebildet, du siehst, immer das folgende Blatt,
> Ausgedehnter, gekerbter, getrennter in Spitzen und Teile,
> Die verwachsen vorher ruhten im untern Organ. (HA 13:108)

> (Simply sleeping was the power within the seed;
> An incipient blueprint, lay folded in the shell,
> Root, leaf, and germ, half-formed and pale;

Kept safe and dry so the nub preserves calm life
Swells, striving upward, trusting to the gentle dew,
Thus rising instantly from the surrounding night.
Yet artless remains the shape of the first appearance,
Called child even among plants, like among human kind.
Instantly rises another shoot that piles new limbs
On limbs, copying always the first form.
But always the same since the succeeding leaves emerge
In full form, you see, their tips and parts shaped more expansively and ornately,
Which previously rested in the lower organ.)

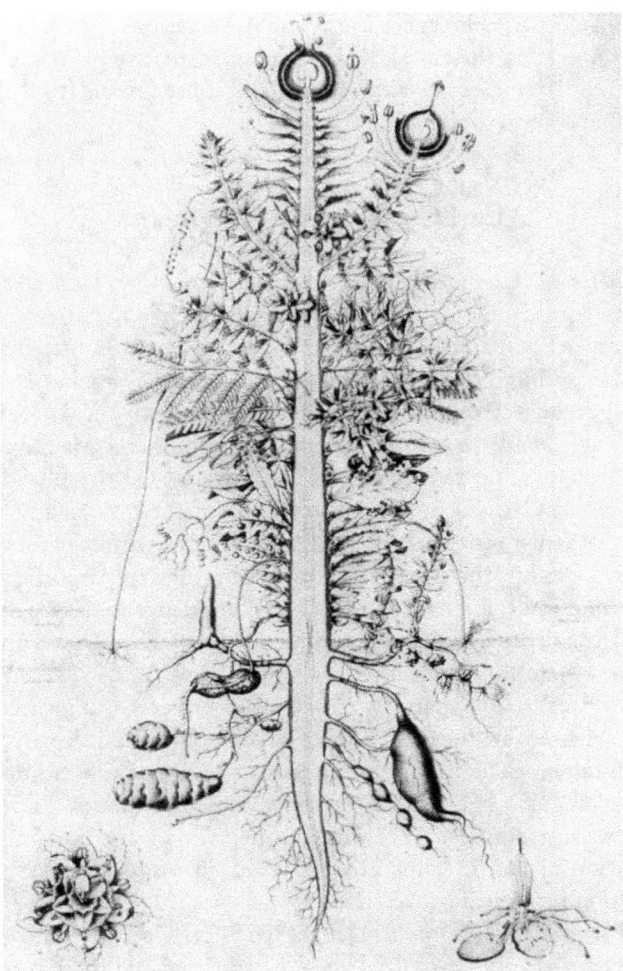

Figure 6.1. Image of the *Urpflanze* (archetypal plant) (1837). Woodcut by Pierre Jean François Turpin according to Goethe's imagination. Wikimedia Commons, public domain.

The aestheticization and idealization of nature is foregrounded in Goethe's "Metamorphose der Pflanzen." It can be seen as a remedial response to nature's progressing demystification in empiricist scientific discourse. Terms such as "höchst bestimmte Vollendung" (highest specific perfection) (HA 13:108), "Wundergebild" (miraculous formation), "Herrlichkeit" (magnificence), "des neuen Schaffens Verkündung" (the new creation's annunciation), "die göttliche Hand" (the divine hand), and "den geweihten Altar" (the holy altar) (HA 13:108) celebrate ontogenesis as a divine, creative process. Nature's productive forces are spiritualized and depicted as both miraculous and full of grace and beauty. The poem's elevated and distinctly poetic style appeals to the recipients' aesthetic and devotional sensibilities. The observation of developing Nature (*natura naturans*) and the art of discovering its formative principle assume the sanctity of a religious service since the divine spirit reveals itself through the transforming power of nature (HA 13:108).

Carl Gustav Carus's Aesthetics

Goethe's poetic representation of nature's all-permeating vital force resonates with Carus's landscape paintings. It is no coincidence that the growing popularity of landscape painting occurs at a time when scientific discourses on nature are becoming more factual and specialized. As previously mentioned, empiricist approaches examine particular physical or chemical processes in isolation. They are unable to account for nature's significance for the human subject or the human subject's role within the universe. Caspar David Friedrich's and Carl Gustav Carus's landscape paintings, on the other hand, attempt to depict living organisms in the context of their formative processes. By directing the observer's gaze to the infinite sky or ocean, they transcend the view of a particular scene and call attention to its correspondence to nature as an organic totality.[20] This spiritualized nature is removed from all practical purposes and now perceived in aesthetic terms as landscape (Ritter 152–53). The aestheticization and idealization of nature is frequently connected to intimate personal encounters with an awe-instilling force when confronted, for instance, with alpine mountains or the infinite vastness of the sea or the limitless sky. The experience of the sublime evokes the spectators' imagination and encourages them to appreciate nature in its entire grandeur as a transcendent power. The aestheticization of nature gains in significance in response to its progressing demystification in scientific discourse.

Carus's *Briefe über Landschaftsmalerei* (1815–35) document how nature becomes re-mystified and is endowed with the spiritual quality that religion possessed before science de-mystified it. Carus suggests that his letters are meant as an instructive tool that would casually guide the reader to a deeper appreciation of the non-utilitarian beauty of nature (BüLM 153). Just as Goethe uses the literary form of an elegy to make the poem's scientific content more personal and easily comprehensible to the non-scientist, Carus resorts to the literary form of letters to give his pedagogical views on landscape painting a more personal and appealing spin. This form allows him to establish a casual and intimate relationship with his readers, avoiding heavy-handed didacticism. According to Carus, nature has not received the respect it deserves as a divine and vital force because it has only been perceived as an object in terms of its practical value for human usage (BüLm; CGS 4:153–54). He emphasizes that it is necessary to liberate nature from the context of its daily use in order to recognize it as an aesthetic entity. For Carus, landscape painting is not merely a realistic reflection of a particular scene of nature. In contrast to mimetic imitation, which depicts a random fragment of nature, a landscape painting aims at capturing nature's creative force. It should be considered as a mediated rendition of nature's totality on a human scale.[21] The incomprehensible vastness of nature has to be translated so that human perception can grasp it. The artist functions as an interpreter and renders the language of nature visible through the depiction of living organisms in their natural environment (BüLm; CGS 4:84). The holistic comprehension of nature, as it is conveyed in landscape paintings, alerts the observers to their role as humans within nature and thus humanizes them.

Figure 6.2. Carl Gustav Carus (1789–1869), *Memory of a Wooded Island in the Baltic Sea (Oak Trees by the Sea)* (1834–35). Wikimedia Commons, public domain.

Figure 6.3. Carl Gustav Carus (1789–1869), *The Goethe Monument* (1832). Wikimedia Commons, public domain.

Even though Carus blamed science for contributing to the fragmentation of nature, he also stressed its importance for a better understanding of nature. For instance, he encouraged artists to pursue scientific training and criticized paintings that did not observe the most fundamental principles of nature's laws, such as gravity (BüLm 141). One of his assumptions was that science allows humans to get closer to nature after they had become alienated from it in the process of civilization. Carus shared with many of his philosophical mentors, such as Schiller and Herder, the idea that being human means having the ability to step outside of nature and reflect on it (CGS 4:64).[22] This capacity enables humans to perceive nature from a dual perspective: its physical appearance and the reflection of it. Thus Carus's bifurcated vision distinguishes classicist aesthetics from mimetic realism and is a prerequisite for the creation of art (CGS 4: 105–7).[23] The mystification of nature in art is a technique of mediation that not only makes nature's inner laws accessible to human perception but also points to their spiritual, eternal meaning (CGS 4:108). Thus science and neoclassical art elevate the depiction of nature from a mere subjectivist rendition of a momentary mood to a level of abstraction that hints at its universal and transcendent quality (CGS 4:91).

The dual perspective of nature also reveals itself in the dialectic of transformation and permanence. In Carus's landscape paintings, the opposition is apparent in the contrast between the change of seasons and the view of the horizon that points to the permanence and infinity of the sky (oaks on the seashore; landscape in spring; cemetery in the moonlight).

Carus's *Naturphilosophie* and His Politics of Race

The assumption of a discernable correspondence between nature's spiritual essence and its physical appearance gave rise to the discipline of physiognomy, of which Carus also became a proponent. Based on the premise that physical appearance is an expression of a person's character, physiognomy utilizes "scientific" observation and description of physical characteristics—such as size, shape, and other traits of body parts—to come to a conclusion about the essential internal qualities of a certain individual or an entire group of individuals. The goal of Carus's efforts to categorize human behavior according to physiognomic traits—laid out in his *Symbolik der Menschlichen Gestalt* (*Symbolism of the Human Form*) (1858)—was to arrive at a reliable distinction between transitory and essential features of the human species: "Eine andere Anforderung geht dahin, dass die Symbolik Zufälliges und Momentanes vom Wesentlichen und Bleibenden gehörig unterscheide" (Another requirement is that symbolism must distinguish between short-lived arbitrary and permanent essential phenomena) (Carus, *Symbolik* 13). Romantic nature philosophy's realization that the human organism is part of a continuously evolving nature, subject to constant transformation even before birth and after death, undermined the subject's autonomy. Hence the desire to compensate for this destabilization by establishing essentialist categories: the more dynamic nature, the stronger the need for stability. This is where Carus's training induced him to use scientific methods of measuring and quantifying to justify speculations about the correspondence of appearance and character. More specifically, Carus divided the human race into four subcategories with a hierarchical ranking: the so-called *Nachtvölker* (nocturnal peoples), *westliche und östliche Dämmerungsvölker* (Western and Eastern twilight peoples), and the *Tagvölker* (daylight peoples). These subcategories follow a hierarchical order in which the so-called *Tagvölker*, equated with the Caucasion race, figure at the top. Accordingly, the intellectual faculties of all the other races were less developed (*Goethe Denkschrift* 58).

Carus's speculative analogies and his categorization of the different human subspecies were certainly not unique in late eighteenth-century literature and culture. Johann Kaspar Lavater (1741–1801), Kant, and Herder have made claims that present the character of Germans and Europeans as morally and socially superior and portray people of color as intellectually inferior.[24] Like Kant and Herder, Carus moderated his ostensibly essentialist categorizations by including all four ethnic groups in the human species, yet he also claimed that the *Nachtvölker Afrikas* behave more like animals than the other groups. He conceded that, under favorable circumstances, individual members of the so-called *Nachtvölker* could be educated and achieve the sophistication of Caucasians, but when left to their own devices they would never realize their mental aptitude (*Goethe Denkschrift* 59–71). On the one hand, Carus compares *Nachtvölker* to a historically earlier stage of civilization; on the other hand, he attributes their alleged lack of abilities to the smaller size of their brain (ibid. 61).

When scientific findings suggested that racial and species distinctions were less well defined than previously assumed, attempts to make sharper distinctions between species, races, and even classes became more prevalent. Western scientists compensated for the loss of their privilege of belonging to the most civilized ethnic group by resorting to taxonomic systems that favored them. Physiognomy provided these privileged groups with the "scientific" tool to justify their social standing as a result of their "natural" superiority. The dwindling difference between human and animal in the wake of the Darwinian model of evolution found antithetical resistance in the taxonomic systems derived from Linnaeus (1707–78), Buffon (1707–88), and Lamarck (1744–1829). This kind of hierarchical taxonomy later developed into the "scientific" validation of the chauvinistic racism and nationalism of the late nineteenth and early twentieth centuries.[25]

The legibility of the body fit perfectly into Carus's *naturphilosophisches* concept that attempted to deduce essential internal characteristics by observing external phenomena. The correspondence of sign and substance also fits "the ideological self-definition of the emergent civil subject" (Gray 74). Richard Gray suggests, for instance, that the assumption of the congruity of external appearance (sign) and internal essence permitted members of the elitist bourgeoisie to distinguish themselves as "self-identical autonomous civil subjects."[26] While the legibility of surface appearances and their classification provided a hermeneutic tool that made it possible to "scientifically" differentiate between fleeting, deceptive disguises and "true" unchanging characteristics, the interpretation of the observations was also considered as a form of art. In this respect, this approach met the classicist goal of unifying art and science and overcoming the tension between transformation and stability, around which middle-class ideology revolves. While internal stability is to guarantee the individual's moral steadfastness and authenticity, the transformational aspect leaves room for *Bildung* or moral self-improvement.

Carus subordinates his empiricist approach to what he deems a human perspective by making analogies between surface appearance and internal qualities of different subcategories of the human species. Vacillating between whether human development can be attributed to nurture or nature, Carus's position reflects the transition from a belief in the subject's individual autonomy, prevalent during the late eighteenth century, to a position that credits nature with a more influential role in shaping the subject's development. In this respect he agrees with the other proponents of different versions of *Naturphilosophie* that humans are part of nature and as such subject to nature's unchanging laws. What was new, and appears modern even from today's perspective, is the genetic principle of evolution and the idea that the creative stimuli inherent in nature preexist human consciousness (both ontogenetically and phylogenetically). This interest in a preconscious, or unconscious, sphere also sparked Carus's writings on the psyche of living organisms. By viewing nature as an all-permeating, infinitely changing process, the human being emerges as a dynamic organism that is part of nature and yet has the ability to transform itself. The ambiguity between predetermination and self-determination addresses the philosophical principle of human freedom and raises the question of humans' relationship to nature.

Ironically, nature's empowerment as a system that predetermines both the mental and physical characteristics of all living creatures, including humans, contributed to the reinforcement of scientific attempts to control and systematize nature's impact. In addition to genealogical and racial generalizations, such attempts also led to gender stereotypes that were "scientifically" founded in nature's "Wechselwirkung" (reciprocity) of male and female forces and sexual procreation, as, for instance, Wilhelm von Humboldt's essay "Über den

Geschlechtsunterschied und dessen Einfluß auf die organische Natur" (1795) ("On the Gender Distinction and Its Influence on Organic Nature") shows (285).[27]

Naturphilosophie and the Poetic Representation of the Preconscious

While the male genius is described as the creative force behind the act of spiritual procreation, nature is portrayed as the maternal, life-giving organism. The gendered portrayal of nature was already a common convention among the proponents of German Idealism and Naturphilosophie.[28] It had serious consequences for the naturalization of gender distinctions both in the workforce and in the private sphere well beyond the nineteenth century, as is obvious in Peter Sloterdijk's portrayal of Schelling as a gynecologist who listens to the belly of pregnant mother earth:

> Tatsächlich lauscht der junge Philosoph wie ein enthusiastischer Gynäkologe am Bauch der geistträchtigen Natur, um in ihrem Inneren die Herztöne des noch nicht zur Welt gebrachten Selbstbewußtseins nachzuweisen. (Sloterdijk, Temperamente 90)
>
> (In fact, the young philosopher listens like an enthusiastic gynecologist to the womb of nature that is pregnant with spirit, in order to discern the heartbeat of the yet undelivered self-consciousness).

In agreement with traditional gender distinctions, Sloterdijk depicts the male philosopher as a scientist in the process of analyzing a pregnant mother nature soon to give birth to a hitherto unknown self-awareness. While this self-awareness had existed before Schelling's Naturphilosophie, the connection of the subconscious and the conscious spheres had not been articulated in this gender-specific fashion. Notably, unconscious organic nature gives birth to consciousness. In fact, Sloterdijk's image of the enthusiastic philosopher who listens to the heartbeat of an unborn child's consciousness is applicable to Carus. Carus's profession as a gynecologist may very well have contributed to his persistent efforts to counteract the separation of the natural and human sciences. His recurring preoccupation with the unconscious sphere of life, which for him often refers to the prenatal development of the human mind, supports this assumption. To be sure, his adherence to Romantic Naturphilosophie became increasingly dated in view of a constantly growing body of empirical knowledge that could not be absorbed by holistic systems. Yet his determination to explore the unknown recesses of the human "soul" also helped prepare the ground for the scientific exploration of the unconscious. His programmatic statement in the introduction to his opus magnum, Psyche (1846), which claims that "Der Schlüssel zur Erkenntnis vom Wesen des bewußten Seelenlebens liegt in der Region des Unbewußtseins" (the key to the awareness of the essence of consciousness lies in the realm of the unconscious) (Carus, *Psyche* 1), illustrates the interdependence of the subjective and the objective, the inner and outer perspective, mind and body of the human self.

Although Carus's philosophy reflects on the dangers of the illusory domination of nature, it employs a myth of a divine totality that grants autonomy to the privileged human subject by virtue of its access to nature's internal laws. Carus creates a Romantic fiction of "a once-upon-a-time wholeness" of nature to counteract the spreading diversity of scientific, philosophical, and aesthetic discourses and to maintain the illusion of a spiritual male human self with access to divine nature's creative forces. His efforts to bring closure to what could have potentially been a dynamic, open philosophical system comes at the price of excluding the heterogeneous elements that contradict his Eurocentric philosophical monism.

The Challenge of Literature and the Arts

The human desire to make sense of an infinitely changing universe constitutes the impetus for both scientific and artistic exploration. The human subject's relationship to nature must be part of the literary and artistic representations of natural phenomena since nature can be understood only from a human point of view. This is where Goethe's poem coincides with the male humanist ideal of *Bildung*. Corresponding to the didactic objective of universal histories discussed in chapters 1 and 2, the pedagogical intention is foregrounded. The minute description of organic plant growth attempts to facilitate the recipients' comprehension by focusing their attention on the development of one single primordial plant that represents all plant species. The anthropomorphisms illustrate aspects of organic growth and formative processes of social integration into a larger meaningful whole. They thus guide the readers by stimulating them to recognize aspects of their own individual developments reflected in nature.

Likewise, Carus's landscape paintings also attempt to facilitate the comprehension of nature's dynamic vital forces. Juxtaposing cyclical alterations, such as the transition from night and day or the change of the seasons with the infinite vastness of the sky, Carus manages to incorporate nature's transformative force. His portrayal of human beings seems marginal in his landscape paintings. His figures are most often minute observers who marvel at nature's overwhelming grandeur. Carus nevertheless adopts a decisively anthropomorphic point of view as Goethe does in his poem on the metamorphosis of plants in the sense that nature is portrayed from the perspective of human sensibilities and with the intention of achieving a certain emotional effect in the observers. While humans are portrayed as small, they are nevertheless part of nature and can partake of its living beauty. The portrayal of nature as an animate organism establishes affinities with the observers who are compelled to perceive themselves as an integral part of it. The affinities between man and living nature create aesthetic effects that appeal to the viewers' empathy rather than their logical understanding. Nevertheless, depictions of nature have to be in agreement with scientific methodologies and knowledge. Just as Goethe's description of the metamorphosis of a plant is a detailed description of botanical processes based on accurate empirical observation, so are Carus's landscape paintings informed by his botanical, zoological, geological, and anthropological studies.

As could be seen in the course of this study, the integration of scientific and aesthetic pursuits in the service of the *Bildung* (formation) of individuals has informed humanist education since the Enlightenment. Goethe's and Carus's literary and visual creations were influenced by this humanist spirit by demonstrating how the dialectical relationship between art and science, between transitory living nature and eternal essence, or life force, manifested itself in the aesthetics that formed the basis of their artistic productions. Moreover, this chapter has argued that both Goethe and Carus regarded anthropomorphic metaphors as an effective tool for conveying their philosophical and scientific ideas. While the humanist mission of educating a growing literate middle class had remained central for all the authors from Lessing to Herder to Goethe, Schiller, and Humboldt, as well as to Carus, the transformations in the life sciences influenced thematic and aesthetic aspects of literary and artistic productions. In conjunction with new scientific concepts and ideas from Oken's and Schelling's *Naturphilosophie*, external natural phenomena and internal instinctual human nature were considered as life-sustaining, powerful, primal forces and as such given greater attention.

The idea that the human faculties, sensory impressions, emotions, and preconscious drives precede and perhaps even predetermine rational thought undermines claims to scientific objectivity. Yet, I would argue, it is the claim of scientific objectivity that undercuts the hermeneutic process and makes apodictic assertions, including racial, ethnic, and characterological prejudices, possible. Carus's desire to delimit individual, national, and racial identity by quantifying distinctive character traits foreclosed the infinite striving for perfection. The citation at the beginning of this chapter from Goethe's *Wahlverwandtschaften* (*Elective Affinities*) describes man as a true Narcissus who delights in seeing his own image everywhere as a foil that undergirds the universe (HA 6:270). Goethe's character, the Captain, who most likely also voices the author's opinion, is aware of the anthropomorphic perspective that informs human ideas in general. One might ask what the reasons and consequences for man's narcissistic self-projections are. The metonymy suggests that the self-reflecting foil provides the grounding for man's universe, an Archimedean point of reference. Yet by exposing this self-referential procedure as narcissistic, Goethe's text reveals human identity or self-certainty ultimately as delusional. In contrast to the Captain's mindfulness of man's limited horizon, Carus's taxonomic hierarchies and physiognomic premises display a self-certainty that attempts to maintain the boundaries between the privileged Western male subject and its others. Whereas the passage from the *Wahlverwandtschaften* opens up the process of interpretation as an experimental, speculative endeavor that always refers back to an illusory self-identity, Carus forecloses this process by insisting on fixed ethnic, national, and individual identities. Carus's physiognomic studies deviate from the dynamic open-endedness of the Romantic philosophy of nature that informs his *Briefe über die Landschaftsmalerei*, an open-endedness that acknowledges humans' subordinate role in Nature. The incongruence between a dominating subject that takes stock and classifies other living beings with a self-certain claim to objectivity, on the one hand, and the subject's integration into Nature as an infinite and all-powerful dynamic organism, on the other, reveals the gap between Carus's scientific discourse and his aesthetics that undermines his desire to unify science and art.

Notes

1. Progress in the life sciences was based on empirical studies that in many instances contradicted the assumption that the mind could control the body. Instead, these studies provided growing evidence of physiological, chemical, and psychological processes that human consciousness could not manipulate, such as the nervous system, dreams, and emotions.
2. Carus distinguishes his Idealist concept of nature from Schelling's Romantic nature philosophy by rejecting the identity of God and nature. Like Goethe, and in contrast to Schelling, Carus views the divine as a purely spiritual concept that transcends nature that can only be intuited but not grasped (Müller-Tamm 15).
3. The translation is borrowed from *Johann Wolfgang Goethe: The Sufferings of Young Werther and Elective Affinities*, edited by Victor Lange (New York: Continuum, 1990), 155.
4. The figure of the *Hauptmann* complements Eduard's remark on the narcissistic image making by saying, "An allen Naturwesen, die wir gewahr werden, bemerken wir zuerst, daß sie einen Bezug auf sich selbst haben" (We recognize first on all natural beings, which we observe that they have a relationship with themselves) (HA 6:271).
5. If not indicated otherwise, all translations from the German are mine.
6. Here are some titles to which I will refer during my discussion: *Grundzüge allgemeiner Naturbetrachtung* (*Foundations of a General Study of Nature*) (1823); "Rezension über Goethes 'Versuch über die Metamorphose der Pflanzen'" ("Review on Goethe's 'Essay on the Metamorphosis of Plants'") (1832); *Lehrbuch der Zootomie* (*Textbook of Zootomy*) (1834); *Zwölf Briefe über das Erdenleben* (*Twelve Letters on Earthly Life*) (1841); *Goethe: Zu dessen näherem Verständnis* (*Goethe: Toward a Better Understanding*) (1843); *Atlas der Cranioscopie oder Abbildungen der Schädel- und Antlitzformen berühmter oder*

sonst merkwürdiger Personen (*Atlas of Cranioscopy or Images of the Skull and Countenance of Famous or Otherwise Remarkable Persons*) (1845); *Physis: Zur Geschichte des leiblichen Lebens* (*Physis [Nature]: Toward a History of the Embodied Life*) (1851); *Symbolik der menschlichen Gestalt* (*Symbolism of the Human Form*) (1858); *Psyche: Zur Entwicklungsgeschichte der Seele* (*Psyche: Toward an Evolutionary History of the Soul*) (1860); *Briefe über die Landschaftsmalerei, Lebenserinnerungen und Denkwürdigkeiten* (*Letters on Landscape Painting, Remembrances of a Life, and Memorable Matters* (1865–66); *Vergleichende Psychology oder Geschichte der Seele in der Reihenfolge der Tierwelt* (*Comparative Psychology or a History of the Soul in the Sequence/Hierarchy of the Animal Kingdom*) (1866).

7. In 2009 the Deutsche Kunstverlag published an essay volume titled *Carl Gustav Carus: Wahrnehmung und Konstruktion*, which honored the painter's legacy. The publication coincided with an exhibition of his works in the National Gallery in Berlin.
8. *Goethe: Zu dessen näherem Verständnis* (1843); *Goethe, dessen Bedeutung für unsere und die kommende Zeit* (*Goethe, His Significance for Our Time and the Future*) (1863).
9. Gray's study provides illuminating insights on Carus's philosophical influences and his "role as a link between the physiognomic tradition . . . and the racial anthropology generated during the period of the Weimar Republic and under Nazi rule" (133).
10. Carus's aesthetics is the pictorial expression of the beauty of nature and its fundamental and divine laws. Beauty is the visual manifestation of these laws in nature: "Schön könnte . . . im sinnlich Erkennbaren nichts genannt werden, worin nicht das Wesen der Gottheit als ewige Vernunft und Gesetzmäßigkeit sich ausspricht" (No sensory manifestation can be called beautiful that does not express the essence of the divine as eternal reason and order) (CGS 4:57).
11. However, Carus distances himself from Schelling's pantheism by siding with Goethe and claiming that the divine spirit both permeates nature and also transcends it. Accordingly, the identity of idea and reality can never be achieved completely. It can only be approximated through the mutual interpenetration of scientific exploration and human imagination (Müller-Tamm 15–16).
12. Carus reduces scientific progress to a human scale—almost rescinding his indebtedness to scientific progress—in his later *Zwölf Briefe über das Erdleben* (1841) and *Von den Naturreichen* (1843). There science originates in a naïve, intuitive comprehension of nature that humanity possessed in earlier stages of its development, and this immediate knowledge of nature is in many ways superior to scientific knowledge.
13. Schiller's journal *Die Horen* (1795), for instance, was also inspired by the idea to reunite the natural and human sciences (Jahn 303).
14. In his essay *Über das Universum als Fortsetzung des Sinnsystems* (1808) (*On the Universe as Continuation of the Sense System*), Oken states that an organism is none other than a combination of all the universe's activities within a single individual body (10). Likewise, complex organisms are reflections of the simpler organisms that constitute them. Applied to complex organisms, such as mammals or the human body, this means that "das Hirn ist ein oben nach vorn umgebogenes Rückenmark" . . . "die Hirnschale kann nichts anderes sein als die ums Hirn fortgesetzte Wirbelsäule . . . der Mund ist der Magen im Kopf, die Nase ist die Lunge, die Kiefer die Arme und Füße . . ." (the brain is a bone marrow, which has been bent forward on top . . . the cranium cannot be anything but the continuation of the spine, supplemented by the brain . . . the mouth is the stomach in the head, the nose is the lung, the jaws [are] the arms and feet . . .). Lorenz Oken, *Lehrbuch der Naturphilosophie* (Zürich: Schulthess, 1843): 298–99. While Carus is

greatly indebted to Schelling and Oken, he distinguished himself from them in that he tried to integrate empirical knowledge with their holistic point of view. Carus, for instance, distances himself from the "seltsamsten Überstürzungen der Naturphilosophie" (strange abstract presumptions) of Schelling's and Oken's nature philosophies (*Natur und Idee* III–V). Yet while Carus deplores the lack of concrete physiological evidence in the medical profession, he is nevertheless convinced that the gathering of empirical facts is only meaningful if it serves as a spiritual point of reference that is comprehensible and suitable to humans (LeuDe; CGS 5:70). In other words, Carus favors a nature philosophy that is grounded on scientific facts but also has universal significance for the human subject. Oken's renowned claim that the skull is just an extension and repetition of the vertebral column results from the application of Schelling's nature philosophy according to which each organism, or part of an organism, mirrors other living organisms or parts of organisms. Oken's homological anatomy provided Carus with the conceptual tools that enabled him to integrate his scientific interests into a comprehensive philosophy of nature as it established analogies between the historical, developmental, and physiological processes of human life and those of the other living organisms of the natural world (LeuDe 66–67).

15. Thomas Pfau's wide-ranging study situates Goethe's phenomenology of knowledge in the philosophical tradition from the fourteenth-century scholastics to twentieth-century phenomenology and points out that the centrality of *Bildung* radically changed the notion of *difference* in late eighteenth-century thought. Under the influence of the emerging life sciences, *difference* was no longer viewed "as sheer heterogeneity" or as description of "static and dissimilar objects or appearances" but rather as "a conceptual tool allowing the scientific observer to trace *relations* as they shift over time" (Pfau 5–6). The prevailing empiricist methodology, which treated phenomena and material things as inert objects in isolation from a superior subject-position, was no longer adequate for the emerging biological sciences as it could explain neither transformations within the same organisms (ontogeny) nor developmental changes within species (phylogeny). As a result, "the empiricist (originally nominalist) conception of difference as static and disjunctive is gradually supplanted by a dynamic and integrative logic of difference as 'transformation'" (Pfau 6).

16. In the introduction to his "Morphologie," Goethe emphasizes Herder's influence on his botanical and zoological studies: "Meine mühselige, qualvolle Nachforschung ward erleichtert, ja versüßt, indem Herder die Ideen zur Geschichte der Menschheit aufzuzeichnen unternahm. Unser tägliches Gespräch beschäftigte sich mit den Uranfängen der Wasser-Erde, und der darauf von altersher entwickelnden organischen Geschöpfe" (My tedious, excruciating research was facilitated, even enraptured, as Herder began to draft his Ideas on the History of Humankind. Our daily conversation focused on the origins of earth as a planet with water and the resulting ancient development of organic beings) (HA 13:63).

17. The translated passages of this poem are taken from *The Metamorphosis of Plants*, ed. Gordon L. Miller, trans. Douglas Miller (Cambridge MA: MIT P, 2009).

18. In his morphological studies, which appeared almost 20 years after his essay "Die Metamorphose der Pflanzen" yet can be read as introductory remarks, Goethe suggests that scientists of all times have been inspired by the desire to recognize living organisms and to comprehend their functions in their environment as signs of their internal lives (HA 13:55). While he acknowledges the accomplishments of scientific methodologies, which examine the parts of the body in isolation, he also points out that these

"trennenden Bemühungen" (separating efforts) do not observe the "lebendigen Bildungen" (living formations) in the context of their physical functions (HA 13:55). In his introductory explanation about the intention of his morphological studies, Goethe relates the scientific desire to mentally grasp organisms to the mimetic drive in artistic pursuits (HA 13:55). Yet like Lessing, Schiller, and Herder, Goethe attributes a much greater appeal to emotional and sensory impressions than to intellectual insights since they capture the interconnections of different organisms in their living environment (HA 13:53).

19. Erich Trunz suggests that the poem was addressed to Christiane Vulpius, who was an avid gardener and shared Goethe's botanical interests by caring for his plants (HA 1:616).
20. Alexander von Humboldt describes nature in philosophical terms, as a universal system and as a worldview in his opus magnum *Kosmos*.
21. "... allein zugleich fühlst du das rechte Kunstwerk als ein Ganzes, als eine kleine Welt (einen Mikrokosmos) für sich und in sich; das Spiegelbild hingegen erscheint ewig nur als ein Stück als ein Theil der unendlichen Natur, herausgegriffen aus seinen organischen Verbindungen und in widernatürliche Schranken geengt, und nicht, gleich dem Kunstwerke als die in sich beschlossene Schöpfung einer uns verwandten, von uns zu umfassenden geistigen Kraft" (... only at the same time you will feel the true work of art as a whole, as a small world (a microcosm) for itself and in itself; the mirror image, however, appears always only as a piece[,] as a part of infinite nature, that has been removed from its organic relations and forced into unnatural boundaries, and unlike the work of art as the self-contained creation of a kindred spiritual force that we are able to comprehend) (BüLm 39–40).
22. In this context, Carus cites a passage from Schiller's poem *Die Künstler* that emphasizes the civilizing effect of art. Accordingly, art creates the necessary distance to nature that liberates the uncivilized subject from his dependence on the senses and thus humanizes him.
23. Carus refers to one of Goethe's late poems—"Howards Ehrengedächtnis" ("In Memoriam to Howard") as an example for the poetic recreation of scientific awareness at a higher spiritual level (CGS 4:105–7). In Carus's words, Goethe's later poetry assumes a mystical quality and "In diesem Sinne erscheint dann die Kunst als Gipfel der Wissenschaft, indem sie die Geheimnisse der Wissenschaft klar erschaut und anmuthig umhüllt" (appears as the pinnacle of science by clearly perceiving the secrets of science and gracefully veiling them) (CGS 4:107).
24. See, for instance, Johann Gottfried Herder, "Ist die Schönheit des Körpers ein Bote von der Schönheit der Seele?," *Werke*, ed. Ulrich Gaier (Frankfurt am Main: Deutscher Klassiker Verlag, 1985), 1:140, 143–44; Immanuel Kant, "Von den verschiedenen Rassen der Menschen," *Werkausgabe*, ed. Wilhelm Weischedel (Frankfurt am Main: Suhrkamp, 1977), 11:23; "Beobachtungen über das Gefühl des Schönen und des Erhabenen," *Werke*, ed. Artur Buchenau (Berlin: Cassirer, 1912), 2:253; Johann Caspar Lavater, *Physiognomische Fragmente zur Beförderung der Menschenkenntnis und Menschenliebe*, ed. Christoph Siegrist (Stuttgart: Reclam, 1984), 317, 325.
25. Samuel Thomas Soemmering (1755–1830) and Pieter Camper (1722–89) also subscribe to an anthropological hierarchy that contrasts the Caucasians and their ideal beauty that manifested itself in the ancient Greeks to the presumed ugliness of the "Negro" race; see for instance Sömmering, *Über die körperliche Verschiedenheit des Negers vom Europäer* (Frankfurt am Main: Varrentrapp, 1785). Retrieved 16 September 2018

from https://books.google.com/books?id=ZQAOAAAAYAAJ&printsec=frontcover&source=gbs_ge_summary_r&cad=0#v=onepage&q&f=false.
26. Critical portrayals that contrasted bourgeois integrity to a courtly life fraught with deception and intrigue had long been in the making in literary works from the Enlightenment onward, especially in the dramas of the *Sturm und Drang* and *bürgerliches Trauerspiel* (domestic tragedies) by Lessing and Schiller: "If the critique of courtly society painted a picture of an artificial world held together by formalized social conventions rather than by genuine sentiment or interpersonal attachment . . . , then physiognomics provided the civil subject with a countermodel that defined individuality precisely in contradistinction to the counterfeit masquerade of courtly life" (Gray 74).
27. Humboldt emphasizes that the purpose of this gendered reciprocity in nature is not confined to procreation but underlies the principle of living nature in general. By universalizing procreation to "eine eigentümliche Ungleichartigkeit verschiedener Kräfte" (a peculiar heterogeneity of diverse forces), which strive toward an ever higher unity, Humboldt depicts gender distinctions as absolute, natural, and eternal. Albeit presented as an objective natural law with a higher purpose that is supposed to educate humans about the truth of their physical and moral condition, Humboldt's universalization of gender distinctions is based on anthropomorphic projections of procreation onto the physical, intellectual, spiritual, emotional, and moral spheres (Humboldt 287–88). Like Goethe's *Metamorphose der Pflanzen* or Herder's philosophical writings, Humboldt's treatise on gender distinctions deliberately seeks to avoid philosophical and scientific terminology (Humboldt 290). Humboldt's anthropomorphic analogies of human thought processes, especially to procreation, stress the human integration into the entirety of the natural world. "Denn auf der Wechselwirkung allein beruht das Geheimnis der Natur. Ungleichartiger Stoff verknüpft sich, das Verknüpfte wird wiederrum Teil eines größeren Ganzen und bis ins Unendliche hin umfaßt immer jede neue Einheit eine reichere Fülle, dient jede neue Mannigfaltigkeit einer schöneren Einheit" (For nature's secret is entirely based on reciprocity. Heterogeneous matter amalgamates. The amalgamation becomes in turn part of a greater whole. Every new unity comprises a richer abundance up to infinity, and each new heterogeneity becomes a more beautiful unity) (Humboldt 285).
28. "Durch seine Natur schreibt [das Genie] Gesetze vor. Nicht wie die Theorie, welche der Verstand langsam auf Begriffe gründet, gibt es die Regel nicht in toten Buchstaben, sondern unmittelbar durch sich selbst, und mit ihr zugleich den Sporn, sie zu üben. Denn jedes Werk des Genies ist wiederum begeisternd für das Genie, und pflanzt so seine eignes Geschlecht fort" (The genius prescribes laws by his nature. Unlike theory, which human understanding slowly bases on terms, it does not provide rules in dead letters, but rather immediately through himself and along with them the impetus to exert them. Every work of the Genius inspires the genius in turn and propagates his own species) (Humboldt, "Geschlechtsunterschied" 290).

CHAPTER 7

Karl Marx's and Ludwig Feuerbach's Materialism in Gottfried Keller's "Kleider Machen Leute"

The socioeconomic transformations in mid-nineteenth-century Europe had a profound impact on "the human condition." In fact, the expression itself became problematic because human existence was increasingly determined by constantly changing socioeconomic factors and had to be viewed in historical rather than ontological terms. Gottfried Keller's novella "Kleider machen Leute" ("Clothes Make People") (1874) encapsulates the shift from the idealized subject-nature relationship to a consumerist subject-object dialectics.[1] The novella's title succinctly illustrates the transformation from the traditional village community, called Seldwyl, where "Leute machen Kleider" (people make clothes), to a striving capitalist society where commodities and possessions define the status of people. This chapter interprets Gottfried Keller's novella against the background of Idealist residues in the materialist philosophies of Ludwig Feuerbach and Karl Marx. My analysis of Keller's novella will present Feuerbach, Marx, and Keller and their engagement with key concepts, such as alienation, objectification, reification, idealization, and nostalgia in the context of bourgeois society's growing consumerism and depletion of spiritual values.

Keller shared with Feuerbach and Marx the conviction that Idealist concepts unduly privileged the power of the human intellect over and against bodily needs and the necessities of the material world. As Hegelian dialectic has shown, antitheses generally contain remnants of the propositions they refute. This is no different for Feuerbach's, Marx's, and Keller's anti-Idealist views. Martin Jay, for instance, points to the Idealist legacy of Western Marxist philosophical ideas by stating apodictically, "Western Marxism recognized its true origin in the tradition of philosophical critique that began with Kant and German Idealism" (Jay 2). Not only is Marxist theory concerned with the physical, economic, and social welfare of human beings, it also promotes ideas that originated in the bourgeois emancipation movement, such as liberty, equality, and social justice. In this sense, one could view it as a radicalization of the humanist philosophies of the Enlightenment, as it extended middle-class emancipation with the aim of empowering a growing, socially and economically disenfranchised segment of the population: the working class or the proletariat.[2] While Idealist philosophies from Kant to Hegel are based on metaphysical assumptions of a meaningful nature, a teleology that to some extent predisposes the human destiny, Marxism ascribes a stronger—and yet in some respects weaker—agency to humans and thus to the consequences of their actions.[3]

A contrastive analysis of a selection of Feuerbach's and Marx's materialist theoretical texts and Keller's novella reveals distinctions between philosophical discourses and literary fiction. It regards Keller's fictitious text as an experiment that enacts the mid-nineteenth-century clash between bourgeois attitudes that are still under the spell of their Idealist traditions and a capitalist economy that threatens to undermine bourgeois romantic fantasies. However, in Keller's novella—and contrary to Marx—the belief in love, individual freedom, and family persists and serves as a background for the narrator's ironic perspective that satirizes Romantic nostalgia in view of an expanding consumerism at the onset of the industrial age. The irony in Keller's text is based on the contradiction between what Marxists would call "false consciousness" and the socioeconomic conditions of capitalist reality.[4] While Marx portrayed the class conflict between the impoverished masses and a capitalist oligarchy as inevitable, Keller's novella focuses on the mental and emotional disposition of concrete, albeit fictional, characters.

Hannah Arendt has pointed to a weakness of materialist theories by suggesting that these discourses are unable to render the imponderables of concrete interactions between unique individuals. By asserting that any given subject's "specific, objective worldly interests ... constitute ... something which *inter-est*, which lies between people" cannot adequately be represented by materialist theories, Arendt puts her finger on a crucial issue of this chapter: namely the significance of literary enactments of specific intersubjective relations and communication (Arendt, *Human Condition* 182). Because this "subjective in-between is not tangible" and is nevertheless "no less real than the world of things we visibly have in common," it can only be adequately rendered through literary or artistic reenactments. I am quoting Arendt's assertion at length because of its relevance for my argument and for this entire study:

> The disclosure of the "who" through speech, and the setting of a new beginning through action, always fall into an already existing web where their immediate consequences can be felt. Together they start a new process which eventually emerges as the unique life story of the newcomer, affecting uniquely the life stories of all those with whom he comes into contact. . . . These stories may then be

recorded in documents and monuments, they may be visible in use-objects or art-works.... Although everybody started his life by inserting himself into the human world through action and speech, nobody is the author or producer of his own life story.... Somebody began it and is its subject in the twofold sense of the word, namely, its actor and sufferer, but nobody is its author. (Arendt, *Human Condition* 184)

Keller's novella illustrates this in-between situation of the human subject by emphasizing the protagonist's insertion into a web of preexisting cultural practices that determine his reactions from the outset. Strapinski, a penniless tailor on his search for employment, is introduced as a quiet, passive antihero who simply reacts to situations by adjusting his behavior toward others in a most accommodating, nearly self-effacing way. He never willfully initiates his actions but instead finds himself caught up in causally interconnected events that take him from episode to episode. The novel begins with the description of his appearance, the most distinctive feature of his otherwise rather modest and unremarkable personality (KSW 5:5). The description introduces him not by name but by profession as a tailor, sporting an elegant black overcoat that belies his economic despair and, together with his long black hair and mustache, gives him a romantic air (ibid.). His pitiable situation as a hungry, weary wayfarer is induced by the bankruptcy of his master tailor and forces him to look for employment elsewhere. In other words, he is from the outset at the mercy of fortune (ibid.). And it is a string of fortuitous events that carries him in the carriage of a "fremden Grafen" (an unknown count) to an inn in the Swiss town Goldach, where he is mistaken for the owner of the carriage, received as a person of high standing, and wined and dined (KSW 5:12–13). Little by little he accepts the role of his fake existence as a count from Poland that the citizens project onto him, partially because he is afraid of both the financial and moral debt that his disclosure of his false identity would exact on him and partially because he is gradually getting used to leading an agreeable and privileged existence for the first time in his life. What complicates matters even further is his romantic involvement with the mayor's daughter, Nettchen, who falls in love with him not knowing his false identity. This intimate love relationship, although it initially prevents him from giving up his forged existence for fear of losing his beloved, eventually forces him to open up and confess his true identity and tell the story of his childhood (KSW 5:51–56).

One could argue that Strapinski's portrayal as a dependent, powerless member of the proletariat is in agreement with Marx's notion of the subject's determination by socioeconomic conditions. After all, the narrator's comments stress the characters' economically and socially conditioned behavior. Yet, in spite of his lack of agency, Strapinski is presented as a human being with a personal history that makes him unique beyond his socioeconomic conditioning. For instance, Strapinski's passivity is motivated by both his mother's disadvantaged social status and her ambition to imitate people of higher standing. Even though she is well meaning in envisioning a better future for her son, she is also portrayed as manipulative. Her overprotective, smothering behavior prevents him from becoming self-reliant, which in turn contributes to his passivity (KSW 5:53–54). In other words, although the protagonist's economic situation determines his life to a large extent, his close relationship to his mother as well as particular incidents of his upbringing are equally important.

The fairy-tale-like love story with a happy ending is nevertheless set against the background of a changing socioeconomic reality. It captures the nostalgic longing for a bygone Romantic era that has been superseded by an alienating consumerism, a consumerism that threatens to relegate the role of the subject to that of a commodity, as the novella's title suggests. The novella is self-reflective as it satirizes the opportunist instrumentalization of bourgeois ideals. Keller's ironic portrayal of the villagers' hypocrisy in an increasingly consumerist world demands a critical distance to bourgeois ideology and its Enlightenment premises. Keller's omniscient third-person narrator creates this distance, vacillating between and commenting on events and characters from a superior perspective on both the consumerist and romantic points of view. Thus the narrator's ironic detachment can be seen as an expression of his transitional position that regards the nostalgic yearning for a bygone nineteenth-century culture as disingenuous but at the same time makes fun of the rising consumerist attitude of the upwardly mobile bourgeoisie.

Keller (1819–90), whose life span coincided with that of Marx (1818–83), shared with the latter a fascination with Ludwig Feuerbach's materialist philosophy. Regardless of Marx's later abandonment of the Feuerbachian framework, Feuerbach's critique of Idealist philosophy and Christianity were significant for Marx's anthropological and philosophical views. In addition, Marx maintained throughout his writings aspects of humanist thought, such as alienation and the notion of a well-educated, free individual. Contrary to widespread popular opinion, Marx's philosophy does not exclusively focus on macroeconomic issues that concern the masses and neglect the individual human being. Marx has often been criticized for his *"credulous faith in human nature"* that ignores its selfishness, greed, and aggressive competition (Eagleton, *Why Marx* 64). According to Terry Eagleton, some Marxists have responded to this critique by claiming that if "Marx overlooked human nature, it was because he did not believe in the idea" (ibid. 79). While it is true that Marx rejects the idea of an unalterable human nature that is independent of social and economic influences, he does believe in distinctive characteristics of the human species. However, his concept of the human is different from that of his Idealist predecessors. For one thing, Marx rejects the essentialist separation of body and mind, which for most neo-humanists, such as Kant, Schiller, and Humboldt, remains the defining difference between animals and humans (MEW 3:21).

In order to illuminate the transition from Idealist concepts to Feuerbach's materialist philosophy, I will briefly summarize some developments that contributed to the reversal of the mind-matter dichotomy, which resonates with Keller's novella's reversal of subject-object relations and eventually leads to a reevaluation of the Idealist ethics and aesthetics. To be sure, eighteenth-century humanists proudly considered themselves as executors of the Platonic legacy, a role that concurred with their mission to transform society through the power of ideas, knowledge, and education, as well as their demand for spiritual freedom and religious tolerance.[5] Moreover, the classical legacy of the mind-body dualism had been reinforced by Christian ethics and the bourgeois code of honor, both of which viewed bodily desires with contempt and aspired to distinguish bourgeois virtues from the moral leniency of courtly society. Consequently, the mind-body duality remained an essential part of neo-humanist thought at a time when the empirical sciences were also trying to maintain categorical distinctions between species, races, genders, and ethnic and social groups that privileged the Caucasian male intellectual. Kant's *Anthropologie in pragmatischer Hinsicht* (*Anthropology from a Pragmatic Point of View*) (1798), Lavater's *Physiognomische Fragmente* (*Physiognomic Fragments*) (1775), and Herder's anthropological studies are only a few examples of such attempts (see also Gilroy 46, 58–61).[6] While Herder and Schiller still adhered to the superiority of the spirit and its Idealist metaphysics, their philosophical and theoretical writings also emphasized the power of instinctual needs that entered into the mind-body dialectic. Yet, in spite of all the efforts to safeguard the holistic Idealism of Romantic *Naturphilosophie*—described in the previous chapter—the scientific advances and social transformations of the industrial age begged for radical changes in conceptualizing the human subject's physical and mental constitution and role in society.

While Keller is still very much indebted to traditional bourgeois values, he nevertheless criticizes their deceptive idealization and their hypocritical invocation to cover up their actual devaluation in a consumerist society. Keller's novella addresses the tension between the Idealist assumption of an essential human nature and the influences of a social, historical, and cultural reality. It challenges the notion of a stable human identity as it portrays the life-transforming socioeconomic influences of an impending modern society, in which individual autonomy was no longer possible (Widdig 110). In spite of its unfavorable view of the growing commercialization, Keller's novella faults capitalist conditions indirectly by exposing their alienating effects on human behavior. More specifically, it addresses the anachronistic discrepancies between the Idealist assumptions of bourgeois ideology and socioeconomic reality.

Keller ironizes the transition from the Romantic privileging of spirituality to the recognition of the urgent and undeniable needs of the body already at the beginning of his novella when the poor journeyman and tailor Wenzel

Strapinski arrives at an inn in a fancy carriage. Strapinski, who is offered a ride in the carriage, looks very distinguished in his elegant black overcoat. His appearance and means of transportation inspire the innkeeper and his employees to think of him as a "geheimnisvoller Prinz oder Grafensohn" (mysterious nobleman) (KSW 5:13). They cling to this presumption and interpret every move and gesture as confirmation of their prejudice. Strapinski's reticence and awkward use of utensils is not interpreted as "Blödigkeit" (bashfulness), as the narrator calls it, but as a sign of his refinement and good manners (KSW 5:17). While Strapinski initially attempts to control his feelings of hunger for fear of being charged for a meal that he cannot afford, his bodily needs eventually win the battle when he, after giving in to the host's encouragement to drink more wine, loses his inhibitions and regains a healthy appetite. The ironic depiction of his failed attempt to maintain his composure reveals the body's undeniable instinctual needs. Keller's critique of Idealist pretentions becomes even more pronounced as the inn's host reinterprets Strapinski's change from reticence to unrestrained gluttony as a sign of "true" commanding power: "... so hab' ich ... nur Generäle und Kapitelsherren essen sehen!" (I have only seen generals and abbots eat like this!) (KSW 5:19).

This first episode of Strapinski's sham performance as a Polish nobleman, like many others that follow, reveals more about the citizens of Goldach and the socioeconomic background of their ulterior motives than about Strapinski himself, who is for the most part silent. The innkeeper is fascinated by the idea of hosting a mysterious celebrity because he and his business could profit from the honor. The host makes every effort to please his guest by offering him the very best and most lavish meal. He does not even heed the cook's warning that the sumptuous dinner may cost too much in order to make a profit (KSW 5:15). While he justifies his generosity with his honor and his professional integrity, he is also motivated by the hope that his hospitality toward his presumed celebrity guest will become known far and wide and raise his own standing:

> Thut nichts, es ist um die Ehre! Das bringt mich nicht um; dafür soll ein großer Herr, wenn er durch unsere Stadt reis't, sagen können, er habe ein ordentliches Essen gefunden, obgleich er ganz unerwartet und im Winter gekommen sei! Es soll nicht heißen, wie von den Wirten zu Seldwyl, die alles Gute selber fressen und den Fremden die Knochen vorsetzen! (KSW 5:15)

> (Never mind, this is a matter of honor! This does not kill me; because a man of high standing who travels through our town should be able to announce that he was served a decent meal, although he arrived unexpectedly and in the winter. No one should be able to say about us what they say about the innkeepers of Seldwyl, who are known to eat all their good food themselves and serve the bones to the foreigners.[7])

The passage not only addresses Goldach's competition with the more traditional and allegedly less-welcoming neighboring town of Seldwyl but also touches on society's transformation due to an expanding economy, which sets the two villages apart. The innkeeper is typical of the Goldach citizens, who consider themselves as cosmopolitan and attempt to gain a good reputation beyond the village's borders. Whereas the more provincial Seldwyler are still upholding their local traditions and care less about what others think of them, the Goldacher's entrepreneurial cosmopolitanism comes with the danger of making them corruptible. For the affluent Goldach society, the mysterious stranger provides a welcome distraction from their comfortable but monotonous daily lives. His professional skill as a tailor allowed him to make his own coat that looks far too elegant and expensive for what a typical artisan could afford. Wearing this coat, Strapinsky projects an image of a mysterious nobleman to those who do not know him. In the Goldach citizens' view, the coat and a Polish fur cap lend him "ein edles und romantisches Aussehen" (a noble and romantic air) (KSW 5:11) and define him as an exotic stranger who embodies a mysterious and possibly adventurous life that the Goldach citizens lack. Thus Strapinski's coat inspires in the citizens a nostalgic longing, a longing that by the mid-nineteenth century has become anachronistic and yet fulfills the modern need for glamour and adventure in a mundane consumerist society. For the citizens of Goldach, the coat means more than simply an expensive piece of clothing, becoming instead a signifier for cultural refinement. Strapinski's black coat is not just a material object but embodies the ideals that society associates with certain objects. In view of the waning of transcendental values in a consumerist society, material objects themselves are endowed with mystique of a bygone era, such as the chivalric qualities associated with nobility. Ironically the idolization of material objects results in the degradation of the human agents to mere objects themselves. In other words, Strapinski's black coat is a symbol of the dialectic between the idealization of material objects and the subject's objectification in a free market economy, as my textual analysis will show.

What makes Strapinski fascinating to the Goldach citizens is his foreignness, his melancholic flair and appearance. Keller obviously parodies clichés of romantic popular novels that were in vogue at the time and appealed to the readers' sentimental yearnings (Widdig 109). Strapinski's delicate features and melancholic looks invite speculations that he might be a Polish piano virtuoso, like Chopin (KSW 5:37), or a nationalist freedom fighter who has been expelled during the November uprising of 1830 (KSW 5:29).[8] Keller's novella obviously satirizes the sentimentality of the town's bourgeois establishment that projects its desires for adventure onto the poor tailor from Seldwyl. At the same time it exposes the commodification of sentimental emotions. The irony is that the bourgeois members of this society judge people and things according to their outward appearances but still cherish romantic fantasies that are out of step with their consumerist values.

In contrast to the Seldwyl citizens' pride in their local traditions, Goldach's entrepreneurship, trade, and manufacturing have created an upwardly mobile society that has resulted in a wealthy bourgeois citizenry. This class is made up of merchants, accountants, entrepreneurs, and civil servants who have a yearning for a less prosaic, more glorious existence. Strapinski fills a void in this respect because Goldachers' affiliation with a member of the Polish nobility or perhaps even an artist would make their own life more illustrious. The narrator's description of the group of regulars at the town inn provides an explanation for the Goldachers' objectification of Strapinski as a mysterious nobleman: "... es waren diejenigen Mitglieder guter Häuser, welche ihr Leben lang zu Hause blieben, deren Verwandte und Genossen aber in aller Welt saßen, weswegen sie die Welt sattsam zu kennen glaubten" (... they were those members of families of good standing, who stayed back home their whole lives long, while their relatives and comrades were placed all over the world, which is why they believed to know the world well enough to be self-satisfied) (KSW 5:20). They offer Strapinski cigars and other tobacco products from all over the world to show their cosmopolitan sophistication (KSW 5:21). They soon invite Strapinski—now called Count Strapinski due to a rumor that the coachman spread—for a ride and introduce him to their favorite pastime: playing cards. The ironic comment of Keller's narrator that the Goldacher treat the tailor like a precious gift underlines Strapinski's objectification (KSW 5:28).

The distinction between a human being's physical manifestation and its idealized essence has also wider implications for the novella's structure, which is based on the principle of *Umkehrung* (reversal) (Honold 67, 70). For instance, the Seldwyl citizens' allegorical reenactment of Strapinski's advancement from tailor to count, which publicly exposes his true identity at the celebration of his engagement to Nettchen, dramatizes the novella's motto, *Kleider machen Leute* (KSW 5:40–43). The reversal of subject and object, or *Sein und Schein*, expands on Marx's assertion that "it is not consciousness of men that determines their being but on the contrary, their social being that determines their consciousness" by depicting this dualistic mind-body relationship as a dialectic process (Marx and Engels, Preface). For instance, Strapinski's coat as an object is not just a precious commodity but also an emblem for his image as Polish count. Likewise his slender, frail appearance is a sign of both the domination of the spirit over the flesh and its physical manifestation in the stereotype of the Romantic artist. The Goldach citizens view the coat as symbol for Strapinski's inner being. Yet their inability to recognize their false assumptions about Strapinski as self-projections has consequences in empirical reality because it determines their social interactions. The reversal of declaring the idealization as real and the subject's lived reality as insignificant, deceptive, and unreliable can be extended to Idealist philosophies as well. While for Idealist philosophers, like Kant and Hegel, the *I* is "an abstract, an only thinking being" whose body does not belong to its essence, Feuerbach's materialist philosophy would claim, "Ich bin ein wirkliches, ein sinnliches Wesen, der Leib gehört zu meinem Wesen; ja der Leib in seiner Totalität ist mein Ich, mein Wesen selber" (I am a real, sensuous being: the body belongs to my essence; indeed, the body in its totality is my self [*mein Ich*], my essence itself) (Feuerbach, *Sämmtliche Werke* 2:325).

The discrepancy between Idealist appearance and plain reality or *Schein* (appearance) and *Sein* (being) is most obvious in a scene where Strapinski takes a walk through the town of Goldach and gets the impression "daß er in ein moralisches Utopien hineingeraten wäre" (that he has been transposed into a moral utopia) (KSW 5:32). Strapinski's own miraculous transformation from poor tailor to Polish aristocrat confirms this impression, and therefore he really believes that the inscriptions and symbols on the fronts of the houses represent the lived reality in the dwellings (KSW 5:30–32). Like Strapinski's coat, the external appearances of the houses do not meet the expectations they evoke. Put in structuralist terms, the signifiers do not necessarily correspond to what they signify, and yet some of them do in unexpected ways (see also Lehrer 576).[9] For instance, the building with the inscription "zur Verfassung" (constitution; literally "framing") houses a cooper who "einfaßte" (framed) little buckets and barrels (KSW 5:31). In other words, the abstract idea of the constitution or framework of a state's political and ethical principles has been taken literally and degraded to the production of material products: the framing of containers. One could also say that the constitution, a symbol of civility and civic pride, has taken the form of an ordinary commodity. The commodification of ethical values is also foregrounded on the building named "zur Geduld" (patience) that has degenerated to housing the "Schuldenschreiber" (debt collector) (KSW 5:31).[10] In contrast, Strapinski literally embodies and wears the product that he made but that has been endowed with an aura that evokes the Romantic imagination. All these discrepancies between *Schein* and *Sein* stress either the denigration of abstract values or the idealization of material objects. Strapinski's illusion of living in a utopian society is caused by the Idealist mottos on the façades of buildings that evoke false expectations. Although bourgeois emancipation materialized in the commercialization of life, the Goldach citizens are determined to hold on to their Idealist beliefs that allow them to justify their leisurely lifestyles. Goldach's obsession with economic prosperity and its euphemistic idealization is also revealed in the inscriptions on the most modern buildings that characterize the "poetic imagination" of their owners, who are "Fabrikanten, Bankiere, Spediteure und ihrer Nachahmer" (factory owners, bankers, owners of delivery services, and their imitators) (KSW 5:31). The names evoke idyllic sceneries and clichéd images such as "Rosenthal, Morgenthal, Sonnenberg, Veilchenburg, Jugendgarten," etc. (ibid.). The narrator emphasizes the economic undercurrent by mentioning that compounds of women's names indicate a "Weibergut" (dowry) (ibid.).

The inversion of the subject-object relations in the novella's title, *Kleider machen Leute*, reflects Feuerbach's influence on Keller. In *Das Wesen des Christentums* (*The Essence of Christianity*), Feuerbach's most well-known work, the philosopher describes the alienating character of religion, which can be attributed to the fact that human beings first project their essence *outside of themselves* before they discover it in themselves. In other words, human beings encounter their own projection as a foreign object—in this case God—and recognize only later that object as their own essence.[11] This type of objectification is a universal human trait and applies to all religions, according to Feuerbach. "Primitive" religions resort more often to anthropomorphisms that the more advanced religions consider idolatrous. For instance, monotheistic religions reject the anthropomorphic depictions of the Greek Gods, which are obviously representations of certain human traits. Monotheistic religions, like Christianity, attempt to conceal divine personifications by prohibiting concrete visual depictions and endowing divinity with purely abstract characteristics.[12] For Feuerbach, the human subject's denial to recognize the anthropomorphic characteristics of the divine being is where alienation takes place. In Keller's novella, the Goldach citizens' inability to recognize "Count Strapinsiki" as an idealized projection of themselves corresponds to Feuerbach's concept of alienation.[13]

Marx transposes Feuerbach's process of alienation onto the process of production. Proletarian subjects are unable to recognize themselves in their products because of the division of labor and the expropriation of the finished product:

> The object, which labor produces—labor's product—confronts it as *something alien*, as a *power independent* of the producer. . . . Under these economic conditions this realization of labor appears as *loss of realization* for the workers; objectification as *loss and bondage* to it, appropriation *as estrangement, as alienation*." (PDF Archive of Marx and Engels; Economic-Philosophic-Manuscripts-1844. pdf, 28; italics in the source)

From an outside point of view, Strapinski's coat is a symbol of alienation because it is a manifestation of the objectification of the subject; in other words, Strapinski's self-worth is closely tied to the clothes that he possesses. However, from Strapinski's point of view, the coat is the true expression of his identity since it is the product of his own labor. In a sense, the coat could be considered as a work of art were it not for the existing web of cultural signifiers that predetermine Strapinski's notion of what he deems to be his distinct, unique identity. Strapinski's "self-expression" through his apparel and appearance has already become a convention. Nevertheless, the coat works as a symbol of alienation on several levels. It does not simply stand for the desire of economic wealth. As mentioned earlier, the coat serves also as a signifier for a Romantic outsider:

> Er nahm sich mit seiner gewölbten Stirne, seinem lieblichen, aber schwermütigen Mundbärtchen, seinen glänzenden, schwarzen Locken, seinen dunklen Augen im Wehen seines faltigen Mantels vortrefflich aus; der Abendschein und das Säuseln der Bäume über ihm erhöhte den Eindruck, so daß die Gesellschaft ihn von Ferne mit Aufmerksamkeit und Wohlwollen betrachtete. (KSW 5:25)
>
> (He appeared magnificent in his undulating creased coat with his arched forehead, his lovely but sentimental little mustache, his shiny black curls, his dark eyes; the evening glow and the softly whispering trees above him enhanced the impression, so that the party observed him from afar attentively and benevolently.)

From the narrator's superior point of view, Strapinski's appearance can no longer be regarded as a genuine form of self-expression, as it imitates an objectified image of the Romantic artist. The Goldach citizens' nostalgic longing to be part of the bygone artistic era points to the void in their consumerist everyday life. The established Goldach citizens, who have both the financial means and free time to spend their time playing cards for money, are certainly not complying with Marx's utopia of a self-determined existence, even though they are not subject to alienating labor conditions and capitalist exploitation. Their economic independence affords them a leisurely lifestyle, which is presented, however, as depleted of meaning. They gamble for money to increase the excitement that their everyday lives lack. Keller underlines their nostalgic indulgence in romantic sentiments by juxtaposing the love story of Wenzel and Nettchen to the depiction of mercantile society. Strapinski's docile acceptance of his assigned new role as a Polish count makes him the perfect antihero, who, in contrast to the protagonists of the *Bildungsromane* (novels of education), is entirely passive. Although he makes some fainthearted attempts to escape the grip of his "benefactors," he is so ashamed of having to disappoint their expectations that he feels he has to accept his new identity.

In a staged allegorical ritual reminiscent of the Swiss *Fastnachtstradition* (carnival tradition) that represents the social estates of a pre-capitalist, feudal society based on rank and order, the Seldwyl citizens expose Strapinski as an impostor (Honold 70). This public humiliation at his engagement celebration leads him eventually to confess and tell the story of his life to his fiancée, who follows him after he leaves the engagement party in shame. No sooner than when the deceived Nettchen asks who he is do we get to know him. Strapinski's narrative establishes the protagonist as someone who deserves empathy rather than punishment. With his confession, the protagonist finds his identity as a human being who must not be reduced to a cultural icon or a representative of a social class. The protagonist's narrative can be taken as an example for literature's ability to capture intangible interactions with other people that disclose the subject's uniqueness through speech. It illustrates the performative advantages of literary texts over what Hannah Arendt criticized as the shortcoming of theoretical materialist discourses, namely that they are unable to do justice to the nuances of human interactions and intersubjective relations (Arendt, *Human Condition* 183). On a diegetic level, Wenzel Strapinski is capable of communicating his individuality by telling the story of his life and thus becoming worthy of Nettchen's love. The narrative indicates the protagonist's individualization by disclosing his first name for the first time, whereas in the past he has always been referred to either as Strapinski, Count Strapinski, or simply as a tailor. On an aesthetic level, Wenzel's confessional mediates the subtleties of interpersonal relationships that theoretical discourses often lack.[14]

The literary presentation of his life story cannot be adequately rendered without repeating it in full length. In view of the limited space I will try to summarize the story that leads up to the climax, which wins over Nettchen's heart after having been deceived into believing Strapinski's fake existence as a count. We learn that young Wenzel decided to stay with his mother out of loyalty in spite of a tempting offer to become the protégé of the lady of the manor, his mother's employer, and receive an education that would have opened the doors to a brighter future in the capital (KSW 5:53). It speaks to Wenzel's integrity that he does not change his mind despite the lady's daughter's pleas to join them. It seems that he rejects the prospects of professional and economic success in view of his indebtedness to his mother and the possibility that she might die lonely. After letting Nettchen know how hard it was to withstand the daughter's pleas, Wenzel recalls her resemblance to Nettchen:

> Wenzel aber streckte den Arm aus, zeigte mit dem Finger auf sie, wie wenn er einen Geist sähe, und rief: "Dieses habe ich auch schon erblickt. Wenn jenes Kind zornig war, so hoben sich so, wie jetzt bei Ihnen, die schönen Haare um Stirne und Schläfe ein wenig aufwärts, daß man sie sich bewegen sah, und so war es auch zuletzt auf dem Felde in jenem Abendglanze." (KSW 5:56)

> (Wenzel extended his arm, pointed a finger at her as if he saw a ghost and exclaimed: "This I have already perceived. Whenever that child was angry her beautiful hair around her forehead and temples lifted itself a little, just as yours right now, so that one could see it move, and this is how it was at last on the field in the evening glow.")

The dramatization of the narrative through verbatim quotations permits the enactment of immediate emotions. The spontaneous identification of the unforgettable "schöne Kind" (beautiful child) with Nettchen is evidence of Strapinski's true love for her and prompts her avowal to never leave him (KSW 5:56–57). The romantic love scene is interrupted, however, by the omniscient narrator's comment: "Die allzeit etwas kokette Mutter Natur hatte hier eines ihrer Geheimnisse angewendet, um den schwierigen Handel zu Ende zu führen" (The always coquettish mother nature applied one of her secret means at this moment to bring this difficult bargain to a conclusion) (KSW 5:56). The contrast between the emotional immediacy of the verbatim re-presentation of the tender moment and the narrator's distancing voice underlines the text's self-reflective irony by playing with Romantic conventions. In other words, the narrator's voice once again provides a critical commentary by exposing the idealization of love as a fictional illusion. Nettchen's matter-of-fact response to Wenzel's suggestion to move to "unbekannte Weiten" (unknown distances) with her and "geheimnisvoll romantisch dort zu leben in stillem Glücke" (lead a mysteriously romantic life in peaceful happiness)—"Keine Romane mehr" (No more romantic storytelling)—underlines the novella's anti-Idealist stance (KSW 5:57).

Although Keller's novella satirizes the citizens' progressing alienation in capitalist society by contrasting the Goldach society to what seems the more "authentic" way of life in the traditional village of Seldwyl, scholarship has pointed out that Strapinski's public outing as an impostor at his wedding shows an uncivilized cruelty that was typical of pre-capitalist feudalism (see, for instance Widdig 111–12). Thus, the self-righteous integrity of the Seldwyl society is by no means presented as flawless. After all, the Seldwyler citizens also seem to be motivated by envy, always looking to outsmart their more openly pretentious rivals. Keller's sympathies seem to lie with his unmasked, inconspicuous protagonist who—despite or rather because of his flaws—has much more in common with the author's mundane contemporary middle-class citizens than the glorified, unique individual the Goldach citizens like to see in him and in themselves. In the end, Strapinski, moves back to Goldach after a successful business career as a *Tuchhändler* (manufacturer of clothes) and becomes part of the town's prosperous society without leaving a penny to the Seldwyl society (KSW 5:62).

Keller's ironic depiction of the Goldach merchant society is, in spite of all its sarcastic asides toward capitalist profiteering, a sympathetic portrayal of human corruptibility. It is therefore less a call for a materialist ideology than a fictitious depiction of a mid-nineteenth-century social microcosm that exposes the disingenuous nature of humanist idealizations in view of an alienating commercialization of society at the dawn of the modern industrial age. While Keller's critique of the hypocritical instrumentalization of humanist values anticipates the anti-Idealist stance of fin-de-siècle literature, the novella also upholds bourgeois values, such as family, and private enterprise. The fact that Wenzel and Nettchen marry, have children, become successful entrepreneurs, and can hardly be distinguished from the rest of the bourgeois establishment does not mean, however, that the novella promotes opportunist conformity. It is Nettchen who stands by Wenzel during his most embarrassing ordeal. She proves her honor by rejecting Melchior Böhni, Wenzel's rival, who offers to marry her after having plotted to expose Wenzel's identity. She counters her father's advice to marry Böhni in order to save her honor with her steadfast response that it is precisely her honor that would prevent her from marrying Böhni (KSW 5:59). In other words, Keller's narrator maintains that it is possible to preserve one's integrity in a consumerist society. The fact that Nettchen is capable of accepting Wenzel, who turns out to be rather modest after the romantic mystique has been stripped away, expresses the belief in middle-class values, such as honesty, loyalty, and self-determination within the boundaries of her preexisting social reality.

Notes

1. Keller's novella has a complicated history of publication. Although the text was completed by 1872, it did not appear until 1874 in the novella collection *Die Leute von Seldwyla*. For a more detailed history of its creation, see KSW 21:39–51.
2. This argument has been made by those who defend Marx against Stalinism. The topic of alienation in the modern age is not only taken up by Marx but becomes a central cultural critique of neo-Marxism from Lukàcs on to the Frankfurt School (Jay 2, 43–55).
3. To be sure, the Enlightenment ideal of individual autonomy bestows inviolability and power on the uniqueness of each human being. This exceptionality is, however, prescribed or even constrained by the divine laws of the universe, as Kant's and Herder's philosophies, as well as many of Goethe's and Schiller's literary works, have demonstrated. Kant's dictum of "the starry heavens above me and the moral law within me" that testifies to a universal order that the individual has to obey; Herder's theodicy that is reflected in history and can be intuited by great geniuses, such as Shakespeare; Goethe's pantheistic view of nature, expressed, for instance, at the end of *Goetz von Berlichingen*; or Hegel's *Zeitgeist* are only a few examples of the quasi-religious metaphysics that prevailed in the literary and philosophical works of the Idealist period.
4. Engels used the term rather than Marx, but Marxists frequently use it to refer to members of the working class who do not want to view themselves as part of the proletariat but identify with bourgeois ideology. This phenomenon is also central to Siegfried Kracauer's study *Die Angestellten (The Salaried Masses)* (1930), which explores the tendency among employees to identify with the bourgeoisie in spite of their economic dependence.
5. The privileging of mind over body goes back to Socrates and has informed Western philosophy ever since. This categorical distinction can be interpreted as a strategy of self-empowerment that legitimizes human hegemony over the entire nonhuman world. Since humans have the power to control the body's instinctual calls, they were considered independent of material necessities. Historian Joseph Fracchia gives a lucid description of the consequences of Western philosophy's omission of the body from the sublime realm of thought: "With the body and material needs deprived of any essential place in the definition of freedom, so, too, was the question of social and economic equality. The locus of freedom was thus effectively displaced onto, and limited solely to, the political sphere in which the individual could appear as a free citizen, not as a materially dependent animal. Thus, along with the definition of the relationship between subject and object as one of knowledge, the definition of freedom in legal and political terms became part of the legacy of philosophy" (Fracchia, *Aufhebung* 156).

6. Humanism can be interpreted as an attempt to establish and preserve Western bourgeois values as the ethical norm. Yet, the intellectual narcissism of Western male literati may have seemed much less obvious from an Enlightenment perspective because their values were also considered revolutionary and liberating. Although the Western philosophical legacy became constitutive for the cultural dominance of the bourgeoisie and the gradual democratization of the feudal order, scientific and social developments began to question the belief in the subject's unity and autonomy, the very center of bourgeois ideology. As shown in previous chapters, advances in the life sciences proved the subject's limited power over the instincts long before Freud. Scientific experiments confirmed the uncontrollable reactions of the nervous system. The specialization of scientific and empiricist methodologies, rapidly advancing industrialization, and the alienating urbanization with its poverty-stricken shantytowns were factors that challenged some of the Idealist premises of neoclassical humanism, such as individual autonomy.
7. If not indicated otherwise, all translations from the German are mine.
8. The Western European bourgeoisie greeted the struggles for national autonomy, especially the Polish uprising against the Russian occupation, with empathy. Gottfried Keller was a member of a committee that supported the Polish liberation movement (Widdig 118; see also Selbmann).
9. Lehrer insinuates that this type of "semiotic thinking[, which] was wholly within the scope of nineteenth-century anthropology," might have been due to Feuerbach's influence on Keller: "Whereas Feuerbach unmasks floating signifiers, so to speak, in the realm of metaphysics and theology, Keller unmasks them in the realm of human society" (576).
10. See also Klaus Jeziorkowski, *Gottfried Keller: Kleider machen Leute* (Munich: Hanser, 1984), 94.
11. "Der Mensch verlegt sein Wesen zuerst *außer sich*, ehe er es in sich findet. Das eigne Wesen ist ihm zuerst als ein andres Wesen Gegenstand. Die Religion ist das *kindliche Wesen* der Menschheit; aber das Kind sieht sein Wesen, den Menschen außer sich—als Kind ist der Mensch sich als ein andrer Mensch Gegenstand. Der geschichtliche Fortgang in den Religionen besteht deswegen darin, daß das, was der frühern Religion für etwas Objektives galt, jetzt als etwas Subjektives, d.h. was *als Gott* angeschaut und angebetet wurde, jetzt als etwas *Menschliches* erkannt wird. Die frühere Religion ist der späten Götzendienst: der Mensch hat sein *eignes Wesen* angebetet. Der Mensch hat sich vergegenständlicht, aber den Gegenstand nicht als sein Wesen erkannt..." (Feuerbach, *Sämmtliche Werke* 7:39–40) (Man first of all sees his nature as if *out of* himself, before he finds it in himself. His own nature is in the first instance contemplated by him as that of another being. Religion is the childlike condition of humanity; but the child sees his nature—man—out of himself; in childhood a man is an object to himself, under the form of another man. Hence, the historical progress of religion consists in this: that what by an earlier religion was regarded as objective is now recognised [sic] as subjective; that is, what was formerly contemplated and worshipped as God is now perceived to be something *human*. What was at first religion becomes at a later period idolatry; man is seen to have adored his own nature. Man has given objectivity to himself, but has not recognised the object as his own nature... [Feuerbach, *Essence*, 13].)
12. While all the visual personifications of deities and relics in Christian religion seem to belie this statement, the biblical prohibition of idolization, "Du sollst Dir kein Bildnis

machen" (You shall not make for yourself an idol) (2. Mose 20:4), exists in most monotheistic religions.
13. The content of Marx's critique of alienated labor did not come, however, from Feuerbach, whose notion of the sensual activity of objectification Marx was beginning to find too "passive." It most likely came from Arnold Ruge, a "left-Hegelian" with whom Marx collaborated from 1842 to 1844.
14. Theoretical and literary discourses often overlap. As we have seen in Lessing's and Herder's philosophies of history, theories often take advantage of literary devices, such as allegories and metaphors.

CHAPTER 8

The End of Pathos and of Humanist Illusions
Schiller and Schnitzler

In the course of the nineteenth century, Friedrich Schiller emerged as Germany's most highly revered dramatist.[1] Schiller's popularity reached its peak in 1859 with "the exuberant festivities" for the one-hundredth anniversary of his birth (Koepke, "Reception" 271). Yet the pathos and moral values of his dramas that appealed to a liberal, middle-class audience in 1848 and 1859 became suspect to modernist writers at the turn of the nineteenth century.[2] Arthur Schnitzler's *Liebelei* (*Flirtation*) (1895), for example, is a scathing critique of the idealization and hypocrisy of the bourgeois code of honor that Schiller upheld. The drama can be read, perhaps even should be read, as a direct response to Schiller's *Kabale und Liebe* (*Intrigue and Love*) (1784).[3] The allusions to Schiller's bourgeois tragedy are too numerous to be regarded as ancillary.[4] In view of the many correspondences to Schiller's play, it is surprising that scholarship gives only cursory attention to these affinities. Taken as a whole, the constellation of characters in Schnitzler's play, the status-induced conflict, the values at stake, and the references to canonical figures, such as Schubert, Hauff, and Schiller, take aim at a humanist cultural tradition that advocated individual autonomy and the supremacy of the mind over the body. As a vehicle for an Idealist image of man, endowed with superior intellectual powers, Schiller's pathos became a target of derision by fin-de-siècle authors.[5] This chapter reads Schnitzler's *Liebelei* as an example of fin-de-siècle responses to the Schillerian concept of pathos and shows how these responses expressed a changing attitude toward love and the mind-body dichotomy. More specifically, it discusses how the spiritualization and glorification of youth and romantic love became untenable according to some fin-de-siècle authors, when sexuality was recognized as an instinctual force and bourgeois morality was unmasked as a smokescreen that served to conceal sexual instincts. Reading the late nineteenth-century drama as a response to some of Schiller's aesthetic assumptions regarding the representation of human nature reveals that Schnitzler's modernist rebellion against the idealization of youth and nature was also accompanied by a melancholy over the loss of ideals.[6] To illustrate Schiller's dualistic construct of culture and nature, the analysis will use his essays "Über das Pathetische" ("On the Melodramatic") (1801) and "Über naive und sentimentalische Dichtung" ("On Naïve and Sentimental Poetry") (1800), and his play *Kabale und Liebe* as points of reference.

Schiller's notion of pathos expresses the spiritual expansion of the human. In his tragedies, human nature is elevated by its capacity to maintain dignity in suffering, even in the face of death.[7] It is ironic that the realization of the ideal can only be achieved in a spiritual realm either at the expense of sensual desires or at the sacrifice of human life. And because of this capacity to relinquish the desire to stay alive in order to preserve one's dignity in the face of death, human nature assumes *erhaben* (sublime) or tragic standing.[8] Pathos served as a rhetorical device to intensify empathy for the heroic suffering of the tragic heroes.[9] As an aesthetic means of ennobling human nature to a level of dignity that contradicted the lived reality in an increasingly mundane civil society, it was gradually perceived as overblown and became the target of irony and ridicule, as one could see in the previous chapter on Keller's *Kleider machen Leute*. It was implausible even in Schiller's time that a musician's sixteen-year-old daughter like Luise Miller of *Kabale und Liebe* would, unlike her father, keep her composure in the most taxing situations and forsake the love of her life to preserve "die Fugen der Bürgerwelt ... und die allgemeine ewige Ordnung" (the cohesion of civility ... and the order of the universe) with heroic gesture (SchW 1:809).[10]

Even though it is fairly obvious that Schiller's heroine serves as little more than as a vessel for the author's lofty ideals, their embodiment in this youthful character has nevertheless been effective in evoking the sympathies of many an audience.[11] And it is precisely Luise's heroic attitude in suffering through numerous injustices, and finally death, that ennobles not only her but also the particular virtues that she represents. Thus, Schiller's play and its young heroine contributed to disseminating middle-class ethics, which manifest themselves in Luise's honesty and ability to foreswear all earthly desires in order to uphold the idea of self-determination and eternal love. What made these moral ideals appealing is the fact that they were embodied in Luise's childlike personality, a personality that appears innocent and naturally free of deception.

The heroic postures of Schiller's tragic figures no longer seemed plausible at the end of the nineteenth century when the suppression of the senses seemed deceptive and constraining. What prompted the recognition of the falseness of Idealist values at the beginning of the industrial age? The rapid transition from a rural to an urban society proved unsettling to many members of the middle classes. City dwellers' feelings of isolation, insignificance, and powerlessness

182 ~: *Beyond Humanism*

Figure 8.1. Luise Miller from *Kabale und Liebe*. Steel engraving by Conrad Geyer (1859). Wikimedia Commons, public domain.

tempered the humanist promise of personal self-fulfillment and made the belief in the uniqueness of the individual more doubtful than ever (Ossar 31–32). The pathos of the tragic hero/heroine and his/her idealist aspirations had become unsuitable to express the condition of the urban middle-class individual in a society whose Romantic ideals had degenerated into a superficial concern for propriety and reputation.[12] The bourgeois code of conduct, which initially advocated self-control as a political tool toward individual autonomy, was now felt as restrictive (Schorske 282). Reading Schnitzler's *Liebelei* as a response to Schiller's idealization of youth, embodied in the heroine of *Kabale and Liebe*, will shed light on the eroticization of love, which became pervasive in both the literary and visual arts at the end of the nineteenth century.[13] Schnitzler's play criticizes what was then perceived as a deceptive pathos and reveals the connections between the idealization of nature, youth, and womanhood.

Looking at late nineteenth-century modernist drama through the lens of Schiller's aesthetic views provides a dual perspective on the aesthetic means by which Schnitzler's drama undermines the pretentions of bourgeois ethics and their false pathos. The modernist emphasis on exposing traditional humanism's euphemistic, prohibitive, prudish discourse should not distract from the fact that Schiller and many of his contemporaries were conscious of the power of affective, instinctual forces and used them to captivate their audiences. One of the conundrums of Schiller's dramatic pathos is that it claims to be in control of the very emotions that it provokes to the point of overwhelming the spectator. It is precisely this duplicity that late nineteenth-century authors were striving to expose.

While late eighteenth- and early nineteenth-century tragedies still upheld heroic self-sacrifice in the name of abstract ethical ideals, late nineteenth-century modernist dramas focused on debunking the false pretensions of these ideals that suppress the bourgeois subject's vital needs and desires.[14] Schiller's pathos is an aesthetic means to promote the human spirit's independence from "base" physical needs and passions. Accordingly, those who are capable of resisting their carnal desires and thus preserve their dignity deserve admiration. Pathos is the expression of the struggle between the sublime human spirit that is capable of asserting its freedom over and against the forces of nature. For Schiller, pathos is an essential constituent of tragedy because it affirms the autonomy of the individual, an autonomy that makes us human and distinguishes us from other species: "Aus aller Freiheit des Gemüts muß immer der leidende Mensch, aus allem Leiden der Menschheit muß immer der selbständige oder der Selbständigkeit fähige Geist durchscheinen" (Through all freedom of mind the suffering human has to be visible, just as through all suffering of humanity the independent spirit or the capability of independence has to be apparent) (SchW 5:527).

A challenge that Schiller faced with his heroine, Luise Miller, was how to endow her with tragic poise and at the same time make her appear natural and innocent. Pathos and the human qualities that accompany it, such as *Würde* (dignity) and *Erhabenheit* (sublimity), do not seem to mix very well with naiveté. And yet it is precisely this quality that Schiller's heroine must possess in order to disclose the pretentious politeness of courtly society through her "natural," childlike honesty. Still, she also reveals a level of poise that makes her worthy of being a tragic figure (Hinderer, *Schiller* 276).[15] Children cannot be regarded as autonomous individuals who have ideals and convictions for which they choose to die a heroic death. And yet Schiller's heroine has an intellectual maturity beyond her years. Schnitzler's youthful protagonists on the other hand have to content themselves with ideals that the adult world has replaced with complacent adherence to convention. *Liebelei* is tragic in that the young protagonists are victims of obsolete middle-class values, the values of a time that still believed in chastity, self-sacrifice, and the suppression of desires and instincts.

In his essay "Über naïve und sentimentalische Dichtung," Schiller reveals his insights into the human psyche by explaining why humans take such pleasure in unadorned nature, and by extension in childlike innocence. Accordingly, the enjoyment of nature is based on a moral idea rather than on sensual pleasure in the aesthetic beauty of form (SW 5:696, 699–700). We humans, so Schiller's argument goes, take delight in nature because nature has an innocent honesty that we once possessed when we were children and that we have lost due to our education and experience. We take joy in the idea of an infinite potential, "die Vorstellung von einer reinen und freyen Kraft, seiner Integrität, seiner Unendlichkeit" (the imagination of a pure and independent force, its integrity, its infinity), which nature and children still possess, and which is bound to be disciplined through reason during the course of our lives (SchW 5:697). In Schiller's thinking, Luise's appeal is the voice of unspoiled nature, and we admire her nature's perfection: "Was [den] Charakter [von Objekten der Natur] ausmacht, ist gerade das, was dem unsrigen zu seiner Vollendung mangelt; was uns von ihnen unterscheidet, ist gerade das, was ihnen zur Göttlichkeit fehlt. Wir sind frei, und sie sind notwendig: wir wechseln, sie bleiben eins" (What distinguishes natural objects from us is precisely what we lack to be perfect; what distinguishes us from them is precisely what they lack to be divine. We are free, and they are necessary: we change, they remain the same one) (SchW 5:695). Children and animals are still part of nature and possess qualities that we lost during the process of becoming civilized but still desire (SchW 5:696). Schiller compares the feeling for nature to the feeling of a sick person for health. In short, the admiration for the innocence of nature is perceived from a sentimental point of view.

Yet a comparison of Luise's childlike behavior to that of Schnitzler's protagonist Christine exposes some differences. For one thing, Christine's naiveté has lost its purity and become suspect of willful ignorance. Her suicide in *Liebelei* is one of those cases in which it is hard to determine whether it is childlike or childish. According to Schiller, it is not easy to distinguish "die kindische Unschuld von der kindlichen" (the childish naiveté from the childlike) and whether such childlike/childish behavior deserves to be ridiculed or to be admired, "indem es Handlungen giebt, welche auf der äussersten Grenze zwischen beyden schweben..." (insofar as there are actions that hover at the extreme limit between both) (SchW 5:702). He distinguishes between two types of naiveté: the naiveté of mental disposition (*Naïve der Gesinnung*) and a naiveté of surprise (*Naïve der Überraschung*). For Schiller, the naiveté of surprise occurs in human beings who have been educated and are surprised about an action that they committed in a moment of forgetfulness. The naiveté of surprise is considered childish and occurs when intentions can no longer be described as "natural." In this case the naïve action becomes a subject of ridicule. Schiller speaks of naiveté of mental disposition if children act in accordance with their unspoiled nature and moral innocence. This type of naiveté deserves admiration when it expresses a "truth" that, because of its "natural" force, is capable of asserting the rights of nature over and against the pretentions of art (SchW 5:698–99).[16]

The discrediting of bourgeois values is one of Schnitzler's pursuits in *Liebelei*. While *Liebelei* can be considered an adaptation of Schiller's *Kabale und Liebe*, Schnitzler made changes that allowed him to criticize Schiller's Idealist views.[17] For instance, he added the figure of Katharina, who represents herself as guardian of bourgeois propriety. Katharina acts as if she serves Christine's best interests by trying to match her with a suitor of her own social class. It becomes obvious, however, that her true motivation is envy. She is characterized as the unhappy wife who married for financial reasons rather than love and is now jealous of all younger women (*Liebelei* 20, 50–52, 55–57).[18] While in Schiller's play Luise's willingness to sacrifice her true love for bourgeois ideals because of ethical considerations and respect for "die Fugen der Bürgerwelt... und die allgemeine ewige Ordnung" (the cohesion of civility... and the order of the universe) (SchW 1:809) is to be considered venerable, Katharina's pragmatic decision to repress her erotic desires and marry a man with a stable income is portrayed as opportunistic, dishonest, and deplorable. Thus Katharina figures as an example of the degeneration of bourgeois ethics (Fritz 304). While Schiller's Luise is presented as an independent, self-determined individual who makes moral decisions that resist a corrupted social environment, Katharina is completely determined by social conventions and the opinion of others. In this respect Schnitzler's sympathies still favor Christine, who, like Schiller's Luise, refuses to let herself be corrupted by marrying a man for opportunistic reasons as Katharina does (*Liebelei* 51–52). Christine is a heroine in the Schillerian mold who holds on to a Romantic ideal against the corrupted social conventions of her day. Neither does she accept the liberal attitude toward sexual relationships of her best friend Mizi nor is she willing to trade "true love" for financial security.

Yet the very same uncompromising faith in "eternal love" that renders Schiller's Luise heroic makes Schnitzler's Christine appear self-delusional, inflexible, and childish. The difference is that Schiller's treatment of Romantic ideals, which once emphasized individual autonomy, are not compatible with the lived reality of fin-de-siècle Vienna.[19] Dagmar Lorenz's point that Christine's suicide, because of her disappointment over "an insincere young man without distinction" whom she barely knows, is "unnecessary" is certainly well taken (Lorenz 133).[20] Yet Christine's actions become more understandable if one considers her not as the autonomous, self-determined heroine that Schiller's Luise Miller represents but as someone who has become beholden to the illusion of "eternal love." All the characters are aware that a lasting romantic relationship between her and the officer Fritz is untenable.[21] It is out of reach, not because of overwhelming external pressures and intrigues, as in Schiller's play, but because of the fin-de-siècle social conventions. The other characters make it perfectly clear that Christine's hopes are unrealistic because relations between upper-class officers and lower-middle-class girls are usually short-lived and certainly do not end in marriage (*Liebelei* 63). Even Christine herself is partially aware that her relationship with Fritz cannot last (*Liebelei* 24, 64). Even though Fritz could not be more evasive whenever she tries to find out about his feelings, she stubbornly clings to the illusion that Fritz must love her. Mizi, her friend, cannot understand Christine's humiliating infatuation and criticizes her: "Er [Fritz] kommt zu spät zu den Rendezvous, er begleit' dich nicht nach Haus, er setzt sich zu fremden Leuten in die Log' hinein, er laßt dich einfach aufsitzen—das laßt du dir alles ruhig gefallen und schaust ihn noch dazu . . . mit so verliebten Augen an (He is late for your dates, he does not walk you home, he prefers to sit with strangers in a loge, he simply stands you up—and you quietly accept it and even look at him with smitten with love) (*Liebelei* 62). In contrast to Schiller's Luise, who remains "true" to herself and her ethical standards over and against the false pretentions of social status, Schnitzler's Christine obviously does not speak in the name of "truth" but rather in the name of wishful thinking. Even though Christine represents the same values as Luise, "eternal love" and faithfulness, it is obvious that she loves a fantasy, as her father attempts to convey: "Hast denn noch nicht gedacht . . . , dass das Ganze ein Irrtum sein könnt.—" (Has it not occurred to you . . . that the whole thing could be an error) (*Liebelei* 81). Christine's error is not only that she loves the wrong person; Weiring's wording, "das Ganze" suggests that the entire notion of eternal love may be mistaken.

This assumption receives further support in the last meeting between Luise and Fritz. Fritz, who in contrast to Christine does not want to talk about eternal love and who seems to live for the enjoyment of the moment, tells her that there may be "Augenblicke, die einen Duft von Ewigkeit um sich sprühen" (moments that radiate a scent of eternity) (*Liebelei* 71) and that this is the only eternity that humans can comprehend. Fritz's statement markedly sets him apart from Christine's belief in eternal love (*Liebelei* 23–24, 72) and the presumption that lovers can transcend the limits of their biological existence and meet at a "dritten Ort" (third place) (SchW 1:835–36), as Luise in *Kabale und Liebe*. While Fritz is also tempted to fall for the seductive "Duft von Ewigkeit" (a scent of eternity), he resists the temptation and pulls himself abruptly away from Christine with the words, "Ich hab dich lieb!—Aber jetzt laß mich fort" (I cherish you!—But now let me go) (*Liebelei* 71). Fritz's fleeting inclination to indulge in the notion of eternal love emphasizes, however, the seductive power of romantic feelings. His momentary relishing in the "atmosphere of eternity" is interrupted by the appearance of his friend Theodor, who, in Mephistophelian fashion, makes Fritz aware of the constraints of time and brings him back to the here and now.[22] In contrast to Christine, who in analogy to Schiller's Luise clings to the promise of eternal love, Fritz is enough of a realist to call the romantic moments a lie (*Liebelei* 74). Yet he also bears some significant similarities to Christine, regardless of his more experienced jaded outlook and his privileged social background that allows for his semi-bohemian lifestyle. Like Christine, he is easily consumed by passionate love relationships. His obligation toward an anachronistic code of honor, which induces him to participate in a duel and to die for his unethical behavior of having an affair with a married woman, derives from the same Idealist belief as Schiller's pathos: namely that ethos is more valuable than human life. Despite dying an honorable death, Fritz cannot be regarded as heroic, as his willingness to engage in the duel happens neither out of conviction nor for a worthy cause. In this regard, Fritz's reluctant willingness to engage in the duel also discloses the anachronism of the Idealist code of honor. By presenting Fritz's and the other characters' moral views and actions as time-dependent derivatives of an obsolete Idealism, Schnitzler undermines Schiller's transcendental truth claim.

The historicity of moral behavior is also connected to the loss of a unique and "whole" individuality. Fritz shares with Christine a tendency to take everything too seriously. He is unable to find enjoyment in the superficial relationship that Theodor has arranged in order to rescue his friend from his obsession with a married femme fatale (*Liebelei* 13). Whereas Christine's fixation on Fritz is presented as spiritual, Fritz's passion for the married woman is purely erotic. Romantic love worship, which according to Karl Guthke and others already took on a quasi-religious character during the period of *Empfindsamkeit*, nourished such obsessive behavior and the expectation of complete self-fulfillment in love throughout the nineteenth century.[23] This obsessive, unconditional love has a strong appeal because it promises liberation from social constraints.[24]

The Romantic idea that true love relationships are made in heaven was compromised, of course, by an oppressive class-based late-nineteenth-century bourgeois morality. Fritz's and Christine's desire for exclusive, unconditional love can be viewed as resistance to societal prohibitions that restrict individual freedom. Even Theodor and Mizi share this longing for spontaneous, romantic love. Their playful arrangement of a coincidental romantic encounter with roses falling accidentally from "heaven" reveals their secret desire for unrestrained, "natural" adventure (*Liebelei* 24, 28, 32). The various characters' desire to resist the domestication of love can be interpreted as a reaction to the loss of an uncompromised fulfillment of their unique individuality.

All the characters are to varying degrees aware of the cultural constraints that prevent them from realizing their desires. Fritz is intellectually aware of the self-destructive nature of his illicit affair and eventually accepts his friend Theodor's suggestion to engage in a flirtatious relationship with Christine to distract himself from the passionate but dangerous liaison with a married woman: "Und du hast ja gar keine Ahnung, wie ich mich nach so einer Zärtlichkeit ohne Pathos gesehnt habe, nach so was Süßem, Stillem, das mich umschmeichelt, an dem ich mich von den ewigen Aufregungen und Martern erholen kann" (And you do not have any idea, how I longed for such affection without pathos, for something so sweet, peaceful, which caresses me, and with which I can relax from the constant commotion and tribulations) (*Liebelei* 12). Fritz's wording betrays that he is not interested in Christine as a person but simply views her as an object of distraction that allows him to recover from his stressful love life. The realization that she does not matter as a person for Fritz leads Christine to commit suicide: "Und ich ... was bin denn ich? was bin ich ihm denn gewesen ... ? (And I ... what am I? what did I mean to him ... ?) (*Liebelei* 86).

Christine's traumatic reaction is symptomatic of the challenges that the loss of individuality at the beginning of modernity posed. One could say that the real tragedy of Schnitzler's play is the lack of a spiritual and deeper meaning of human existence.[25] Christine's obstinate attempts to maintain the fantasy of personal fulfillment in an exclusive love relationship can be attributed to her upbringing in a relatively sheltered *Biedermeier* atmosphere. The mention of cultural icons, such as Schubert, Hauff, and Schiller, that grace the shelves of Christine's petit-bourgeois home, explain her Romantic view of love. After all, Gustav Klimt, for instance, depicted Schubert as the symbol of the simplicity of the bygone *Biedermeier* era.[26] Hauff can be read as an allusion to Christine's longing for the fairy tales of her childhood, and Schiller's Idealism and the promise of transcending the limits of her sordid reality in a love relationship contribute at least in part to Christine's anachronistic insistence on the fulfillment of her dream.

Christine's sheltered upbringing in the privacy of the modest home is contrasted to Fritz's aimless and fragmented everyday life: "Ich geh in Vorlesun-

Figure 8.2. Gustav Klimt (1862–1918), *Schubert at the Piano* (1899). Wikimedia Commons, public domain.

gen—zuweilen—dann geh ich ins Kaffeehaus ... dann les ich ... zuweilen spiel ich auch Klavier—dann plauder ich mit dem oder jenem—dann mach ich Besuche ... das ist doch alles ganz belanglos" (I go to lectures—at times—then I go to cafés ... then I read ... at times I play the piano—then I chat with this or that person—then I visit people ... this is all very insignificant) (*Liebelei* 69). Even though Fritz has an ulterior motive to depict his everyday life as "ganz belanglos" (very insignificant) and "langweilig" (boring), these terms are characteristic of the aimless daily lives of officers in turn-of-the-century Vienna.[27] Both Fritz's and Christine's obsessive relationships provide them with an emotional intensity that compensates for the lack of meaning to their lives and allows them to escape the ennui of modern existence.[28] As controlled forms of aggression and sexuality, Fritz's dueling and Christine's worship of eternal love reveal the clandestine connection between instinct and morality. While Fritz and Christine appear morally more sincere than Theodor and Mizi, as they are bound by social conventions, they are at the same time more enthralled to their instincts.

The ambiguous relationship toward nature also figures prominently in *Liebelei*. For instance, the "süße Mäderl" (sweet little girl) who provides "Erholung" (distraction) as the idealized and domesticated version of nature is contrasted to the demonic "interessantes Weib" (interesting woman) or the wild and uncontrollable force of nature (*Liebelei* 12–13). When Fritz visits Christine, in a scene reminiscent of Faust's secret visit of Gretchen's living quarters, he is fascinated by her home and explains his "spontaneous" appearance with his longing for "diesem lieben Gesichtel" (this cute little face) (*Liebelei* 65). Fritz's choice of the demonstrative pronoun "diesem" rather than "deinem" is, of course, another indication for his objectification of Christine. Fritz's fascination with Christine's domestic surroundings is obviously not a yearning for Christine but for the aura of naiveté and purity.[29] Fritz can be compared to a tourist visiting a more pristine, less civilized culture. Christine's idyllic home evokes in him sentiments that allow him to yearn for a bygone, more "natural" world from the point of view of the decadent yet superior observer. While the pictures in Christine's home, titled *Abschied—und Heimkehr* and *Verlassen* (*Farewell—and Homecoming* and *Abandonment*) (*Liebelei* 66–67), reveal the kitschy reification of romantic sentiments, Fritz's perspective can be described as an ironic duplication of this reification. For Fritz these pictures do not have an aesthetic appeal. When Christine apologizes for the pictures' ugliness, he does not contradict her (*Liebelei* 67). While Christine still indulges in the mood that the pictures portray, Fritz relishes in observing Christine's naïve yearning from an aloof point of view. Yet, for a moment, Fritz yields to the appeal of sentimentality, although he is partially aware of its artificiality. Sentiment takes precedence over reason as it connects the characters with the illusory belief of their individual uniqueness by letting them physically experience that they are alive. Schnitzler reveals how the narcissistic self-indulgence in sentimentalities has become part of the characters' psyche. Fritz's empty promise to replace Christine's dusty artificial flowers with fresh and fragrant ones shows that he does not completely comprehend the reification of sentiments in bourgeois conventions (*Liebelei* 68).[30] The freshly cut flowers are just another attempt to nourish the illusion of romantic love. Freshly cut flowers are neither natural nor alive, no matter how natural and alive they appear. In this regard, the dusty artificial flowers of Christine's room are more truthful because they exhibit both the artificiality and the anachronism of social conventions. Weiring's consoling words, with which he tries to suggest to Christine that Fritz does not know the difference between "echt und unecht," could be directed at the other characters as well, as they, too, either pretend or deceive themselves (*Liebelei* 83).

Whereas Theodor and Mizi seem much more capable of coping with the illusory nature of "true love," they carefully arrange the romantic get-together that takes up the first part of the play. Theodor as the "geborene Festarrangeur" (natural organizer) sees to it that the roses do not look like an arrangement, and Mizi helps him to make them appear as if they had accidentally fallen from the sky (*Liebelei* 20, 24, 28). Theodor then drinks to the "glücklichen Zufall" (fortunate coincidence) even though he carefully planned their get-together (*Liebelei* 32). While Theodor criticizes Fritz for his risky affair with the married woman, he also entertains the illusion of adventure that a romantic love affair promises. Mizi surprises him by disheveling his hair, and he responds by calling her "Du Katz, du!" (*Liebelei* 27), hinting at her unpredictability as a domesticated version of a cat of prey. Theodor and Mizi play with the idea of romantic adventure in a controlled way. Schnitzler's play seems to follow Schiller's dictum that humans are only free when they play. The characters are able to maintain the illusion of freedom as long as they can control the game of love in the confined space of a carefully arranged candlelight atmosphere. Yet the illusion of an unproblematic love relationship comes to an abrupt ending with the ring of the doorbell and the entrance of the husband of Fritz's lover (*Liebelei* 35). Even though the tragedy is exclusively motivated by the characters' actions, their actions are determined by beliefs and desires that influence their behavior beyond their control. These beliefs are often expressed in seemingly superficial conversations (see, for example, *Liebelei* 21–35).[31]

Schnitzler's drama takes it upon itself to expose the characters' false illusions, which become conventionalized and lead to obsessive, erroneous, and pretentious behavior. Yet the play also evokes a melancholy feeling over the loss of humanistic ideals that are embodied in Christine's father, Weiring. The realization that modern existence is incompatible with humanism's metaphysical assumptions, such as the human individual's ability to control life through reason and to transcend a biologically determined existence through a commitment to universal and eternal moral values, is hardly acceptable to individuals who have been steeped in and brought up with these values. Christine is such a character who cannot accept a reality that has abandoned the idea of eternal love: "Und wann kommt dann der nächste Liebhaber?" (And when is it time for the next lover?) (*Liebelei* 90). While Schnitzler's play makes it clear that her stubborn belief in this ideal is selfish and unrealistic, it does not present any alternatives to the sincerity and hope that Christine's Romantic ideals provide. After all, the other characters are perplexed when they find out how seriously Christine took the fling with Fritz. Fritz's, Theodor's, and Mizi's lives seem aimless and shallow. While Christine's suicide on the one hand seems to be based on unrealistic expectations, it embarrasses her more-experienced friends and guardians, almost like Schiller's Luise embarrasses Lady Milford by asserting nature's rights over and against a corrupted reality. Yet by underlining that Christine's expectations are illusory, Schnitzler shows that her behavior is not asserting nature's rights but replicating bourgeois conventions and concealing uncontrollable desires.

A critique of the anachronistic humanist ideology had to confront the repression of the instincts and therefore required a different aesthetics, an aesthetics that could no longer portray the bourgeois individual as rational, autonomous, and whole. Traditional tragedy is unsuitable for portraying fragmented and ideologically mediated modern existence because it is based on the notion of individual autonomy. Protagonists who succumb to unconscious desires and mediated ideologies cannot be considered heroic. While it is possible to feel sympathy for the victimized protagonists—Fritz and Christine—their youthful naiveté is not glorified as pure, good, and true, as is Schiller's Luise Miller's. Their language is not endowed with pathos, and their deaths do not serve a higher purpose or eternally true values. To the contrary, their sufferings and deaths are caused by the belief in such humanist moral principles that no longer corresponded to the lived reality at the end of the nineteenth century.

Notes

This chapter appeared in a longer version that included an analysis of Frank Wedekind's *Frühlings Erwachen* as an article in the *Journal of Austrian Studies* 46, no. 4 (2013): 1–22.
 1. Schiller was particularly suitable as a national icon of German culture for both conservative liberals of the *Biedermeier* and the progressive liberals of the *Vormärz*. He could be claimed, on the one hand, for the national cause as founder of a "native tradition of drama" and, on the other, as promoter of the ideas of the French Revolution (Pugh 25). While the Idealist tradition of the early 1800s had been regarded as outdated by the mid-nineteenth century, it nevertheless prevailed and even became canonized in the years after 1850: "Die idealistische Ästhetik, die nach 1850 zum Bildungsgut aufstilisiert, ja geradezu kanonisiert wird, ist argumentativ immer gegenwärtig.... So sind zwar die idealistischen Formen als hohl durchschaut, vergangen zudem; aber überall beweisen sie ihre Macht" (The Idealist aesthetics that has been promoted to become part of the educational canon is always present in discourse.... While idealist forms are perceived as hollow, and in addition as outdated, they nevertheless ubiquitously demonstrate their power) (Schanze 377). If not indicated otherwise, all translations from the German are mine.
 2. "Das Schillerjahr 1859 hebt den Schiller der roten Pappnasen aufs Schild, in Erfüllung des Büchnerschen Diktums. Er wird nach der unerfüllbaren politischen Einigung ein Surrogat 'im Geiste,' wozu sich der halbe Schiller, der Dichter der 'Ideale' hoch droben, besonders zu eignen schien. Und so ist es nur konsequent, wenn die Kritiker der Zeit, nicht einverstanden mit dem idealistischen Getue unter realistischer Flagge, immer wieder Schiller und sein Drama zum Ziel ihrer Angriffe machten" (Schiller's anniversary of 1859 advertises the aspect of Schiller that is known for the clichéd red-nosed puppets in agreement with Büchner's saying. After the unachievable political unification he becomes a surrogate "in spirit," which appeared suitable only for half the Schiller, the poet of lofty ideals. And thus it is logical if the critics of his time object to the idealist histrionics under a realist banner, and keep attacking his dramas) (Schanze 377–78).
 3. Max Ophüls's film adaptation of Schnitzler's play also emphasizes the similarities to Schiller's *Kabale und Liebe* by foregrounding Christine's father in his professional environment, which underlines the parallel to Luise's father, Miller. Ophüls also adds a scene with a rival suitor who, regardless of his minor role, bears some resemblance to Luise's rejected and conspiring suitor, Sekretär Wurm.
 4. Axel Fritz situates Schnitzler's *Liebelei* in the tradition of the *bürgerliches Trauerspiel* and notes numerous correspondences to Schiller's *Kabale und Liebe* (Fritz 306, 307, 308, 312, 313).

5. For Schiller, suffering in tragedy is only justified if it serves an ethical purpose. Pathos emphasizes the hero's ability to preserve his composure in view of his suffering and thus emphasizes his freedom over and against the physical inclination to give expression to pain (SchW 5:512; see also 517, 521). These and all future references to the German version of Schiller's works are taken from *Sämtliche Werke*, ed. Peter-André Alt et al., 5 vols. (Munich: dtv, 2004).
6. Karl Heinz Bohrer contradicts Hegelian and post-Hegelian assertions of Peter Szondi and George Steiner that declare the end of tragedy in the modern age by claiming that tragic pathos is not only subject to dramatic action but can also be an expression of a frenetic style of representing the suffering subject's horror (Bohrer 386). Accordingly, tragedy is not limited to the genre of drama and can be detected in existentialist prose, such as in Camus's *L'étranger* (1942) or Sartre's *Les mouches* (1943) or in Baudelaire's poetry. Tragedy has taken on a different quality rather than disappearing. In Bohrer's view, modern tragedy expresses and radiates an intensity of emptiness. While the tragic hero still exists in the greatness of his loneliness, he has lost his heroism (Bohrer 388).
7. In his essay "Über das Pathetische," Schiller invokes Winckelmann's description of *Laokoon* to explain his definition of pathos as an assertion of the human mind's freedom over and against the instincts: "'Laokoon,' sagt uns Winckelmann ... 'ist eine Natur im höchsten Schmerze, nach dem Bilde eines Mannes gemacht, der die bewußte Stärke des Geistes gegen denselben zu sammeln sucht'" ("Laokoon," says Winckelmann, ... "is a manifestation of nature in its utmost pain in the image of a man who has sought to gather the conscious power of the mind against this pain") (SchW 5:521–22). Schiller concurs with Winckelmann and admires Laokoon's successful suppression of the natural inclination to escape death in order to protect his sons. The depiction of the suppression of the instincts becomes the aesthetic expression for the strength of the human will that can withstand the strongest assault of physical nature (SchW 5:526).
8. Luise Miller, Marquis von Posa, and Maria Stuart are examples of this tragic grandeur.
9. Schiller is aware, of course, that language can reveal the contestation between the free will and affect (SchW 5:519). Those human beings who are capable of keeping their composure and who resist the inclination to express their physical suffering deserve our admiration. The pathos arises from the tension between their suffering and their heroic effort to preserve their moral independence by resisting the urge to give in to their suffering (SchW 5:521).
10. As mentioned before, Karl-Philipp Moritz and other reviewers criticized Schiller's play for Luise's implausibly grandiose rhetoric (Henning 184; see also pp. 185 and 234). Even Schiller must have been aware of the improbably high level of abstraction of which his youthful heroine was capable. This is why he has her rival, Lady Milford, marvel at the astonishing maturity and wisdom pouring from a young person's mouth: "Unerhört! Unbegreiflich! Nein Mädchen! Nein! Diese Größe hast du nicht auf die Welt gebracht, und für einen *Vater* ist sie zu jugendlich" (Unheard of! Incomprehensible! No, my dear! No! This magnanimity is not your own, and your passion is too youthful to be inspired by your father) (SW 1:829).
11. As mentioned earlier, I will use Schiller's *Kabale und Liebe* only as a starting point. For interpretations of Schiller's play and Luise Miller's function as a tragic heroine, see, for instance, Walter Hinderer, *Schiller und kein Ende*. Hinderer points out that Schiller's heroines do not conform to gender expectations as they are characterized as sublime rather than beautiful (271–97). See also Guthke, "Tragödie der Säkularisation: Schillers *Kabale und Liebe*," *Das Abenteuer der Literatur* (210–41).

12. In this context, Axel Fritz points out "daß die bürgerliche Familienmoral immer weniger idealistisch und immer mehr ideologisch wird, immer weniger mit wirklicher Moral und immer mehr mit 'Reputation,' bürgerlichem Ansehen, zu tun hat wie in Hebbels *Maria Magdalene*" (... that bourgeois morals became increasingly ideological, and had less and less to do with real ethical values but rather with "reputation," bourgeois respectability, as in Hebbel's *Maria Madalene*) (Fritz 304).
13. The focus on sexuality and loss of innocence during adolescence is also apparent in Schnitzler's *Reigen* (1900); in Hofmannsthal's *Der Tod des Tizian* (1892), *Das Märchen der 672. Nacht* (1895), and *Knabengeschichte* (1906); and in the paintings of Erich Heckel and Ernst Kirchner, for instance.
14. While the idealization of love at the beginning of the nineteenth century was to show the moral superiority of a love governed by "natural" emotions over the "arranged" aristocratic marriage of convenience, the bourgeoisie of the late nineteenth century tended to downplay that many bourgeois marriages were also arranged. In Schnitzler's *Liebelei*, for instance, Katharina Binder's admonition that Christina should date someone of her own class reveals the bourgeoisie's status-based, discriminatory marriage practices. At the same time, Katharina is offended by Weiring's implication that her marriage was calculated and therefore neither virtuous nor based on true love (*Liebelei* 56–57).
15. The incongruity between childlike naiveté and the mature self-assurance required of a tragedy also comes across in Wedekind's *Frühlings Erwachen*. Wedekind called his play "eine Kindertragödie" (a children's tragedy), an oxymoron according to the premises of classical tragedy.
16. Schiller emphasizes that the naiveté of mental disposition is only possible if we forget the fact that children are incapable of simulation as naiveté: "Die Handlungen und Reden der Kinder geben uns daher auch nur so lange den reinen Eindruck des Naïven, als wir uns ihres Unvermögens zur Kunst nicht erinnern und überhaupt nur auf den Kontrast ihrer Natürlichkeit mit der Künstlichkeit in uns Rücksicht nehmen. Das Naïve ist eine Kindlichkeit, wo sie nicht mehr erwartet wird, und kann ebendeswegen der wirklichen Kindheit in strengster Bedeutung nicht zugeschrieben werden" (The actions and words of children impress us as naïve, only as long as we do not recall their inability to simulate and only as long as we focus on the contrast between their natural and our pretentious behavior. Naiveté is a childlike behavior where it is no longer expected. It can therefore in its strictest sense not be attributed to actual childhood) (SchW 5:699).
17. *Liebelei*'s indebtedness to the genre of bourgeois tragedy has been recognized in secondary literature, especially by Axel Fritz. Yet the affinities between Schiller's *Kabale und Liebe* and Schnitzler's *Liebelei* have been mentioned only in passing. Michael Ossar noted that "there is indeed disproportionately little scholarly literature on Schnitzler and nearly none on *Liebelei*" (19).
18. This and all future references to the German version of *Liebelei* are taken from *Liebelei*, ed. Michael Scheffel (Stuttgart: Reclam, 2002). The page numbers will be cited parenthetically in the text.
19. Luise's infatuation with Ferdinand may have been spurred by her reading of romantic novels. Luise's father, Miller, is concerned that his daughter has come under the bad influence of the writers of romantic fiction. Guthke points out that already in the second half of the eighteenth century one could detect the "'enthusiastische' Überhöhung des Eros zum quasi-religiösen Erlebnis" ("enthusiastic" elevation of Eros that likens it to a quasi-religious experience) and that Miller criticizes the "Scheinlogik der Säku-

laren Frömmigkeit" (the deceptive logic of secular piety) with his condemnation of the "'überhimmlische Alfanzereien' of the 'Bellatristen'" ("superlunary tomfooleries" of the "belletrists") (Guthke, 211; Schw1:758).
20. Lorenz also stresses that "in light of the relaxed sexual mores of her environment and her father's liberal views, there is no need to become a tragic heroine" (133). She emphasizes with good reason that Christine's suicide "would seem grotesque were it not in keeping with [the Victorian moral code], a code alive on Vienna's stages" (133). In other words, Christine's obsession with Fritz, whom she barely knows, only becomes understandable if one considers her cultural conditioning by an outdated repressive bourgeois code of honor that for many of her peers is no longer binding.
21. While Axel Fritz's statement is true that Christine is aware from the start "daß die Beziehung zu Fritz nicht von Dauer sein kann" (that [her] relationship with Fritz cannot last) (315), Christine's later reaction to Mizi's suggestion that Fritz will sooner or later leave her, shows her reluctance to accept this possibility (79).
22. Axel Fritz also points out the play's numerous allusions and similarities to the Gretchen scenes in Goethe's *Faust* (311).
23. As mentioned earlier, Guthke analyzes Schiller's *Kabale und Liebe* in the context of secularization. He shows very convincingly how Ferdinand and Luise view their love as a form of religious worship. Ferdinand's attempts to convince Luise of his theology of love are contrasted with Luise's doubts of committing blasphemy by violating the God-given social order (Guthke 220–23).
24. This is why Luise Miller longs for a "dritten Ort" that is free from social constraints.
25. In this respect, Schnitzler's play resembles Karl Heinz Bohrer's description of the altered form of a modern tragedy with its "Pathos der entfremdeten Existenz.... Es gibt noch den tragischen Helden, der, obwohl sein Heroismus verschwunden ist, dennoch existiert in der Größe seiner Einsamkeit" (pathos of the alienated mode of existing. ... There is still the tragic hero, who, although his heroism has vanished, nonetheless exists in the splendor of his loneliness) (Bohrer 388).
26. Schubert's songs, in typical *Biedermeier* fashion, would be played in the privacy of the bourgeois home: "For Klimt and his bourgeois contemporaries, the once hated age of Metternich was recalled now as the gracious-simple age of Schubert—a *Biedermeier* Paradise Lost" (Schorske 221).
27. Schnitzler's depiction of Willi Kasda's everyday life in *Spiel im Morgengrauen* is another example of the boredom and aimlessness of officers in turn-of-the-century Vienna.
28. Imke Meyer's study *Männlichkeit und Melodram* identifies pressures with which Schnitzler's male protagonists had to struggle in late nineteenth-century Habsburg society. Accordingly, the alienating loss of social coherence and recognition compelled many of Schnitzler's male protagonists to compensate for their insecurities by representing themselves as victims (177–79). Fritz's sentimental longing for an all-consuming love relationship can be seen as another expression for the wish to cling to an imagined male identity.
29. The reification of emotions is, however, not limited to the male characters. For instance, it is also apparent in Mizi's fascination with uniforms and the picture of Fritz in uniform (*Liebelei* 17, 25).
30. In Schnitzler's *Liebelei*, all that is left of nature is a sentimental yearning for it—for example, the freshly cut flowers used for decorative purposes (*Liebelei* 28, 68) and the branch of the lilac bush that Weiring picked from a public park (53). The characters have internalized bourgeois norms and values to such an extent that "nature" is always

culturally mediated. Schnitzler's *Liebelei* exposes the dangerous nature of obsessive disorders. While these disorders are all but natural, they can be regarded as failed attempts to control human instincts: Theodor's envy of Mizi's memories of male relationships, Katharina's envy of Christine's and Mizi's relationships to young gentlemen, Fritz's obsession with the unobtainable married woman, Christine's obsession with Fritz. These obsessions reveal the unsolvable tensions arising from the attempt to control unfulfilled desires.

31. This may be one of the reasons why the play did not receive much scholarly attention.

CHAPTER 9

Blurring the Human/Animal Boundary
Hofmannsthal's Andreas

Introduction

Hugo von Hofmannsthal and other fin-de-siècle writers explored the increasingly fluid boundaries between "the Human" and "the Animal" in their fiction.[1] Their works undermine the Cartesian idea of man as a "rational animal" that prevailed during the Idealist paradigm of the late eighteenth and early nineteenth centuries. Hofmannsthal achieves the blurring of the boundaries through narrative techniques, depictions of fluid, dreamlike transformations of scenery, and shifting points of view, as well as by emphasizing the hybridization of human and animal sensations from the characters' perspective. Hofmannsthal's exposure to the latest developments in the life sciences stimulated his literary probes of the human mind's alleged control of the instincts that prevailed during the first half of the nineteenth century and beyond. My analysis of an episode in Hofmannsthal's fragmentary novel *Andreas* will show how this posthumously published text reflects and transcends scientific fin-de-siècle perspectives by revealing the protagonist's dependencies on subconscious predispositions.

I will first briefly sketch out some post-Darwinian theories that criticized certain limitations of empiricist research methods. Ironically, it was the realization of the unreliability of the human perception that stimulated the literary recreation of subjective experiences because the sciences had to rely exclusively on objective criteria and thus leave the representation of subjective states of mind to the arts and letters. This did not mean, however, that literary representations of internal, emotional processes were to ignore scientific points of view but rather to make use of the latest developments in the natural sciences, as philosopher, art historian, and writer Wilhelm Bölsche (1861–1939) explained in his *Die Naturwissenschaftlichen Grundlagen der Poesie* (*The Scientific Fundamentals of Poetry*).[2]

According to Bölsche, this new realist aesthetics had to expel the sentimental idealization of love (Bölsche, *Naturwissenschaftlichen* 43). Condemning the spiritualization of erotic feelings with obvious roots in Christian metaphysics, Bölsche calls for an unsentimental depiction of the motivating instinctual forces of love, "die den Menschen mit Bewusstsein zu der folgenreichsten und tiefsten aller physischen Functionen hinleitet, zum Zeugungsacte" (which directs the human being to the most consequential and fundamental of all physical functions, to the reproductive act) (ibid. 45). Bölsche's plea for a "realist" acknowledgment of the biological origins of romantic feelings has broader philosophical implications for the human position in nature in general. In his volume titled *Hinter der Weltstadt* (*Behind the Metropolis*), which appeared in 1901, Bölsche deplores our human tendency to regard ourselves as separate from nature. Instead of viewing nature as uncanny, dead matter, which threatens to overcome us, Bölsche urges contemporary writers and readers to regard nature as a living organism, which "alles Menschliche als Möglichkeit in ihrem Schoße umschloß von Urtagen an" (harbored in its womb from the beginning of time every human trait as a possibility) (Bölsche, *Weltstadt* 185).

Bölsche was by no means the only philosophically minded writer who worshiped organic monism.[3] After all, the mind-body duality became questionable after Darwin's evolutionary theory had made it clear that our affinity to the animal species has a much longer history than the mental capacities that distinguish us from them. Another important factor that contributed to the blurring of the animal-human distinction was Ernst Haeckel's assertion that each individual organism (ontogeny) repeats its species' evolutionary development (phylogeny). Accordingly, we humans are for the most part animals because we prenatally live through all the developmental stages from mononuclear organism to primate. In this context, Arthur Schopenhauer's *Die Welt als Wille und Vorstellung* (*The World as Will and Representation*) deserves to be mentioned, as it is grounded on the survival instincts that humans share with other species. Claiming that all living organisms are driven by a common "Will to Live," it anticipated Darwin's and Haeckel's discoveries of what Carl Gustav Jung later called the collective subconscious, which predetermines rational decisions of the human mind.[4]

These scientific and philosophical developments had consequences for modernist aesthetics as well.[5] As numerous scholars have shown (Sprengel, *Darwin*; Riedel *Homo*; Bohnen, Fick, Winter), the sciences, and especially the life sciences, fundamentally changed philosophical and literary views of human life. For instance, the Darwinian theory of evolution as well as the mechanistic viewpoint of scientific empiricism resulted in a rather gloomy outlook that resonated not only with Schopenhauer's pessimistic philosophy but also with fin-de-siècle art and literature. Philosophers Rudolph Hermann Lotze (1817–81) and Gustav Theodor Fechner (1801–87) responded to this lack of a posi-

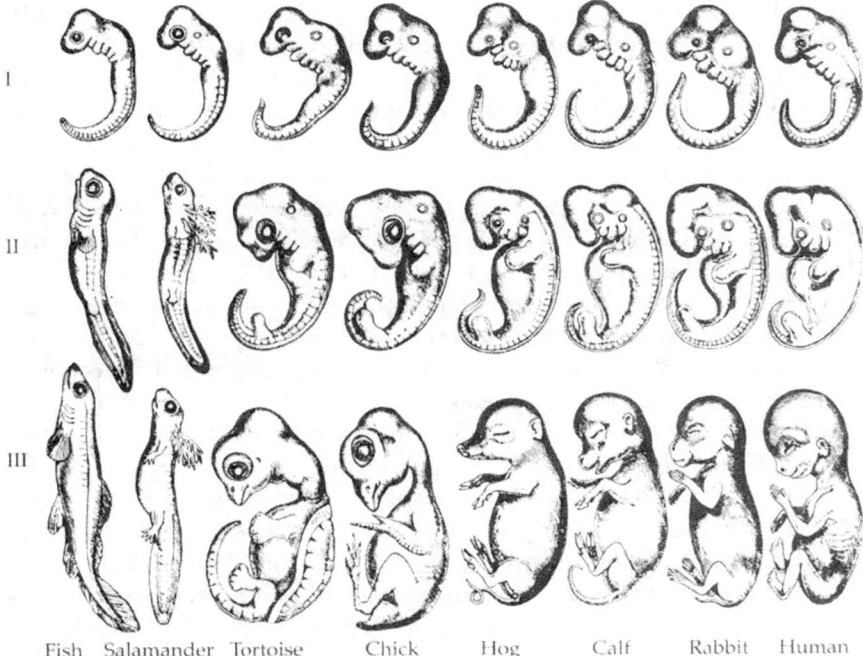

Fish Salamander Tortoise Chick Hog Calf Rabbit Human

Figure 9.1. Romanes's 1892 copy of Ernst Haeckel's alleged embryo drawings. Romanes's version is often attributed incorrectly to Haeckel. Wikimedia Commons, public domain.

tive worldview by spiritualizing nature as an aesthetically organized organism. Their pantheistic philosophies, inspired by Leibniz's *Monadology*, attempted to counteract the empiricist segmentation of life by equating nature to a divine living being that reflects our internal, spiritual experiences (Riedel, *Homo* 68).[6]

It would be misleading, however, to characterize their monistic systems as antirational. Both Fechner and Lotze strove to overcome metaphysics by attempting to anchor their theories in contemporary science.[7] While Fechner's *Elemente der Psychophysik* (*Elements of Psychophysics*) received much praise for its scientific precision at the time of its appearance, its author's goal was to defy the natural science's alienating abstraction. Modern scientific methods went beyond the limited scope of human sensory perception by proving its fallibility or subjective distortions (Fick 42). Fechner and Lotze were trying to restore trust in the human senses by stressing the existential meaning of individual sensory experiences. Yet while Fechner and Lotze are still caught in nineteenth-century anthropocentrism, their focus on the human subject no longer privileges the mind but assigns a spiritual quality to physical bodies. Fechner sharply opposes scientific empiricism, which presumes a world made up of dead objects that can only be observed from an external perspective. His contemporary Lotze goes even further by asserting that we can know other human beings only by deducing from our own inner experiences and projecting our emotions and sensations onto these individuals. Schopenhauer, on the other hand, deviates from this hierarchical distinction between *res cogitans* (essence) and *res extensa* (surface) by viewing the neurosensory apparatus as an intrinsic part of human physiology (Riedel, *Homo* 76–77). His philosophy presumes that the universe is not a human projection but consists of an all-pervasive dynamic force, called "Will," which permeates all living organisms and predetermines the human individual.

Biologist and philosopher Ernst Haeckel (1834–1919), who popularized Darwin in Germany, agreed with Schopenhauer's assumption that both humans and animals share common preconscious instincts and emotions. In view of the neurophysiological kinships and the Darwinian realization of a common evolutionary history between humans and animals, many fin-de-siècle literary texts explore their affinities. These works challenge earlier Idealist philosophies that upheld human intellectual self-determination. Hofmannsthal's story focuses on human-animal relations and explores to what extent the presumed freedom of will distinguishes humans from other species. In line with Fechner's, Lotze's, and Schopenhauer's monistic pantheisms, Hofmannsthal's aesthetics also aims at expressing emotional and corporeal experiences from a subjective point of view that scientific investigations are unable to represent.[8]

The continuing attempts by philosophers and scientists to establish procedures that were intended to guarantee the universal validity of scientific findings deepened the rift between "objective" science and "subjective" literature during the course of the nineteenth century (Daston and Galison 254). Scientists, such as Herman von Helmholtz (1821–94), became aware that human perceptions are by no means reliable representations of external reality but "are only signs of external objects" and that "even the Kantian *a priory* intuition of space was simply a 'subjective form of intuition [*Anschauungsform*], like the sensory qualities of red, sweet, cold'" (ibid.). They concluded that scientific objectivity could not be achieved through mere observation of nature; "instead, objectivity lay in the invariable relations among sensations, read like the abstract signs of a language rather than as images of the world" (ibid. 253). The unreliability of human perception resulted in efforts to exclude or neutralize the scientists' subjective observations in order to preserve universal validity. These efforts were accompanied by the progressing specialization of scientific research, the abstraction of scientific language, and the scientists' willful suppression of subjective impressions, or, in Schopenhauerian terminology, the "will to willnessless" (ibid. 203). It is not surprising that these developments contributed to the separation of the two cultures of *Natur-* and *Geisteswissenschaften*. Literary explorations then focused with greater intensity on the domains that were excluded from scientific observations: namely impressions, sensations, and emotions, that is, human subjectivity.

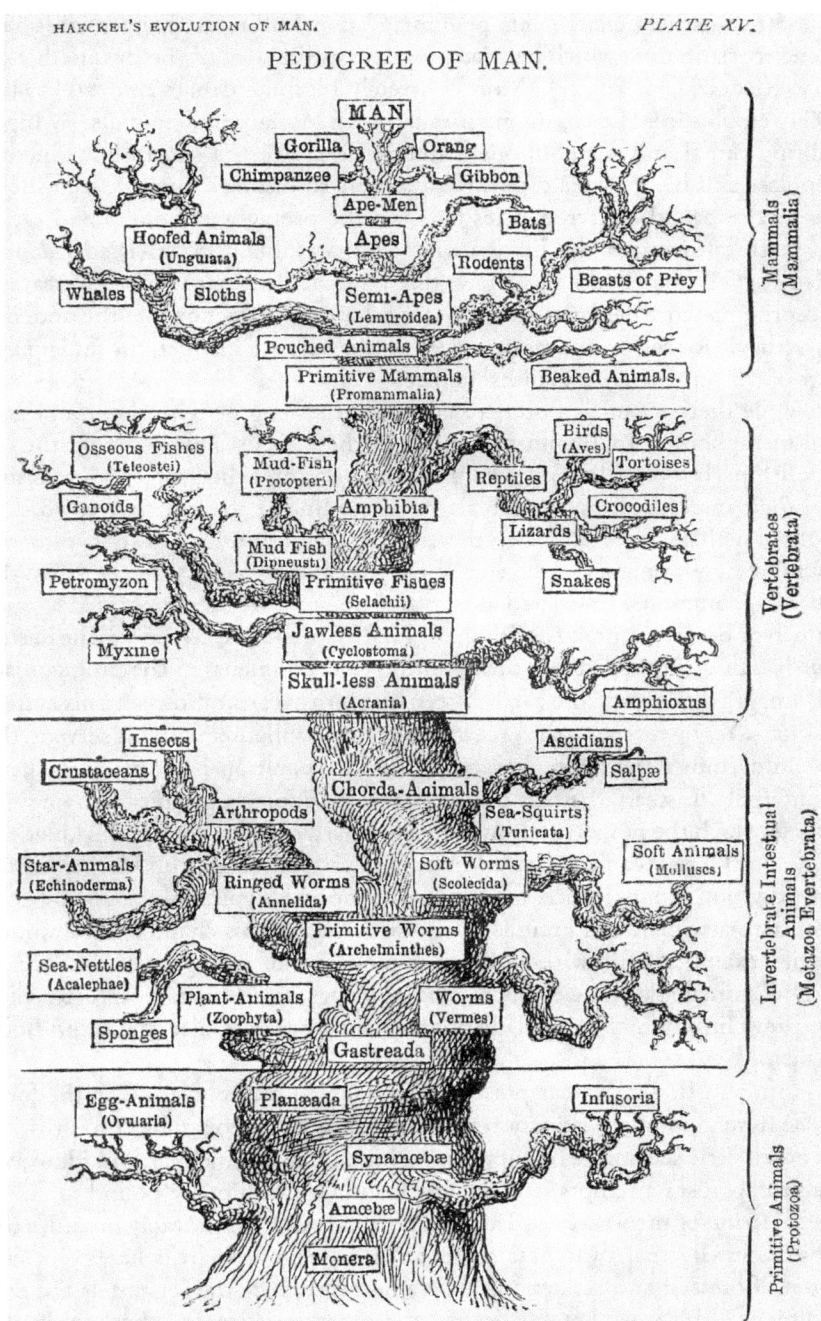

Figure 9.2. Ernst Haeckel (1834–1919), *Tree of Life*. Wikimedia Commons, public domain.

Hofmannsthal's enactments of human-animal affinities point to this aesthetic reorientation, which became prevalent at the turn of the twentieth century (Riedel, *Homo* xii–xv).[9] More concretely, Hofmannsthal's *Andreas* (1913/1931) emphasizes the commonalities between humans and animals. By highlighting verbal and surreptitious connections between a servant's instinctual impulses and his master's ostensible attempts to distance himself from these, the text reveals the discrepancies between the protagonist's moral and rational justifications and the hidden motivations of his actions (Riedel, *Homo* 32–34).[10] Ultimately, the text shows that rational discourse inevitably creates a deceptive distance between the illusive ideal of self-perfection and the underlying struggle for self-preservation driven by the survival instinct, the undeniable part of the human being's animal nature.

While there have been numerous studies that engage with the use of animal metaphors in Hofmannsthal, none of these focuses explicitly on the relationships between the protagonists, the servants, their objects of desire, and their interactions with animals.[11] My reading of the Finazzer episode in Hofmannsthal's *Andreas* views the fragmentary novel as a response to the scientific developments at the end of the nineteenth century. In the story, the *Knecht*—commonly translated as "servant" or "groom"—is represented as subhuman or between human and animal (HoSW 30:48, 51, 54, 66).[12] The bestial *Knecht* can be interpreted as the haunting abject figments of the protagonist's self-images that expose the gap between his spiritual aspirations and his animal instincts. Yet by revealing the protagonist's close affiliation with his servant, the text undermines the main character's willful separation from his animalistic counterpart. Instead, the text points to the continuity and unity of living nature, of which the human is always already a part, even before its individuation. In short, the text can be read as an attempt at subverting the Idealist mind-body division that prevailed as an imago of the archetypical human being even after its Darwinian and Freudian demystifications. This chapter will examine specific examples of how the literary employment of the figure of the servant and his animalistic agencies, such as horses, dogs, snakes, cats, and eagles, blur the prevailing human-animal distinction and therefore also the mind-body dualism.[13]

Hofmannsthal's Andreas presents this dualism metaphorically in the form of the human-animal distinction that allows the bourgeois subject to preserve his narcissistic self-image by suppressing his animalistic inclinations. However, the protagonist's attempts to overcome his inner disunity are bound to fail as the abjection of the unacknowledged animalistic Other inevitably precedes the subject's intellectual awareness thereof.[14] This is why Andreas has a glorified vision of himself and his actions and cannot recognize the servant as the embodiment of his unacceptable desires and characteristics. In other words, the subject's identity depends on the suppression of his instincts. The narrative underlines the subject's ignorance of its preexisting animalistic nature by letting the figures of the *Knecht* suddenly emerge out of the blue without the protagonist's anticipation.[15]

In contrast to Hofmannsthal's literary explorations of this topic, the monistic philosophies of Fechner, Haeckel, Bölsche, and Schopenhauer suggest that the subject can potentially overcome its inner division either through subjective sensory and physical awareness (*Einfühlung*; Fechner, Bölsche, Haeckel) or through self-abnegation (Schopenhauer). Sexual copulation, during which the subject abandons its individuality in favor of a higher unison, would be the prime example for the successful unification of the un-identical. However, the dissolution of the mind-body division can only be experienced temporarily in states of ecstasy or in complete self-annihilation (Schopenhauer). Hofmannsthal's *Andreas* can be read as an allegory that bears witness to both the suppression of the instincts and the intellect's inaptitude to overcome the mind-body schism. The novel also depicts the failure of the humanist concept of *Bildung* and its promise to liberate the bourgeois subject through self-tutelage.

While the bestial *Knecht* claims to facilitate the protagonist's travels, he takes control of his master's journey and leads him on a terrifying ride to unfamiliar locations. This servant, Gotthelf, is depicted as brutish and is linked to the sexual assault of his master's potential lovers and objects of desire.[16] The following textual analysis will show how fictional enactments of fantastic and yet imaginable constellations can problematize and destabilize theoretical assumptions by reenacting fluid, unsettled, and dreamlike experiences.

Hofmannsthal's *Andreas*

In Hofmannsthal's *Andreas*, the servant named Gotthelf is a diabolical creature, who—like Mephistopheles in Goethe's *Faust*—attempts to take advantage of the protagonist under the pretext of offering his services to Andres von Ferschengelder,[17] a young traveler of the lower Viennese nobility (Miles 123). Gotthelf, a name that literally means "God's help,"[18] appears all of a sudden and recommends himself by bragging about his professional experiences having allegedly served under the most illustrious masters of German aristocracy. While Andres becomes suspicious, even disgusted by Gotthelf's brashness, he feels nonetheless compelled to come up with excuses for his reluctance to employ the pushy loudmouth in view of his seemingly outstanding references (HoSW 30:47–48). Andres's insecurities, his vanity and respect for people of higher standing, provide Gotthelf with an opportunity to exploit the inexperienced traveler's weaknesses (HoSW 30:49). In short, Gotthelf manipulates Andres to take him into his services and to buy a second horse for their *Grand Tour* to Italy.

Hofmannsthal's fragmentary novel has often been interpreted as a type of *Bildungsroman*, a genre that typically portrays the journey of a young male protagonist and his development toward maturity, commonly ending with his integration into society after a string of potentially hazardous adventures (Miles 3–136, Mayer 130–31, 137). Situated in the 1770s when the *Grand Tour* was customary for young gentlemen of the upper classes, Hofmannsthal's novel both imitates and undermines the conventional *Bildungsroman*. As someone who has been brought up with this ideal of an education—after all, the *Grand Tour* is financed by his parents (HoSW 30:63)—Andres perceives Gotthelf as a bestial creature who poses a threat to his civility and reputation. Consequently, he attempts to distance himself from his eerily deceitful companion by comparing him to a raging fox and a spider (HoSW 30:51). Yet Gotthelf displays the same condescending name-calling of people. He equates the women with whom he allegedly had intercourse to animals who are completely beholden to their base instincts. For instance, he describes one of them as a "kranke Hündin" (sick bitch) (HoSW 30:50) and likens amorous women to female foxes, in analogy to Andres who fancies Gotthelf to a raging fox (HoSW 30:50–51). Andres's and Gotthelf's inclinations to degrade human objects of scorn by describing them as animals underline the affinity of their fantasies. Their degrading name-calling resonates, of course, with the mind-body division that removes human beings from the animal world and subjects the physical and sensory capacities to the control of the intellect. Andres's unsuccessful attempts to keep Gotthelf at a distance, their spatial proximity, and the similarity of their sensual imagination suggest an indomitable codependence between master and servant. As an unconscious force that succeeds in manipulating the protagonist's "free will,"[19] Gotthelf can be seen as a manifestation of the protagonist's unconscious or id[20]:

> So hatte denn Andres einen Bedienten der hinter ihm ritt und seinen Mantelsack übergeschnallt hatte, ehe er es recht wußte und wollte. . . . es wäre ihm lieber gewesen (den) ersten Tag nicht wieder durchzumachen. Aber da fruchtete kein Wollen. (HoSW 30:49)
>
> (So Andres had a servant riding behind him, who strapped his coat bag over his shoulder before he knew it and wanted it. . . . He would have rather wanted not to repeat his first day. But wanting did not amount to anything in this case.)

Hofmannsthal juxtaposes Andres's feebly expressed intentions to the servant's coercive determination that conceals sexual desire with seemingly cogent reasoning (HoSW 30:49). Although the sexually inexperienced Andres is appalled by Gotthelf's bragging about his sexual humiliation of women, he remains silent because he is ashamed of his ignorance with regard to women. When confronted with his instincts—and in this case Gotthelf represents the sexual drive—Andres is powerless. Put differently, Andres secretly desires to be the kind of womanizer that Gotthelf boasts to be.

Hofmannsthal's narrative stresses the dominance of the unconscious through sudden shifts from chronological narration to the protagonist's fantasies that reveal his secret desires (HoSW 30:51–52; 54; 60; 69–71). These imaginations are at times prompted by Gotthelf's pugnacious behavior that offends Andres's ethical sensibilities. At one point Gotthelf's vulgarities stimulate Andres to fancy himself as "der beste Schütz" (the best shooter) whose hunting skills make him the target of a beautiful duchess's glances: "... wie er schießt spielt [der] Blick [der Gräfin] so mit ihm wie er mit dem Leben der Waldtiere" (... as he shoots, the duchess's gaze plays with him as he plays with the lives of the animals of the forest) (HoSW 30:51). This enticingly daring foreplay soon ends in a "wildes Tun" (wild activity), with a common "Weib" (wench), an activity that is far from beautiful and resembles "ein Morden im Dunkeln" (a killing in the dark) in an isolated chamber with thick walls (HoSW 30:51). Significantly, this fantasy also ends in an abhorrent vision of Gotthelf shooting "mit aufgerissenem Maul auf ein Weib, das im Hemd zu ihm geschlichen ist" (with his gaping maw at a wench who came crawling to him in her nightshirt) (ibid.). At that point, Andres can still blame his servant and his cunning lewdness for animalistic cruelties. However, the story's almost seamless blending of fantasy and perceived reality suggests with mounting evidence that Andres and his servant are indeed one and the same person (see also Le Rider 98–99).[21]

Andres's gradual awareness of his loss of innocence is connected to a rest stop at an isolated *Gehöft* (estate) on their journey toward Italy. The estate is surrounded by a stone wall, and life in the family is presented from Andres's perspective as an idyllic, self-sufficient paradise where humans and animals live in harmony. Romana, the young daughter of the family Finazzer, who appears to Andres "in ihrem bedachten Ernst ... wie ein Kind, im Unbewußten aber und in der Lieblichkeit und Größe wie eine Jungfrau" (in her thoughtful sincerity ... as a child, and yet unconsciously in her gracefulness and size as a virgin), proudly tells Andres the history of her family (HoSW 30:55). The fact that Andres perceives the family's incestuous relationships as innocuous and affectionate not only shows his naiveté but also his surreptitious proclivity to imagine his sexual desire for Romana as pure and innocent. Andres's initial idealization of life at the Finazzer estate is underlined by the natural cohabitation of humans and animals (HoSW 30:54–56, 58). The colorful depiction of these idyllic scenes stands in stark contrast to Andres's moral ruminations. When he becomes aware that Romana's mother observes his and Romana's intimacies and presumes her to disapprove of their "freier Umgang" (uninhibited conduct), the mother's face appears to him "trüb und streng" (dreary and stern) (HoSW 30:58). The ambiguities and stark contrasts are significant semantic elements and permeate the entire story, from the characterization of the figures to the representation of nature. While the narration renders Andres's infatuated imagination in the most vivid and beautiful colors, it portrays Gotthelf's interaction with the maid as crude and repulsive, emphasizing the maid's unkempt hair, heated cheeks, and suggestive giggle. Andres cannot help noticing that Gotthelf was "mehr auf ihr drauf als ihr" (rather on than next to) the maid (ibid.) and that the slob was barely able to assume "eine manierliche Stellung" (a seemly posture) (ibid.).

So, as I have shown, the objects of male desire in Hofmannsthal's story are split into two figures that are nonetheless closely affiliated: an ostensibly innocent Romana and a lewd maid. Yet, Hofmannsthal's narrative destabilizes this juxtaposition of the two women characters in various ways. Romana, for instance, not only complies in responding to Andres's desires but actively seduces him (HoSW 30:56, 59). In addition, their love scene immediately succeeds Gotthelf's brutish intimacies with the maid. Another juxtaposition of scenes that links Edenic purity and erotic transgression depicts Romana's seductive supine position that lures a female goat to stand above her and let her drink (HoSW 30:56–57). The following analogous scene emphasizes the seemingly naive yet sexually motivated union of Andres and Romana by depicting Romana as an innocent seductress:

> Flink schwang sie die großen leichten Glieder in das Bett und lag der Länge nach darin und berührte mit der Fußspitze nur leise das untere Bettholz. Andreas war über sie gebeugt. So fröhlich und arglos lag sie unter ihm, wie sie sich auch unter die Geiß hingestreckt hatte. Andreas sah auf ihren halboffenen Mund, sie streckte die Arme nach ihm aus und zog ihn leise an sich, daß seine Lippen die ihren berührten.... Sie ließ ihn und zog ihn wieder sanft zu sich und nahm und gab wieder einen Kuß und dann auf die gleiche Weise zum dritten und vierten Mal. (HoSW 30:59)

> (Swiftly she bounced her big light limbs into the bed and lay there lengthwise. Her tip of the toes softly touched the wooden frame of the bed. Andreas hunkered over her. She lay underneath him so cheerfully and artlessly, just as she had lain down under the goat. Andreas looked at her parted lips. She reached her arms out to him and pulled him softly closer, so that his lips touched hers.... She released him and pulled him again softly closer and received and bestowed a kiss and then did the same for a third and fourth time.)

The love scene reveals Andres's self-portrayal as an innocent spectator and passive participant in a child's game. Reading the Romana episode from a fin-de-siècle perspective, one cannot fail but notice the ironic discrediting of the idealization of bourgeois love. The narrator's initial effort to portray this love scene as playful and innocent is diluted by Romana's passionate involvement in the erotic action. While the narrative describes the love scene from Andres's perspective, it also exposes his biased point of view.[22] Moreover, the sudden shift from innocent playfulness to erotic enrapture captures the immediacy of sexual impulses, which, in view of their uncontrollable inception, evade moral judgment. Precisely because moral censure of instinctual behavior is only possible from hindsight, it must be seen as a deceitful attempt to safeguard the human by rejecting its "animal" nature. Likewise, Andres tries to preserve his human ethos in conformity with his bourgeois upbringing. Andres's point of view suffers precisely from this delusional separation of innocent love from immoral sex. His attempts at distancing himself from the lecherous Gotthelf, his idealization of Romana as pure and guileless, his perception of a paradisiac nature on the Finazzer estate, his obliviousness to the Finazzer family's incestuous behavior, his indebtedness to his parents' fiscal and moral mandate of becoming a responsible, educated human being, all of this forces him to reject his unconscious actions upon reflection. His *Grand Tour*'s directive of maturation leads, however, to self-delusion as it requires the suppression of his animal nature.

The unfortunate consequences of this Idealist concept of a rational humanity that is thought capable of self-improvement are illustrated in an allegorical saying uttered by Gotthelf. When Andres and Romana interrupt Gotthelf and the maid in brewing a nefarious concoction, which in Gotthelf's words can "ein krankes Ross gesund und einen gesunden Hund krank machen" (cure a sick horse and make a healthy dog sick) (HoSW 30:58), the narrative reaches an important turning point. Read in allegorical terms, the association of horse and dog constitutes an important link between Andres's idealization of Romana and condemnation of Gotthelf. While the concoction allows Gotthelf to give the horse he sold to Andres a healthy appearance, the same "medicine" later poisons the Finazzers' dog. One could read the brew as a metaphor for the idealization of living creatures, which on the one hand superficially changes the horse's appearance but also leads to the suppression of animal instincts symbolized by the poisoning of the dog. Andres can be considered complicit in the deceptive or lethal abuse of animals. His traumatic flashbacks to his youth that remind him of his killings of a cat and of a little dog support this assumption (HoSW 30:64, 71). Andres half-heartedly admits to the repression of these reminders of his sadistic instincts yet does not fully acknowledge them:

> Ihm war unsicher ob ers gethan hatte oder nicht, aber es kommt aus ihm. So rührt ihn das Unendliche an. Die Erinnerung war martervoll, trotzdem wandelte ihn Heimweh an nach dem zwölfjährigen Knaben Andres der das begangen hatte. Alles schien ihm gut was nicht hier war; alles lebenswert außer der Gegenwart. (HoSW 30:71)

> (It seemed uncertain whether he did it or not, but it comes from within. This is how the infinite touches him. The memory was painful, and yet he was longing for the twelve-year-old boy who had done this. Everything that was not here seemed good; everything was worth living for except for the present.)

It is noteworthy that in this interior monologue the narrator empathizes with the protagonist and equates the subconscious with the infinite. Infinity as a superhuman transcendent phenomenon dwarfs human agency and therefore presents the *I* as a victim rather than as a perpetrator. Distant memories seem, albeit painful, impersonal ("es kommt aus ihm") and provide an opportunity for self-excuse by blaming an independent "It." The longing for the childhood past can also be seen in this context of repression because it diminishes the protagonist's responsibility for his actions.[23] Although these subconscious flashbacks can be painful, the time lapse permits for personal self-justification. By deceitfully changing the horse's appearance (idealization) and abusing the dog of his childhood, because he could not bear seeing that it was submissive not only to him but also to other dogs, he destroys the possibility of a personal friendship with animals. In addition, he also makes it impossible to accept his own animal nature. This repressive mechanism can be extended to his human relationships as well: by idealizing Romana, Andres is incapable of acknowledging his own inner Gotthelf. Therefore Andres is completely taken aback and speechless when Gotthelf points out the similarities of his and his master's sexual relationships (HoSW 30:60): "Dem Andres war eine Hitze in der Brust und stieg gewaltsam die Kehle herauf, aber keine Rede löste sich ihm von der Zunge; er hätte dem mit der Faust ums Maul schlagen wollen—warum tat er es nicht?" (Andres felt the heat in his chest rising up his throat, but nevertheless he remained tongue tied; he had wanted to hit Gotthelf's muzzle with his fist—why didn't he do it?) (HoSW 30:60). The question of why he did not silence Gotthelf is left unanswered—a lacuna that suggests the inadmissible validity of Gotthelf's allusion. The imagined opposition between the Finazzers' idyllic family life and Gotthelf's violent atrocities allow Andres to blame his own sexual fantasies on his bestial other and preserve his innocence. Not surprisingly, Gotthelf disappears after he poisons the dog, as the action sharpens Andres's senses and reminds him of his own cruelty toward animals. His guilt feelings are interspersed with haunting fantasies about Romana, which he initially tries to legitimize by imagining Romana as his wife and as the mother of his children (HoSW 30:63). Bourgeois respectability is undermined, however, in his dreams.

One of his dreams connects his desire for a fleeing Romana to his childhood home in Vienna. He finds himself in a *"Durchhaus,"* a house that connects two streets through a passage (HoSW 30:64). In front of the door that leads to Romana is a dying cat whose back he had broken with a drawbar and who had been unable to die for a long time (ibid.). The connection of pain and desire ("Wollust") is unacceptable to Andres. Its instinctual erotic undertones conflict with his bourgeois ideals. However, the subconsciously repressed instinctual gratification that connects violence with pleasure haunts him in his dreams. His sadistic torturing of the animals is projected onto his victims, appearing in its distorted form as a horrifying image. The cat approaches him like a snake. As he attempts to step over the animal "mit unsäglicher Qual, trifft ihn der Blick des verdrehten Katzenkopfes von unten, die Rundheit des Katzenkopfes aus einem zugleich katzenhaften und hündischen Gesicht, erfüllt mit Wollust und Todesqual in gräßlicher Vermischung" (the gaze of a twisted cat's head meets him from below with unspeakable pain, the roundness of the cat's head in a simultaneously feline and canine face full of lust and agony horribly blended together) (HoSW 30:64). The cat that he maimed is linked to the dog that Gotthelf poisoned, and his erotic fantasies about Romana are connected to Gotthelf's sexual abuse of the maid, whose desperate sobbing wakes him from his dream. The sound of the maid's "unaufhörliche Klagen" (endless weeping) are matched by the "maßlosen Schrecken" (boundless horror) on Romana's face, and Andres "ahnte nun einen gräßlichen Zusammenhang, dass es ihn kalt überlief" (now felt a terrible connection, so that he had to shudder) (HoSW 30:66).

In this dream Andres anxiously pursues Romana, but he also must conceal that he is chasing her. The dream highlights the resemblance of the imagined Romana and the Romana who suddenly appears in a niche of the raped maid's room with a terrified expression on her face and a trembling body as if she had been raped herself (HoSW 30:66). Moreover, Andres's earlier attempt to have sex with Romana and his ominous guilt feelings of having committed "etwas Schweres" (something grave) (HoSW 30:65) provides further indication that Gotthelf can be understood as Andres's alter ego.

Andres's repression of his erotic desires becomes manifest as he refuses to acknowledge the similarity between himself and his groom. Yet while Romana invites his romantic thoughts by leading him on through both her insinuations during their conversations and her seemingly natural, uninhibited behavior (HoSW 30:57; 59), Andres is not as passive as he appears initially when he lets himself be dominated by Gotthelf. For instance, he deliberately forgets having ordered Gotthelf to carry his coat bag up to his room. He carries it up himself, so that he has the opportunity to be alone with Romana. The text makes Andres's duplicitous behavior obvious: "Andres nahm den Mantelsack er that als hätte er vergessen, was er dem Burschen [Gotthelf] anbefohlen hatte, er grübelte selber vor wem er so that, vor sich, vor dem Kerl oder vor Romana" (Andres took the coat bag. He acted as if he had forgotten what he had ordered his servant. He wondered himself for whom he had put on this appearance, for himself, for the lad, or for Romana) (HoSW 30:59). The fact that Andres is not sure whether he is deceiving himself, Gotthelf, or Romana makes all three characters the objects of his duplicity. Andres cannot be trusted because he deceives himself in order to manipulate both his object of disdain (Gotthelf), and of desire (Romana), as well as his idealized view of himself. The triangular relationship between Andres, Gotthelf, and Romana is symbiotic because Gotthelf and Romana have become part of Andres's distorted perception. It is worth mentioning that Andres and Romana's love scene immediately succeeds Gotthelf's intimacies with the maid. Andres's distancing from Gotthelf is linked to his desire of having a pure love relationship with Romana. His clandestine knowledge of his deceptive behavior must be censured because it would compromise his personal integrity as well as the preservation of his romanticized love relationship with Romana.

Romana's association with the violent dream sequence and her sudden, half-naked appearance at the rape scene also undermines the deceptive separation of the two protagonists and their love objects:

> Traumartig, als hätte er nun hier gesehen, was er wollte, ging er durch die Knechte und Mägde durch, die ihm stillschweigend Platz machten; da stand hinter allen, in eine Türnische geduckt, Romana halb angezogen, mit bloßen Füßen und zitternd. Fast so wie ich sie im Traum gesehen habe, dachte es in ihm. Als sie ihn gewahr wurde, nahm ihr Gesicht den Ausdruck maßlosen Schreckens an. (HoSW 30:66)
>
> (Dreamily, as if he had now seen what he wanted to see, he made his way through the servants and maids, who silently made room for him; there, bent into a door niche, Romana was standing partially dressed with bare feet and trembling. When she noticed him, her face assumed the expression of boundless horror.)

While Andres becomes partially aware of his inadmissible desires expressed by his close affiliation with his servant, which are made apparent through authorial interventions such as "wie der Herr so der Knecht" (HoSW 30:67), the experiences at the Finazzer *Gehöft* bring back memories of his youth as a twelve-year-old. Especially Gotthelf's poisoning of Finazzer's dog, which Andres then buries out of guilt feelings, reminds him of his terrible torture and killing of his own little dog. Although these memories are *martervoll* (painful), they also instill in him a yearning for his younger self (HoSW 30:71). Both these experiences are connected to Andres's lost innocence that no longer allows him to have an animal companion (HoSW 30:70). His intuition, that there was a connection "between him and the dead dog" as well as "between him and Gotthelf" (HoSW 30:72), is more fully revealed in another dream, in which Romana utters the proverbial phrase, "ich weiß nicht, wo der Hund begraben liegt" (HoSW 30:72–73), which can be rendered as "I do not know where the bones are buried." In this dream Romana "sank halb zu Boden wie ein verwundetes Reh" (swooned like a wounded deer) and believed that Andres was both Gotthelf and yet not Gotthelf. She then begged Andres not to strip her naked and bind her to the bedpost as Gotthelf had done with the maid (HoSW 30:73). All these connections between master and servant suggest Gotthelf is indeed Andres's instinctual beastly other. Gotthelf disappears precisely at the point when Andres is in danger of becoming aware of his own brutish nature. In spite of his guilt feelings, Andres never fully acknowledges his secret sadist desires.

When Andres continues his *Grand Tour*, he leaves behind the Finazzer family and the memory of his darker self by sublimating his love affair with Romana. His imagined spiritual self becomes manifest again through an animal metaphor. In overcoming the experiences at the Finazzer *Gehöft*, he identifies with an eagle that soars high above the valley: "Andres umfing den Vogel, ja er schwang sich auf zu ihm mit einem beseligten Gefühl. Nicht in das Tier hinein zwang es ihn diesmal, nur des Tieres höchste Gewalt und Gabe fühlte er auch in seine Seele fließen" (Andres embraced the bird, yes he ascended to it with a blissful feeling. This time he was not forced into the animal, instead he felt his soul imbibing the animal's highest power and gift) (HoSW 30:76). In short, Andres does not identify with the eagle's body but only with its idealized, symbolic powers. He projects the elation that he is able to experience by connecting his identification with the soaring bird to his love relationship with Romana: "Wie jener in gewaltigen Räumen das zarte Reh hegte, mit Schattenkühle es deckte, mit bläulichem Dunkel es vor dem Verfolger barg, so lebte in ihm Romana" (Like that eagle protected the dear in mighty spaces, covered it with his cool shadow, and hid it with bluish darkness from [its] persecutor, this is how Romana lived inside of him) (HoSW 30:76). Andres's romantic fantasy of an eagle that protects and shelters a tender fawn from its persecutor is in stark contrast to the violent animal relationships that he experienced during his stay at the Finazzer estate. Likewise his love affair with Romana has been purged of the sadistic sexual violence that his bestial other, Gotthelf inflicted on the maid. Although Andres's "overcoming" of the Finazzer episode by glorifying the eagle may seem like a happy ending, it is a sublimation that keeps him from acknowledging that his bodily desires predetermine his thoughts, regardless of his attempts to control them. Consequently, one can read Hofmannsthal's narrative as a fictional enactment of the humanist ideal of self-improvement—the goal of the *Grand Tour* on which Andreas and so many bourgeois intellectuals embarked. While Hofmannsthal's critique thwarts the idea of bourgeois aspirations of individual autonomy, it can nevertheless be read as an extension of the mandate of an increased self-awareness, albeit with a significantly diminished trust in the rational faculties. After all, the demystification of the faith in autonomy of the individual has its parallel in the Enlightenment's demystification of religion. Simply put, the loss of bourgeois ideals means a gain in self-awareness. Yet this greater awareness of the human subject's irrational instincts does not translate into its empowerment as it is accompanied by a loss of orientation and self-control. The fact that the ego is no longer master in its own house has even greater consequences than Freudian psychoanalysis assumed. In this respect, Hofmannsthal's fictional narrative goes further than the Freudian attempt to grasp the power of the unconscious with rational means, as it illustrates the predetermining powers of the subject's cultural conditioning in an exemplary way. Andres does not make progress because his humanist upbringing with its ideal of individual autonomy allows him to distance himself from the dark forces of his animalistic desires.

In the context of fin-de-siècle Vienna's rebellion against the false idealization of traditional bourgeois notions of romantic love, Hofmannsthal's *Andreas* can be read as an anti-*Bildungsroman*, in which the protagonist matures by sublimating desires and experiences that do not conform to bourgeois moral standards. Andres's development is presented from a quasi-Nietzschean perspective that views civilization as a repression of the instinctual nature of the human. In other words, Hofmannsthal's *Andreas* is a travesty of the humanist belief in self-mastery and self-improvement. By associating the carnal aspect of love with the servant and maid while reserving its spiritual qualities for the "master," Hofmannsthal exposes the fabrications of a conventional bourgeois aesthetics. This tradition projected the dependence on the instincts on the lower ranks in order to preserve the ideal of an autonomous bourgeois subject.

Read together with Schnitzler's *Liebelei*, discussed in the previous chapter, Hofmannsthal's *Andreas* is another expression of the fin-de-siècle critique of Idealist metaphysics. However, the texts also resonate with the humanist legacy by trying to overcome the repressive aspects of what was perceived as the tyranny of Christian middle-class morality and the overvaluation of reason. Many texts of this period focus on the exploration of uncanny distortions of consciousness that could not be mediated adequately in rational or factual terms. Schnitzler and Hofmannsthal expanded on Marx's, Nietzsche's, and Freud's exposure of the overpowering socioeconomic, cultural, and phylogenetic forces that led to the individual's demystification. Their literary enactments of the consequences of neo-humanist ideology for the bourgeois subject's anachronistic and illusory self-perceptions are central to these works and many others of this period.

Notes

1. In works such as Hofmannsthal's *Reitergeschichte* (*A Rider's Story*), *Brief des Lord Chandos* (*Lord Chandos Letter*), and *Märchen der 672. Nacht* (*Tale of the 672nd Night*), or Kafka's *Bericht für eine Akademie* (*A Report to an Academy*), *Eine Kreuzung* (*A Crossbreed*), and *Die Verwandlung* (*The Metamorphosis*), to name just a few with a focus on human-animal relations, many fin-de-siècle writers challenge the notion of a clearly definable human-animal boundary.
2. "Eine Anpassung an die neuen Resultate der Forschung ist durchweg das Einfachste, was man verlangen kann. Der gesunde Realismus ermöglicht diese Anpassung. Indem er einerseits die hohen Güter der Poesie wahrt, ersetzt er andererseits die veralteten Grundanschauungen in geschicktem Umtausch durch neue der exacten Wissenschaft entsprechende" (The simplest thing one can demand is an adaptation to the new results

of research. A healthy realism makes this adaption possible. Preserving the assets of poetry on the one hand, it conveniently replaces anachronistic assumptions for new ones that are compatible with exact science") (Bölsche, *Grundlagen* 5).
3. Bölsche belonged to the *Friedrichshagener Dichterkreis*, a literary society that included other well-known writers of the time, such as Bruno Wille and the Hart brothers.
4. Both Hofmannsthal and Kafka were introduced to Schopenhauer's ideas via Nietzsche's philosophy, which they had both read at a young age (Riedel, *Homo* 25; Robertson 109).
5. Although the depiction of subconscious processes had already been explored in Romantic literature, the distrust in the rational faculties and the skepticism regarding the scientific disclosure of nature's secrets had grown stronger. This does not mean, however, that the major developments in the sciences did not exert any strong influences on late nineteenth-century literature.
6. While these metaphysical systems were able to both overcome the antagonism of science and religion as well as provide meaning to an otherwise meaningless accumulation of seemingly unrelated scientific facts, they also smacked of pseudoscientific speculation (Riedel, *Homo* 69). Nevertheless, they pointed to a lacuna that the sciences were unable to fill.
7. Bölsche invokes Fechner as a prime example of the attempt to complement the scientific materialism with a spiritual outlook that was inspired by Schelling's and Oken's Romantic *Naturphilosophie*. Bölsche's materialist philosophy had an optimistic outlook (Bölsche, *Weltstadt* 283–93) in contrast to Schopenhauer's pessimistic nihilism.
8. Certainly the long tradition of fables endows animals from an anthropocentric point of view; however, this portrayal of human behavior through animal characters is very much steeped in the moral and rational discourse of the Enlightenment, which assumes that behavior is based on the human ability to make ethical choices and can be judged according to objective moral criteria. This assumption had become untenable with the realization that preconscious desires and survival instincts predetermine our moral understanding.
9. The publication dates of the two texts do not coincide with the dates of composition. The main fragment of Hofmannsthal's *Andreas* was written either before or in 1913. After that, Hofmannsthal kept working on the text, but he was never able to integrate the several hundred notes that he amended. The sketchy and random notes do not provide a coherent outline of the novel's planned trajectory or ending and contain revisions that contradict earlier plans. John Zilcosky relies on these notes in his Freudian study on uncanny encounters with the exotic foreign. He examines Hofmannsthal's text in view of the author's development after 1918, which claims with good reason that "Hofmannsthal's post-1918 expansion suggests that he, like [his protagonist] Andreas, imagines a new geographic space . . . that will grant his character an imperial ego and himself a finished Bildungsroman" (150). While Hofmannsthal's notes suggest indeed that the protagonist visits Africa and Egypt and "completes his *nostos* by returning to Austria, marrying Romana, and having many children," the Hofmannsthal fragment of 1913 provides no indication of this development. In fact, the ending of a traditional *Bildungsroman* seems to contradict my interpretation, which reads the Finazzer episode as a fin-de-siècle criticism of the humanist ideal of *Bildung*.
10. David H. Miles views Hofmannsthal as a Neoplatonist who attempts in *Andreas* "to fuse the modern sensibility of a Rilke or a Kafka with the ideals and outlook of Goethe" (Miles 10). In contrast to Miles's study, my investigation claims that the protagonist's

attempts to sublimate his unconscious desires are presented as self-serving delusions and prevent the protagonist's self-knowledge.

11. See, for instance, Helen Frink, *Animal Symbolism in Hofmannsthal's Works* (New York: Lang, 1987); Eva Hoffmann, "'Jede unserer Seelen lebt nur einen Augenblick': Erzählperspektive, Wahrnehmung und Animalität in Hofmannsthal's Reitergeschichte, *Studia Austriaca* 23 (2015): 51–64; Konrad Heumann, "Mensch und Tier: Zum Problem der Objektfindung bei Ganghofer und Hofmannsthal; Mit einem Jagdbilderbogen von Max Arco Zinneberg," *Deutsche Vierteljahrsschrift für Literaturwissenschaft und Geistesgeschichte* 78, no. 4 (2005): 602–33; Elke-Maria Clauss, "'. . . und weiss nicht Mensch und Tier zu unterscheiden': Zur Funktionsweise der Tierbilder in Hofmannsthal's *Elektra*," in *Die Zoologie der Träume: Studien zum Tiermotiv in der Literatur der Moderne*, ed. Dorothee Römhild (Opladen: Westdeutscher, 1999), 59–83; Kyle Wanberg, "The Writer's Inadequate Response: Elizabeth Costello and the Influence of Kafka and Hofmannsthal," *European Journal of English Studies* 20, no. 2 (2016): 152–65; Jacques Le Rider, *Modernity and Crises of Identity: Culture and Society in Fin-de-Siècle Vienna* (New York: Continuum, 1993): 97–100. This selection is by no means comprehensive.
12. All subsequent references to Hofmannsthal's *Andreas* are taken from Hugo von Hofmannsthal, *Sämtliche Werke: Kritische Ausgabe*, vol. 30, ed. Manfred Pape (Frankfurt am Main: S. Fischer, 1982), and appear parenthetically in the text.
13. Although Miles points out that the Freudian or Jungian influences on Hofmannsthal's Andreas are fairly obvious, he does not fully acknowledge their impact on the antibourgeois aesthetics. While he identifies the Finazzer episode's major theme as "Andreas' inability to come to terms with the dark side of love, with his own unconscious erotic desire" (165), he views the protagonist's later sublimation of his erotic desires by identifying with an eagle in the air as successful in connection with the "overall pattern of love in the Bildungsroman" (149). By comparing the protagonist's romanticized image of Romana to Natalie and Mathilde, the idealized heroines of Goethe's *Wilhelm Meister* and Novalis's *Heinrich von Ofterdingen*, Miles interprets this spiritualization of love as an inherent trait of the classical *Bildungsreise*. The question remains, however, to what extent Hofmannsthal's text adheres to this romanticization of love. Whereas Miles views the novel on a trajectory that eventually balances the protagonist's instinctual drives with his spiritual aspirations (153), my analysis emphasizes the novel's deviations from the classical *Bildungsroman*.
14. Jacques Lacan has illustrated this mechanism of identity formation in his pivotal essay on the "Mirror Stage." See also my monograph *Narcissism and Paranoia in the Age of Goethe* where I discuss enactments of bourgeois identity formation in literary texts of the eighteenth and nineteenth centuries.
15. The *Doppelgänger* motif, enacted in the master-slave relationship, occurs time and again in Romanticism and in the literature of the turn of the century, often capturing this paradox of the subject's un-identical identity. Other texts by Hofmannsthal and Kafka also make use of the *Doppelgänger* motif: for instance, Hofmannsthal's "Reitergeschichte," Kafka's "Das Urteil" or "Bericht für eine Akademie," Theodor Storm's *Ein Doppelgänger*, Oscar Wilde's *The Picture of Dorian Gray* (1890), Guy de Maupassant's "Le Horla" (1887). The motif was particularly popular in Romantic literature. Novalis, E. T. A. Hoffmann, Jean Paul, Heinrich Heine, Ludwig Tieck, and Adalbert von Chamisso all employ the *Doppelgänger* motif. For a more comprehensive list, see Otto Rank, *Der Doppelgänger: Psychoanalytische Studie* (Leipzig: Psychoanalytischer Verlag, 1925).

16. The servant's sexual violence is associated with a dungeon-like horse shed reminiscent of the pigsty in Kafka's "Ein Landarzt." Yet the often-noticed insinuation to the Freudian id is only of limited significance as the story's dynamics transcends the boundaries of theoretical and philosophical frameworks by establishing a complex web of fictitious relations.
17. Hofmannsthal uses the alternative first name "Andres" instead of Andreas throughout the texts. The name "Ferschengelder" can be associated with the term *Fersengeld* (literally: heel money). Usually the term is used as an idiom as "jemand Fersengeld geben" (to make someone take to one's heels). For Andres this metaphor is quite suitable because he is constantly trying to escape his servant or other. He also was paid literally by his parents to take to his heels and embark on a *Grand Tour*.
18. God's help also plays a role in Kafka's "Ein Landarzt," where the protagonist ironically calls the horses a godsend.
19. The emphasis on "Wollen" resonates with Kafka's "Ein Landarzt" where the country doctor refers to the groom as someone who assists the protagonist out of his own "free will." In other words, it is the servant whose will can be characterized as "free" rather than that of the protagonist.
20. Both Miles and Leonhard Fiedler have already pointed out Gotthelf's affinity to the protagonist's unconscious (Miles 164–69; Fiedler 62–65).
21. Le Rider: "The cleft of subjectivity of Andreas is expressed in the story through the omnipresent theme of double personality. Gotthilf, the manservant whom Andreas rashly engages while staying at Villach, turns out to be a satanic double" (98).
22. Zilcosky emphasizes the narrator's shifting perspective that permits both distance from and intimacy with the protagonist (142–46).
23. In anticipation of the Freudian paradigm, Andres's repressive tendencies also provide an example for the association of infinity/transcendence/superego and the subconscious (id). Since present reality is not acceptable to the ego in view of the superego's demands, its distorted, repressed content returns later from the past and haunts the subject.

CHAPTER 10

Humanism and Ideology
Thomas Mann's Writings (1914–30)

Introduction

The last two chapters of this volume will focus on how the political changes before and during the Weimar Republic affected Thomas Mann's (1875–1955) and Hermann Hesse's (1877–1962) humanist perspectives. Their development as authors during these years lends itself to a comparative analysis. This is why the introduction to this chapter on Mann also refers to Hesse in anticipation of chapter 11, which deals more specifically with the latter. Hesse and Mann shared many biographical, aesthetic, and philosophical commonalities. Before the end of the 1920s, their intellectual exchange was virtually nonexistent. Therefore very little has been written on their sparse correspondence before and during the Weimar Republic. Yet, their biographical, political, and literary orientations drew the authors closer together during these years. An exploration of their early political and aesthetic views provides insights into their struggles and changing positions concerning the humanist tradition. As Theodore Ziolkowski points out, Mann and Hesse were conditioned by their common experience as educated bourgeois citizens (*Bildungsbürger*) who under the influence of Nietzsche became disillusioned with the exceedingly optimistic promises of Idealist philosophy. Not surprisingly, their ambivalent relationship toward their bourgeois origins became a major theme and permeated their entire work, despite their numerous differences, such as Mann's "Weltbürgertum" (cosmopolitanism) and Hesse's "Einsiedelei" (hermitic lifestyle) (Ziolkowski, ix).

Mann and Hesse reflected on their cultural heritage in both their fiction and essayistic works. Educated in the authoritarian school system of Wilhelminian society, they initially defended their elitist status against the democratization of culture at the advent of modernity.[1] One could say that, like many literati in pre–World War I Germany, they considered themselves as representatives of the nobility of the mind, or *Adel des Geistes*, as the title of one of Mann's essay collections suggests.² Yet they also struggled with the constraining pomposity and intolerance of their privileged background. Because of their ambivalent feelings toward the educational and philosophical traditions that shaped them, their intellectual elitism was fraught with self-doubt and self-irony. In other words, both Mann and Hesse subject their protagonists to a profound critique of the cultural milieu that conditioned them. This critique also entails a self-criticism as internalized humanist values inform their entire personalities. The protagonists' confrontations with their anachronistic biases manifest themselves in their probing of familiar assumptions by viewing them from different, even contradictory, perspectives.

Mann's and Hesse's conflicted relationships toward their humanist education can be attributed in part to their adolescent rebellion against the authoritarian school system, which resulted in their premature abandoning of school.³ While their failure to complete a traditional high school education may have enhanced their intellectual independence as well as their literary ambitions, it also contributed to their heightened awareness of the educational system's shortcomings, which had taught them humanist ideas in an authoritarian fashion. Their critique of bourgeois ethics was undoubtedly reinforced by their enthusiasm for Nietzsche's "Umwertung aller Werte" (revaluation of all values). Next to countless references to Nietzsche and Schopenhauer in both their essayistic and literary works, they also share a common love for the same authors, such as Goethe, Schiller, Keller, Fontane, Storm, C. F. Meyer, Tolstoy, Dostoevsky, among many others that belonged to the literary canon of an educated late nineteenth-century *Bildungsbürger* (educated bourgeois) (Ziolkowski iii; Carlsson 29, 85). Perhaps even more important for this inquiry than their shared intellectual and cultural horizon is their literary indebtedness to Romantic irony. The question of how their ironic, multiperspectival narratives both challenge and reaffirm their aesthetic and ideological representations of the humanist tradition is of central concern in this chapter. Read together, the two chapters will show the distinctions in how Mann and Hesse used irony to liberate themselves from the constrictions of the legacy of the Idealist mind-body and nature-spirit dualisms in their literary and essayistic writings. The writers' essays and speeches will reveal to what extent their humanist concerns responded to the political and social events to which the writers were exposed.⁴ While the authors' common aesthetic interests date back to the Wilhelminian period, their ostensibly deviating views toward the German war effort seem to set them politically far apart. In contrast to Hesse, who was opposed to the senseless carnage of World War I and preferred to live in Swiss exile, Mann remained a staunch supporter of the German monarchy until the end of the war (Kontje, *Cambridge* 55).

Mann's Humanist Plight

This chapter focuses in particular on Mann's gradual emancipation from the anti-humanist influences of Schopenhauer and Nietzsche and his vociferous commitment to the humanist cause in view of the disastrous outcome of World War I and the rise of fascism.[5] I will draw on Mann's early novella *Tonio Kröger* (1912) and his novel *Der Zauberberg* (*The Magic Mountain*) (1924), as well as various essays written before, during, and after World War I. In view of Mann's essayistic writings before and during the war, especially "Gedanken im Kriege" ("Thoughts during War") (1914), "Gute Feldpost" ("Good News from the Trenches") (1914), "Friedrich und die große Koalition" (Frederic and the Grand Coalition) (1914), and *Betrachtungen eines Unpolitischen* (*Reflections of an Unpolitical Man*) (1915–18), scholarship often assumed that Mann had always had aristocratic leanings at the beginning of his career. However, close examinations of Mann's early essays have shown that the author's position during the years prior to World War I was not as nationalist and antidemocratic as often presumed. Heinrich Detering, for instance, points out that Mann—except for some passages of provocative, anti-Semitic rhetoric with Nietzschean overtones—by no means fits the distinctly conservative label that critics often attached to him (GKFA 14.2:590–98).[6] Detering calls the years between 1900 and 1912 a phase of essayistic experimentation during which the author tried to find himself by adopting various roles (GKFA 14.2:582–83). Accordingly, Mann's early essays are probingly inquisitive rather than argumentative and resemble the multiperspectival representations of diverse opinions that characterize his fiction. Other critics suggest that the influence of Schopenhauer and Nietzsche prevented Mann from adopting dogmatic positions and ideologies (Lehnert 7). In view of Mann's playful enactment of contradictions and polarities, Lehnert argues, it would be reductive to pigeonhole the author according to a political affiliation or specific worldview.

Mann's liberal or democratic leanings disappear, however, with Germany's mobilization for World War I.[7] In "Gedanken im Kriege," Mann praised the German virtues of "Begeisterung und Ordnung" (enthusiasm and order) (GKFA 15.1: 29), which correspond to the Nietzschean categories of the "Dionysian" and "Apollonian." Mann's vacillations between these two poles— inchoate irrational yearnings on the one hand and the artistic desire to sublimate the incommensurable by lending it form on the other—link the aesthetic and ideological reflections that prevail in both his fictional and his essayistic prose at the time. After all, Mann emphasizes the literary qualities of his *Betrachtungen* by calling them a *Künstlerwerk* in which he lets others speak as in a novel (GKFA 13.1:13–14).[8] He follows the programmatic objectives of Romantic irony by giving each of the two poles equal weight. Thus, he counterbalances his unbridled enthusiasm for the war frenzy with an emphasis on

"Organisation." His assumed German national characteristics, such as "Solidität, Exaktheit, Umsicht, Tapferkeit, Standhaftigkeit" (solidity, precision, circumspection, courage, persistence) are complemented by "Schonungslosigkeit gegen sich selbst, moralischer Radikalismus, Hingebung bis aufs Äußerste, *Blutzeugenschaft*" (uncompromising self-discipline, moral radicalism, devotion to the utmost, *blood sacrifice*) (GKFA 15.1:30). While his chauvinistic praise of Prussian militarist qualities was narrow-minded and racially prejudiced, Mann's patriotism was by no means extreme at the time. It fed on a literary and cultural tradition that forged a notion of German national identity based on allegedly superior German characteristics. Herder's, Goethe's, and Schiller's *Sturm und Drang* works, Lavater's physiognomic writings, as well as Kant's anthropology all present the abovementioned "manly" virtues as naturally inherent in the German national character. In contrast to these presumed masculine virtues, effeminacy, deceit, weakness, lack of integrity, or superficiality had long been attributed to the decadent French courts and then portrayed as French character traits (Mathäs, *Narcissism* 102–24).

While Mann invokes his humanist education to justify his patriotic sentiments, he nevertheless distances himself from the humanist ideology of Germany's western neighbors. For instance, he refers to the Neoplatonic distinction between profound inner truth and insubstantial surface to contrast German morality, spirituality, and culture from French political verbosity, everyday life, and civilization. He presents himself in the tradition of Protestant *Innerlichkeit* (inwardness) from Luther to Kant, claiming that the spiritual revolutions caused by these iconic figures—namely the emancipation of the individual before God and the Critique of Pure Reason—were much more radical than the French Revolution (GKFA 15.1:38). The authoritative source for Mann's antithesis is the Kantian distinction between instrumental reason and true morality. Accordingly, the German soul is more truthful and complex than what the English and French uphold as the major achievement of civilization: the Proclamation of Human Rights (GKFA 15.1:38). Mann portrays German culture and morality as deep and genuine in contrast to the shallow political charades of Germany's western neighbors (GKFA 15.1:37). He follows the Nietzschean mission of debunking manipulative rhetoric by exposing the Western coalition's propagandistic claim to be on the just side of history (GKFA 15.1:42–44).

Mann's reluctance to yield to the increasing pressure of being on the "politically correct" side after the tide in favor of war had turned against it could be interpreted as an attempt to save face by refusing to change his opinion yet again for advantageous reasons, as he had done at the beginning of the war (Kurzke GKFA 13.2:10). After all, he repeatedly presents himself as a lone wolf rather than as a member of the herd (Nietzsche) of opportunistic intellectuals who take sides against their own compatriots so that they can be on the winning side of history. His defense of the strong personality over and against political mass movements can also be read as a final attempt to uphold the autonomy of the individual in the transition toward a more egalitarian, democratic society. He resists the prospect of a democratic government even as it becomes increasingly clear that Germany is going to lose the war (Kurzke, GKFA 14.2:14).[9]

To be sure, Mann seems to take a distinctly conservative political position by considering humanism's democratic agenda unsuitable for Germany and by defending the "vielverschriene 'Obrigkeitsstaat'" (much-derided autocratic state) (GKFA 13.1:33–34). Yet calling his *Betrachtungen eines Unpolitischen* strictly reactionary would not do justice to his probing ruminations. Mann's epitaph, taken from Goethe's *Torquato Tasso*—"Vergleiche dich! Erkenne was du bist!" (Compare yourself, recognize what you are!)—alludes to the discursive, literary open-endedness of these reflections. Mann's *Betrachtungen* should rather be read as a self-interrogation that takes stock of his political, philosophical, and aesthetic views. These reflections are intended as a dialogic consideration of opposing ideological positions and, as such, an expression of the ambiguous nature of German culture and history (GKFA 13.1:23). Likewise Mann himself introduces his notorious *Betrachtungen* by characterizing the book as "Darstellung eines innerpersönlichen Zwiespaltes" (the depiction of an inner conflict) and instructs his readers to discern the *Vielstimmigkeit* (equivocality) of the text (Lehnert 16).[10]

Mann's juxtapositions of *Sein* and *Meinen*, *Künstlertum* and *Bürgertum*, *Einsamkeit* and *Öffentlichkeit* (Being and meaning, artist and bourgeois, solitude and gregariousness) (GKFA 13.1:19) provide his framework for "die eigentliche Bahn des Lebens . . . , die Rücksprünge, Widersprüche, Spannungen . . . ohne die das Drama des Lebens nicht vorwärts geht" (the actual course of life . . . , the throwbacks, contradictions, tensions . . . , without which the drama of life does not evolve) (GKFA 13.1:23). With reference to *Tonio Kröger* he calls his method ironic, that is, open to either of the two poles between which his texts vacillate: "Ironie aber ist immer Ironie nach beiden Seiten hin, etwas Mittleres, ein Weder-Noch und Sowohl-Alsauch" (Irony is always irony toward both sides, something in between, a neither-nor and as well as) (GKFA 13.1:100). Kurzke points out that Mann always expresses his "angreifbaren Äußerungen" (controversial statements) in the form of a "Rollenrede" (subjective opinion) that invites an opposing voice (Kurzke, GKFA 13.2:13–14).

As mentioned earlier, Mann emphasized the distinction between German culture and French civilization. This opposition can be substituted by the categories of "Geist" (spirit) vs. "Leben" or "Bürger" vs. "bourgeois." Accordingly "Germanness" means culture, soul, freedom, and art as opposed to French civilization, society, the right to vote, and literature (GKFA 13.1:35). Mann presents the humanist belief in the perfectibility of the human being through education as wishful thinking. Instead, he acknowledges the Dionysian, irrational aspect of human existence and claims that the German national character is incompatible with the "superficial" egalitarianism of the French, American, and British civilizations. In Mann's opinion, the so-called *Zivilisationsliterat*, who, like his brother Heinrich, sees only the good and reasonable humanitarian side of humanity, ignores that one also must experience hate both as a perpetrator and as a victim (GKFA 13.1:486). The philanthropic writer is for Mann a *Menscheitsschmeichler* (flatterer of humanity) who claims to be concerned about human dignity but depicts a kitschy travesty of life that is deprived of all sincerity, poise, solemnity, and responsibility (GKFA 13.1:483–84). As opposed to the *Zivilisationsliteraten*'s self-serving identification with the humanist belief in an inherently good and perfectible human nature, Mann tried to dig deeper to find out to what extent "Man" is free and to what extent he is determined (GKFA 13.1:24).

By portraying the "authoritarian German character" in the larger context of Germany's philosophical tradition from Luther via Kant to the end of the nineteenth century, Mann is able to support his contention that German skepticism toward a truly democratic system is rooted in German history. Accordingly, the Lutheran Reformation provoked the prevailing dichotomy between an "inner," universal freedom of spirit and an "outer" subordination to the political order of the state. This philosophical dualism was embedded in Germany's supranational unit of the Holy Roman Empire, which embodied the ideal of a *Kulturnation* and the reality of a fragmented agglomeration of territories, each of which had its own particular political order. In other words, religious and philosophical ideals existed in an autonomous realm that remained untouched by a debased political reality. In Mann's view, it was a mistake to believe that universal philosophical ideals could be transposed to the actual political situation, as the American Declaration of Independence and the French Revolution attempted to do (GKFA 13.1:302–6).[11] The assumption that individual freedom and happiness could be achieved by imposing a universal democratic political system ignored the far-reaching impact of German history on the nation's genuinely introverted apolitical nature, according to Mann.

Mann justified his pro-war sentiments by making his self-esteem dependent upon the war effort of the German nation. He regarded war as a useful means to prevent both the destabilization of both Germany's national culture and his own personal integrity. Yet his identification with the German nation went beyond the current political reality and had its roots in a presumed glorious German past. This "eigentliche Glanzzeit der deutschen Geschichte" (actual heyday of German history) reaches back to the emergence of the *Bürgertum* at the waning of the Middle Ages when northern German cities blossomed and expanded their trade with the outside world through their strong fleet and alliance, the Hansa (GKFA 13.1:125). Despite their strong international ties, these free cities remained truly patriotic because of their loyalty to the German emperor during the Holy Roman Empire until 1806. This long-standing patriotic commitment distinguishes the German *Bürgertum* from the bourgeoisie of the Western entente.[12]

Mann's peculiar blend of humanist and authoritarian views are partially due to his upbringing as a member of the privileged upper middle class that had its origins in the pre-democratic hierarchical order of the estates. His German brand of republicanism distinguished itself from American or French post-revolutionary bourgeois egalitarian models in that it envisioned a more rigid and hierarchical social order. Mann considered himself to be a representative of this tradition, which set him apart from the growing number of nouveau-riche citizens who rose to the ranks of the upper middle class, simply because of their affluence.

Tonio Kröger

Mann's first major literary successes, *Buddenbrooks* (1901) and *Tonio Kröger* (1903), draw heavily on the author's biography. *Tonio Kröger* is of significance in the context of this study because the novella is beholden both structurally and thematically to the humanist legacy. The novella is to be considered as a variation of the *Bildungsroman* (novel of education), a genre that works toward the humanist goal of cultivating male bourgeois individuals to become responsible citizens, as was already pointed out in previous chapters. The novella's binary structure, which reflects the protagonist's inner conflict, can be considered as a classic example of the neo-humanist mind-body dichotomy. Tonio's inner division between his father's cerebral, northern German sense of bourgeois propriety and his mother's southern artistic receptivity for the sensory pleasures of life is a barely disguised echo of this duality, which is also recognizable in Tonio's name.

Torn between his indebtedness to his respectable bourgeois upbringing and his somewhat questionable artistic calling, Tonio's inner division is typical of the divided loyalties of artists like Mann and Hesse. Their humanist education led them to adopt the values of the privileged *Bildungsbürgertum* and contributed to their cultural elitism. However, the confrontation with the post-Darwinist, Nietzschean, and Freudian critiques of the humanist paradigm enabled intellectuals to view their education from a critical point of view and reflect on its prejudices and limitations. Kröger's return to his hometown and his realization of its parochial restrictions illustrate his artistic and intellectual emancipation from his bourgeois past (GKFA 2.1:286–87). It is not without irony that Kröger is unable to cast off the shackles of his bourgeois upbringing in the bohemian, antibourgeois climate of the south. His discussion with the painter and confidante Lisaweta helps him realize that he can distance himself from his bourgeois identity, but he can neither ignore nor reject it. Cutting off his relationship to his past would mean to forsake all the experiences that are the lifeblood of his art. In order to find an artistic point of reference that permits him to depict his development, he needs to revisit the familiar surroundings of his origin. It is not sufficient to simply replicate his biography, however. Instead of rendering merely a realistic account of his bourgeois upbringing, Tonio needs distance, an outside point of view, which allows him to rise above the limitations of his ingrained bourgeois values. In order to gain this loftier vantage point, he travels further north rather than staying in his hometown.

Although Tonio declares his empathy for the average citizens, such as his childhood friends Hans Hansen and Inge Holm, he also retaliates for the humiliations he suffered in the past by satirizing the narrow-minded bourgeois etiquette (GKFA 2.1:261). Critics of Mann's irony might say that his narrator ridicules the awkward attempts of the uneducated petit bourgeoisie to imitate the privileged bourgeois elite of Mann's heritage. Mann's humanism can therefore be regarded—at least until his commitment to the Weimar Republic in the early 1920s—as a superior posture that enables him to pledge his empathy with the average citizens from a discriminating, elitist point of view. After all, the narrator sympathizes with Tonio as the intellectual outsider and ridicules some of the lower-class petit bourgeois minor characters, such as the inebriated, traveling young merchant from Hamburg, whose northern German substandard pronunciation he mocks (GKFA 2.1:297–98).

In spite of the arrogant sarcasms that make fun of "little" people, the narrator does not spare the protagonist and the intellectuals from ironic comments, as his affinity to the awkward but intellectual Magdalena Vermehren shows.[13] Tonio's "superior" posture does not prevent him from developing an awareness of his ambiguous role as an artist on the one hand and as a bourgeois citizen on the other, which induces him to vacillate between both positions and ironize them from oppositional points of view. Thus he considers himself eventually as "ein Bürger, der sich in die Kunst verirrte, ein Bohémian mit Heimweh nach der guten Kinderstube, ein Künstler mit schlechtem Gewissen" (a bourgeois who lost his way into art, a bohemian who is homesick for his well-mannered upbringing, an artist with a guilty consciousness) (GKFA 2.1:317).

While the narrator claims that the empathy with his bourgeois characters derives from "love for blond, blue-eyed, and fair-skinned, happy, amiable, and common people" (GKFA 2.1:318), one cannot help but notice that his irony is patronizing, as he considers himself superior to them. The narrator excuses his and Tonio's lofty irony by portraying his protagonist as an exceptional human being who is able to transform his former role as an outsider into the ability to observe and illustrate their bourgeois conventions with a sharp eye for their awkward efforts to imitate the upper class. Tonio's intellectual elitism, which is presented as his retribution for his former status as a victim of humiliation, can be related to the author's defense of Germany's alleged national exceptionality. In his *Betrachtungen eines Unpolitischen*, he supports Germany's war effort as an attempt to defend itself and its role as a nation that has been treated as an underdog because of its antidemocratic national character.[14] In analogy to Tonio's exceptionality as an introverted outsider, Mann justifies Germany's uniqueness also with its introspective, basically apolitical national character, "die deutsche Trennung von Geist und Politik" (the German separation of spirit and politics) (GKFA 13.1:303).

Mann justifies his political development with his commitment to the humanist cause in his legendary speech "Von deutscher Republik" ("Concerning a German Republic") (GKFA 15.1:535). In order to explain his political transformation and to preempt accusations of being a turncoat, he continued to stress Germany's exceptional history that distinguishes it from the victorious Western powers of the entente. In this speech of 1922, he still characterizes himself as conservative and emphatically sets himself apart from the revolutionary forces that initially helped topple the monarchy (GKFA 15.1:533). Historian Friedrich Meinecke called Mann a "Herzensmonarchist" (monarchist at heart) who, despite his public declaration of support for the Republic, remained emotionally tied to his elitist way of thinking (Kurzke, GKFA 15.1:347). Thus, Mann can be regarded as a classical case of a *Vernunftrepublikaner*, a person who supported the Weimar Republic on rational grounds but not on emotional ones. Mann's affiliation with democracy did not come easy, as some of his essays between 1918 and 1922 show. Pleading with Schiller and Dostoevsky (1848–80) "that the question of the human cannot be solved politically but only morally through either Christian self-perfection or through the 'aesthetic education' and liberation of the individual," he distinguishes his German type of humanism from the civilizing spirit of the Enlightenment (GKFA 15.1:212). Mann continues to separate this personal and "apolitical" humanism from the "Tugenddünkel" (conceited righteousness) of the victorious Western allies or the "Zivilisationsliteraten" who, like his brother Heinrich, sided with them during World War I (GKFA 15.1:238). In a letter to Hermann Kayserling, he tries to favor the "kulturbildende Kraft des deutschen Geistes" (the power of the German spirit's foundation of culture) by situating himself in the Romantic tradition (GKFA 15.1:293). For Mann, "apolitical" German culture is based on introspective soul-searching. It implies that this type of self-reflection has more integrity than the ideological slogans connected to what he calls the rational radicalism in the wake of Rousseau and the French Revolution (GKFA 15.1:489, 521).[15]

Mann's speech "Von deutscher Republik" is generally viewed as the author's first endorsement of Weimar democracy and as a clear break with the antidemocratic views expressed in his *Betrachtungen eines Unpolitischen* (GKFA 15.2:348). Although he had already voiced his support for the Weimar Republic in 1919 in his essays titled "Zuspruch" ("Encouragement") and "Für das neue Deutschland" ("In Favor of the New Germany"), he felt compelled to publicly engage in the politics of his day after numerous politically motivated murders, most notably the one of Foreign Secretary Walther Rathenau by right-wing anti-Semites (GKFA 15.2:345). Mann gave the speech on 13 October 1922 on the occasion of Gerhart Hauptmann's sixtieth birthday. In view of the politically motivated violence by the growing right-wing nationalist movement, Mann took the opportunity to address Germany's young generation in order to win their support for the fledgling democracy (GKFA 15.2:514). He presented Gerhart Hauptmann's work as a prime example of a humane national literature. Humane meant for Mann neither "völkisch simpel noch völkisch ungeschlacht, und randalierend, sondern liberal im menschlichsten Sinn..." (neither folkish [in the sense of xenophobic] and simplistic, nor folkish, crude, and violent, but liberal in the most human sense) (GKFA 15.2:517). While Mann strongly condemned monarchist and radical reactionary tendencies (GKFA 15.2:522), he also distanced himself from the legacy of the French Revolution by situating his democratic leanings in the German Romantic tradition rather than the Enlightenment.[16]

Mann cites Georg Philipp Friedrich Freiherr von Hardenberg aka Novalis (1772–81) and Walt Whitman (1819–92) in support of his idiosyncratic views of a democratic German state.[17] Linking Novalis and Whitman, the American poet whose great epic free verse poem, *Leaves of Grass* (1855), heralded the spirit of the common man, permitted Mann to support democracy without abruptly abandoning his former elitist and aristocratic inclinations. While he conceded that Novalis was hardly a democrat, he also discovered textual evidence of a "democratic-republican aspect" in the poet's philosophy of the state (GKFA 15.1:539). The nexus between the life-negating Romantic mystic and the life-affirming prophet of democracy is that they both recognize the idea of humanity in each individual member of the state:

> Deutsch aber, oder allgemein germanisch, ist jedenfalls der Instinkt eines staatsbildenden Individualismus, die Idee der Gemeinschaft bei Anerkennung der Menschheit in jedem ihrer Einzelglieder, die Idee der Humanität, die wir innerlich menschlich und staatlich, aristokratisch und sozial zugleich nannten und die von der politischen Mystik des Slaventums gleich weit entfernt ist wie vom anarchischen Radikal-Individualismus eines gewissen Westens: die Vereinigung von Freiheit und Gleichheit, die "echte Harmonie," mit einem Worte: die Republik. (GKFA 15.1:540)
>
> (German, however, or generally Germanic is the instinct of a state-constituting individualism, the idea of community that recognizes the humanity in each of its members, the idea of humaneness, which we called genuinely humane and public, aristocratic, and social at the same time, and which is as far from the political mysticism of Slavism as from the anarchist radical individualism of a particular

Western ideology: the unification of freedom and equality, "genuine harmony," in a word: the republic.[18])

This passage is essential to Mann's rhetorical strategy as it presents his "genuinely German" republicanism as a moderate philosophy that can mediate between East and West, between the individual and the state, between the human desire for freedom and the yearning for integration into a hierarchical structure. Mann's strategy to position himself both in between and yet above the extreme left-wing socialist and right-wing nationalist tendencies that posed a threat to Weimar democracy is reminiscent of Tonio Kröger's wavering between the petit bourgeois citizen and the intellectual, elitist artist. Mann's elitism makes itself felt through his insistence on the intellectual superiority of German Romanticism. On the upside, his elitism induces him to forsake the Nietzschean admiration of "the blond beast" and show greater sensibility to its inhumane excesses (GKFA 15.1:541).

Regardless of Mann's rejection of Nietzsche's anti-humanist and anti-Christian idolization of the "Herrenmensch" (natural ruler) (GKFA 15.1:541), his speech contains aspects of Nietzschean thought that go beyond the Idealist humanism of the Enlightenment. The rebellion against repressive forms of propriety or etiquette, which he calls "der Tod aller freien Humanität" (death of all free humanness), and the significance of the body figure prominently in Mann's portrayals of the human (GKFA 15.1:549). Remarkably, Mann discovers the erotic dimensions of human existence not only in Nietzsche or Whitman but also in Novalis and Goethe (GKFA 15.1:548–53). By emphasizing the erotic aspects of love and death, Mann sets the German notion of *Menschlichkeit* (humanness) apart from its Western, especially French, concept of humanism, which in his view is predominantly abstract and ideological. Since Novalis and Whitman incorporate the emotional and physical aspects of *Menschlichkeit* in their philosophies of the state, Mann can use them as *Eideshelfer* (guarantors) for his argument that the German national notion of *Humanität* shows a more comprehensive and deeper understanding of the human than the Western Enlightenment tradition that focuses exclusively on the rational, ethical dimension (GKFA 15.1:559).

Der Zauberberg

In Mann's novel *Der Zauberberg* (1926) the protagonist, Hans Castorp, is conceived as a mediator between "Zivilisationsliterat" Settembrini's curtailed Enlightenment humanism—or what critic Antal Mádl termed "Teilhumanismus" that excludes the emotional aspects of human existence—and Jesuit Naphta's yearning for death (Mádl 65–67). In contrast to Tonio Kröger, however, Castorp is not an intellectual outsider but resembles Hans Hansen in his bourgeois "normalcy." As a young protagonist who has no clear convictions, Castorp is exposed to the ideas that the other characters represent. Castorp's malleability encourages Settembrini and Naphta to convince the passive protagonist of their strong convictions. While Castorp is receptive to the erudite arguments of their disputes, he does not take sides or come to any conclusive decisions in favor of either Settembrini's optimistic affirmation of life or Naphta's passivity and love of the beyond. Castorp's intermediate position thus parallels Tonio Kröger's inner conflict not only between north and south, the Apollonian and Dionysian, Enlightenment rationality and its Romantic transcendence but also between east and west, augmented by the figures of Madame Chauchat and Peeperkorn. While these characters are more nuanced than the conceptual categories that Mann develops in his essays "Goethe und Tolstoi" (1921), "Bekenntnis und Erziehung" (1922) and "Von deutscher Republik" (1922), they can certainly be recognized as representative spokespersons for the ideas that informed these essays.

Mann's position as an author and narrator resembles Castorp's refusal to take sides. He characterizes his reluctance to take a stand and advocate a certain point of view very succinctly in a letter to Hermann Hesse: "In Wahrheit ist meine Produktion ein Spielen zwischen geliebten und ironisierten Gegensätzen,—wie mir überhaupt dieser Zwischenraum recht eigentlich als der Spiel-Raum der Kunst und Ironie erscheint" (In truth, my production is a playful vacillation between beloved and ironized antagonisms—as this space in-between appears to me as the genuine "play space" of art and irony) (Carlsson and Michels 28). On the one hand, Mann justifies his refusal to side with the adulation of the Dionysian with his reluctance to become associated with the irrational nationalist mysticism of the National Socialists (ibid.). On the other hand, he also feels that art has to preserve its autonomy in view of its growing socialist activist politicization (ibid. 272–73). In view of his resistance to commit himself politically either to the socialist activism of the left or the nationalistic mysticism of the right, Mann willingly concedes his somewhat indecisive stance, regardless of the danger of being called a "dürr-humantären Rationalisten" (half-hearted humanitarian rationalist) (ibid. 28).

In the *Zauberberg* Mann's main protagonist enacts this wavering between Naphta's irrationalist praise of the natural instincts and Settembrini's dogmatic, moralist rationalism. Like his author, the protagonist becomes increasingly aware of the contradictions that both these opposing ideologies harbor (GKFA 5.1:704–5). Given *Tonio Kröger*, the vacillation becomes manifest both in the protagonist's reflections on the opposing philosophies and literally, in his geographical movements. Just as Kröger travels from his hometown to Copenhagen and then further north to Aalsgard in order to gain distance from the bourgeois rationalism and the artistic irrationalist aspects of his personality,[19] Castorp has to set himself physically apart from Naphta and Settembrini in order to develop his own point of view. While Kröger has to reach Aalsgard in order to observe his bourgeois peers from a detached ironic perspective, Castorp distances himself from his fellow patients at the sanatorium by climbing upward on a snow-covered mountain. In both cases the protagonists seek an elevated vantage point from where they can contemplate and gain clarity with regard to their own position. The outcome of their reflections is perhaps less surprising than the manner in which these metaphorical enactments of Mann's irony are depicted. Both protagonists maintain their independence of thought, which allows them to playfully represent two opposing philosophies in an ironic way. For instance, Castorp's decision to climb the mountain in inclement weather is irrational, yet he proceeds with a rational purpose, namely to preserve his individual point of view. Likewise, his insight comes to him as a dream, as a seemingly irrational sequence of exaggerated and distorted images. Yet the dream images of a harmonious life, "von ihrer Jugend, ihrer Hoffnung, ihrem Glück und Frieden" (of its youth, its hope, its happiness and freedom), as well as its dark side, graphically depicted as an infernal devouring of children (GKFA 5.1:745–46), capture human fears and hopes that underlie Naphta's and Settembrini's ideological abstractions. Mann's text addresses literature's ability to evoke archetypal human feelings and experiences that induce Castorp to ask himself where he had already encountered these hopes and fears before he dreamt them (GKFA 5.1:746). The fact that these feelings exist in him before he becomes aware of them characterizes them as part of the human subconscious that always revolves around longing and fear, or love and death.

Mann reformulates eighteenth- and nineteenth-century traditional humanist concepts in light of contemporaneous medical findings and the biological and chemical processes that determine both the physical and mental constitution of human nature. While the narrator's awareness of the body's increasing significance, foregrounded in the *Zauberberg* as a leitmotif through extensive and detailed discussions of medical discoveries and conditions, contributes to the demystification of the humanist idealization of the human spirit, Castorp's plea *"Der Mensch soll um der Güte und Liebe willen dem Tode keine Herrschaft einräumen über seine Gedanken"* (Man shall not leave control of his thoughts to death) reaffirms neo-humanist values (GKFA 5.1:748). The difference is, however, that Castorp acknowledges the power of death and eros and that he belittles the moral value of reason because in his view it does not foster benevolent thoughts. Instead, he promises to uphold "Liebe" (caritas) and "Güte" (kindness).

Castorp's separation of reason and ethics leaves open whether ethical dispositions like love and kindness are natural qualities and cannot be controlled by reason, just as eros cannot be ruled by it either. Mann's discourse on love is somewhat problematic as it differentiates between eros on the one hand and caritas on the other, and yet claims that sexual love cannot entirely be separated from platonic love. The narrator's authoritative explanation provides some insight into Mann's seemingly ambiguous position:

> Das ist vollkommene Eindeutigkeit in der Zwiedeutigkeit, denn Liebe kann nicht unkörperlich sein in der äußersten Frömmigkeit und nicht unfromm in der äußersten Fleischlichkeit, sie ist immer sie selbst, als verschlagene Lebensfreundlichkeit wie als höchste Passion, sie ist die Sympathie mit dem Organischen, das rührend wollüstige Umfangen des zur Verwesung Bestimmten,—Charitas ist gewiß in der bewunderungsvollsten oder wütenden Leidenschaft. (GKFA 5.1:907–8)
>
> (This is perfect clarity in ambiguity, as love cannot be disembodied even in its most pious form, nor can it be impious even in its most bodily incarnation. Love is always itself, both as a sly friendliness toward life or as utmost passion. Love is our empathy with organic life, the movingly lustful embrace of what is destined to decay—caritas is certainly inherent in the most admirable or irate passion.)

The narrator's insistence on the inseparable cohesion of physical attraction and empathy is compatible with his references to Novalis and Walt Whitman in his essay "Von deutscher Republik." There he invokes the two poets in praise of a personal, emotional, human, and, in the case of Whitman, even homoerotic passion for a democratic society: "Eros als Staatsmann, als Staatsschöpfer ..." (GKFA 15.1:555). Citing Mann's introductory lecture to the *Zauberberg* for students at Princeton University, Thomas Rendall has pointed out the connection between Mann's concept of *Steigerung* (intensification, elevation), which characterizes the protagonist's process of maturation, and Goethe's use of the same concept in his essay *Die Metamorphose der Pflanzen* (Rendall 92–93). Rendall suggests that Castorp's relationship to Madame Chauchat develops in analogy to Goethe's scientific description of the development and differentiation of plants as a process of refinement and purification (ibid.) as it changes from an initially sexual liaison to a friendship. In view of Castorp's preference of caritas over eros and his process of maturation, one can assume that the platonic love relationship is portrayed as superior precisely because it is not associated with the death wish, as eros is (Rendall 93–94). Castorp simply gives love a higher ethical meaning without necessarily suppressing or rejecting the erotic aspect (Myers 600). In Hegelian terms one could probably say that eros is both included and transformed or sublated (*aufgehoben*) in caritas. This point of view is consistent with Castorp's premise to prevent death from taking control over human thought while keeping in mind that the desire to be consumed in love or to die nevertheless exists.

Mann's text also exposes erroneous eighteenth-century anthropological assumptions by consulting early twentieth-century scientific discourses. For instance, when Hofrat Behrens talks about his knowledge of Madame Chauchat's "inwendig" (interior) "subcutaneous" characteristics, he is not referring to the internal secrets of her soul but to very measurable physiological data, such as her blood pressure or movements concerning her "Lymphbewegung" (lymphatic tissue). In other words, the apotheosis of the human soul has become obsolete by the end of the nineteenth century. Mann's novel describes the scene of Joachim Zimßen's and Hans Castorp's *Durchleuchtung* (screening) as a sobering insight into a human being's organic inside that reveals nothing but "leeres Gebein" (empty bones) (GKFA 5.1:330). The medical reduction of the human to its functional aspects augmented already-existing doubts about the exceptional role of the human among the living creatures. While the screening process implies a scientific objectification and thus contributes to the demystification of the human subject, Mann's narrative also makes it clear that science is by no means objective. When Hofrat Behrens explains that the screening only works if one isolates the human body and blocks out daylight, he implies that the scientific experiment requires a manipulation of human perception: "Erst müssen wir uns mal die Augen mit Finsternis waschen, um so was zu sehen, das ist doch klar" (First we must wash our eyes in darkness in order to see something like this, that is evident) (GKFA 5.1:329–30). Mann stresses the pseudo-religious signification of science even more by having Behrens suggest that one should meditate in silent prayer: "Ich finde es sogar gut und richtig, daß wir uns vorher ein bißchen sammeln, sozusagen in stillem Gebet" (GKFA 5.1:330). In other words, one has to believe in science in order to make it work.

Mann's *Zauberberg* indirectly discredits the unfounded claims of physiognomy by having Hofrat Behrens point out that the surface of the skin harbors deceptive features that lead to false assumptions about racial differences. External appearances can be deceptive and therefore do not relate to the state of a human being's inner qualities as physiognomic studies and racial theories claimed (GKFA 5.1:391). Both the classical assumption that a healthy human body signifies a beautiful soul and the physiognomic claim that physical malformations indicate mental or moral defects were scientifically proven to be baseless. While physiognomic assertions of definite mind-body correlations had been contested throughout the nineteenth century and had hardly any credibility among scientists, proponents of racist or chauvinist philosophies resorted to such claims well into the twentieth century.[20] In fact, there was a "truly phenomenal resurgence of physiognomic theories" in Weimar Germany (Gray 177). This trend is significant for my argument because physiognomy attempted to scientifically justify the interpretive methodology of the *Geisteswissenschaften* (human sciences) by adopting the quantifying methodologies of the *Naturwissenschaften* (natural sciences).

Mann's Political Transformation

The revival of physiognomic theories during the 1920s must be seen in the context of the social, economic and political upheavals that plagued the Weimar Republic from its beginning in 1918. The industrial revolution and the fast-paced technological progress, the emergence of a democratic civil society in a formerly hierarchical state with distinct class boundaries, the mass migration to the cities that led to the ghettoization of the working poor and unemployed in the industrial urban areas, the hyperinflation of 1923 and other economic difficulties such as high unemployment, the political instability, and the humiliating Treaty of Versailles raised the level of anxiety among large parts of the population, especially among the impoverished middle class. In this climate of existential uncertainty, physiognomy promised to provide a sense of security or predictability by establishing laws that allowed individuals to classify other people and draw conclusions about their hidden internal characteristics.[21]

The compensation for the loss of traditional religious beliefs and metaphysics becomes a target of both Mann's and Hesse's essayistic works during the 1920s. Both authors explain the emergence of obscurantist political prophecies that were affiliated with extremist movements on the right and left as a result of the religious vacuum and the search for meaning, a phenomenon that has a very similar explanation as the revival of physiognomy. By 1922 Mann's political perspective had indeed changed considerably since his pro-war sentiments in *Reflections of an Unpolitical Man*, where he had portrayed war as an inevitable tool for Germany to preserve its national autonomy and where he had argued that democracy was incompatible with the German national character. Whereas in 1914 he made fun of the "englische Humanitätsgleisnerei" (English hypocritical humanitarianism) and distanced himself from the humanist agenda of the Western alliance by claiming that the German soul possessed something deep and irrational in contrast to the less sincere character of other peoples (GKFA 15.1:45), he now aligns himself and the German nation with Western democracy under a humanist banner (GKFA 15.1:522). He condemns the obscurantist nationalist war rhetoric, which he himself admittedly defended before and during the war. His intention to win over the young generation for the Weimar Republic also challenges his previous position of the "apolitical" artist, who attempted to preserve his moral freedom by focusing on universal existential questions rather than politically relevant issues that are subject to change. In the following years Mann pursued his gradual but steady attempts to integrate Germany and its culture into the European community of democratic nations by denouncing the romanticist aberrations that had led to Germany's anti-humanist nationalism.

Mann's essay "Deutschland und die Demokratie" (1925) is exemplary for his political transformation. He still distinguishes between the French and German humanism, emphasizing that France was more entrenched in its "bürgerlich-klassischer Tradition" and thus was able to view its engagement in World War I as a legitimate effort to defend its classical humanist legacy (GKFA 15.1:939–40). In other words, nationalism and humanism are identical in France in Mann's opinion. German nationalism, on the other hand, could easily be labeled as anti-humanist because of the Western powers' self-representation as bona fide heirs of the classical humanist tradition. For Mann, the fascist movement plays into the hands of Germany's enemies' propaganda by paying homage to a barbarian "Wotanskult" (anti-humanist cult) (GKFA 15.1:944). He attempts to counteract the fascist appropriation of German nationalism by invoking Germany's own humanist tradition, citing Goethe's *Iphigenie* and appealing to the "höhere Deutschtum" (the elevated German spirit), "das immer 'das Land der Griechen mit der Seele gesucht' hat" (whose soul had always been in search of the classical Greek spirit) (GKFA 15.1:945). Mann is fully aware that his invocation of Goethe's *Iphigenie* as a prime example of the German neo-humanist tradition serves the ideological goal of refashioning Germany as a highly civilized nation that puts the stereotype of Germany's barbarianism to shame. He even admits to his attempt to give new meaning to the "Begriff der Humanität der zur leeren Worthülse geworden, zum akademischen Gerümpel geworden war, mit neuem Inhalt zu erfüllen" (the term humanism which [in his opinion] had become a platitude, academic verbiage) (GKFA 15.1:946).

Mann's changing political position reflects the socioeconomic upheavals and political ups and downs of the Weimar Republic. In view of a short period of economic stability due to the Dawes Plan and Foreign Minister Gustav Streseman's (1878–1929) successful foreign policy resulting in Germany's full sovereignty and admission to the League of Nations (Schulze 216), Mann expressed his confidence in the endurance of bourgeois culture in his speech "Lübeck als geistige Lebensform" of 1926 (*Essays* 3:36). At that point he believed in the continuing preeminence of the humanist cultural tradition, which in his opinion was to prevail in spite of the enormous "moral, scientific, economic, political, technical, aesthetic revolutions" (ibid.). He still defended the supremacy and integrity of the mind of the educated and privileged *Bildungsbürgertum* (bourgeoisie) against the economic interests of a growing petite bourgeoisie and proletariat who threatened his belief in the integrity of a purely spiritual humanist legacy: "Der Geist ist etwas sehr Reines, und wer eine Lebensform im Geistigen hält, der hält sie rein, der schützt sie vor jeder Entartung und Verhärtung, die sie in der Wirklichkeit erleiden mag" (The spirit is something very pure, and whoever leads a spiritual way of life preserves its purity and protects it from any degeneration and ossification, which it may suffer in reality)

(*Essays* 3:37). He also changed his formerly nationalist disposition to a more sophisticated cosmopolitan attitude: "Weltbürgerlichkeit, Weltmitte, Weltgewissen, Weltbesonnenheit" (cosmopolitanism, world center, world conscience, world civility) were the catchwords that he preferred to attach to the German bourgeoisie (ibid.). In Mann's opinion, this cosmopolitan humanism would find its aesthetic expression in a sublime form of irony that transcends all class distinctions.

Mann's confidence in the humanist legacy was shattered with the onset of the Great Depression. In his speech "Ein Appell an die Vernunft" ("An Appeal to Reason") of 1930, he concedes that in these times of economic hardship "die spielend leidenschaftliche Vertiefung ins Ewig-Menschliche" ([the artist's] immersion in the apolitical realm of the eternally human) would be frivolous (*Essays* 3:260). The strong showing of the NSDAP at the general election to the Reichstag on September 14 was a wake-up call that convinced Mann of the economic conditions' impact on the political convictions of the vast majority of people. Mann addresses the bourgeois aversion to a socialist class-consciousness and revises his distaste for ideologies that are based on socioeconomic considerations. In contrast to his former elitist detachment from the socialist working class, he now lauds its "unzweifelhaft besseren und lebendigeren Willen" (undoubtedly better and more lively willingness) to engage with intellectual and spiritual matters than the bourgeoisie (*Essays* 3:273). Mann's political transformation is also accompanied by his unequivocal commitment to the Western entente in spite of the harsh conditions of the Treaty of Versailles that in his opinion contributed to the weakness of the Weimar Republic. While Mann recalls his bourgeois heritage in an attempt to portray the German national character as politically averse to the fanatic extremism that threatened Weimar democracy, he recognizes the danger that the "Abkehr vom Vernunftglauben" (turning away from the rationalism) and the irrational regression into a chaotic nature mysticism poses for the Weimar Republic (*Essays* 3:266).

The identification of a pitiless rationality with the widely despised victorious alliance and the loss of national pride, ethical ideals, and traditional religious beliefs resulted in a widespread demoralization of the Germans and left a spiritual vacuum that explains the emotional appeal of extremist grassroots movements. Such movements, and especially the NSDAP, welcomed the unemployed, uprooted, uneducated, and impoverished members of society into a *Volksgemeinschaft* (national community), which promised a radical change and a return to a more authentic way of life that was for many much more appealing than the uninspiring pragmatism of the established parties. In short, the extremism of the right was appealing not only because it claimed to restore national pride by retaliating for the humiliation at the hands of the allied powers but also because it promised a spiritual home and appealed to the masses' emotional needs. While Mann in his *Betrachtungen eines Unpolitischen* (*Reflec-*

tions of an Unpolitical Man) also followed such anti-modern nationalist ideologies to distinguish himself from the mindset of the victorious Western powers (GKFA 15.1:559), he now sides with the rationalist attitude that he used to condemn as superficial and calculating.

This ideological shift is also noticeable in his fiction, especially *Der Zauberberg* and *Mario und der Zauberer* (*Mario and the Magician*) (1930). Yet Mann's political transformation does not result in a distinct aesthetic transformation. Mann continues to write from the perspective of an omniscient narrator, who, despite his sometimes self-deprecating gestures, depicts the foibles and human shortcomings of his characters from a sympathetic yet superior point of view. The following passage from the final pages of the *Zauberberg* illustrates Mann's self-ironical attitude toward his gradual retraction from the views expressed in "Deutschland und die Demokratie," and in "Lübeck als geistige Lebensform," namely those of Germany's distinctly spiritual form of democracy and its mediating position between east and west. The passage also exemplifies how Mann's irony can both expose and withstand the tension between an untrustworthy humanist tradition and a profane, gruesome, and hostile reality, between the euphemistic generalities of ideological rhetoric and the very specific and complicated occurrences of everyday life:

> Er sprach mit schwacher Stimme, aber viel, schön und von Herzen über die Selbstvervollkommnung der Menschheit auf gesellschaftlichem Wege. Seine Rede ging wie auf Taubenfüßen, aber bald, wenn er etwa von der Vereinigung der befreiten Völker zum allgemeinen Glücke sprach, so mischte sich—er wollte und wußte es wohl selber nicht—etwas wie Rauschen von Adlersschwingen hinein, und das machte zweifellos die Politik, das großväterliche Erbe, das sich mit dem humanistischen Erbe des Vaters in ihm, Lodovico, zur schönen Literatur vereinigt hatte,—genau wie Humanität und Politik sich vereinigten in dem Hoch- und Toastgedanken der Zivilisation, diesem Gedanken voll Taubenmilde und Adlerskühnheit, der seinen Tag erwartete, den Völkermorgen, da das Prinzip der Beharrung würde aufs Haupt geschlagen und die Heilige Allianz der bürgerlichen Demokratie in die Wege geleitet werden... (GKFA 5.1:1076–77)

> (He spoke in a weak but heartfelt voice, and had much to say about self-perfection of humanity by way of social reform. His speech began as if on dove's feet, but as soon as he talked, for instance, about the liberated peoples' unification for universal happiness, a sound like that of an eagle's rushing pinions colored his voice—not that he wanted it or knew it—and that was undoubtedly due to the politics that he had inherited from his grandfather, which had then blended with the humanistic legacy of his father to create beautiful literature in him— just as humanity and politics were blended in the lofty and celebrated idea of civilization, an idea full of the mildness of a dove and the boldness of an eagle, which was awaiting its day, the dawn of peoples, when the principle of obstinacy would be struck down and the gateway opened to the Holy Alliance of bourgeois democracy.)

This passage satirizes Lodovico Settembrini's "schönen Gesinnung" (beautiful ethos), which for the most part coincides with that of the *Zivilisationsliteraten* or proponents of Western "Francophile" democracy. Mann's narrator distances himself from Settembrini's somewhat naïve belief in a *Völkermorgen* (dawn of peoples) by emphasizing the latter's grandiose rhetoric and thus illustrating his overblown humanist expectations for a civilized, democratic, bourgeois society. A sudden change in style unmasks Settembrini's naïve belief that long-standing anti-democratic sentiments could be put to rest by simply "hitting the principle of persistence on its head"—a belief that recalls Mann's earlier opinion on the enduring authoritarian tradition that shaped the German national character.

The narrator's sarcastic tone exposes Settembrini's starry-eyed intellectualism and calculating self-representation as a humanist aesthete with well-meaning intentions. He also expresses doubt as to whether Settembrini would remain impartial and shy away from bloodshed, "wo die Menschlichkeit sich begeisterungsvoll mit der Politik zur Sieges- und Herrschaftsidee der Zivilisation verband" (where humaneness enthusiastically joined forces with politics to promote the idea of victory and domination of civilization) (GKFA 5.1:1077).[22]

Settembrini's opportunistic wavering whenever political reality is in conflict with his ideological principles makes his ideological position even more questionable. The omniscient narrator, who acts as the author's critical representative, stresses time and again the inadequacies of humanist ideology in the face of political reality and its hypocritical misappropriation for political purposes. While the irony of these interventions prevents a one-sided didacticism and points to the inconsistencies of ideological dogmas, these interferences also reflect a manipulative authorial subtext. Narrative irony dominates because it acts as a superior voice that reduces the characters to agents with limited capacity and insight. In short, Mann's irony provides the authorial counterpoint to the characters' insufficiencies. In spite of its interrogative, nondidactic nature, it speaks from a sovereign, nondiegetic point of view that is off-limits to criticism. While the narrator's sardonic remarks occasionally mock his authority and thus challenge the humanist assumptions of the nineteenth-century *Bildungsroman*, the novel could be regarded as a satirical response to humanism—and as such as posthumanist—insofar as it reduces the characters to caricatures and thus reveals the opportunist appropriation of humanist ideals. Yet the narrator's sovereignty surreptitiously validates the notion of individual autonomy. While the authorial subtext undermines humanist values by exposing their rhetorical exploitation for politically expedient purposes, such as the violent suppression of authoritarian ideas, it does so without breaking with the aesthetic conventions that represent them. Hesse's *Steppenwolf*, which will be the focus of the next chapter, deviates more substantially from the conventions of the *Bildungsroman* and entails a more radical critique of the humanist premises of human nature.

Notes

1. In *Reflections of an Unpolitical Man*, Mann connects his defense of his German cultural background to his nationalism, which he compares favorably to his brother's Francophile leanings. Hesse's cultural elitism is mediated through the perspective of the narrators of *Steppenwolf*. Although one must not equate the perspective of these fictional characters with those of their authors, the autobiographical similarities between authors and narrators suggest strong affinities.
2. The essay collection *Adel des Geistes: Sechzehn Versuche zum Problem der Humanität* was published in 1945 but contains essays that were written over a span of thirty-five years.
3. See, for instance, Stephan Zweig's *Die Welt von Gestern* (Frankfurt: Fischer, 1985), 44–85; also York-Gothart Mix, *Die Schulen der Nation: Bildungskritik in der Literatur der Moderne* (Stuttgart: Metzler, 1995).
4. All future references to Thomas Mann's works will be taken from the *Große Kommentierte Frankfurter Ausgabe* and cited parenthetically in the text as GKFA including volume and page number.
5. See, for instance, Kontje, *Cambridge Introduction to Thomas Mann*, 54–100; Freedman, *Hermann Hesse: Pilgrim of Crisis*, 353–69.
6. Hermann Kurzke mentions in his commentary to Mann's *Betrachtungen* that Mann's jingoist war frenzy was surprising and is often explained as an aberration of the otherwise highly civilized and sophisticated author (GKFA 13.2:10).
7. Several critics link Mann's aggressive patriotism and warmongering to his insecurities about being exposed as an effeminate bluestocking and a homosexual (GKFA 14.2:591–92; Kontje, *Cambridge* 56; Kurzke, GKFA 13.2:10).
8. Niels Werber points out the similarities to Mann's *Zauberberg*, in which the author conveys his contradictory pro- and antidemocratic views through the two opponents, Settembrini and Naphta (235–36).
9. Although Mann liked to portray himself as a political outsider among intellectuals, he was by no means the only one who favored an autocratic hierarchical state over democracy. The conservative cultural philosopher Paul de Lagarde (1827–91); the literary scholar Ernst Bertram (1884–1957), Mann's friend who later collaborated with the Nazis; and the historian and philosopher Oswald Spengler (1880–1936), to name just a few intellectuals, voiced similar views and can be regarded as Mann's ideological guides during this phase of his life (Kontje, *Mann's World* 65–66, 70–71, 103).
10. Mann's ambivalent position toward Germany's democratic future has been widely acknowledged in scholarship. Lothar Pikulik, for instance, views the *Betrachtungen* as both an involuntary inclination toward and a distancing from Germany's inevitable future democratization (13). Consequently, Pikulik points out that Mann's opponent, the politicized *Zivilisationsliterat*, a pseudonym for his brother Heinrich, figures only seemingly as a serious antagonist since Mann himself shares many character traits with his rival (13).
11. Markus Kartheiniger attributes this generalization to Locke's and Rousseau's interpretations of Hobbes's natural rights (244).
12. While Mann portrayed the German war effort as a fight for the preservation of Germany's national identity, Mann's claim that his support of the war had nothing to do with imperialist or expansionist tendencies is hard to believe. After all, he was reminiscing about the restoration of a German Reich that was much bigger and more powerful.

13. For instance, the protagonist criticizes the essay of a famous French writer as "recht feines Geschwätz" (finely spun verbiage) (297). The narrator also comments on the protagonist's foray into the ivory tower of the arts and on the "Hochmut der Erkenntnis" (arrogance of knowledge) (264).
14. Mann refers to Paul de Lagarde in disputing the suitability of the motto of the French Revolution for the German national character (GKFA 13.1:300–301).
15. In his essay "Goethe und Tolstoi," Mann sets up the same opposition between Rousseau and German humanism. For Mann, Goethe and Tolstoy distinguish themselves from Rousseau because they saw no reason to long for nature as they embodied nature themselves (GKFA 15:1:388). He also views both Goethe and Tolstoy as truly national populist poets: "Goethe ist, wie Tolstoi, darum der volkhaft echteste Dichter seines Landes, ein wahrer Ausbruch des Volksgeistes, gleich Luther, gleich Bismarck" (Goethe is, like Tolstoy, the most genuinely populist poet, a true eruption of the populist spirit, like Luther, like Bismarck) (ibid. 416).
16. With regard to Germany's particular history, Mann's argument of a distinctly authoritarian German national character bears some justification. After all, the perceived loss of a genuinely German cultural tradition in view of the increasing internationalization and homogenization of national and regional customs reinforced nationalist and anti-Semitic sentiments at the beginning of the twentieth century. The presumed erosion of national identity was particularly strong and consequential because of the overpowering influence of the Western entente on a politically and economically weakened Germany after World War I (GKFA 13.1:127–28). The devastating loss had both a humiliating and a disorienting effect for many Germans (Zweig, Troeltsch).
17. While Novalis seems like an odd choice for justifying democratic leanings, his linking of the German Romantic poet to the American herald of democracy may be considered an astute strategic move that allowed Mann to portray his political transformation as a logical development. Both poets extrapolate from their individual experiences to the universality of human existential sensitivities and thus justify their individual subordination and participation in the social entity of the state. Mann distinguishes these poets from what he considers radical Enlightenment philosophy since they promote equality without neglecting the individuality of each human being (GKFA 15.1:540). The focus on personal experience was essential for Mann's democratic conviction.
18. If not indicated otherwise, all translations from the German are mine.
19. Mann refers to Aalsgard in his essay "Luebeck als geistige Lebensform" (1926) as the place where he spent a vacation in 1899 "wo der 'Tonio Kröger' unbewußt entworfen wurde" (where "Tonio Kröger" was subliminally conceived) (Mann, Essays 3:21).
20. For a discussion of "German Physiognomic Thought from Lavater to Auschwitz," see Richard T. Gray, About Face (Detroit: Wayne State University Press, 2004).
21. The most extreme forms of physiognomic prejudice can be detected "in the proto-fascist racial anthropologies of the 1920s and 1930s, which sought to draw distinct lines of racial kinship and clearly segregate the unified racial community from the racial Other" (Gray 205).
22. Settembrini's lack of concern for the common soldier is further emphasized by the contrasting, realistic description of a fighting Hans Castorp whose survival in the trenches remains doubtful (GKFA 5.1:108–85).

CHAPTER 11

Between Humanism and Posthumanism
Hermann Hesse's Steppenwolf

Introduction

In contrast to Thomas Mann, Hermann Hesse distanced himself from the war euphoria already in 1914. Yet he also expressed sympathetic feelings toward the German side in World War I and considered war as a necessary evil that had to be fought (HSW 15:10).[1] He even wrote several war poems in which he identifies with the soldiers in the trenches (Schwilk 183–86). However, in his opinion, nationalism should never serve as an end in itself but rather as "eine Art Vorschule zum Ideal der Menschheit" (a kind of preschool for an ideal humanity) (HSW 15:17). By way of introduction to my analysis of Hesse's novel *Steppenwolf*, I will summarize the author's political development as it is represented in his numerous essays that appeared between 1914 and 1922. These essays will shed light on the interests and intellectual background that Hesse shared with Mann in spite of their different biographies and developments as authors. It will also explain Hesse's nontraditional humanism.

In a newspaper article titled "O Freunde, nicht diese Töne" ("Oh Friends, Don't Speak like That"), published in the *Neue Zürcher Zeitung* in 1914, Hesse emphasized that he could not be happy about the war and that it would be important to establish friendly ties to the adversaries after the war (HSW 15:15). Hesse refers to Schiller's "An die Freude" ("Ode to Joy") with the admonition to intone something more pleasant and joyful. The citation of Schiller's poem was his response to the excessive nationalism and the denigration of non-German literature. Hesse positioned himself squarely in the Enlightenment tradition when he admonished his fellow Germans to heed humanist values, such as "Gerechtigkeit, Mäßigung, Anstand, Menschenliebe" (justice, restraint, integrity, philanthropy) (HSW 15:13). He also emphasized that the ultimate goal must be the overcoming of war in the name of a peaceful coexistence of all of humanity. His relatively mild but nevertheless courageous criticism was met with a flurry of vehemently hostile reactions in the German press. Hesse received an abundance of hate mail at this time of patriotic fervor (Schwilk 187; HSW 15:290–96). After a trip through Germany he was attacked as a draft dodger and coward because he expressed his relief in his travelogue over not being drafted (Schwilk 189; HSW 15:118–22). These accusations and defamations are noteworthy in view of Hesse's attempts to volunteer for military service and being rejected twice because of his nearsightedness and advanced age. After these rejections, he tried to lend his moral support to those in the trenches by distributing literature to the soldiers through the German Red Cross. His ambivalent feelings toward Germany's war effort by no means characterize him as a staunch war opponent or pacifist. To the contrary, he was convinced that aggression is part of human nature and that war is part of life and cannot be abolished by fiat (HSW 15:114; 135–39). Nevertheless, Hesse condemns in the strongest terms the senseless continuation of the "Massenwürgen, Todschlägerei, Schlächterei" (mass slaying, slaughter, massacring) after the peace negotiations of Brest-Litowsk in 1917, which in his opinion benefitted only a "kleine Schicht von Geschäftemachern" (a small group of profiteers) and ignored humanity's call for peace (HSW 15:182–87).

Hesse's criticism of such warmongering permeates his political and feuilleton writings of the early 1920s. He lamented, for example, the nationalist invocation of the "deutsche Pseudogeist" (German pseudo-spirit), which the world had identified justifiably as the culprit of the war (HSW 15:295). The selfish incantation of ideological slogans was also the target of Hesse's political pamphlet *Zarathustra's Wiederkehr* (*Zarathustra's Return*), first published anonymously in Switzerland in 1919. Ironically, Hesse appealed to "einen deutschen Geist, einen deutschen Mut, eine deutsche Mannhaftigkeit" (a German spirit, a German courage, and a German manhood) (HSW 15:220), as if he were in agreement with the patriotic fervor that deplores the loss of Germany's glory after World War I.[2] However, in the historical context of its appearance in 1920, *Zarathustra's Wiederkehr* must be seen as an exhortation to the defeated German people, especially the demoralized soldiers, to face their own guilt and be accountable for the disastrous outcome of the war. Instead of succumbing to the victim's self-pity and longing for revenge, as so many patriotically minded Germans did after the Treaty of Versailles, Hesse's Zarathustra suggests that the Germans accept their fate and their responsibilities for their past actions.

Although Hesse's text addresses the nationalist fervor in this specific historical situation, its archaic language in the allegorical style of Nietzsche's *Zarathustra* transcends the particular context of postwar chauvinism by striking a philosophical tone that applies to human behavior in general. Nietzsche's concept of *amor fati*, which demands introspective self-questioning with the goal of understanding and accepting the inevitable truths of one's fate and ultimately of knowing oneself, has an aesthetic dimension that becomes apparent in Hesse's fictional works.[3] This type of introspection aims at the Socratic imperative of self-knowledge (*gnothi seauton*), which supposedly leads to becoming true to oneself. However, this self-interrogation also results in realization that to live means to suffer (HSW 15:231).[4]

The realization that much of human suffering originates in the self rather than in the hostile actions of others is no reason for being despondent, Hesse claims. While blaming others no longer promises relief from one's suffering, it is much more realistic to learn how to accept one's own fate than to know how to change the world. The human compulsion to be active by doing things just for the sake of doing something is at the core of a self-deceptive escapism, according to Zarathustra, who can be seen as a sounding board for the author. In his opinion, humans try to escape their suffering by attempting to change the world. In view of Hesse's introspective soul-searching, it is not surprising that the author's philosophical and political development differed from Mann's increasing political involvement. Although Hesse remained an antifascist and despised any form of authoritarianism and subordination, he had no illusions about his political influence. His psychologically and philosophically informed writings sought to uncover the reasons for political conflicts and warfare at the base of human nature rather than in ideological rhetoric, which in his opinion was often used for ulterior purposes. This explains the interweaving of political, philosophical, psychological, and homiletic discourse evident in *Zarathustra's Wiederkehr*.

In "Die Sehnsucht unserer Zeit nach einer Weltanschauung" ("The Longing of our Time for a World View"), which first appeared in the journal *Uhu* in 1926, Hesse implies that one cannot expect the average individual to have a genuinely personal philosophy of life, as he had argued in *Zarathustra's Wiederkehr*. Hesse acknowledges that the vanishing authority of the churches, industrialization and the development of new technologies, as well as rapid demographic shifts have caused a spiritual vacuum that manifests itself in a widespread longing for binding ethical norms and a universally recognized philosophical or religious foundation (HSW 15:479–81). He explains the blossoming of countless religious sects, self-styled prophets, fortune-tellers, charlatans, and other manifestations of superstitious beliefs as a consequence of these social, economic, and demographic transformations.[5] His welcoming openness to new spiritual experimentation, however, reveals his vitalist and cyclical understanding of cultural progress, which views each beginning with fascination and is expressed in his poem "Stufen": "Und in jedem Anfang wohnt ein Zauber inne" (In each beginning dwells its magic) (HSW 5:400–401). This idea of rejuvenation and rebirth, which can also be found in Nietzsche's *Zarathustra*, is a leitmotif in many of Hesse's works, such as *Peter Camenzind*, *Unterm Rad*, *Gertrud*, *Roßhalde*, *Demian*, and *Steppenwolf*.

Hesse's ambivalence toward his humanist education is not only central to his novel *Steppenwolf* but also a concern that he shares with Thomas Mann. Both authors problematize their pride in their humanist erudition and their somewhat elitist condescension toward their less educated, seemingly superficial contemporaries in their fictional works. For instance, Mann's parodies of simple people correspond to Hesse's alter ego's contempt for popular culture. The intellectual characters' self-importance, however, is also discredited through irony and self-criticism.

Yet there are certain characteristics that distinguish the narrators' positions toward their characters. While the narrators of Mann's *Tonio Kröger* and *Zauberberg* reveal a close affinity to their author and maintain sovereignty throughout the texts, the narrative authority of Hesse's narrators in *Steppenwolf* is by no means unassailable. The first-person narrator Harry Haller does not judge the characters from a superior distance, like Mann's omniscient narrators, but remains constrained by the limited perspective of the protagonist. Moreover, the omniscient narrator of the "Tractatus" section of the novel certainly knows more than Haller by giving a psycho-philosophical analysis of the Steppenwolf, but he also knows less than the protagonist because he is incapable of adopting Haller's subjective point of view. In short, the novel's multiperspectival account of Haller's life, the open-ended conclusion and nonlinear, antirational development of the protagonist deconstruct the idea of individual autonomy that has been an essential assumption of humanist ideology. I will devote the remainder of this chapter to an analysis of *Steppenwolf* in order to show that Hesse's novel can be regarded as a more radical, posthumanist response to the conventions of the *Bildungsroman* than Mann's *Zauberberg*.

Hesse's *Der Steppenwolf*

Hermann Hesse's *Der Steppenwolf* (1927) criticizes the humanist tradition to which it is indebted. It also aspires to overcome the Nietzschean antihumanism of its protagonist and, for several reasons, anticipates posthumanist tendencies. Hesse's *Der Steppenwolf* is *post*humanist in a temporal sense as it confronts the nineteenth-century humanist legacy from a twentieth-century perspective. The novel's critique of traditional bourgeois values does not simply reject humanism and its philosophy of individual autonomy. It dislodges Idealist concepts of wholeness and self-perfection and replaces them with a multiperspectival view of a continuously changing human consciousness in an open-ended process of self-searching. One might say that the novel is "as much *post*-humanist as it is post-*humanist*" (Badmington, "Theorizing" 15). While *post*humanism succeeds the humanist paradigm, it still must engage with the humanist tradition, even "acknowledge its persistence," from a critical perspective (ibid.). The protagonist of Hesse's novel, Harry Haller, becomes gradually aware that his anti-humanist point of view is predisposed by the German humanist tradition with which he was brought up. Haller also realizes that the Cartesian dichotomy of mind and body is a myth.[6] The multiperspectival debunking of both the humanist premises of bourgeois individuality and the protagonist's anti-humanist opposition to these premises leads to the dissolution of a definable personhood, which in turn calls for a posthumanist awareness of the human subject's fluidity and evanescence.

The following analysis focuses on the novel's subversion of both the humanist education and the protagonist's anti-humanist rebellion against it. It discloses how Hesse's novel undermines universalist philosophical claims, regardless of whether they belong to the Idealist or anti-Idealist Nietzschen philosophy that influenced both the protagonist and his author. Hesse's novel reveals how German nineteenth-century humanist philosophy is based on a mind-body hierarchy that is no longer justifiable at the beginning of the twentieth century. The Steppenwolf metaphor illustrates how traditional humanism established the supremacy of the spiritual over the animal nature of "Man" and serves to expose binary reasoning, foregrounded in the protagonist's man-animal division, as a hypothetical construct. More precisely, the Steppenwolf metaphor takes on an emblematic function that encapsulates both the protagonist's personal dilemma as an artist and social outsider and the human conundrum in general created by traditional humanism's suppression of the abject biological reality of life. Yet it also provokes the protagonist's vacillation between the repression and acknowledgment of the subconscious and reveals multifaceted dimensions of human existence. Although Harry Haller has to realize that the Steppenwolf metaphor is a narcissistic self-projection, it plays a catalytic role as the gradual acceptance of Haller's dark animal side leads him on a path that aims at overcoming the mind-body dualism. While Haller eventually fails to liberate himself completely from the stifling, parochial moralist views of his bourgeois upbringing, his humiliating punishment of being laughed at for taking life too seriously forces him to witness the dismantling of his imaginary personality.

In the case of Hesse's novel, traditional humanist assumptions are contested by an array of diegetic and nondiegetic devices, such as multiple narrative perspectives, that dispute or relativize the actuality of the protagonists and their claims. Moreover, they include contradictory accounts by the characters; the dissolution of fixed boundaries between individual characters, i.e., the blending, mixing, and multiplying of characters as, for instance, in doubles or gender-bending fusions of characters; and the disassembling of personalities. Hesse's *Der Steppenwolf* seeks to reveal the human dependence on an instinctual, subconscious nature beyond rational control, thus exposing the myth that individuals are superior to other living beings by virtue of their ability to rationally know themselves. Irony as an inconclusive dialogic mode of self-reflection is an effective device for communicating the perpetual human striving toward an elusive self-recognition. To be sure, one could argue that these narrative strategies can also be detected in humanist novels of education. However, within the humanist paradigm they do not serve the overall purpose of deconstructing the unity and agency of the human subject as a fiction, as Hesse's *Der Steppenwolf* does. Moreover, the posthumanist paradigm distinguishes itself from anti-humanist approaches (i.e., by Freud, Marx, or Nietzsche) in that it reflects on these and reveals that all attempts at delimiting the subject ontologically are arbitrary.

Conceding the difficulty of defining posthumanism, Badmington detects the incipient impulses for anti-humanist and posthumanist tendencies already in Marxist and Freudian thinking (*Posthumanism* 4–6). Accordingly, the Marxist rejection of "the humanist belief in a natural human essence, which exists outside history, politics, and social relations" (ibid. 5), implicitly defies the sovereignty of human reason expressed in Descartes's "Cogito ergo sum." Assuming that human thinking is contingent on social, political, and cultural conditions, Marxism discards both the notion of individual autonomy and the supremacy of mind over body. The Freudian challenge to Cartesian dualism and the humanist paradigm is even more radical than its Marxist counterpart as it ultimately disputes the very existence of the *I* as a reliable entity. With the acknowledgment of the subconscious, instinctual sphere, however, the authority and independence of the human mind is not only contested from the world outside but also from within the human subject. Jacques Lacan emphasizes the diminishing power of the Freudian ego in his essay on the mirror stage by detecting the self-deluding image-making process in the early stages of ego formation. Accordingly, the Cartesian mind-body duality proposed in traditional eighteenth-century humanist philosophy fails to recognize that the human subject is conditioned by a series of *méconnaissances* that constitute the ego from the very beginning of its development (Lacan 6). Hesse's novel focuses on the inadequacy of the mind-body division and its continuing influence on the conceptualization of the human. The protagonist's binary perspective is typical for intellectuals at the time and prevailed well into the twentieth century.

As a writer who was sensitive to the challenges that bourgeois intellectuals had to face in view of the rapid social transformations after World War I, Hesse became increasingly aware that the humanist beliefs of his education were anachronistic.[7] With its numerous autobiographical references, *Der Steppenwolf* can be considered as a fictional portrayal of the author's gradual disillusionment with the humanist worldview.[8] Giving a detailed account of the deconstruction of his personality, Hesse's alter ego, Harry Haller, gradually comes to realize after his soul-searching process that the Cartesian mind-body division is a simplification, inadequate to grasp the complexities of modern existence. Moreover, the protagonist's self-interrogation reveals that his personality does not consist of a spiritual essence but dissolves into an accumulation of acquired conventions, habits, cultural and philosophical traditions, even specific historical events and constellations. Hesse's novel inverts the traditional *Bildungsroman* by turning the protagonist's progress toward completion upside down, into a process of self-dissolution (Schwarz, "Erklärung" 197).[9] The novel not only undermines the humanist belief in the perfectibility and homogeneity of the individual, it also questions the Enlightenment assumption that civilization means progress. By revealing the constructedness of cultural hierarchies and the increasing fragmentation of twentieth-century individuals, it anticipates current notions of posthumanism.

Hesse's novel disrupts the humanist aesthetics of the *Bildungsroman* in several respects, including its form. Rather than presenting a linear narrative, the author chooses three different viewpoints that account for the novel's multiperspectivity. It consists of an editor, who represents the bourgeois foil for Haller, also known as Steppenwolf; a first-person narrator, who depicts Haller's development from a personal point of view; and the third-person narrator of the *Tractat* or treatise, who analyzes Haller's human condition from a quasi-objective, philosophical and psychological perspective. The complexity of the narrative perspective illustrates the fragmentation of the self.[10] The novel's formal and semantic structure is by no means traditional, although it does not take advantage of the stream-of-consciousness technique or experiment with syntactical and morphological structures.[11] The insertion of dream sequences, a long epistolary passage of mysterious origin, philosophical discourses, and the disintegration of the novel's main character into a multiplicity of hybrid characters that oscillate between fact and fantasy reveal the novel's indebtedness to the Romantic tradition. By integrating ideas of Nietzsche, Carl Gustav Jung, as well as intermedial discourses on cinema, radio, and mass culture, Hesse transforms, criticizes, and plays with the conventions of *Bildungsroman* and *Künstlernovelle* in an attempt to overcome and question a fossilized Idealist tradition (Herwig and Trabert 9).[12]

The fragmentation of the main character is pointedly connected to the disintegration of the mind-body dualism. In Idealist philosophy, "Man" is portrayed as a rational animal. Likewise, the Steppenwolf is, of course, not an actual animal but a metaphor that refers to the protagonist Harry Haller. It characterizes its protagonist as a lonesome drifter who roams the streets at night and despises the false pretenses of civility. It also evokes the animalistic side of human existence that has been suppressed in the civilizing process.[13] Thus the Steppenwolf, as a symbol with manifold meanings, stands for "the Animal" in general, and as such for the human other, in that it both distinguishes itself from the human but also embodies it. The Steppenwolf, on the one hand, marks the uncivilized abject, and on the other a purportedly more genuine, uncorrupted human nature worthy of preservation. However, this nature dualism, which represents Haller's initial philosophy, is deconstructed during the course of the protagonist's vacillating development and with it the entire mind-body duality of the Cartesian tradition.

Haller's philosophy, laid out by the third-person narrator in the "Treatise on the Steppenwolf," attributes the Steppenwolf's personal tragedy to the incompatible "zwei Naturen, eine menschliche und eine wölfische ... sie lagen in ständiger Todfeindschaft gegeneinander" (HSW 4:46) ("two natures, a human and a wolfish one," within himself that "were in continual and deadly enmity" [HS 41]). Raised in a bourgeois family, "those who brought him up had declared a war of extinction against the beast in him" [HSW 4:45; HS 41]). The Steppenwolf regards himself "als eine Bestie ... nur mit einem dünnen Überzug von Erziehung und Menschentum" (HSW 4:45) ("as a beast with only a thin covering of the human" [HS 41]). While he "weit über das dem Bürger mögliche Maß hinaus zum Individuum entwickelt ... ist er dennoch ein Zwangshäftling des Bürgertums und kann ihm nicht entrinnen" (HSW 4:56) ("developed far beyond the level possible to the bourgeois ... he is nevertheless captive to the bourgeoisie and cannot escape it" [HS 53]). In other words, the third-person narrator of the treatise is convinced that Haller cannot liberate himself from the damaging effects of his bourgeois education and that "[s]tatt seine Persönlichkeit zu vernichten, war es nur gelungen, ihn sich selbst hassen zu lehren" (HSW 4:14) ("instead of destroying his personality ... succeeded only in teaching him to hate himself" [HS 11]). His view of himself as a caged animal is the main reason for his despair and leads to his decision to commit suicide on his fiftieth birthday. At the bottom of his suffering is the Cartesian dichotomy of mind and body. It instills in him a yearning for pure spirituality on the one hand and "eine wilde Begierde nach starken Gefühlen" (HSW 4:28) ("a wild longing for strong emotions" [HS 27]) on the other. Yet neither of these routes of escape from the self-imposed restraint is available to him because the internal struggle between his instinctual needs and his desire to be rid of them has become part of his disposition.[14] Although Haller knows that his inner division and unhappiness are the result of his bourgeois upbringing, he is also aware that "he can never turn back again and become wholly wolf" (HSW 4:65; HS 63).

Viewing himself as the victim of a repressive education that failed to civilize him, Haller suffers from the lonely existence of an outsider. Yet he also clings to the image of the misunderstood intellectual as it allows him to preserve the illusion of being a nonconformist, self-determined, exceptional human being. Competing with the Nietzschean notion of "the savage born too late, born in the midst of a civilized society" (Lingis 13) who can ennoble himself by asserting the atavistic rights of the wolf-man and his healthy animal instincts, are other monistic notions that no longer view the individual as an essentialist albeit divided entity. As I will show later, references in Hesse's text to monistic and scientific theories by Charles Darwin, Ernst Haeckel, and Carl Gustav Jung as well as Hinduist concepts resonate with these competing philosophies. While they all promise to overcome Idealist metaphysics by viewing the mind as a result of evolution, they also try to counteract the fragmented, split subject. Yet at the conclusion of the open-ended novel, not any one of the philosophies mentioned above can adequately represent the fragmentation, ambiguities, and transformational dynamics of human existence. The open-ended form portrays Haller's life as an inconclusive example with many possibilities.

As the protagonist realizes, however, in the course of his development, viewing human nature according to the simplistic Steppenwolf dualism cannot do justice to the complexities and inconsistencies of his existence (HSW 4:122). Therefore, he has to abandon his Steppenwolf posture that has allowed him to identify with a narcissistic self-image as both a maverick and a victim. As the novel's title suggests, the animal—the inhuman other, whether perceived as an enemy from outside, a threat from within, or a desired ideal—takes the role of a catalyst in the deconstruction of the protagonist's personality that coincides with the demise of his traditional humanist worldview.

Haller gradually comes to realize that what he deems to be the most frivolous leisure activities of modern civilization, such as dancing, have deep roots in earlier stages of the evolution of the human psyche.[15] While he notices that he has unfulfilled sensual and spiritual needs, the inhibitions of his elitist education prevent him initially from enjoying life. By introducing his Faust-like protagonist—a highly educated but pessimistic intellectual—to the sensual pleasures of life, Hesse lets him reconnect with basic instinctual needs that he had lost in the process of his strict upbringing. Haller's cynicism with regard to his middle-class principles, such as decency, modesty, and propriety, is, of course, linked to Nietzsche's cultural critique of nineteenth-century humanism: "We no longer derive man from 'the spirit' or 'the deity'; we have placed him back among the animals" (*Portable Nietzsche* 580).[16] Like Nietzsche, whom Haller esteems as a role model and brother, who was also born into an era that did not understand him, Haller admires the wild, strong animal species rather than the domesticated ones.[17]

Haller's confrontation with the nineteenth-century cultural heritage that informs his entire persona is not simply a matter of intellectual or moral reorientation. It is both painful and liberating because his education has become his second nature. In other words, the metaphysical presumptions of the humanist legacy have conditioned the protagonist to the extent that he perceives himself and the world through the lens of the essentialist biases of his Protestant, middle-class upbringing. The association with a group of nonintellectual bohemians and *bon vivants* teaches him that his relationship to his changing environment cannot simply be understood from an intellectual point of view but must be relearned from a sensual, even sexual, level of experience. As a symbol of a primeval, untamed nature that has been lost in the process of civilization,[18] the Steppenwolf image is a reminder of the protagonist's dependence on a dualist worldview and at the same time becomes a stepping-stone on his path to emancipation from his limiting perspective.

The fact that the protagonist reconnects to his bourgeois origins through his olfactory sense reveals that his upbringing has not just influenced him on an intellectual level but also on an instinctual one (HSW 4:8). Haller has internalized the bourgeois standard of cleanliness to the extent that it becomes fully embodied. It is ironic that the Steppenwolf as a creature of the wild is attracted to the scent of cleanliness, the odor of civilization. In other words, the instincts have been civilized to the point that they reject their own "animalistic" nature. This domestication of the instincts is at the core of Haller's self-hatred because the instinctual side of his being has been trained to reject its very disposition.[19] Haller is partially aware of this self-denying aspect of his bourgeois upbringing and therefore rebels against all forms of superficial propriety as it represses his true feelings and sensual desires.[20] Yet he initially does not comprehend the extent of modern civilization's transforming influence on the individual psyche, including his own. This is why he clings to his Steppenwolf personality as a possible route of escape from the constraints of civilization, not knowing that civilization also controls his sensual perception.[21]

Haller's fascination with the "naïve, redliche Sinnlichkeit" (HSW 4:38) ("simple honest sensuality" [HS 37]) of jazz music must also be seen in this context of the mind-body dualism. While his attraction to the "raw and savage gaiety" of jazz may come as a surprise, his explanation leads back to the clash between the old humanist education of his upbringing and the "knabenhaft frisch und kindlich" (HSW 4:38–39) ("unashamedly primitive and childishly happy" [HS 38]) American brand of music.[22] In other words, Haller's secret fascination with the boyishly fresh and childlike is still connected to his desire to gain access to an exclusive circle of immortals, of "kingly men" (HS 64; HSW 4:66). Although Haller is intellectually aware that he is a "Zwangshäftling des Bürgertums und kann ihm nicht entrinnen" (HSW 4:56) ("captive to the bourgeoisie and cannot escape it" [HS 53]), he does not fully comprehend that his anti-bourgeois rebellion against the "Wichtigtuerei der Wissenschaft, der Zünfte, der Künste" (HSW 4:70) ("pomposity of the sciences, societies and arts" [HS 69]) is influenced by the epistemic assumptions of these discourses. Haller's dualistic view of the human privileges the mind over the body regardless of his fascination with the sensual allure of raw emotions conveyed in jazz music. After all, the "Magic" of the senses promises a means to gain access to a spiritual realm (HSW 4:31, 33–34; HS 30, 32–33).[23]

The domestication of Haller, the wolf, is enacted when Haller accepts the invitation of an acquaintance—a professor with whom he used to discuss oriental mythology—out of sheer politeness and against his genuine inclination (HS 74–75; HSW 4:76–77). Hesse's first-person narrator emphasizes the dishonest repression of will by comparing his, Haller's, meek politeness to the submissive behavior of a "starved dog" ("verhungerter Hund") that "laps up" the professor's praise and cordiality. The Steppenwolf's behavior has been conditioned to succumb to flattery and recognition like a domesticated animal: "Ich blickte dem artigen Mann in sein gelehrtes Gesicht, fand die Szene eigentlich lächerlich, genoß aber doch wie ein verhungerter Hund den Brocken Wärme, den Schluck Liebe, den Bissen Anerkennung" (HSW 4:76) ("And while I looked into the good fellow's bookish face pondering the ridiculously stilted conversation and yet basking in the warmth, gulping the kindness, and the bit of recognition" [HS 75]). The metaphors of "Brocken Wärme," "Schluck Liebe," and a "Bissen Anerkennung" call attention to the self-abnegation brought about by the taming of the instincts. Haller's servile desire to be liked takes the place of the untamed animal's drive for self-preservation, like hunger and thirst, so much so that his learned behavior assumes the function of the instincts: "Gerührt grinste der Steppenwolf Haller, im trockenen Schlunde lief ihm der Geifer zusammen, Sentimentalität bog ihm wider seinen Willen den Rücken" (HSW 4:76) ("The Steppenwolf stood there and grinned as his animal instincts filled his dry mouth with slobber and sappy feelings began to bend his spine against his will" [HS 75]). Here the narrator follows Nietzsche in stressing the continuity between animal and human phylogeny by implying that human characteristics and moral values stem from the instinctual behavior of animals (NW 1:1032; 26). Accordingly, Haller's deceptively submissive behavior toward the professor has its origins in the tamed animal's desire for praise. The difference between the tamed wolf and Haller is, however, that Haller can reflect on his domestication. While this capacity of self-reflection seems to increase the protagonist's suffering because he must watch helplessly how his will gets broken and his spine gets bent, the process of spiritual and physical degeneration does not necessarily end in utter despair as the ability to reflect on his situation also provides Haller with a certain distance that allows him to laugh about his quandary.

Haller's unwitting adherence to the mind-body dichotomy is also evident in his interactions with Hermine, whose name and appearance reminds Haller of a friend from his youth, or younger self, named Hermann (HSW 4:88, 107). Hermine, who calls Haller "little brother" and "my boy" (HS 109; HSW 4:107) and who plays with him a game "for life and death" (HS 109; HSW 4:107) embodies Haller's thinly disguised alter ego. Her androgynous appearance, her youth, her maternal wisdom, intellectual acumen, and philosophical mind underline her ambiguity as well as diverse roles as Haller's mother figure, promiscuous seductress, and younger self (SW 110). Hermine views herself as a kind of mirror ("eine Art Spiegel") for Haller, "weil in mir innen etwas ist, was dir Antwort gibt und dich versteht" (HSW 4:106) ("because there is something in me that answers you and understands you" [HS 108]). Haller agrees with Hermine's self-assessment but also recognizes her as someone who is "so ganz und gar anders als ich!" ("And yet you are so entirely different from me") (ibid.). Hermine's intangible, scintillating personality appears to Haller as his "Gegenteil" ("opposite") that has "alles was mir fehlt" (HSW 4:106) ("all that I lack" [HS108]). Indeed, with her sensuality and her social skills, she seems to embody Haller's narcissistic fantasy of a self that complements his impoverished, ascetic reclusiveness. Hermine assumes the role of Haller's guide, and in this sense she is similar to his other mentor figures, such as Mozart and Goethe, who teach him to overcome his bourgeois inhibitions. Like these so-called immortals, Hermine initiates the transformation of Haller's personality that will eventually liberate him from the limitations of his dualistic point of view. Hermine's ability to transcend seemingly fixed borders between man and woman, child and teacher, mother and seductress make her appear to Haller "wie das Leben selbst: stets nur Augenblick, nie im voraus zu berechnen" (HSW 4:109–10) ("like life itself, one moment succeeding to the next, and not one to be foreseen" [HS 112]). In contrast to traditional masculinist representations of Woman, Hermine is not presented as childlike. On the contrary, Hermine is in control of the effect that she has on Haller and able to use it to her advantage. Her personality that is both highly sensual and youthful, albeit worldly-wise, seems puzzling and defies characterization in terms of Haller's Idealist categories.[24]

When Haller tells Hermine about his inner division between man and wolf, she replies that his self-image as a Steppenwolf is a poetic fantasy (HSW 4: 111; HS 113). She sets him straight by telling him that, in contrast to human beings, animals never act embarrassed or pretentious to impress their audience. To her, animals belong to nature and therefore act in agreement with their natural disposition (HSW 4:111; HS 113). In Hermine's opinion there are moments, however, when human beings resemble animals (HSW 4:112; HS 114). For Hermine, animals are more in touch with the sincerity of existence than humans. Culture and civilization, on the other hand, enable humans to deceive themselves about the inevitable realities of life. While human existence on the whole seems less genuine than that of animals, it does have a much wider range of modes of experience. Hermine's observation that Haller had the looks of an animal when she first met him confirms a human's ability to experience multiple states of mind: ("Heute bist du kein Wolf, aber neulich, ... da warst du schon so ein Stück Bestie, gerade das hat mir gefallen") (HSW 4:111) ("You are no wolf today, but the other day ... there was really something of the beast about you. It is just what struck me at the time" [HS 113]). Introducing Haller to a whole range of sensual experiences that he had repressed because of his education, Hermine, both as a dancing teacher and at the same time a spiritual mentor, represents the revaluation of Idealist philosophy at the turn of the twentieth century. Echoing Darwin, Haeckel, Nietzsche, Freud, and Jung, Hermine rejects Kantian dualism. She serves as a mediator between Haller's Idealist outlook and his later, more unprejudiced attitude that is able to appreciate the sensual aspects of life. In her multifaceted roles as Haller's complementary other—as his soul sister (HSW 4:122; HS 126), a mother figure (HSW 4:115; HS 118), a worldly-wise philosopher, a youthful prostitute, and a dance teacher—her seemingly incompatible characteristics defy the very notion of a specific individuality, the metaphysical hallmark of Idealist philosophy. Her dazzling personality (HSW 4:106–8; HS 108–10) is living proof for her philosophy that a human being is devoid of a definable essence. Hermine opens Haller's eyes to the heterogeneity and instability of human existence. Her constant presence allows him to perceive a much fuller spectrum of life. She and Haller eventually come close to viewing the human subject as "constituted by evolutionary stratification" (Wolfe, *Animal* 3). While such a posthumanist point of view still presents the evolution toward the human as progress toward a more complex organism of a higher rank, "the 'animalistic' or 'primitive' determinations inherited from our evolutionary past … coexist uneasily in a second-order relation of relations, which the 'human' surfs or manages with varying degrees of success or difficulty" (ibid.). The "Tractatus's" narrator's hypothesis, "daß [der Mensch] in der Tat eigentlich eine Bestie sei, nur mit einem dünnen Überzug von Erziehung und Menschentum darüber" (HSW 4:45) ("that [a human] being was actually a beast with only a thin covering of the human" [HS 41]) testifies to the influence of late-nineteenth-century paleontology and biological anthropology.

Hesse makes use of another scientific discovery, namely that ontogeny recapitulates phylogeny (Haeckel, Jung). According to this hypothesis of Haeckel, every individual undergoes a primeval transformation from primitive mononuclear organism to primitive animal, to mammal to primate to human. This theory, of course, resonated with Jung's theory of the collective unconscious, according to which each living organism inherited primordial states of consciousness.[25] Biologists like Darwin and Haeckel, for instance, kept stressing that human civilization developed very late in the history of the species. Their historical point of view was to counteract human hubris and its narrow-minded moral values (Haeckel 26).[26] Haeckel's eschewing of Kant's dualist Idealism in favor of a dynamic monism resonates in Hesse's novel and especially in the idea that every human being does not consist of one or two souls "sondern aus zehn, aus hundert, aus tausend Seelen" (HSW 4:122) ("of ten or a hundred or a thousand souls" [HS 126]).

Pablo is another figure whose appearance changes in Haller's perception. Pablo represents, to some extent, a contrast to Harry as he is introduced as a superficial bon vivant and jazz musician whose main goal in life is to make his audience happy by playing popular tunes to which they can dance. His carefree lifestyle and "loose morals" resemble those of Hermine, yet he seems to lack her philosophical perspicacity. Haller is reluctant to befriend Pablo because he considers the latter's hedonism frivolous and immoral. He also feels envious of this young, easygoing crowd-pleaser who possesses all the social skills and popularity that he himself lacks. If it were not for Hermine, the elitist intellectual recluse, Haller, would never have befriended Pablo. Only after Hermine introduces him to the sensual aspects of his personality by teaching him to dance to Pablo's music is Haller prepared to get to know the musician.

Hesse's novel associates Pablo's naive, anti-intellectual, uninhibited "nature" with the Steppenwolf's characterization of jazz as "wild, launisch und kraftvoll." Moreover, jazz is described as a musical style that has the advantage of being at least "[von] einer großen Aufrichtigkeit, einer liebenswerten, unverlogenen Negerhaftigkeit und einer frohen, kindlichen Laune" (HSW 4:38–39) ("sincere, unashamedly primitive, and childishly happy" [HS 38]). These descriptions point to Haller's Romantic and Eurocentric concept of a history that associates earlier stages of civilization with the ignorance and innocence of childhood. Haller's belief in a hierarchical progression of human civilization that reaches its apex in the European culture of the eighteenth and nineteenth centuries echoes Idealist narratives of human development by Kant, Lessing, Herder, and Schiller, among others.[27] Although these accounts differ, they all share a Euro- and logocentric point of view and make an essentialist distinction between humans and animals. As Derrida points out in his essay *The Animal That Therefore I Am*, for many philosophers from Descartes to Lacan and Heidegger "the animal" is simply defined as the other of the human or vice-versa so that the definition of the human depends on delineating what the human is not: the animal (Derrida 27).

Haller looks at jazz as an expression of a primeval form of art because it appeals to uncivilized, instinctual nature in contrast to the spiritual refinement of his musical idols, such as Mozart.[28] His ambivalent feelings toward jazz betray a perplexity toward modern culture that he tries to cover up with his patronizing, condescending posturing as a misunderstood intellectual. Although Haller seems to admire the disposition of the "Negro" and the "American," "der uns Europäern in all seiner Stärke so knabenhaft frisch und kindlich erscheint" (HSW 4:39) ("who with all his strength seems so boyishly fresh and childlike to us Europeans" [HS 38]), he also looks down on the culture of the new world as a deplorable regression. Haller's perception of Pablo as a representative of Europe's cultural decadence on the one hand and as a happy and carefree child on the other confirm the protagonist's wavering between disgust and secret admiration when he is confronted with an incomprehensible modernity. While the Steppenwolf's philosophy and self-image as it is represented in the "Tractatus" is also based on the distinction between human and animal, Haller's first-person narrative questions and subverts this distinction by confronting the protagonist with characters like Pablo and Hermine.

After all, Hermine's and Pablo's surprising transformations are meant to prepare Haller for the eventual rejection of his Steppenwolf identity (HSW 4:165; HS 176). Pablo introduces Haller to his magic theater, a sequence of dreamlike scenes that lets Haller look at different aspects of his multifaceted personality with the intention of teaching him to laugh about himself. More concretely, Pablo's theater has a multiplicity of doors, behind each of which is a segment or theme that is connected to Haller's life. Most of the episodes are linked to the themes that have been addressed earlier in the narrative, such as the war of mankind against the machine, the suppression or justification of instinctual needs through reason, the debunking of the myth of the unity of the subject, the taming of the Steppenwolf, the role of art in contemporary society, and finally the possibility of escaping the Steppenwolf existence through humor. Haller fails in the effort to laugh at himself because he takes Pablo's theater as reality and kills Hermine in a bout of jealousy. While it would be intriguing to examine the connections of the various segments of the magic theater, I will limit myself to examining the episode titled "Wunder der Steppenwolfdressur" (HSW 4:182–85) ("Marvelous Taming of the Steppenwolf" [HS 194–96]).

In this episode, Haller watches an animal tamer who looks like him leading a tamed wolf to do tricks that resist its animal nature. The wolf has been trained to refrain from eating a rabbit and a lamb placed before him. The clenching of his teeth, the saliva dripping from his mouth, and his trembling body reveal, however, that the wolf's abstinence is achieved under extreme repression of its instincts. The wolf displays a canine submissiveness that Haller finds painful to watch (HSW 4:183; HS 195). In the second part of the act, the roles are reversed. Now it is the wolf that forces the animal tamer to act like a tamed wolf. However, the docile wolf-man then begins to act like a wild beast mauling and killing the rabbit as well as the lamb. Haller flees the scene deeply shocked, commenting, "Dieses magische Theater, sah ich, war kein reines Paradies, alle Höllen lagen unter seiner hübschen Oberfläche" (HSW 4:184) ("This magic theater was clearly no paradise. All hell lay beneath its charming surface" [HS 196]). The allegorical episode reiterates Hesse's Nietzschean critique of a civilization that has established itself through the repression of nature. After Haller has been socialized and educated to control his instincts, nature asserts itself and returns with a vengeance as the tamer's beastly behavior is a result of the taming of nature. To distract himself after the horrific scene, Haller spontaneously hums the first line of the fourth movement of Beethoven's ninth symphony: "O Freunde nicht diese Töne" (HSW 4:184) ("O Friend[s], not these notes" [HS 196]).[29] In this context the citation can be read as an ironic comment on the regressive beastliness of the docile animal tamer. There is no benevolent God who created a meaningful cosmic order and the human being according to his image as in Schiller's poem. Compare, for instance, the lines "Brüder—überm Sternenzelt / Muß ein lieber Vater wohnen" (brothers above the starry canopy / There must dwell a loving father) (SchW 1:133)[30] to the cold laughter and childish behavior of the immortals of Hesse's novel. In other words, the quasi-Christian belief in a meaningful universal order of the Schiller poem—"Freude heißt die starke Feder / In der ewigen Natur / Freude, Freude treibt die Räder / In der großen Weltenuhr" (Joy is the name of the strong spring / in eternal nature / Joy, joy drives the wheels / in the great clock of worlds) (SchW 1:134)—has been replaced by a cold, inhuman universe and an image of organic nature that is driven by aggression and self-preservation. The deceptive optimism of German Idealist philosophy is contrasted to Haller's memories of photographs from World War I that disturb his longing for "erträglichere, freundlichere Bilder" (HS 196) ("more bearable, friendlier pictures" [HSW 4:184]). While humming the Beethoven tune, he is reminded of "jene Haufen ineinander verknäuelter Leichname, deren Gesichter durch Gasmasken in grinsende Teufelsfratzen verwandelt waren" (HSW 4:184) ("those heaps of bodies entangled with each other whose faces were changed to grinning ghouls by their gas masks") [HS 196]). It is significant that the dead soldiers are not depicted as innocent victims but as grinning ghouls. Haller thinks that he was naïve to be appalled about these horrific pictures as a former war opponent because aggression appears to be simply part of human nature. His comment, "Heute wußte ich, daß kein Tierbändiger, kein Minister, kein General, kein Irrsinniger Gedanken und Bilder in seinem Gehirn auszubrüten fähig war, die nicht ebenso scheußlich, wild und böse, ebenso roh und dumm in mir selber wohnten" (HSW 4:184) ("Today I knew that no tamer of beasts, no general, no insane person could hatch a thought or picture in his brain that I could not match myself with one every bit as frightful, every bit as savage and wicked, as crude and stupid" [HS 196]), expresses his disillusionment with the belief in a good and true humankind.

Does this mean that Haller's development ends in a state of utter despair over the evil disposition of the human species? This would imply that German humanism and its "immortal" representatives, such as Mozart and Goethe, were nothing but a vain fantasy. To be sure, Hesse's novel exposes traditional humanism's suppression of the instinctual, irrational, and immoral side of human nature. However, reading Hesse's text merely as a criticism of humanism's alleged hypocrisy from a Nietzschean point of view would neglect the ambiguities, incongruities, and conflicting voices that the novel articulates. Such a reading would not do justice to the text's historical dimension, such as the changing roles of bourgeois intellectuals and artists in modern mass culture, the loss of spiritual belief systems in an increasingly violent, war-stricken world that shattered the faith in a unified subject and meaningful universal order.

Haller's ambivalent relationship toward his humanist education, which causes his internal struggle and arduous suffering, has meaning although he has to abandon the purportedly eternal values on which he based his identity. While he has to dispose of his elitist belief in the immortal's spiritual purity for a much less stable outlook that considers human fallibility, he manages to detect the spiritual dimension of art in the midst of the modern age that he despises. After all, Mozart admonishes Haller to accept the changing times and listen to the music of the immortals as it is transmitted in the new technological invention of the radio because this seemingly profane technology "cannot destroy the spirit of this music" (HSW 4:198–99; HS 213).

Another example of the spirit of art in modern disguise is Haller's epiphany triggered by the dancing letters of the "electric sign" that announces the magic theater (HS 32; SW 4:34). Certainly, the novel is ripe with unflattering remarks about modern civilization and popular culture, but Haller's skepticism toward the mass culture of the modern age is also subject to investigation and as such cannot be seen as Hesse's final word.[31] While the protagonist criticizes modern mass culture from a sentimental point of view, he is also aware of his reductive idealization of the past. The fact that "*The Steppenwolf* is a text that keeps on commenting on itself, talking about itself" characterizes it as a multiperspectival work in the tradition of Romantic irony (Swales 180). The denigration of Hesse's work as "schematic, simplificatory, perilously close to earnest kitsch" by German academic critics during the 1950s certainly does not do justice to the novel's complexity and multiperspectivity (ibid. 184). Swales's contention that the text "is worryingly uni-vocal" because "the three narrative strands tend to merge into one" also conflates the different and often contentious points of view of the various characters. Although Hermine and Pablo turn out to be all projections of the protagonist, Haller's inner voices are far from homogenous and continue to vacillate between the yearning for a universal ethics and the desire to overcome the limiting fiction of his Steppenwolf existence that he inherited with his Idealist education.[32] Harry's development is an open-ended process of disillusionment. It does not have a static objective, but the objective is the protagonist's development itself, a process that exposes the illusion of the mind-body dichotomy, embodied in the Steppenwolf metaphor, as a deceptive hypothesis that both veils and unveils the plethora of intangible possibilities that reside in human existence. Thus, the novel seems to probe the attempt to define what is human along the lines of the narrator of the "Tractatus":

> Der Mensch ist ja keine feste und dauernde Gestaltung (dies war, trotz entgegengesetzter Ahnungen ihrer Weisen, das Ideal der Antike), er ist vielmehr ein Versuch und Übergang, er ist nichts andres als die schmale, gefährliche Brücke zwischen Natur und Geist. (HSW 4:63)[33]

(Man is not by any means of fixed and enduring form [this, in spite of suspicions to the contrary on the part of their wise men, was the ideal of the ancients]. He is much more an experiment and a transition. He is nothing else than the narrow and perilous bridge between nature and spirit. [HS 61])

The attempt at defining what is human at the same time defies an ontological definition. While the human subject as bridge between nature and spirit seems to take the mind-body dichotomy for granted, it remains unclear whether this dichotomy only exists because of the bridge. Taking into account the precariousness and transience of the mediation between nature and spirit, one can infer that the dichotomy does not exist without human effort. The Steppenwolf is always already humanized, regardless of whether he denotes the wild, uncontrollable beast that we fear or the trapped, tamed creature that we pity. Yet the human itself is still defined as what Idealist philosophers called a mixture between animal and angel. What has changed is, however, the dynamic and unstable nature of the human subject that makes human existence more uncertain. Being sentenced to be the object of ridicule at the end, Hesse's protagonist is not allowed to assume the subject-centered agency that the humanist paradigm presumes. Haller's humiliation as punishment for taking life too seriously is an expression of the posthumanist condition that condemns the subject to witness the debunking of its humanist illusion of self-importance.

Hesse's protagonist and first-person narrator is struggling to achieve an ironic point of view that allows him to laugh at himself. However, he has undergone a development that allows him to face his inadequacies and bear being laughed at. After all, he does not let the humiliation with which the novel ends demoralize his future efforts to subject himself to the eternal cycle of life that will most likely consist of other challenges and humiliations: "Einmal würde ich das Figurenspiel besser spielen. Einmal würde ich das Lachen lernen" (HSW 4:203) ("One day I would be a better hand at the game. One day I would learn how to laugh" [HS 218]). Haller's situation as an eternally striving subject may also entail an affirmation of the attempt of the hermeneutical, never-ending search for meaning.

Notes

A part of this chapter has been previously published as "From Anti-humanism to Post-humanism: Hermann Hesse's *Steppenwolf,*" *Konturen* 7 (2014): 179–209. Web: http://journals.oregondigital.org/konturen/article/view/3500/3305.

1. Subsequent references to this edition of Hesse's works will be cited parenthetically as HSW, including volume and page number. References to the English translation are taken from Hesse, *Steppenwolf*, trans. Josef Mileck and Horst Frenz (New York: Picador, 1963) will be cited parenthetically as HS followed by the page number.

2. It is not the spirit of 1914 that Hesse implores, but rather the spirit of Nietzsche, whose anti-German iconoclasm he praises. Hesse particularly admires Nietzsche's courage to withstand the nationalist mass hysteria of the Wilhelmenian Empire. The motto of his original pamphlet cites Nietzsche's preface to volume 2 of *Menschliches, Allzumenschliches* (1886) (HSW 15:221). It describes what Freud would later term the "superego" as "Jenes verborgene und herrische Etwas, für das wir lange keinen Namen haben, bis es sich endlich als unsere Aufgabe erweist" (that hidden and commanding thing, for which we have no name until it finally turns out to be our duty). Nietzsche's admonishment to obey this inner tyrant in view of the punishing disease, which in Hesse's opinion results from any attempts to avoid personal responsibility, anticipates the Freudian concept of *Verdrängung* (repression).
3. *Zarathustra's Wiederkehr* is, after all, in its allegorical form ultimately a fictional text, although it alludes to a concrete historical situation. The godlike Zarathustra, on the one hand, takes on the function of a mentor, or in Freudian terms the superego, and, on the other hand, rejects the role of being a teacher (HSW 15:225–26). The paradox of the nonteaching teacher is not as aporetic as it may seem. Notwithstanding Nietzsche's contempt of Socrates's dialectic rationality, the Socratic method of questioning can be seen as an antecedent of Zarathustra's "pedagogy." Like Socrates, Zarathustra does not consider it his task to impart knowledge but rather to stimulate his audience to learn what is human by interrogating themselves: "Warum wollt ihr nicht einmal suchen, ob der Schmerz nicht in euch selber sitzt?" (Why don't you explore, if the pain originates from within you?) (HSW 15:228). If not indicated otherwise, all translations from the German are mine.
4. "Gut zu leiden wissen, ist mehr als halb gelebt. Gut zu leiden wissen ist ganz gelebt! Geborenwerden ist Leiden, Wachstum ist Leiden.... So, meine Freunde, leidet der Mensch Schicksal.... Schicksal tut weh." (Knowing how to suffer well means more than having lived halfway. Knowing how to suffer well means having lived completely. Being born is suffering, growth is suffering.... In this way, my friends, the human being suffers fate.... Fate hurts.)
5. His faith in the strong individual who opposes the mentality of the majority and is capable of creating and following his own philosophy of life seems to have weakened since he now concedes that most individuals need spiritual guidance to give their lives meaning (HSW 15:480).
6. While most neo-humanist philosophers and writers of the German Idealist tradition, such as Kant, Herder, Schiller, Humboldt and Hegel, deviated from the Cartesian claim of *cogito, ergo sum*, they nevertheless adhered to the mind-body dichotomy, despite their attempts to harmonize the body-mind division.
7. The bourgeois intellectuals had to contend a loss of status after World War I. The popularization of culture and the mass media contributed to this development as it made the boundaries of high culture and popular culture more fluid.
8. Hesse wrote the novel to overcome a crisis after two painful separations from his partners, Mia Bernoulli and Ruth Wenger. Likewise, Hesse's protagonist finds himself in a midlife crisis that triggers the self-finding process. Both Hesse and his protagonist publish newspaper articles criticizing Germany's nationalism and involvement in World War I. Like Harry Haller, Hesse had to confront the challenges of a rapidly changing society. For a more comprehensive description of the *Steppenwolf*'s autobiographical allusions, see Schwilk 284–305.

9. In this context, it is noteworthy that Goethe's *Wilhelm Meister* made a deep impression on Hesse (Schwilk 74–76).
10. The subordination of the body to the mind in German Idealism was very much indebted to the Cartesian "I think, therefore I am." The mind remained the defining characteristic of humanity as the biological and genetic differences between human and animal became less obvious. Likewise, Jacques Derrida states that "logocentrism is first of all a thesis regarding the animal, the animal deprived of the logos, deprived of the *can-have-the*-logos: this is the thesis, position, or presupposition maintained from Aristotle to Heidegger, from Descartes to Kant, Levinas, and Lacan" (*Animal*, x).
11. For instance, Henriette Herwig and Florian Trabert challenge Thomas Mann's claim that the *Steppenwolf*'s "experimentelle Kühnheit" (experimental audacity) (Mann, HSW 13:840–43) was comparable to James Joyce's *Ulysses* or André Gide's *Faux Monnayeurs* (Herwig and Trabert 9). They point out that Hesse's novel makes use of neither the stream-of-consciousness technique nor of "Auflösung morphologischer und syntaktischer Strukturen" (the dissolution of morphological and syntactic structures) as Joyce's novel does (ibid.). According to their opinion, the *Steppenwolf* also lacks a fragmentation of the plot when compared to André Gide's *Les Faux-Monnayeurs*.
12. While one can certainly find reasons for calling Hesse's works traditionalist—reasons that may be responsible for Hesse's waning presence in academic scholarship in recent years—there have also been some innovative approaches that challenge the conventional wisdom among critics. In their introduction to a collection of essays, Herwig and Trabert point out that the self-reflective nature of Hesse's work and the inclusion of intermedial discourses, such as cinema, music, and visual arts, shows Romanticism's affiliation to modernist tendencies (9). They call the author therefore a "Grenzgänger der Moderne" (12). In view of the novel's ironic commentary on the modern era of Hesse's own time, its open-ended dialectical reflections on traditional humanism and modernist anti-humanism, as well as its contrastive and playful juxtaposition of competing discourses of mass and high culture, I would go further and place the novel on the cusp of postmodernist/posthumanist tendencies. The discussions surrounding the reception of cultural icons such as Goethe and Mozart, as well as their ironic defamiliarization, are vital for Hesse's critical revision of Germany's humanist legacy.
13. The narrator of the "Tractatus of the Steppenwolf" emphasizes that the "Zweiteilung in Wolf und Mensch, in Trieb und Geist, durch welche Harry sein Schicksal verständlicher zu machen versucht" (the dichotomy of wolf and "Man," of instinct and spirit, through which Harry attempts to make his fate more understandable) is a fictional simplification, which does not do justice to a human being's inner contradictions. Instead of the Faustian "Zwei Seelen wohnen, ach, in meiner Brust!," each I consists of "eine höchst vielfältige Welt, ein kleiner Sternenhimmel, ein Chaos von Formen, von Stufen und Zuständen, von Erbschaften und Möglichkeiten" (a highly variegated world, a little starry sky, a chaos of shapes, of levels and states, of legacies and possibilities) (HSW 4:59).
14. By advocating that the abyss between mind and body is a human construct that teaches more about humans than about animals, and that the man/nature opposition needs to be overcome through a monistic philosophy, Hesse is following Nietzschean and Darwinian perspectives of looking at human development in terms of a continuum of the animal species. Hesse's *Steppenwolf* also anticipates Deleuze and Guattari's claim that

"each individual is an infinite multiplicity, and the whole of Nature is a multiplicity of perfectly individuated multiplicities" (*Thousand*, 254).
15. This is why the narrator of the Tractatus comments that Harry deludes himself over the borders between the human and animal aspects in his soul: "Harry rechnet, so fürchten wir, ganze Provinzen seiner Seele schon zum 'Menschen,' die noch lange nicht Mensch sind, und rechnet Teile seines Wesens zum Wolfe, die längst über den Wolf hinaus sind" (HSW 4:63) ("[Harry] assigns, we fear, whole provinces of his soul to the "man" which are a long way from being human, and parts of his being to the wolf that long ago have left the wolf behind" [HS 61]).
16. For an in-depth analysis of the textual correspondences between Nietzsche's philosophy and Hesse's *Steppenwolf* see Dagmar Kiesel's essay "Das gespaltene Selbst: Die Identitätsproblematik in Hermann Hesses *Steppenwolf* und bei Friedrich Nietzsche." Kiesel points out that many of the novel's underlying themes, such as the division of the self, self-hatred, suicide, loneliness, and the individual's relationship to the bourgeoisie are also important aspects of Nietzsche's criticism of Idealist philosophy.
17. Nietzsche removes the terms "noble" and "servile" from their historical context of feudal society and presents them as natural traits of animal species. According to Alphonso Lingis, this "transference of the identifying characteristics of the noble animal upon the human animal that rises from the herd is far older than feudal class society; we see the falcon-man, lion-man, stallion-man, eagle-man, bull-man, cobra-man in the necropolises of Egypt, on the temple friezes of the Assyrians, the Hittites, and on the seals of Mohohendo-daro and Harrappa on the Indus two thousand years older still" (*Animal Philosophy* 9).
18. The writings of Rousseau exerted a significant influence on Hesse (Schwilk 68, 143). Yet Hesse takes issue with Rousseau's nature/culture division by claiming that Rousseau's return to nature is no longer a possibility for the Steppenwolf.
19. Sigmund Freud's *Das Unbehagen in der Kultur* (1930) (*Civilization and Its Discontents*) connects the diminished importance of the sense of smell in humans to a repression that is connected to the process of civilization (Freud, SA 9:229). Cary Wolfe has also pointed out this connection (*Animal Rites* 2).
20. Haller's disdain for politeness is first mentioned by the editor (HS 9). There the editor interprets Haller's contemptuous "look which criticized both the words and the speaker of them" in the spirit of a Nietzschen critique of civilization: "'See what monkeys we are! Look such is man!' and at once all renown, all intelligence, all the attainments of the spirit, all progress toward the sublime, the great and the enduring in man fell away and became a monkey's trick!" (HS 9). A second instance is when Harry is a guest at a professor's house and insults his hosts with his blunt criticism of their bourgeois taste (HS 81–83).
21. Gilles Deleuze and Félix Guattari have focused on what they call the theme of "becoming-animal" as a kind of escape from preconceived notions of identity and sameness: "To become animal is to participate in movement, to stake out the path of escape in all its positivity, to cross a threshold, to reach a continuum of intensities that are valuable only in themselves, to find a world of pure intensities where all forms are undone as do all the significations, signifiers, and signifieds to the benefit of an unformed matter of deterritorialized flux, of nonsignifying signs" (see Calarco and Atterton, *Animal Philosophy* 96). In view of the later deconstruction of the Steppenwolf image, one could say that Hesse coincides with Deleuze and Guattari by attempting to disrupt oversimplified abstractions, correspondences, dichotomies, analogies.

22. From today's perspective, Haller's characterization of jazz as a type of music that he liked because of "einer großen Aufrichtigkeit, einer liebenswerten unverlogenen Negerhaftigkeit und einer frohen kindlichen Laune" (a great honesty, an endearing primitive quality with something of the negro in it and childishly happy) certainly appears racist. However, Haller displays the arrogance of the nineteenth-century German intellectual elite that looks down on all non-European races and cultures. It characterizes Haller as a protagonist who has not reflected on his own biases but who, in the course of the novel, has to reconsider his prejudices.
23. A flashing neon sign that advertises the magic theater turns out to be Haller's access to a new experience that eventually lets him transcend the confinement to his dualist worldview.
24. Some feminist approaches may not agree with this assertion because Hermine still reveals the masculinist division of mother and whore. On the one hand, Harry perceives her as an all-knowing mother figure, and on the other, she is introduced as a prostitute. In her article on "Hesse, Women, and Homoeroticism," Kamakshi P. Murti argues "that the female characters in Hesse's works," including *Der Steppenwolf*, "are either reduced to an object or allegorical status ... or become increasingly hermaphroditic to reflect and enable the consummation of the protagonist's homoerotic desires, both processes resulting in the annihilation of woman as a subject" (270). While Murti's observation is indeed very well taken, Hermine differs from traditional masculinist fantasies as the novel exposes her as the male protagonist's projection. Moreover, the blurring of the boundaries between Hermine's spiritual and sensual qualities calls the mind-body split as well as the gender division into question.
25. Hesse had already undergone psychiatric treatment with Josef Bernhard Lang, a student of Jung, beginning in April 1916. Hesse also studied the dualism of the gnostic worldview with its dual divinities for light and darkness, spirit and body. According to Heimo Schwilk, Hesse is fascinated by the Manichean teachings and their ascetic rejection of bodily pleasures. He is particularly intrigued by the idea of a creator that unites both the good and the bad (Schwilk 201). Likewise, for Jung, the self is divine, which erases the distinction between good and bad. One could read the *Steppenwolf* as a literary response to his examination of these ideas.
26. In spite of all their deviances from the Darwinian point of view, as well as from each other, Nietzsche and Jung agreed with Darwin's anti-creationist, anti-transcendental, and seemingly anti-Idealist views. Their philosophies exerted great influence on Hesse.
27. See, for instance, Kant's "Mutmaßlicher Anfang der Menschengeschichte," Lessing's *Die Erziehung des Menschengeschlechts*, Herder's "Auch eine Philosophie der Geschichte zur Bildung der Menschheit," and Schiller's "Was heißt und zu welchem Ende studiert man Universalgeschichte?" Herder's narrative deviates from the other accounts as it replaces the Enlightenment model of linear progress with an organic development that views the phylogenesis of mankind in analogy to the ontogenesis of an individual human being. It anticipates Haeckel's claim that ontogenesis repeats phylogenesis even though it was still beholden to Christian creationism and did not espouse the theory of evolution.
28. As in Schiller's *Universalgeschichte*, for instance, the pristine cultures of non-European parts of the world, especially Africa, were equated to those of prehistorical Europe.
29. As mentioned before, Hesse published an article with the same title on 3 November 1914 in the *Neue Züricher Zeitung*, in which he pleads "for a civil tone among intellectuals" in view of the heated nationalistic fervor at the beginning of World War I (Cornils, "Introduction" 4).

30. The references to Schiller's works are taken from *Sämtliche Werke*, edited by Peter-André Alt et al. 5 vols. Munich: dtv, 2004. They are cited parenthetically as SchW followed by volume and page number.
31. Haller's sarcastic comments about the movie *The Ten Commandments* (1923) by Cecil B. DeMille condemn the technological make believe of cinema that serves a superficial sensationalism and commercialization of art (HSW 4:153; HS 162).
32. The irony and self-irony with which both the third- and first-person narrators ridicule Haller's elitist adulation of spiritual qualities and his concomitant desire to overcome these sentimental yearnings also contradicts Jörg Drews's contention that Hesse's novel is something for "Ratsuchende" (Drews 26).
33. Swales points out the similarity to a passage in section four of the first part of Nietzsche's *Also sprach Zarathustra*: "Der Mensch ist ein Seil geknüpft zwischen Tier und Übermensch—ein Seil über einem Abgrunde. / Was gross ist am Menschen, das ist, dass er eine Brücke und kein Zweck ist" (Man is a rope stretched between the animal and the Superhuman—a rope above an abyss. / What is great in man is that he is a bridge and not a purpose) (Nietzsche, *Werke* 2:281).

Conclusion

In view of the title of this volume, one might justifiably ask why the study does not include any contemporary literature. Recalling previous chapters, it is obvious that posthumanism includes a temporal aspect. As numerous literary responses to the neo-humanist ideology under discussion have shown, eighteenth-century humanism became inadequate to describe or represent the lived experience of late nineteenth- and early twentieth-century subjects. The idealization of the individual was put to the test in literature, already at the inception of neo-humanism during the last quarter of the eighteenth century. Thus, literature served as a testing ground for the dualist privileging of the mind over the body throughout the nineteenth century. The literary enactments of humanist ideas often criticized or undermined the bourgeoisie's austere moral standards by portraying the rationalist imperative to control one's bodily instincts as the cause of human suffering. Lessing, Schiller, Herder, and Goethe illustrated the human subject's inner tensions by dramatizing the conflict between emotional and moral demands. Recognizing the power of the senses and emotions, their theoretical essays blur the boundaries between allegorical fiction and rational discourse, thereby differentiating the humanist assumption of the humanist premise of individual autonomy. So, one may ask whether the term "posthumanist" could be applied to earlier periods than those from the late twentieth century onward that we usually associate with it.[1] This study has intended to trace humanism's emancipatory trajectory by revealing how post-Kantian literary, scientific, and philosophical revisions of the mind-body dualism showed an increasing awareness of the influences of the senses and exposed restrictive norms of bourgeois morality as well as Eurocentric racial and gender biases that eventually led to what is now called posthumanism.

While this investigation does not call for a revision of posthumanism's time frame, it has made the case that the literary engagements with humanist ideals contest an unambiguous distinction between posthumanism and neo-humanism. For this and other reasons, a definition of posthumanist literature would ultimately be reductive, although it can serve as a provisional guide to the goals of posthumanist approaches. Just as eighteenth- and nineteenth-century literary representations of neo-humanist ideas challenge and transcend programmatic definitions, literature in general defies prescriptive standards that restrict the autopoietic logic of fiction. The situational context, the figural constellations and the characteristics of the protagonists, in short, the complex demands of plausibility problematize even those literary works with specific didactic intentions. As my study has tried to argue, literary fiction illustrates examples of general ideas in specific contexts that allow explorations of human characteristics unconstrained by programmatic or ideological demands. Because of their embeddedness in specific plausible contexts, the literary works of this study have been shown to be more nuanced, ambiguous, and inconclusive than the premises of neo-humanist ideological, aesthetic, and philosophical treatises.[2] By illustrating how unachievable ideological and ethical premises, such as the control over one's instincts, affect the fictional characters' behavior, literary works can challenge these unrealistic demands as they contradict human nature.

J. M. Coetzee's novel *Elizabeth Costello* (2003) is a contemporary example that addresses the discrepancy between humanism's unrealistic ideals and the lived reality. The title figure is a well-known Australian writer who attends the award ceremony for an honorary doctorate bestowed on her sister, Blanche. On this occasion Blanche has to give a lecture addressed to faculty at the University of Johannesburg in South Africa. Blanche, also known as Sister Bridget, a nun and devout Catholic, takes a critical look at the origin and purpose of the institutionalized humanities. She traces the ethical dimension of the humanities during the Renaissance back to their religious origins and their goal of finding the true meaning of the biblical scriptures by studying the classical languages. In her lecture she deplores the loss of the search for the "True Word" when the study of classical languages became part of the university curriculum (Coetzee 22). She argues that at that point, the humanities no longer deserved that name but should have been called "textual scholarship," since this was what the humanities turned into from the fifteenth century onward (119–20). Instead of the search for the "True Word," it was about "the recovery of the true text, then the true translation of that text. . . . This is how the studies, literary studies (as studies in interpretation), cultural studies and historical studies—the studies that form the core of the so-called humanities—came together" (120). For Blanche the humanities lost their way of finding the "redemptive word" five centuries ago and "have taken a long time to die, but now, at the end of the second millennium of our era, they are truly on their deathbed" (122).

Blanche's speech, which was received "with a murmur of puzzlement," is followed by a dinner that the two sisters attend (123). During the dinner conversation, Elizabeth brings up Blanche's speech to an English professor named Godwin who took offence with what he perceived as Sister Bridget's attempt to turn back the clock in a secular age (124). Elizabeth supports her sister, contending that she did not want to turn back the clock but was instead arguing "that there has been something misconceived in the study of the humanities from the start. . . . Something wrong with placing hopes and expectations on the humanities that they could never fulfill" (124). She lends further backing to Blanche's argumentation by suggesting that she is well aware of the sorry state of the humanities today, whose mission has been reduced to "moneymaking" (124). Nevertheless, Elizabeth does not agree with her sister's dire predictions. While she knows that the "Hellenistic" type of humanism—the type that Winckelmann, Schiller, and Goethe represented—"was just a phase in the history of the humanities" (131) and that the wide gap among posthumanist visions of a society without "poverty, disease, illiteracy, racism, sexism, homophobia, xenophobia" are far from becoming a reality, she still believes in these ideals by declaring "that people cannot live without hope, or perhaps without illusions" (131). This is why she advocates "more inclusive visions of what human life can be," although she is aware that the humanisms of the past have not been able to live up to what they proposed.

This leads us back to the fundamental question of whether the humanities still have a place in an educational system that tends to become more and more specialized and geared toward providing preparatory training for students in their chosen professions. The idea of a broad, general education that enables students to reflect on their roles as citizens in an increasingly complex and diverse society is perhaps more important than ever. In a society that may be prone to disintegrate due to ideological polarization, economic disparity, technological specialization, and social fragmentation, a reflection on the humanist tradition based on representative literary works can perhaps make a small contribution to keeping a dialogue on common human values alive. While all of the analyzed works are part of the German literary canon and may not be familiar to an American audience, their philosophical backgrounds and their impact transcend national boundaries. A diachronic narrative on the development of humanist discourses situates the literary works in the larger context of the Western civilizational process during the past two hundred years. Yet the literature under analysis was not meant to function as an illustration of a preconceived trajectory. On the contrary, the close readings of selected representative works were intended as interventions that show ruptures, gaps, and modifications in discourses on humanism that have often been viewed as homogenous.

Philosopher Peter Sloterdijk's blanket statement on the failure of the humanist enterprise in his controversial speech of 1999, titled "Regeln für den Menschenpark" ("Rules for the Human Park") is just one example among many that witnesses the posthumanist trend of demanding a radical departure from humanism's unrealistic goals.[3] In light of traditional humanism's parochial prohibitions and its numerous invocations for ideological purposes, Sloterdijk calls for a fundamentally different approach to "improve" on the nature of human beings. He considers genetic modification as a promising alternative to what he views as a repressive humanist didacticism that has failed over the long duration of the civilizing process since the French Revolution. For Sloterdijk, the European bourgeoisie used the humanist literary canon during the nineteenth century to indoctrinate generations of students by forcing them to read the classics in order to generate nationalist narratives that presented their nations as natural successors to the Greeks and Romans. This is how the humanist study of the classics served to establish patriotic communities of readers all over Europe, according to Sloterdijk. He also rejects the premise that reading can tame human nature by pointing out—not unlike Hesse's *Steppenwolf*, discussed in the previous chapter—that the repressed instinctual side would always find a way to erupt under duress.

Sloterdijk goes on to argue by selectively citing Nietzsche that humans have been able to use a combination of genetics and ethics to domesticate themselves under the tutelage of clerics and teachers. He sketches out a tentative alternative to this humanist self-abasement that allegedly has led the human species to forsake its full potential. Plato's *Statesman* serves Sloterdijk as an example that envisions the active cultivation of a superhuman species, which in light of the genetic revolution has become an imaginable reality. Sloterdijk refers to Heidegger's "Brief über den Humanismus" ("Letter on Humanism") (1947) as the first posthumanist text that abandons the human-animal dualism.[4]

It is easy to acknowledge Sloterdijk's point that humanist education has not led to the intended qualitative moral betterment of humankind in view of the countless atrocities of recent human history. Yet civilizational progress has also undeniably led to a reduction of everyday violent aggression that is characteristic of ancient or less-civilized societies where the rights of brute force prevail. One may be willing to concede that literary canons have contributed to the enhancement of ethical sensibilities despite the daily outbreaks of atavistic violence that seem to confirm Sloterdijk's presumed revenge of a repressed human animality. Similarly, his call for a posthumanist turn neglects the plurality and flexibility of humanist discourses, which the literary examples helped to reveal.

As adumbrated above, the examples under discussion, their characters, and their dilemmas are for the most part multifaceted and focus on topics that are still relevant today, not least because of their ambiguities, as the chapters on Moses and the Sublime have shown. Likewise, Lessing's Enlightenment pedagogy is far from dogmatic and requires the readers' active participation. His dramatizations of ethical questions humanize Enlightenment premises by personifying them, which allows the audience to identify with the protagonists. Empathy is essential for self-recognition and the goal of self-improvement. Lessing's pedagogy of self-tutelage is a prime example of the dialogic open-endedness of neo-humanist principles as it challenges dogmatism and the primacy of expedience.

Regardless of the outdated aspects of their anthropological assumptions and ethical norms, many of these early works strove to explore the full spectrum of human sensibility, a probing that eventually also questioned some of the foundational premises of humanism, such as the preeminence of the intellect. Another significant blind spot of neo-humanist ideology is its gender bias, which excluded "the fair sex" from an education that allows the male subject to achieve its full potential as self-determined individual. The *Bildungsroman* therefore generally depicts the development of a male protagonist, with few exceptions, such as Sophie de la Roche's *Fräulein von Sternheim*. The gender bias is apparent in Kant's and Schiller's dualisms that project the mind-body separation onto the gender division. Likewise, racist, nationalist, and Eurocentric hierarchies that privilege the members of the educated European elite over all other members of humanity are obviously in violation of humanism's egalitarian premises.

In addition, the literary texts illustrate the power of metaphors. As is obvious from the texts under consideration, the poetic qualities of the written word are by no means restricted to fiction, nor are they limited to the effective communication of abstract ideas. The analyses of all the texts under discussion have demonstrated the communicative advantages of metaphoric expression. Because of their sensory appeal, images, metaphors, and allegories are able to reach nonspecialists. They make a more immediate and thorough impression on the recipients than theoretical abstractions do. The comparison of Johann Gottfried Herder's humanist writings to those of the anti-humanist ego-theory of contemporary neuroscientist Thomas Metzinger has shown that even today's scientists rely on allegories that have been handed down from the Western classics to describe their theoretical abstractions in a tangible fashion. Ironically and perhaps more importantly, Metzinger's reliance on canonized traditional allegories undermines his denial of the human subject's agency and confirms to the contrary that the ancient Greek practice of *paideia* (education), the pedagogical foundation of the humanist tradition, is alive and well.

As some of the texts have shown, such as Lessing's and Schiller's (*Universalgeschichten*) (Universal Histories), Herder's historical, anthropological, and philosophical essays, Goethe's drama *Torquato Tasso* or his poem "Metamorphose der Pflanzen," or Carus's *Briefe über Landschaftsmalerei*, poetic language can not only anticipate or illustrate scientific discoveries but also present these in the larger context of their effects on human beings, human nature, and nature in general. For instance, Lessing's *Die Erziehung des Menschengeschlechts* not only tells the story of how Jews and Christians used the Bible to civilize themselves, but it also conveys in allegorical form the significance of human sensory perception for the process of learning in general. Lessing's text shares with all the other texts in this volume a self-reflective element that scientific discourses often lack. Yet scientific discoveries also inspire the poetic imagination, as we have seen in Mann's *Der Zauberberg* or Hesse's *Steppenwolf*. Literary responses to scientific discoveries often explore the ethical dimensions and effects of technological or civilizational progress by enacting them in real-life situations. Another distinguishing characteristic between scientific and literary discourses can be detected in the historical dimension. While scientific approaches, such as humoral pathology, become obsolete, once they are superseded by "more accurate" methods, they can have an extended life span as historical documents in the humanities.

Even if one agrees with Coetzee's protagonist that the eighteenth-century "Hellenist" versions of humanism are dated and that more "inclusive visions of what life can be have emerged since then" (131), they should nevertheless have a place in the humanities. Certainly, along with new discoveries about human nature in the life sciences, socioeconomic conditions changed vastly throughout the nineteenth century. In view of these transformations that affected virtually every aspect of civic life, many fin-de-siècle writers, such as Schnitzler and Hofmannsthal, considered many neo-humanist assumptions inadequate. Darwin, Marx, Nietzsche, and Freud contributed to radically transformed views about "human nature," a term that in itself became questionable. The paradigm shift affected all academic disciplines, even the natural sciences. Nevertheless, humanist ideals still lingered in the background either in the form of a nostalgic longing for a more humane past or in the form of a discredited ideology that was invented by a hypocritical bourgeois establishment. In the twentieth century, humanism regained relevance in view of the unprecedented atrocities of World War I. While Thomas Mann and Hermann Hesse were perhaps the most prominent advocates of a more peaceful, humane, democratic society, they also sarcastically exposed the anachronisms of a humanist elitism that prevailed in the educational institutions and among intellectuals. Both Mann and Hesse attempted to liberate themselves from the restrictions of a dualist view of the human being as a rational animal; they nevertheless remained indebted to their nineteenth-century educational backgrounds. Yet in contrast to the escapist humanist nostalgia after World War II that led the conservative establishment to return to the Weimar classics to divert attention away from the uncomfortable reminders of the recent past, Mann and Hesse were looking to adapt the humanist agenda for the present. While this study did not discuss any literary works during the second half of the twentieth century—this could be the subject of a future study—it attempted to shed light on the cultural transformations in the humanist enterprise that deserve continued attention through ongoing adjustments to an increasingly diverse and culturally fragmented social reality.

Notes

1. As mentioned in the introduction to this volume, a recent collection of essays, titled *Posthumanism in the Age of Humanism* (2019), examines posthumanism in eighteenth- and nineteenth-century philosophical, scientific, and literary texts as "an attempt to critically interrogate the status of the human as exceptional, as autonomous, as standing outside a web of relations, or even as a subject or object of knowledge corresponding to a determinate set of practices" (Landgraf et al. 2). In contrast to my study, the essay collection focuses mainly on developments in the life sciences predominantly in scientific, philosophical texts (ibid. 3).
2. Elizabeth Costello, the protagonist of J. M. Coetzee's novel with the same name and accomplished novelist, argues in a similar vein. Her son, the narrator, challenges Costello because she chose Kafka's *Report to an Academy* (*Ein Bericht für eine Akademie*) (1917) in an award ceremony to speak about realism. Her audience seems somewhat perplexed after her lecture because she explained that in Kafka's story it is impossible to tell "what is really going on in this story: whether it is a man speaking to men or an ape speaking to apes . . ." (18). Most readers who know Kafka's story will probably agree with the narrator that it is an odd example of realist literature and would like to ask Costello what Kafka has to do with realism. She answers this question later by saying, "Kafka's ape is embedded in life. . . . That ape is followed through to the end, to the bitter, unsayable end . . ." (32). Costello's point is that literature has to be embedded in a situational context that defines its premises in order to be believable regardless of the ideological reservations that the readership may have (33).
3. Other examples can be found in Nietzsche's debunking of the repressive underpinnings of the humanist idealization of human nature, or Horkheimer and Adorno's *Dialectic of Enlightenment*. See also, Herbert Marcuse, "Humanismus—gibt's den noch?" *Neues Forum* 196, no. 1 (1970): 349–53.
4. Instead of worshiping the human as the apex of creation that can rule over nature, Heidegger views the human as the "Hüter des Seins" (steward of being) who inhabits the house of language: "Vielmehr ist die Sprache das Haus des Seins, darin wohnend der Mensch ek-sistiert, indem er der Wahrheit des Seins, sie hütend, gehört" (24) ("Rather, language is the house of being, in which the human being ek-sists by dwelling in that he belongs to being, guarding it"). Translation borrowed from "Letter on 'Humanism,'" translated by Frank Capuzzi in *Pathmarks*, ed. William McNeill (Cambridge UP, 1998), 254. Heidegger's ontology categorically rejects the two-thousand-year-old tradition of defining the human as a rational animal. Instead, he postulates a radical ontological distinction between the human and the animal. Although Heidegger does away with a metaphysical humanism, he still adheres to a metaphysics of presence by enthroning Being. Moreover, man is still "the result of a simultaneous division and articulation of the animal and the human, in which one of the two terms was also what was at stake in it" (Agamben 92).

Works Cited

Abel, Jacob Friedrich. *Eine Quellenedition zum Philosophieunterricht an der Stuttgarter Karlsschule (1773–1782)*, edited by Wolfgang Riedel. Würzburg: Königshausen & Neumann, 1995.
Adler, Hans. "Humanität—Autonomie—Souveränität: Bedingtheit und Reichweite des Humanitätskonzepts J. G. Herders." In *Kontroversen, alte und neue*, edited by Albrecht Schöne, 8:161–66. Tübingen: Niemeyer, 1985.
———. "Einführung: Denker der Mitte; Johann Gottfried Herder 1744–1803." *Monatshefte* 95, no. 2 (2003): 161–70.
———. "Autonomie versus Anthropologie: Schiller und Herder." *Monatshefte* 97, no. 3 (2005): 408–16.
———. "Herder's Concept of Humanität." In *A Companion to the Works of Johann Gottfried Herder*, edited by Hans Adler and Wulf Koepke, 93–116. Rochester, NY: Camden House, 2009.
———. "Ästhetische und anästhetische Wissenschaft: Kants Herder-Kritik als Dokument moderner Paradigmenkonkurrenz." *Deutsche Vierteljahrsschrift für Literaturwissenschaft und Geistesgeschichte* 68, no. 1 (1994): 66–76.
Adler, Hans, and Wulf Koepke, eds. *A Companion to the Works of Johann Gottfried Herder*. Rochester, NY: Camden House, 2009.
Adorno, Theodor W. "Zum Klassizismus von Goethe's Iphigenie." In *Gesammelte Schriften: Noten zur Literatur*, edited by Rolf Tiedemann, 11:495–514. Frankfurt am Main: Suhrkamp, 1974.
Agamben, Giorgio. *The Open: Man and Animal*. Translated by Kevin Attell. Stanford, CA: Stanford UP, 2004.
Agocs, Andreas. *Antifascist Humanism and the Politics of Cultural Renewal in Germany*. Cambridge: Cambridge UP, 2017.
Aguado, María Isabel Peña. *Ästhetik des Erhabenen: Burke, Kant, Adorno, Lyotard*. Vienna: Passagen Verlag, 1994.
Alt, Peter-André. *Schiller: Leben—Werk –Zeit*. 2 vols. Beck: Munich, 2004.
———. "Kommentar." In *Friedrich Schiller: Sämtliche Werke; Historische Schriften*, edited by Peter-André Alt, 4:1001–69. Munich: dtv, 2004.
———. "Natur, Zivilisation und Narratio: Zur triadischen Strukturierung von Schillers Geschichtskonzept." *Zeitschrift für Germanistik* 18, no. 3 (2008): 530–45.
Altenhofer, Norbert. "Geschichtsphilosophie, Zeichentheorie und Dramaturgie in der 'Erziehung des Menschengeschlechts': Anmerkungen zur patristischen Tradition bei Lessing." In *Nation und Gelehrtenrepublik: Lessing im europäischen Zusammenhang*.

Sonderband zum Lessing Yearbook, edited by Wilfried Barner and Albert M. Reh, 25–36. Detroit, MI: Wayne State UP, 1984.
Althaus, Thomas. *Das Uneigentliche ist das Eigentliche: Metaphorische Darstellung in der Prosa bei Lessing und Lichtenberg*. Münster: Aschendorff, 1991.
Arendt, Hannah. *Von der Menschlichkeit in Finsteren Zeiten: Gedanken zu Lessing*. Hamburg: Hauswedell, 1960.
———. *The Human Condition*. 2nd ed. Chicago: U of Chicago P, 1998.
Arens, Katherine. "History as Knowledge: Herder, Kant, and the Human Sciences." In *Johann Gottfried Herder: Academic Disciplines and the Pursuit of Knowledge*, edited by Wulf Koepke, 106–19. Columbia, SC: Camden House, 1996.
Arnold, Günter. "Herder's Interdisciplinary Conjectures on the Origin of Human History." In *Johann Gottfried Herder: Academic Disciplines and the Pursuit of Knowledge*, edited by Wulf Koepke, 98–105. Columbia, SC: Camden House, 1996.
Assmann, Jan. *Moses the Egyptian: The Memory of Egypt in Western Monotheism*. Cambridge, MA: Harvard UP, 1997.
———. "Nachwort." In *Die hebräischen Mysterien oder die älteste religiöse Freymaurerei*, edited by Jan Assmann, 157–99. Neckargmünd: Edition mnemosyne, 2001.
———. "Über das Erhabene: Schiller im Licht von Kant und Mozart." *Jahrbuch der deutschen Schillergesellschaft* 51 (2007): 166–82.
Badmington, Neil, ed. *Posthumanism*. Houndmills: Palgrave, 2000.
———. "Theorizing Posthumanism." *Cultural Critique* 53 (2003): 10–27.
Baumgarten, Alexander Gottlieb. *Metaphysica*. New York: Olms, 1982.
Beiser, Frederick C. *German Idealism: The Struggle against Subjectivism, 1781–1801*. Cambridge: Harvard UP, 2002.
Beller, Stephen, ed. *Rethinking Vienna 1900*. New York: Berghahn, 2001.
Benda, Oskar. *Die Bildung des dritten Reiches: Randbemerkungen zum gesellschaftlichen Sinnwandel des deutschen Humanismus*. Vienna: Deutscher Verlag für Jugend und Volk, 1931.
Benner, Dietrich. *Wilhelm von Humboldts Bildungstheorie*. Weinheim: Juventa, 2003.
Bennett, Benjamin. "Reason, Error and the Shape of History: Lessing's Nathan and Lessing's God." *Lessing Yearbook* 9 (1977): 60–80.
———. "Trinitarische Humanität: Dichtung und Geschichte bei Schiller." In *Friedrich Schiller: Kunst, Humanität und Politik in der späten Aufklärung*, edited by Wolfgang Wittkowski, 164–77. Tübingen: Niemeyer, 1982.
———. *Goethe's Theory of Poetry*. Ithaca: Cornell UP, 1986.
Bergel, Kurt. "Review of *Stefan George und Thomas Mann: Zwei Formen des dritten Humanismus* by Hans Maier." *Modern Philology* 46, no. 2 (1948): 142–44.
Bergengruen, Maximilian, et al., eds. *Die Grenzen des Menschen: Anthropologie und Ästhetik um 1800*. Würzburg: Königshausen & Neumann, 2001.
Berger, Thomas. *Der Humanitätsgedanke in der Literatur der deutschen Spätaufklärung*. Heidelberg: Winter, 2007.
Blumenbach, Johann Friedrich. *Über den Bildungstrieb*. Göttingen: Dietrich, 1791.
Bod, Rens, Julia Kursell, Jaap Maat, Thijs Weststeijn. "Introduction: The Humanities and the Sciences." *Isis* 106, no. 2 (2015): 337–40.
Böhme, Gernot. *Für eine ökologische Naturästhetik*. Frankfurt am Main: Suhrkamp, 1989.
Böhme, Hartmut. "Das Steinerne: Anmerkungen zur Theorie des Erhabenen aus dem Blick des 'Menschenfremdesten.'" In *Das Erhabene: Zwischen Grenzerfahrung und Größenwahn*, edited by Christine Pries, 119–41. Weinheim: Acta humanora, 1989.

Bölsche, Wilhelm. *Hinter der Weltstadt: Friedrichshagener Gedanken zur ästhetischen Kultur.* Leipzig: Diedrichs, 1901.
———. *Die naturwissenschaftlichen Grundlagen der Poesie: Prolegomena einer realistischen Ästhetik,* edited by Johannes Braakenburg. Tübingen: Niemeyer, 1976.
Bohnen, Klaus. "Lessings 'Erziehung des Menschengeschlechts' und Charles Bonnets 'Palingenesie.'" *Germanisch-Romanische Monatsschrift* 31, no. 3 (1981): 362–65.
Bohrer, Karl Heinz. *Das Tragische: Erscheinung, Pathos, Klage.* Munich: Hanser, 2009.
Borchmeyer, Dieter. "Politische Betrachtungen eines angeblich Unpolitischen: Thomas Mann, Edmund Burke und die Tradition des Konservatismus." *Thomas-Mann-Jahrbuch* 10 (1997): 83–104.
———. *Weimarer Klassik: Porträt einer Epoche.* Weinheim: Beltz, 1998.
———. "Iphigenie auf Tauris." In *Goethes Dramen,* edited by Walter Hinderer, 117–57. Stuttgart: Reclam, 1999.
———. "'Marquis Posa ist große Mode': Schillers Tragödie 'Don Carlos' und die Dialektik der Gesinnungsethik." In *Die Weimarer Klassik und ihre Geheimbünde,* edited by Walter Müller-Seidel and Wolfgang Riedel, 127–44. Würzburg: Königshausen und Neumann, 2002.
Bovenschen, Silvia. *Die imaginierte Weiblichkeit: Exemplarische Untersuchungen zu kulturgeschichtlichen und literarischen Präsentationsformen des Weiblichen.* Frankfurt am Main: Suhrkamp, 1979.
Braidotti, Rosi. "Posthuman, All Too Human: Towards a New Process Ontology." *Theory, Culture & Society* 23, nos. 7–8 (2006): 197–208.
———. *The Posthuman.* Malden, MA: Polity, 2013.
Breidbach, Olaf. *Goethes Metamorphosenlehre.* Munich: Fink, 2006.
Breithaupt, Fritz. "Narcissism the Self and Empathy: The Paradox That Created Modern Literature." In *The Self as Muse: Narcissism and Creativity in the German Imagination 1750–1830,* edited by Alexander Mathäs, 39–57. Lewisburg, PA: Bucknell UP, 2011.
Brockmann, Stephen. *German Literary Culture at the Zero Hour.* Rochester, NY: Camden House, 2004.
Buchwald, Reinhard. *Das Vermächtnis der deutschen Klassiker.* Frankfurt am Main: Insel-Verlag, 1962.
Buck, August. *Humanismus: Seine europäische Entwicklung in Dokumenten und Darstellungen.* Freiburg: Alber, 1987.
Bunge, Wiep van. "Spinoza and the Idea of Religious Imposture." In *On the Edge of Truth and Honesty: Principles and Strategies of Fraud and Deceit in the Early Modern Period,* edited by T. van Houdt, 105–25. Boston: Brill, 2002.
Bürger, Christa. *Der Ursprung der bürgerlichen Institution Kunst im höfischen Weimar: Literatursoziologische Untersuchungen zum klassischen Goethe.* Frankfurt am Main: Suhrkamp, 1977.
———. "Der bürgerliche Schriftsteller im höfischen Mäzenat: Literatursoziologische Bemerkungen zu Goethes 'Tasso.'" In *Deutsche Literatur zur Zeit der Klassik,* edited by Karl Otto Conrady, 141–53. Stuttgart: Reclam, 1977.
Burckhardt, Jacob. *Die Kultur der Renaissance in Italien.* Frankfurt am Main: Deutscher Klassiker Verlag, 1989.
Burke, Edmund. "A Philosophical Inquiry into the Origin of Our Ideas of the Sublime and Beautiful, with an Introductory Discourse Concerning Taste." In *Works.* Vol. 1. London: George Bell and Sons, 1897.
Butler, Judith. *Senses of the Subject.* New York: Fordham UP, 2015.

Calarco, Matthew, and Peter Atterton, eds. *Animal Philosophy*. New York: Continuum, 2004.
Carlsson, Anni, and Volker Michels, eds. *Hermann Hesse—Thomas Mann: Briefwechsel*. Frankfurt am Main: Fischer, 1975.
Carus, Carl Gustav. *Symbolik der menschlichen Gestalt: Ein Handbuch zur Menschenkenntnis*. Dresden: Rohrmoser, 1938.
———. *Lebenserinnerungen und Denkwürdigkeiten*. Edited by Elmar Jansen. 2 vols. Weimar: Kiepenheuer, 1966.
———. *Gesammelte Schriften*. Edited by Olaf Breidbach. 10 vols. Hildesheim: Olms, 2009.
Caruth, Cathy. "Afterword: Turning Back to Literature." *PMLA* 125, no. 4 (2010): 1087–95.
Cassirer, Ernst. *An Essay on Man: An Introduction to a Philosophy of Human Culture*. New York: Doubleday, 1954.
Césaire, Aimé. *Discourse on Colonialism*. Translated by Joan Pinkham. New York: Monthly Review Press, 2000.
Clauss, Elke-Maria. "'... und weiss nicht Mensch und Tier zu unterscheiden': Zur Funktionsweise der Tierbilder in Hofmannsthal's *Elektra*," in *Die Zoologie der Träume: Studien zum Tiermotiv in der Literatur der Moderne*, edited by Dorothee Römhild, 59–83. Opladen: Westdeutscher Verlag, 1999.
Coates, Wilson, Hayden White, and Salwyn Shapiro. *The Emergence of Liberal Humanism*. New York: McGraw Hill, 1966.
Coetzee, J. M. *Elizabeth Costello*. Vintage Digital, 2003.
Colvin Sarah. "Leaning In: Why and How I Still Study the German." *German Life and Letters* 69, no. 1 (2016): 123–41.
Cornils, Ingo, ed. *A Companion to the Works of Hermann Hesse*. Rochester, NY: Camden House, 2009.
———. "Introduction: From Outsider to Global Player; Hermann Hesse in the Twenty-First Century." In *A Companion to the Works of Hermann Hesse*, 1–16. Rochester, NY: Camden House, 2009.
Cornils, Ingo, and Osman Durrani, ed. *Hermann Hesse Today: Hermann Hesse heute*. Amsterdam: Rodopi, 2005.
Cotter, Jennifer, et al., eds. *Human, All Too (Post)Human: The Humanities after Humanism*. Lanham, MD: Lexington, 2016.
Curtius, Ernst Robert. *Europäische Literatur und Lateinisches Mittelalter*. Bern: Francke, 1948.
———. *Kritische Essays zur europäischen Literatur*. Frankfurt am Main: Fischer, 1984.
Damasio, Antonio. *Descartes' Error: Emotion, Reason, and the Human Brain*. New York: Putnam's Sons, 1994.
———. *Looking for Spinoza: Joy, Sorrow, and the Feeling Brain*. Orlando, FL: Harcourt, 2003.
Daston, Lorraine, and Peter Galison. *Objectivity*. New York: Zone Books, 2010.
Davies, Tony. *Humanism*. London: Routledge, 1997.
DeGrazia, David. *Human Identity and Bioethics*. New York: Cambridge UP, 2005.
Deiters, Franz Josef. "Goethes 'Iphigenie auf Tauris' als Drama der Grenzüberschreitung oder: Die Aneignung des Mythos." *Jahrbuch des freien deutschen Hochstifts* (1999): 14–51.
Deleuze, Gilles, and Félix Guattari. *Kafka: Toward a Minor Literature*. Translated by Dana Polan. Minneapolis: U of Minnesota P, 1986.

———. *A Thousand Plateaus: Capitalism and Schizophrenia*. Translated by Brian Massumi. London: Athlone, 1988.
De Man, Paul. "Kant and Schiller." In *Aesthetic Ideology*, edited by Paul De Man, 129–62. Minneapolis: U of Minnesota P, 1997.
Demant, Alexander. *Metaphern für Geschichte: Sprachbilder und Gleichnisse im historisch-politischen Denken*. Munich: Beck, 1978.
Demetz, Peter. *Die süße Anarchie*. Frankfurt am Main: Ullstein, 1945.
———. "Zur Situation der Germanistik: Tradition und aktuelle Probleme." In *Die deutsche Literatur der Gegenwart*, edited by Manfred Durzak, 347–61. Stuttgart: Reclam, 1971.
Dennis, John. "Letter Describing His Crossing the Alps, Dated from Turin, Oct 25, 1688." In *The Critical Works*. Vol. 2, edited by Edward Niles Hooker, 380–82. Baltimore: Johns Hopkins UP, 1939–43.
Derrida, Jacques. "Violence and Metaphysics: An Essay on the Thought of Emmanuel Levinas." In *Writing and Difference*, translated by Alan Bass, 79–153. London: Routledge, 1978.
———. *The Animal That Therefore I Am*. Translated by David Wills. New York: Fordham, 2008.
Descartes, René. *Über den Menschen (1632) sowie Beschreibung des menschlichen Körpers (1648)*. Translated by K. E. Rothschuh. Heidelberg: Lambert & Schneider, 1969.
Detering, Heinrich. *Das offene Geheimnis: Zur literarischen Produktivität eines Tabus von Winckelmann bis Thomas Mann*. Göttingen: Wallstein, 1994.
———. *"Juden, Frauen und Litteraten": Zu einer Denkfigur beim jungen Thomas Mann*. Frankfurt am Main: Fischer, 2005.
Dilthey, Wilhelm. *Einleitung in die Geisteswissenschaften: Versuch einer Grundlegung für das Studium der Gesellschaft und der Geschichte. Gesammelte Schriften*. Vol. 1. Edited by Bernhard Groethuysen. Leipzig: Teubner, 1923.
———. *Introduction to the Human Sciences: Selected Works*. Vol. 1. Edited by Rudolf A. Makkreel and Frithjor Rodi. Princeton, NJ: Princeton UP, 1989.
Dörr, Volker, und Michael Hofmann, eds. *"Verteufelt human"? Zum Humanitätsideal der Weimarer Klassik*. Berlin: Schmidt, 2008.
Drews, Jörg. "'. . . bewundert viel und viel gescholten . . .': Hermann Hesses Werk zwischen Erfolg und Mißachtung bei Publium und Literaturkritik." In *Hermann Hesse Today: Hermann Hesse Heute*, edited by Ingo Cornils and Osman Durrani, 21–31. Amsterdam: Rodopi, 2005.
Drexler, Hans. *Der Dritte Humanismus: Ein kritischer Epilog*. Frankfurt am Main: Diesterweg, 1942.
Dülmen, Richard van. *Der Geheimbund der Illuminaten: Darstellung, Analyse, Dokumentation*. Stuttgart Bad-Cannstatt: Frommann-Holzboog, 1975.
Durzak, Manfred, ed. *Die deutsche Literatur der Gegenwart: Aspekte und Tendenzen*. Stuttgart: Reclam, 1971.
———, ed. *Deutsche Gegenwartsliteratur: Ausgangspositionen und aktuelle Entwicklungen*. Stuttgart: Reclam, 1981.
Eagleton, Terry. *The Ideology of the Aesthetic*. Malden, MA: Blackwell, 1990.
———. *After Theory*. New York: Basic, 2003.
———. *Sweet Violence: The Idea of the Tragic*. Malden, MA: Blackwell, 2003.
———. *Why Marx Was Right*. New Haven, CT: Yale UP, 2011.
Eckardt, Georg, Matthias John, Temilo van Zantwijk, and Paul Ziche. *Anthropologie und empirische Psychologie um 1800*. Köln: Böhlau, 2001.

Ehrhardt, Gundula. "'Meine natürliche Aufgabe in dieser Welt ist erhaltender Art': Thomas Manns kulturkonservatives Denken (1919–1922)." *Thomas-Mann-Jahrbuch* 16 (2003): 97–118.
Eibl, Karl. "Lauter Bilder und Gleichnisse: Lessings religionsphilosophische Begründung der Poesie." *Deutsche Vierteljahrsschriften* 59, no. 2 (1985): 224–52.
Emrich, Wilhelm. *Franz Kafka*. Frankfurt: Athenäum, 1960.
Engelberg, Ernst. "Schiller als Historiker." In *Die deutsche Geschichtswissenschaft vom Beginn des 19. Jahrhunderts bis zur Reichseinigung von oben*, edited by Joachim Streisand, 11–31. Berlin: Deutsche Akademie der Wissenschaften, 1969.
Erhart, Walter. "Verbotene Bilder? Das Erhabene, das Schöne und die moderne Literatur." *Jahrbuch der deutschen Schillergesellschaft* 41 (1997): 79–106.
Ette, Ottmar. "Literature as Knowledge for Living, Literary Studies as Science for Living." *PMLA* 125, no. 4 (2010): 977–93.
Fechner, Frank. *Thomas Mann und die Demokratie: Wandel und Kontinuität der demokratierelevanten Äußerungen des Schriftstellers*. Berlin: Duncker & Humblot, 1990.
Feuerbach, Ludwig. *Sämmtliche Werke*. 10 vols. Leipzig: Wigand, 1846–66.
———. *The Essence of Christianity 1890*. 2nd ed., translated by Marian Evans. London: Paul, Trench, Trübner, 1890.
Fick, Monika. *Sinnenwelt und Weltseele: Der psychophysische Monismus in der Literatur der Jahrhundertwende*. Tübingen: Niemeyer, 1993.
Fickert, Kurt. "The Significance of the Epiphany in *Der Steppenwolf*." *International Fiction Review* 29 (2002): 1–10.
Fiedler, Leonhard M. "Hofmannsthal und Kafka." *Hofmannsthal-Blätter* 27 (1983): 62–65.
Fiero, Petra S. "New Humanism." In *The Feminist Encyclopedia of German Literature*, edited by Friederike Eigler and Susanne Kord, 363–64. Westport, CT: Greenwood, 1997.
Fischer, Bernd. "Herder heute? Überlegungen zur Konzeption eines transkulturellen Humanitätsbegriffs." *Herder Yearbook* 8 (2006): 175–93.
Fischer, Klaus P. "Schopenhauer und Hesse: Über den Einfluß von Arthur Schopenhauer auf Hermann Hesses Steppenwolf." *Stimmen der Zeit* 115 (1990): 353–57.
Fish, Stanley. "The Crisis of the Humanities Officially Arrives," *New York Times*, October 2010. Retrieved 14 August 2018 from https://opinionator.blogs.nytimes.com/2010/10/11/the-crisis-of-the-humanities-officially-arrives.
Fleischer, Helmut. *Marxism and History*. Translated by Eric Mosbacher. New York: Harper & Row, 1973.
Forster, Michael N., ed. *Johann Gottfried von Herder: Philosophical Writings*. Translated by Michael N. Forster. Cambridge: Cambridge UP, 2002.
Fortmann, Patrick. "Brain Matters in the German Enlightenment: Animal Cognition and Species Difference in Herder, Soemmering, and Gall," in *Posthumanism in the Age of Humanism*, edited by Edgar Landgraf, Gabriele Trop, and Leif Weatherby, 37–52. New York: Bloomsbury, 2019.
Fracchia, Joseph. "Marx's *Aufhebung* of Philosophy and the Foundation of a Materialist Science of History." *History and Theory* 30, no. 2 (1991): 153–79.
———. "Organisms and Objectifications: A Historical-Materialist Inquiry into the 'Human and Animal.'" *Konturen* 6 (2014): 41–61.
Frank, Manfred. *Selbstgefühl*. Frankfurt: Suhrkamp, 2002.
———. "Der Mensch bleibt sich ein Rätsel." Interview. *Die Zeit*, 27 August 2009.
Freedman, Ralph. *Hermann Hesse: Pilgrim of Crisis*. New York: Fromm, 1997.
Freud, Sigmund. *Studienausgabe*. 11 vols. 4th ed. Frankfurt am Main: Fischer, 1994.

Frierson, Patrick R. *What Is the Human Being?* Hoboken, NJ: Taylor and Francis, 2013.
Frierson, Patrick R., and Paul Guyer, eds. *Immanuel Kant: Observations on the Feeling of the Beautiful and Sublime and Other Writings.* Cambridge: Cambridge UP, 2011.
Frink, Helen. *Animal Symbolism in Hofmannsthal's Works.* New York: Lang, 1987.
Fritz, Axel."Vor den Vätern sterben die Töchter: Schnitzlers *Liebelei* und die Tradition des bürgerlichen Trauerspiels." *Text und Kontext* 10, no. 2 (1982): 303–18.
Fueter, Eduard. *Geschichte der neueren Historiographie.* Zürich: Füssli, 1935. [Reprint: 1985].
Gaier, Ulrich. "Gesellschaftsstruktur, Denkform, Klassizität: Widersprüche im letzten Drittel des 18. Jahrhunderts und ihre Lösungen (am Beispiel Herder, Goethe, Schiller und Hölderlin)." In *Literarische Klassik,* edited by Hans-Joachim Simm, 371–409. Frankfurt am Main: Suhrkamp, 1988.
———. *Herders Sprachphilosophie und Erkenntniskritik.* Stuttgart: Fromman Holzboog, 1988.
———. "Poesie oder Geschichtsphilosophie? Herders erkenntnistheoretische Antwort auf Kant." In *Johann Gottfried Herder: Geschichte und Kultur,* edited by Martin Bollacher, 1–17. Würzburg: Königshausen & Neumann 1994.
———. "The Problem of Core Cognition in Herder." *Monatshefte* 95, no. 2 (2003): 294–309.
Gatterer, Johann Christoph. "Vom historischen Plan und der darauf sich gründenden Zusammenfügung der Erzählungen." In *Allgemeine Historische Bibliothek I,* 15. Halle: 1767.
———. *Abriß der Genealogie.* Edited by Friederich Heinz F. [Nachdruck]. Göttingen: Degener, 1960.
Geras, Norman. *Marx and Human Nature: Refutation of a Legend.* London: Verso, 1983.
Gessinger, Joachim."'Das Gefühl liegt dem Gehör so nahe': The Physiological Foundations of Herder's Theory of Cognition." In *Johann Gottfried Herder: Academic Disciplines and the Pursuit of Knowledge,* edited by Wulf Koepke, 32–52. Columbia, SC: Camden House, 1996.
Gilmore, Myron P. *The World of Humanism,* 1453–1517. New York: Harper and Row, 1962.
Gilroy, Paul. *Against Race: Imaging Political Culture beyond the Color Line.* Cambridge, MA: Harvard UP, 2000.
Girschner, Gabriele. "Zum Verhältnis zwischen Dichter und Gesellschaft in Goethes *Torquato Tasso*." *Goethe-Jahrbuch* 101 (1984): 162–87.
Gliboff, Sander. "Ascent, Descent, and Divergence: Darwin and Haeckel on the Human Family Tree." *Konturen* 6 (2014): 103–30. Retrieved 3 October 2016 from http://journals.oregondigital.org/index.php/konturen/article/view/3523/3287.
Goethe, Johann Wolfgang von. *Werke: Hamburger Ausgabe.* Edited by Erich Trunz. 14 vols. Munich: dtv, 1998.
Grassi, Ernesto, and Thure von Uexkull. *Von Ursprung und Grenzen der Geisteswissenschaften und Naturwissenschaften.* Bern: Francke, 1950.
Gray, Richard T. *About Face: German Physiognomic Thought from Lavater to Auschwitz.* Detroit, MI: Wayne State UP, 2004.
Greif, Stefan. "'Unsere Humanität ist nur Vorübung …': Herders Widerlegung doktrinärer Menschlichkeit." In *"Verteufelt human"? Zum Humanitätsideal der Weimarer Klassik,* edited by Volker C. Dörr and Michael Hofmann, 31–45. Berlin: Erich Schmidt, 2008.

Grosche. Stefan. *"Zarten Seelen ist gar viel gegönnt."* Göttingen: Wallstein, 2001.
Grusin, Richard A. *The Nonhuman Turn*. Minneapolis: U of Minnesota P, 2014.
Guillory, John. *Cultural Capital*. Chicago: U of Chicago P, 1993.
Guthke, Karl S. *Das Abenteuer der Literatur*. Munich: Francke, 1981.
Györffy, Miklós. "Thomas Mann und Hermann Hesse: Thematisch-Motivische Beziehungen." In *Hermann Hesse und die Moderne: Diskurse zwischen Ästhetik, Ethik und Politik*, edited by Detlef Haberland and Géza Horváth, 223–33. Vienna: Praesens, 2013.
Habermas, Jürgen. *The Future of Human Nature*. Malden, MA: Blackwell, 2003.
Hadot, Pierre. *Plotinus or The Simplicity of Vision*. Translated by Michael Chase. Chicago: U of Chicago P, 1993.
Haeckel, Ernst. *Die Welträtsel*. Hamburg: Nikol 2009.
Hahn, Karl-Heinz. "Schiller als Historiker." In *Aufklärung und Geschichte*, edited by Erich Bödeker et al., 388–415. Göttingen: Max-Planck-Institut für Geschichte, 1986.
Haller, Albrecht von. "Untersuchung den empfindlichen und reizbaren Theilen des menschlichen Körpers." *Der Königlich Schwedischen Akademie der Wissenschaften Abhandlungen* 15 (1756): 14–39; 96–127. Retrieved 4 March 2019 from: https://books.google.com/books?id=0GFmAAAAcAAJ&pg=PA96&lpg=PA96&dq=Untersuchung+der+empfindlichen+und+reizbaren+Theile&source=bl&ots=KPz0SeJyU8&sig=L80iTH3zYsmb3ixbMGz6sR8NbSY&hl=en&sa=X&ved=0ahUKEwjPttzaq7XWAhVJ72MKHc7iAz4Q6AEIMzAC#v=onepage&q=Untersuchung percent20 der percent20empfindlichen percent20und percent20reizbaren percent20Theile&f=false.
Halliwell, Martin, and Andy Mousley. *Critical Humanisms: Humanist/Anti-Humanist Dialogues*. Edinburgh: Edinburgh UP, 2003.
Hamburger, Käte. "Das Opfer der delphischen Iphigenie." *Wirkendes Wort* 4 (1953/54): 221–23.
Haraway, Donna J. "A Manifesto for Cyborgs: Science, Technology, and Socialist Feminism in the 1980s." *Socialist Review* 80, no. 15, 2 (March–April, 1985): 65–107.
———. *Primate Visions*. New York: Routledge, 1989.
———. *The Haraway Reader*. New York: Routledge, 2004.
Hartwich, Wolf-Daniel. *Die Sendung Moses: Von der Aufklärung bis Thomas Mann*. Munich: Fink, 1997.
Hayden-Roy, Priscilla. "Refining the Metaphor in Lessing's 'Erziehung des Menschengeschlechts.'" *Monatshefte* 95, no. 3 (Fall 2003): 393–409.
Hayles, Katherine N. "The Human in the Posthuman: Afterword." *Cultural Critique* 53 (Winter 2003): 134–37.
———. *How We Became Posthuman: Virtual Bodies in Cybernetics, Literature, and Informatics*. Chicago: U of Chicago P, 1999.
Heidegger, Martin. *Brief über den Humanismus*. Frankfurt am Main: Klostermann, 1949.
Heinz, Marion. "Grundzüge von Herders Psychologie: 'Uebers Erkennen und Empfinden der Menschlichen Seele.'" In *Johann Gottfried Herder: Academic Disciplines and the Pursuit of Knowledge*, edited by Wulf Koepke, 137–51. Columbia, SC: Camden House, 1996.
Heise, Wolfgang. "Realistik und Utopie in Herders Humanitätskonzept." *Weimarer Beiträge* 25, no. 5 (1979): 47–81.
Helbing, Lothar. *Der Dritte Humanismus*. Berlin: Die Runde, 1932.
Heller, Peter. "Lessing's Historical Dialectic." *Lessing Yearbook* 13 (1981): 159–73.
Henkel, Arthur. "Die 'verteufelt humane' Iphigenie." *Euphorion* 59 (1965): 1–17.

Henning, Hans. *Schillers "Kabale und Liebe" in der zeitgenössischen Rezeption*. Leipzig: Zentralantiquariat der Deutschen Demokratischen Republik, 1985.
Herbrechter, Stefan. *Posthumanismus*. Darmstadt: Wissenschaftliche Buchgesellschaft, 2009.
Herder, Johann Gottfried. *Werke in zehn Bänden*. Edited by Martin Bollacher et al. 10 vols. Frankfurt am Main: Deutscher Klassiker Verlag, 1985–2000.
Hermand, Jost. "Zur politischen Polarisierung der westdeutschen Literatur seit 1961." In *Deutsche Gegenwartsliteratur*, edited by Manfred Durzak, 299–313. Stuttgart: Reclam, 1981.
———. *Geschichte der Germanistik*. Hamburg: Rowohlt, 1994.
Herrmann, Hans Peter. "Musikmeister Miller, die Emanzipation der Töchter und der dritte Ort der Liebenden." *Jahrbuch der deutschen Schillergesellschaft* 28 (1984): 223–47.
Herwig, Henriette, and Florian Trabert, eds. *Der Grenzgänger Hermann Hesse: Neue Perspektiven der Forschung*. Freiburg i. Br.: Rombach, 2013.
Hesse, Hermann. *Steppenwolf*. Translated by Josef Mileck and Horst Frenz. New York: Picador, 1963.
——— *Sämtliche Werke*. Edited by Volker Michels. 21 vols. Frankfurt am Main: Suhrkamp, 2001–2007.
Heumann, Konrad. "Mensch und Tier: Zum Problem der Objektfindung bei Ganghofer und Hofmannsthal; Mit einem Jagdbilderbogen von Max Arco-Zinneberg." *Deutsche Vierteljahrsschrift für Literaturwissenschaft* 79, no. 4 (2005): 602–33.
Himma, Kenneth Einar. Review of *Being No One: The Self-Model Theory of Subjectivity*, by Thomas Metzinger. *Metapsychology Online Reviews* 7, no. 21 (2003). Retrieved 15 Aug 2018 from http://metapsychology.mentalhelp.net/poc/view_docph p?type=book&id=1720&cn=394.
Hinderer, Walter. "Zur Situation der westdeutschen Literaturkritik." In *Die deutsche Literatur der Gegenwart*, edited by Manfred Durzak, 325–46. Stuttgart: Reclam, 1971.
———. "Die Räuber." In *Interpretationen: Schillers Dramen*, edited by Walter Hinderer, 11–63. Stuttgart: Reclam, 1972.
———. *Schiller und kein Ende: Metamorphosen und kreative Aneignungen*. Würzburg: Königshausen & Neumann, 2009.
Hinske, Norbert. "Das stillschweigende Gespräch: Prinzipien der Anthropologie und Geschichtsphilosophie bei Mendelssohn und Kant." In *Moses Mendelssohn und die Kreise seiner Wirksamkeit*, edited by Michael Albrecht et al., 135–56. Tübingen: Niemeyer, 1994.
Hobson, Irmgard W. "Goethe's 'Iphigenie': A Lacanian Reading." *Goethe Yearbook* 2 (1984): 51–67.
Hoffmann, Eva. "'Jede unserer Seelen lebt nur einen Augenblick': Erzählperspektive, Wahrnehmung und Animalität in Hofmannsthal's Reitergeschichte." *Studia Austriaca* 23 (2015): 51–64.
Hofmann, Michael. "Zur Aktualität des Erhabenen: Schiller, Hugo, Johnson, Tabori." *Weimarer Beiträge* 49, no. 2 (2003): 202–18.
———. *Schiller: Epoche, Werk, Wirkung*. Munich: Beck, 2003.
———. "Die Wege der Humanität: Krise und Erneuerung des Humanitäts-Paradigmas im Werk Goethes und Schillers." In *"Verteufelt human"? Zum Humanitätsideal der Weimarer Klassik*, edited by Volker Dörr und Michael Hofmann, 141–59. Berlin: Schmidt, 2008.
Hofmann, Michael, et al. *Schiller und die Geschichte*. Munich: Fink, 2006.

Hofmannsthal, Hugo von. *Sämtliche Werke: Kritische Ausgabe*. Vol. 30, edited by Manfred Pape. Frankfurt am Main: S. Fischer, 1982.

Hohendahl, Peter Uwe. *Literaturkritik und Öffentlichkeit*. Munich: Piper, 1974.

Holub, Robert C. "The Enlightenment of the Dialectic: Jürgen Habermas's Critique of the Frankfurt School." In *Impure Reason: Dialectic of Enlightenment in Germany*, edited by W. Daniel Wilson and Robert Holub, 34–47. Detroit: Wayne State UP, 1993.

Honold, Alexander. "Kleider machen Leute." In *Gottfried-Keller-Handbuch: Leben-Werk-Wirkung*, edited by Ursula Amrein, 67–71. Stuttgart: Metzler, 2016.

Horkheimer, Max, and Theodor W. Adorno. *Dialektik der Aufklärung*. Frankfurt: Suhrkamp, 1988.

Holzhey, Christoph. "On the Emergence of Sexual Difference in the 18th Century: Economies of Pleasure in Herder's *Liebe und Selbstheit*." *German Quarterly* 79, no. 1 (2006): 1–27.

Hull, Isabel. *Sexuality, State, and Civil Society in Germany 1700–1815*. Ithaca, NY: Cornell UP, 1996.

Humboldt, Wilhelm von. "Über die Aufgabe des Geschichtsschreibers." In *Werke*, edited by Andreas Flitner und Klaus Giel, 1:585–606. Stuttgart: Cotta, 1960–81.

———. *Gesammelte Schriften*. Vol. 1, edited by Königlich Preußische Akademie der Wissenschaften. Nachdruck. Berlin: De Gruyter, 1968.

———. "Über den Geschlechtsunterschied und dessen Einfluß auf die organische Natur." In *"Ob die Weiber Menschen sind": Geschlechterdebatten um 1800*, edited by Sigrid Lange, 284–308. Leipzig: Reclam, 1992.

Hutchinson, Peter, "Der Steppenwolf." In *Landmarks in the German Novel*, edited by Peter Hutchinson, 151–66. Bern: Lang, 2007.

Irmscher, Hans Dietrich. "Beobachtungen zur Funktion der Analogie im Denken Herders." *Deutsche Vierteljahrsschriften* 55 (1981): 64–97.

———. "Nationalität und Humanität im Denken Herders." *Orbis Litterarum* 49, no. 1 (1994): 189–215.

Israel, Jonathan. *Enlightenment Contested: Philosophy, Modernity, and the Emancipation of Man 1670–1752*. New York: Oxford UP, 2006.

Jaeger, Werner. "Antike und Humanismus." In *Humanismus*, edited by Hans Oppermann, 18–32. Darmstadt: Wissenschaftliche Buchgesellschaft, 1970.

Jahn, Ilse. *Geschichte der Biologie: Theorien, Methoden, Institutionen*. Jena: Fischer, 1985.

Jahn, Karl-Heinz. "Schiller und die Geschichte." *Weimarer Beiträge* 16 (1970): 29–69.

Janik, Allan, and Stephen Toulmin. *Wittgenstein's Vienna*. New York: Touchstone, 1973.

Janßen, Johannes. *Schiller als Historiker*. Freiburg: Herder, 1879.

Jaspers, Karl. *Existentialism and Humanism*. Translated by E. B. Ashton. New York: Moore, 1952.

Jauß, Hans Robert. "Racines und Goethes Iphigenie." In *Rezeptionsästhetik: Theorie und Praxis*, edited by Rainer Warning, 353–400. Munich: UTB, 1975.

Jay, Martin. *Marxism and Totality: The Adventures of a Concept from Lukács to Habermas*. Berkeley: U of California P, 1984.

Jens, Walter, and Hans Küng. *Anwälte der Humanität: Thomas Mann, Hermann Hesse und Heinrich Böll*. Munich: Kindler, 1989.

Jeziorkowski, Klaus. *Gottfried Keller: "Kleider machen Leute": Text, Materialien, Kommentar*. Munich: Hanser, 1984.

Johnson, Mark. *The Meaning of the Body: Aesthetics of Human Understanding*. Chicago: U of Chicago P, 2008.

Joosten, Heiko. *Selbst, Substanz und Subjekt: Die ethische und politische Relevanz der personalen Identität bei Descartes, Herder und Hegel*. Würzburg: Königshausen und Neumann, 2005.
Kain, Philip J. *Schiller, Hegel, and Marx: State, Society, and the Aesthetic Ideal of Ancient Greece*. Montreal: McGill-Queen's UP, 1982.
Kant, Immanuel. *Schriften zur Anthropologie, Geschichtsphilosophie, Politik und Pädagogik: Werkausgabe*. Vols. 11–12, edited by Wilhelm Weischedel. Frankfurt: Suhrkamp, 1977.
———. *Anthropologie in pragmatischer Hinsicht*. Edited by Wolfgang Becker. Stuttgart: Reclam, 1983.
———. *Schriften zur Geschichtsphilosophie*. Stuttgart: Reclam, 1985.
———. *Kritik der Urteilskraft*. Edited by Gerhard Lehmann. Stuttgart: Reclam, 1986.
———. "Of Duties to Animals and Spirits." In *Lectures on Ethics*, translated by Peter Lauchlan Heath and John Lachs, 212–13. New York: Cambridge UP, 1997.
Karalaschwili, Reso. "Harry Hallers Goethe-Traum: Vorläufiges zu einer Szene aus dem *Steppenwolf* von Hermann Hesse." *Goethe Jahrbuch* 97 (1980): 224–34.
———. *Hermann Hesse: Charakter und Weltbild*. Frankfurt am Main: Suhrkamp, 1993.
Kartheininger, Markus. "Bewahrung der menschlichen Natur: Zum Problem von geistiger Freiheit und Demokratie in den *Betrachtungen eines Unpolitischen*." *Literaturwissenschaftliches Jahrbuch* 45 (2013): 227–63.
Keller, Gottfried. *Sämtliche Werke: Historisch-kritische Ausgabe*. 10 vols. Edited by Walter Morgenthaler et al. Zürich: *Neue Züricher Zeitung*, 1996–2013.
Kelsch, Wolfgang. *Licht, Liebe, Leben: Johann Gottfried Herder und die Freimaurer*. Bayreuth: Quatuor Coronati, 1994.
Kiesel, Dagmar. "Das gespaltene Selbst: Die Identitätsproblematik in Hermann Hesses Steppenwolf und bei Friedrich Nietzsche." *Nietzsche Studien* 39 (2010): 398–433.
Klinger, Cornelia. "The Concepts of the Sublime and Beautiful in Kant and Lyotard." In *Feminist Interpretations of Immanuel Kant*, edited by Robin May Schott, 191–211. University Park: Pennsylvania State UP.
Klingmann, Ulrich. "Arbeit am Mythos: Goethes Iphigenie auf Tauris." *German Quarterly* 68, no. 1 (1995): 19–33.
Knodt, Eva. "Hermeneutics and the End of Science: Herder's Role in the Formation of *Natur-* and *Geisteswissenschaften*." In *Johann Gottfried Herder: Academic Disciplines and the Pursuit of Knowledge*, edited by Wulf Koepke 1–12. Columbia, SC: Camden House, 1996.
Knoeferl, Eva. *Thomas Mann's World: Empire, Race, and the Jewish Question*. Ann Arbor: U of Michigan P, 2011.
———. *"Dies Glasperlenspiel mit schwarzen Perlen": Musik und Moralität bei Hermann Hesse und Thomas Mann*. Würzburg: Ergon, 2012.
Koch, Manfred. "Von der vergleichenden Anatomie zur Kulturanthropologie: Wilhelm von Humboldts Hermeneutik fremder Kulturen im Kontext der zeitgenössischen Wissenschaft vom Menschen." *Zeitschrift für Germanistik* 3 (1993): 80–98.
Koelb, Clayton, ed. *Thomas Mann's "Goethe and Tolstoy": Notes and Sources*. Birmingham: U of Alabama P, 1984.
Koenen, Gerd. *Das rote Jahrzehnt: Unsere kleine deutsche Kulturrevolution 1967–1977*. Frankfurt am Main: Fischer, 2007.
Koepke, Wulf. "Das Verhältnis individueller und kollektiver Kräfte." In *Johann Gottfried Herder: Language, History and the Enlightenment*, edited by Wulf Koepke, 163–74. Columbia, SC: Camden House, 1990.

———. "Introduction." In *Johann Gottfried Herder: Academic Disciplines and the Pursuit of Knowledge*, edited by Wulf Koepke, ix–xii. Columbia, SC: Camden House, 1996.

———. "The Reception of Schiller in the Twentieth Century." In *A Companion to the Works of Friedrich Schiller*, edited by Stephen D. Martinson, 271–96. Rochester, NY: Camden House, 2005.

Kondylis, Panajotis. *Der Niedergang der bürgerlichen Denk- und Lebensform: Die liberale Moderne und die massendemokratische Postmoderne*. Weinheim: VCH, Acta Humaniora, 1991.

Kontje, Todd. "Socialization and Alienation in the Female *Bildungsroman*." In *Impure Reason: Dialectic of Enlightenment in Germany*, edited by W. Daniel Wilson and Robert Holub, 221–41. Detroit: Wayne State UP, 1993.

———. *The Cambridge Introduction to Thomas Mann*. Cambridge: Cambridge UP, 2011.

———. *Thomas Mann's World: Empire, Race, and the Jewish Question*. Ann Arbor: U of Michigan P, 2011.

Konzett, Matthias. "The Difficult Rebirth of Cosmopolitanism: Schnitzler and Contemporary Austrian Literature." In *A Companion to the Works of Arthur Schnitzler*, edited by Dagmar C. G. Lorenz, 349–69. Rochester, NY: Camden House, 2003.

Koopmann, Helmut. *Thomas-Mann-Handbuch*. Stuttgart: Kröner, 1990.

Kost, Jürgen. *Wilhelm von Humboldt—Weimarer Klassik—Bürgerliches Bewusstsein: Kulturelle Entwürfe in Deutschland um 1800*. Würzburg: Königshausen und Neumann, 2004.

Kracauer, Siegfried. *Die Angestellten*. Frankfurt am Main: Suhrkamp, 1971.

Kramer, Olaf. "'Es spricht kein Gott; es spricht dein eignes Herz': Kommunikative Autonomie und rhetorische Typologie in Goethes *Iphigenie*." *Rhetorik* 33, no. 1 (2014): 114–30.

Kraushaar, Wolfgang. *Acht Und Sechzig: Eine Bilanz*. Berlin: Ullstein, 2008.

Kroll, Joe P. "Conservative at the Crossroads: 'Ironic' vs. 'Revolutionary' Conservatism in Thomas Mann's Reflections of a Non-political Mann." *Journal of European Studies* 34, no. 3 (2004): 225–46.

Kuhlmann-Hodick, Petra, ed. *Carl Gustav Carus: Wahrnehmung und Konstruktion*. Dresden: Deutscher Kunstverlag, 2009.

Kuhse, Helga, and Peter Singer, eds. *A Companion to Bioethics*. Oxford: Blackwell, 2001.

Kurzke, Hermann. *Thomas Mann: Das Leben als Kunstwerk*. Munich: Beck, 1999.

———, et al. *Kommentar: Betrachtungen eines Unpolitischen*, vol. 13.2 of *Große kommentierte Frankfurter Ausgabe*. Frankfurt am Main, Fischer, 2009.

Lacan, Jacques. "The Mirror Stage as Formative of the Function of the I as Revealed in Psychoanalytic Experience." *Écrits: A Selection*, 1–7. New York: Norton, 1977.

Lakoff, George, and Mark Johnson. *Metaphors We Live By*. Chicago: U of Chicago P, 1980.

Landgraf, Edgar, Gabriel Trop, and Leif Weatherby, eds. *Posthumanism in the Age of Humanism: Mind Matter and the Life Sciences after Kant*. New York: Bloomsbury, 2019.

Landgren, Gustav. "'Untergangsmusik war es, im Rom der letzten Kaiser mußte es ähnliche Musik gegeben haben': Hesses Verhältnis zur Musik in *Der Steppenwolf*." In *Der Grenzgänger Hermann Hesse: Neue Perspektiven der Forschung*, edited by Henriette Herwig and Florian Trabert, 111–22. Freiburg, i.Br.: Rombach, 2013.

Lange, Sigrid, ed. *"Ob die Weiber Menschen sind . . .": Geschlechterdebatten um 1800*. Leipzig: Reclam, 1992.

Lehleiter, Christine. *Romanticism, Origins, and the History of Heredity*. Lewisburg, PA: Bucknell UP, 2014.

Lehnert, Herbert, and Eva Wessel. *Nihilismus der Menschenfreundlichkeit: Thomas Manns "Wandlung" und sein Essay Goethe und Tolstoi.* Frankfurt am Main: Klostermann, 1991.
Lehrer, Mark. "Keller's Anthropological Realism: The Scientific Underpinnings of the Early Prose." *German Quarterly* 60, no. 4 (1987): 567–81.
Le Rider, Jacques. *Modernity and Crises of Identity: Culture and Society in Fin-de-Siècle Vienna.* Translated by Rosemarie Morris. New York: Continuum, 1993.
Lessing, Gotthold Ephraim. *Werke und Briefe in zwölf Bänden.* Edited by Wilfried Barner et al. Frankfurt am Main: Deutscher Klassiker Verlag, 1985–2003.
Librett, Jeffrey S. "Enlightenment beyond Teleology: Religious Familiality and the Fundamental Gift in G. E. Lessing." *German Studies Review* 41, no. 2 (2018): 235–51.
Lingis, Alphonso. "Nietzsche and Animals." In *Animal Philosophy*, edited by Matthew Calarco and Peter Atterton, 7–14. New York: Continuum, 2004.
Litt, Theodor. *Das Bildungsideal der deutschen Klassik und die moderne Arbeitswelt.* Bochum: Kamp, 1965.
Loechte, Anne. *Johann Gottfried Herder: Kulturtheorie und Humanitätsidee der Ideen, Humanitätsbriefe und Adrasta.* Würzburg: Königshausen & Neumann, 2005.
Lorenz, Dagmar C. G. "The Self as Process in an Era of Transition: Competing Paradigms of Personality and Character in Schnitzler's Works." In *A Companion to the Works of Arthur Schnitzler*, edited by Dagmar C. G. Lorenz, 129–47. Rochester, NY: Camden House, 2003.
Lovibond, Sabina. "Meaning What We Say: Feminist Ethics and the Critique of Humanism." *New Left Review* 220, no. 1 (1996): 98–115.
Lützeler, Paul Michael. *Kontinentalisierung: Das Europa der Schriftsteller.* Bielefeld: Aisthesis, 2007.
———. "The Role of Literature in the German Studies Association." *German Studies Review* 39, no. 3 (2016): 505–14.
Lyotard, Jean-François. "Das Interesse des Erhabenen." In *Das Erhabene: Zwischen Grenzerfahrung und Größenwahn*, edited by Christine Pries, 91–118. Weinheim: Acta humanora, 1989.
———. "The Sublime and the Avant-Garde." In *The Inhuman*, translated by Geoffrey Bennington and Rachel Bowlby, 89–107. Stanford, CA: Stanford UP, 1991.
———. *Lessons on the Analytic of the Sublime.* Translated by Elizabeth Rottenberg. Stanford, CA: Stanford UP, 1994.
Maier, Hans Albert. *Der dritte Humanismus im Werke Stefan Georges und Thomas Manns.* Luzern: Universität Bern, 1946.
Malter, Rudolf. "Schiller und Kant." In *Schiller-Handbuch*, edited by Helmut Koopmann, 687. Stuttgart: Kröner, 1998.
Mann, Bonnie. *Women's Liberation and the Sublime: Feminism, Postmodernism, Environment.* Oxford: Oxford UP, 2006.
Mann, Thomas. *Adel des Geistes: Sechzehn Versuche zum Problem der Humanität.* Stockholm: Bermann-Fischer, 1945.
———. *Essays.* Vol. 3, edited by Hermann Kurzke and Stephan Stachorski. Frankfurt am Main: Fischer, 1994.
———. *Große kommentierte Frankfurter Ausgabe: Werke, Briefe, Tagebücher.* Edited by Heinrich Detering et al. Frankfurt am Main: Fischer, 2002–18.
Marcuse, Herbert. "Humanismus—gibt's den noch?" *Neues Forum* (1970): 349–53.
Markworth, Tino. "Das 'Ich' und die Geschichte: Zum Zusammenhang von Selbstthematisierung und Geschichtsphilosophie bei J. G. Herder." In *Johann Gottfried Herder:*

Academic Disciplines and the Pursuit of Knowledge, edited by Wulf Koepke, 152–97. Columbia, SC: Camden House, 1996.

Marx, Karl, and Friedrich Engels. *Economic and Philosophic Manuscripts of 1844*. Translated by Martin Milligan. Moscow: Progress Publishers, 1959. Retrieved 25 September 2018 from https://www.marxists.org/archive/marx/works/download/pdf/Economic-Philosophic-Manuscripts-1844.pdf.

———. Preface of *A Contribution to the Critique of Political Economy*, [1859] 2002. Retrieved 25 September 2018 from https://www.marxists.org/archive/marx/works/1859/critique-pol-economy/preface-abs.htm.

Mathäs, Alexander. *Narcissism and Paranoia in the Age of Goethe*. Newark: U of Delaware P, 2008.

Matthias, Bettina. "Arthur Schnitzler's *Fräulein Else* and the End of Bourgeois Tragedy." *Women in German Yearbook* 18 (2002): 248–66.

Maurer, Michael. "Geschichte zwischen Theodizee und Anthropologie: Zur Wissenschaftlichkeit der historischen Schriften Herders." In *Johann Gottfried Herder: Language, History and the Enlightenment*, edited by Wulf Koepke, 120–36. Columbia, SC: Camden House, 1990.

Mayer, Hans. *Stefan George und Thomas Mann: Zwei Formen des dritten Humanismus in kritischem Vergleich*. Zürich: Speer, 1947.

———. "Der Steppenwolf und der Unpolitische: Hermann Hesse und Thomas Mann im Briefwechsel." In *Vereinzelt Niederschläge: Kritik—Polemik*, 51–61. Pfullingen: Neske, 1973.

Mayer, Mathias. "Nachwort." In *Hugo von Hofmannsthal: "Andreas,"* 127–48. Stuttgart: Reclam, 2000.

McCarthy, John A. *Crossing Boundaries: A Theory and History of Essay Writing in German, 1680–1815*. Philadelphia: U of Pennsylvania P, 1989.

———. "*Verständigung und Dialektik*: On Consensus Theory and the Dialectic of Enlightenment." In *Impure Reason: Dialectic of Enlightenment in Germany*, edited by W. Daniel Wilson and Robert C. Holub, 13–33. Detroit: Wayne State UP, 1993.

McCarthy, John A., Stephanie M. Hilger, Heather I. Sullivan, and Nicholas Saul, eds. *The Early History of Embodied Cognition 1740–1920: The Lebenskraft-Debate and Radical Reality in German Science, Music, and Literature*. Leiden: Brill, 2016.

McNeely, Ian F., and Lisa Wolverton. *Reinventing Knowledge: From Alexandria to the Internet*. New York: Norton, 2008.

Mehring, Reinhard. *Das Problem der Humanität: Thomas Manns politische Philosophie*. Paderborn: Mentis, 2003.

Mendelssohn, Moses. *Philosophical Writings*. Translated by Daniel O. Dahlstrom. Cambridge: Cambridge UP, 1997.

Mendelssohn, Peter de. *Der Zauberer: Das Leben des deutschen Schriftstellers Thomas Mann*. 3 vols. Frankfurt am Main: S. Fischer, 1996.

Menges, Karl. "Erkenntnis und Sprache: Herder und die Krise der Philosophie im späten achtzehnten Jahrhundert." In *Johann Gottfried Herder: Language, History and the Enlightenment*, edited by Wulf Koepke, 47–69. Columbia, SC: Camden House, 1990.

Merleau-Ponty, Maurice. *The World of Perception*. London: Routledge, 2004.

Metzinger, Thomas. "Introduction." In *Neural Correlates of Consciousness*, edited by Thomas Metzinger, 1–12. Cambridge, MA: MIT P, 2000.

———. *Being No One: The Self-Model Theory of Subjectivity*. Cambridge, MA: MIT P, 2003.

———. *The Ego Tunnel*. New York: Basic Books, 2009.

Meyer, Imke. *Männlichkeit und Melodram: Arthur Schnitzlers erzählende Schriften*. Würzburg: Königshausen & Neumann, 2010.
Michels, Volker. "'Spitzbübischer Spötter' und 'Treuherzige Nachtigall'? Zur Genese der Freundschaft von Thomas Mann und Hermann Hesse." Frankfurt am Main: Faust Kultur, 2014.
———. *Materialien zu Hermann Hesses Der Steppenwolf*. Frankfurt: Suhrkamp, 1972.
Michelsen, Peter. "Schiller's Fiesko: Freiheitsheld und Tyrann." In *Schiller und die höfische Welt*, edited by Achim Aurnhammer et al., 341–58. Tübingen: Niemeyer, 1990.
Michler, Werner. *Darwinismus und Literatur: Naturwissenschaftliche und Literarische Intelligenz in Österreich: 1859–1914*. Wien: Böhlau, 1999.
———. "Darwinismus, Literatur und Politik: Robert Müllers Interventionen." *Akten des X. Internationalen Germanistenkongresses Wien 2000. Zeitenwende—Die Germanistik auf dem Weg vom 20. ins 21. Jahrhundert.* Vol. 6: *Epochenbegriffe: Grenzen und Möglichkeiten; Aufklärung-Klassik-Romantik; Die Wiener Moderne*, edited by Peter Wiesinger et al. Bern: Lang, 2002.
Miles, David H. *Hofmannsthal's Novel "Andreas": Memory and Self*. Princeton, NJ: Princeton UP, 1972.
Mix, York-Gothart. *Die Schulen der Nation: Bildungskritik in der Literatur der Moderne*. Stuttgart: Metzler, 1995.
Moran, Dermot. *Introduction to Phenomenology*. London: Routledge, 2000.
Mueller-Vollmer, Kurt. "From Sign to Signification: The Herder-Humboldt Controversy." In *Johann Gottfried Herder: Language, History and the Enlightenment*, edited by Wulf Koepke, 9–24. Columbia, SC: Camden House, 1990.
Müller, Joachim. "Das humanistische Programm der deutschen Klassik." *Wissenschaftliche Zeitschrift der Friedrich-Schiller-Universität Jena* 11, no. 2 (1962): 167–71.
———. "Hermann Hesse und Thomas Mann im Briefgespräch: Über ihre freundschaftliche Beziehung." In *Gesammelte Studien*, 119–28. Halle: Niemeyer, 1974.
Müller-Michaels, Harro. "'For His Own Self-Formation'—On the Educative Effect of Autobiography about 1800." In *Johann Gottfried Herder: Academic Disciplines and the Pursuit of Knowledge*, edited by Wulf Koepke, 220–31. Columbia, SC: Camden House, 1996.
Müller-Seidel, Walter, and Wolfgang Riedel, eds. *Die Weimarer Klassik und ihre Geheimbünde*. Würzburg: Königshausen & Neumann, 2002.
Müller-Sievers, Helmut. *Self-Generation: Biology, Philosophy, and Literature Around 1800*. Stanford, CA: Stanford UP, 1997.
Müller-Tamm, Jutta. *Kunst als Gipfel der Wissenschaft: Ästhetische und wissenschaftliche Weltaneignung bei Carl Gustav Carus*. Berlin: De Gruyter, 1995.
Mukherjee, Ankhi. "'What Is a Classic?': International Literary Criticism and the Classic Question." *PMLA* 125, no. 4 (2010): 1026–42.
Murti, Kamakshi. "'Ob die Weiber Menschen Seyn?': Hesse, Women, and Homoeroticism." In *A Companion to the Works of Hermann Hesse*, edited by Ingo Cornils, 263–99. Rochester, NY: Camden House, 2009.
Myers, David. "Sexual Love and Caritas in Thomas Mann." *JEPG* 96 (October 1997): 567–90. JSTOR.
Nayar, Pramod K. *Posthumanism*. Cambridge: Polity, 2014.
Neis, Cordula. *Anthropologie im Sprachdenken des 18. Jahrhunderts*. New York: De Gruyter, 2003.

Nethersole, Reingard. "Twilight of the Humanities: Rethinking (Post)Humanism with J. M. Coetzee." *Symploke: A Journal for the Intermingling of Literary, Cultural and Theoretical Scholarship* 23, nos. 1–2 (2015): 57–73.
Neubauer, John. "Sprache und Distanz in Goethes 'Iphigenie.'" In *Verlorene Klassik?*, edited by Wolfgang Wittkowski, 27–39. Tübingen: Niemeyer, 1986.
Neugebauer-Wölk, Monika. *Esoterische Bünde und Bürgerliche Gesellschaft.* Göttingen: Wallstein, 1995.
Neumann, Bernd. "'Ganzer Mensch' und 'innerweltliche Askese': Zum Verhältnis von Citoyen-Utopie und Bourgeoiser Wirklichkeit in Gottfried Kellers Seldwyla-Novellen." *Monatshefte* 71, no. 2 (Summer 1979): 145–60.
Nietzsche, Friedrich. *Werke in drei Bänden.* Edited by Karl Schlechta. Munich: Hanser, 1966.
———. *The Portable Nietzsche.* Translated by Walter Kaufmann. New York: Viking, 1968.
———. *Daybreak.* Edited by Maudemarie Clark and Brian Leiter. Cambridge: Cambridge UP, 1997.
Nisbet, H. B. *Herder and the Philosophy and History of Science.* Cambridge: Modern Humanities Research Association, 1970.
———. *Gotthold Ephraim Lessing: His Life, Works, and Thought.* Oxford: Oxford UP, 2008.
Nordhalm, Jens. "'Die Demokratie. Wir haben Sie ja schon!': Thomas Manns Bewegung zur Republik in den 'Betrachtungen eines Unpolitischen.'" *Literaturwissenschaftliches Jahrbuch der Görres-Gesellschaft* 47 (2006): 253–76.
Nussbaum, Martha. *Cultivating Humanity: A Classical Defense of Reform in Liberal Education.* Cambridge, MA: Harvard UP, 1999.
———. *Not for Profit: Why Democracy Needs the Humanities.* Princeton: Princeton UP, 2010.
Oken, Lorenz. *Über das Universum als Fortsetzung des Sinnensystems: Ein pythagoräisches Fragment.* Jena: Frommann, 1808.
———. *Lehrbuch der Naturphilosophie.* Zürich: Schulthess, 1843.
Oliver, Kelly. "Animal Pedagogy: The Origin of 'Man' in Rousseau and Herder." *Culture, Theory and Critique* 47, no. 2 (2006): 107–31.
Ossar, Michael. "Individual and Type in Arthur Schnitzler's *Liebelei.*" *Modern Austrian Literature* 30, no. 2 (1997): 19–34.
Otto, Regine. "Herder's Academy Conception—Theory and Practice." In *Johann Gottfried Herder: Academic Disciplines and the Pursuit of Knowledge*, edited by Wulf Koepke, 199–211. Columbia, SC: Camden House, 1996.
Pape, Manfred, ed. *Hugo von Hofmannsthal: Sämtliche Werke.* Vol 30. Frankfurt: Fischer, 1982.
Pfabigan, Alfred. "Freud's 'Vienna Middle.'" In *Rethinking Vienna 1900*, edited by Stephen Beller, 154–70. New York: Berghahn Books, 2001.
Pfau, Thomas. "'All is Leaf': Difference, Metamorphosis, and Goethe's Phenomenology of Knowledge." *Studies in Romanticism* 49, no. 1 (2010): 3–41.
Pfotenhauer, Helmut. "Anthropologische Ästhetik und Kritik der ästhetischen Urteilskraft oder Herder, Schiller, die antike Plastik und Seitenblicke auf Kant." In *Um 1800: Konfigurationen der Literatur. Kunstliteratur und Ästhetik*, edited by Helmut Pfotenhauer, 201–20. Tübingen: Niemeyer, 1991.
Pikulik, Lothar. *Thomas Mann und der Faschismus: Wahrnehmung—Erkenntnisinteresse—Widerstand.* Hildesheim: Olms, 2013.

Plant, Sadie. "On the Matrix: Cyberfeminist Simulations." In *The Gendered Cyborg: A Reader*, edited by Gill Kirkup et al. 265–75. London: Routledge, 2000.
Platner, Ernst. *Anthropologie für Ärzte und Weltweise*. 1772. Hildesheim: Olms, 2000.
Port, Ulrich. *Pathosformeln: Die Tragödie und die Geschichte exaltierter Affekte (1755–1888)*. Munich: Fink, 2005.
Prang, Helmut. *Der Humanismus: Sein Wesen und Wandel in Deutschland*. Bamberg: Meisenbach, 1948.
Pries, Christine, ed. *Das Erhabene: Zwischen Grenzerfahrung und Größenwahn*. Weinheim: Acta humaniora, 1989.
Proß, Wolfgang. "'Ein Reich unsichtbarer Kräfte': Was kritisiert Kant an Herder?" *Scientia Poetica* 1 (1997): 62–119.
Pugh, David. *Schiller's Early Dramas: A Critical History*. Rochester, NY: Camden House, 2000.
Rank, Otto. *Der Doppelgänger: Eine psychoanalytische Studie*. Leipzig: Psychoanalytischer Verlag, 1925.
Rasch, William. "Mensch, Bürger, Weib: Gender and the Limitations of Late 18th Century Neohumanist Discourse." *German Quarterly* 66, no. 1 (1993): 20–33.
Rasch, Wolfdietrich. *Goethes Iphigenie auf Tauris als Drama der Autonomie*. Munich: Beck, 1979.
———. "Schillers Aufsatz über die Anfänge der Menschheitsgeschichte." In *Friedrich Schiller: Kunst, Humanität und Politik in der späten Aufklärung*, edited by Wolfgang Wittkowski, 220–27. Tübingen: Niemeyer, 1982.
Rath, Norbert. *Zweite Natur: Konzepte einer Vermittlung von Natur und Kultur in Anthropologie und Ästhetik um 1800*. Münster: Waxmann, 1996.
Reill, Peter H. "Science and the Construction of the Cultural Sciences in Late Enlightenment Germany: The Case of Wilhelm von Humboldt." *History and Theory* 33, no. 3 (1994): 345–66.
———. "Herder's Historical Practice and the Discourse of Late Enlightenment Science." In *Johann Gottfried Herder: Academic Disciplines and the Pursuit of Knowledge*, edited by Wulf Koepke, 13–21. Columbia, SC: Camden House, 1996.
Reinhold, Karl Leonhard. *Die hebräischen Mysterien oder die älteste religiöse Freymaurerei*. Edited by Jan Assmann. Neckargmünd: Edition mnemosyne, 2001.
Rendall, Thomas. "Thomas Mann's Dantesque *Zauberberg*." *Monatshefte* 108, no. 1 (2016): 85–98.
Richter, Karl. "Wissenschaft und Poesie 'auf höherer Stelle' vereint: Goethes Elegie *Die Metamorphose der Pflanzen*." In *Gedichte und Interpretationen: Klassik und Romantik*, edited by Wulf Segebrecht, 156–68. Stuttgart: Reclam, 1984.
Richter, Simon. "Medizinischer und ästhetischer Diskurs im 18. Jahrhundert: Herder und Haller über Reiz." *Lessing Yearbook* 25 (1993): 83–95.
Riedel, Wolfgang. *Die Anthropologie des jungen Schiller: Zur Ideengeschichte der medizinischen Schriften und der "Philosophischen Briefe."* Würzburg: Königshausen und Neumann, 1985.
———. "Introduction." In *Eine Quellenedition zum Philosophieunterricht and der Stuttgarter Karlsschule (1773–1782)*, edited by Wolfgang Riedel, 402–50. Königshausen & Neumann, 1995.
———. *"Homo Natura": Literarische Anthropologie um 1900*, 1–39. Berlin: 1996.
———. "Aufklärung und Macht: Schiller, Abel und die Illuminaten." In *Die Weimarer Klassik und ihre Geheimbünde*, edited by Walter Müller-Seidel und Wolfang Riedel, 9–26. Würzburg: Königshausen & Neumann, 2002.

Rigby, Kate. "Art, Nature, and the Poesy of Plants in the Goethezeit: A Biosemiotic Perspective." *Goethe Yearbook* 22 (2015): 23–44.
Ritter, Joachim. *Subjektivität: Sechs Aufsätze*. Frankfurt am Main: Suhrkamp, 1989.
Rothschuh, K. E. *Geschichte der Physiologie*. Berlin: Springer, 1953.
Rudolf, G. "Hallers Lehre von der Irritabilität und Sensibilität." In *Von Boerhaave bis Berger: Die Entwicklung der kontinentalen Physiologie im 18. Und 19. Jahrhundert*, edited by K. E. Rothschuh, 14–34. Stuttgart: Fischer, 1964.
Safranski, Rüdiger. *Schiller oder die Erfindung des deutschen Idealismus*. Munich: Hanser, 2004.
Said, Edward W. *Humanism and Democratic Criticism*. New York: Columbia UP, 2004.
Sandel, Michael J. *The Case against Perfection: Ethics in the Age of Genetic Engeneering*. Cambridge, MA: Belknap, 2007.
Sanders, Helke. "Rede zur Befreiung der Frau (1968)." In *Die 68er: Schlüsseltexte der globalen Revolte*, edited by Angelika Ebbinghaus, 154–59. Vienna: Promedia, 2008.
Savage, Robert. "Menschen/Affen: On a Figure in Goethe, Herder, and Adorno." *Zeitschrift für deutsche Philologie. Sonderheft: Texte, Tiere, und Spuren* 126 (2007): 110–25.
Scaglione, Aldo. "A Note on Montaigne's *Des Cannibales* and the Humanist Tradition." In *First Images of America: The Impact of the New World and the Old*, edited by Fredi Chiappelli, Michael J. B. Allen, and Robert L. Benson, 63–70. Berkeley: U of California P, 1976.
Schanze, Helmut. "Theorie des Dramas im bürgerlichen Realismus." In *Deutsche Dramentheorien*, edited by Reinhold Grimm, 2:374–93. Frankfurt am Main: Athenäum, 1971.
Schauer, Markus. "Friedrich Immanuel Niethammer und der Bildungspolitische Streit des Philanthropinismus und Humanismus um 1800." *Pegasus-Onlinezeitschrift* V/1 (2005): 28–45. http://www.pegasus-onlinezeitschrift.de/erga_1_2005_schauer.html.
Schiffer, Werner. *Theorien der Geschichtsschreibung und ihre erzähltheoretische Relevanz*. Stuttgart: Metzler, 1980.
Schieder, Theodor. "Schiller als Historiker." *Historische Zeitschrift* 190 (1960): 31–54.
Schiller, Friedrich. *Werke: Nationalausgabe*. Edited by Julius Petersen and Gerhard Fricke. 42 vols. Weimar: Hermann Böhlaus Nachfolger, 1943–.
———. *Sämtliche Werke*. Edited by Peter-André Alt et al. 5 vols. Munich: dtv, 2004.
Schilson, Arno. "'Kommentar' to *Die Erziehung des Menschengeschlechts*." In *Gotthold Ephraim Lessing: Werke 1778–1781*, edited by Arno Schilson and Axel Schmitt, 10:794–879. Frankfurt am Main: Deutscher Klassiker Verlag, 2001.
Schings, Hans-Jürgen. "Die Illuminaten in Stuttgart: Auch ein Beitrag zur Geschichte des jungen Schiller." *Deutsche Vierteljahrsschrift für Literaturwissenschaft und Geistesgeschichte* 66, no. 1 (1992): 48–87.
———. *Die Brüder des Marquis Posa: Schiller und der Geheimbund der Illuminaten*. Tübingen: Niemeyer, 1996.
Schlözer, August Ludwig. *Vorstellung seiner Universal-Historie*. Edited and introduced by Horst Walter Blanke. Waltrop: Spenner, 1997.
Schmidt, Alfred. *The Concept of Nature in Marx*. London: NLB, 1971.
———. *Kritische Theorie, Humanismus, Aufklärung*. Suttgart: Reclam, 1981.
Schmitz, Heinz-Gerd. *Die Ironie des Konservativen: Philosophische Untersuchungen zu einem Diktum Thomas Manns*. Berlin: Duncker & Humblot, 2011.
Schneider, Helmut J. "The Cold Eye: Herder's Critique of Enlightenment Visualism." In *Johann Gottfried Herder: Academic Disciplines and the Pursuit of Knowledge*, edited by Wulf Koepke, 53–60. Columbia, SC: Camden House, 1996.

Schnitzler, Arthur. *Liebelei*. Edited by Michael Scheffel. Stuttgart: Reclam, 2002.
Scholes, Robert. "Presidential Address 2004: The Humanities in a Posthumanist World." *PMLA* 120, no. 3 (2005): 724–33.
Schomers, Walter Ludwig. *Thomas Mann und der französische Zeitgeist der zwanziger Jahre*. Würzburg: Königshausen & Neumann, 2012.
Schonauer, Franz. "Literaturkritik in der Bundesrepublik Deutschland." In *Deutsche Gegenwartsliteratur*, edited by Manfred Durzak, 404–23. Stuttgart: Reclam, 1971.
———. "Sieburg & Co. Rückblick auf eine sogenannte konservative Literaturkritik." In *Literaturmagazin 7*, edited by Nicolas Born and Jürgen Manthey, 237–52. Reinbek: Rowohlt, 1977.
Schorske, Carl E. *Fin-De-Siècle Vienna: Politics and Culture*. New York: Vintage: 1981.
Schröter, Klaus, ed. *Thomas Mann im Urteil seiner Zeit. Dokumente 1891–1955*. Frankfurt am Main: Klostermann, 2000.
Schulz, Karlheinz. *Goethe: Eine Biographie*. Stuttgart: Reclam, 1999.
Schwarz, Egon. "Zur Erklärung von Hesses 'Steppenwolf.'" *Monatshefte* 53, no. 4 (1961): 191–98.
———. *Hermann Hesses Steppenwolf*. Königstein: Taunus, Athenäum, 1980.
———. "Hermann Hesse: Der Steppenwolf." In *Interpretationen: Romane des 20. Jahrhunderts*, 128–57. Stuttgart: Reclam, 1993.
Schwilk, Heimo. *Hermann Hesse: Das Leben des Glasperlenspielers*. Munich: Piper, 2012.
Seeba, Hinrich C. "Lessings Geschichtsbild: Zur ästhetischen Evidenz historischer Wahrheit." In *Humanität und Dialog: Lessing und Mendelsohn in neuer Sicht*, edited by Erhard Bahr et al., 289–303. Boston: Twayne, 1981.
———. "Historiographischer Idealismus? Fragen zu Schillers Geschichtsbild." In *Friedrich Schiller: Kunst, Humanität und Politik in der späten Aufklärung*, edited by Wolfgang Wittkowski, 229–49. Tübingen: Niemeyer, 1982.
Seidlin, Oskar. "Goethes Iphigenie—'verteufelt human?'" *Wirkendes Wort* 5 (1954/55): 272–80.
Sharpe, Lesley. *Schiller and the Historical Character: Presentation and Interpretation in the Historiographical Works and the Historical Drama*. Oxford: Oxford UP, 1962.
Shaw, Philip. *The Sublime*. New York: Routledge, 2006.
Siefken, Hinrich. "Thomas Manns Dienst an der Zeit in den Jahren 1918-33." *Thomas-Mann-Jahrbuch* 10 (1997): 167–86.
Sloterdijk, Peter. *Regeln für den Menschenpark: Ein Antwortschreiben zu Heideggers Brief über den Humanismus*. Frankfurt am Main: Suhrkamp, 1999.
———. *Philosophische Temperamente: Von Platon bis Foucault*. Munich: Diedrichs, 2009.
Snow, C. P. *The Two Cultures and the Scientific Revolution*. New York: Cambridge UP, 1959.
Soper, Kate. *Humanism and Anti-humanism*. LaSalle, IL: Open Court, 1986.
———. "The Humanism in Posthumanism." *Comparative Critical Studies* 9, no. 3 (2012): 365–78.
Spitta, Dietrich. *Menschenbildung und Staat: Das Bildungsideal Wilhelm von Humboldts angesichts der Kritik des Humanismus*. Stuttgart: Mayer, 2006.
Spivak, Gayatri Chakravorty. *Death of a Discipline*. New York: Columbia UP, 2003.
Spranger, Eduard. *Der gegenwärtige Stand der Geisteswissenschaften und die Schule*. Leipzig: Teubner 1922.
Sprengel, Peter. *Darwin in der Poesie: Spuren der Evolutionslehre in der deutschsprachigen Literatur des 19. und 20. Jahrhunderts*. Würzburg: Königshausen & Neumann, 1998.

———. "Tierliebe und Sadismus als Diskurs der Wiener Moderne." *Akten des X. Internationalen Germanistenkongresses Wien 2000. Zeitenwende—Die Germanistik auf dem Weg vom 20. ins 21. Jahrhundert*. Vol. 6: *Epochenbegriffe: Grenzen und Möglichkeiten; Aufklärung-Klassik-Romantik; Die Wiener Moderne*, edited by Peter Wiesinger et al., 503–9. Bern: Lang, 2002.
Staiger, Emil. *Die Kunst der Interpretation*. Zürich: Atlantis, 1961.
Steiner, George. *Death of Tragedy*. New York: Knopf, 1961.
———. "The Muse's Farewell." *Salmagundi* 135–36 (2002): 148–56.
Stiening, Gideon. "'Und das Ganze belebt, so wie das Einzelne, sei': Zum Verhältnis von Wissen und Literatur am Beispiel von Goethes *Die Metamorphose der Pflanzen*." In *Literatur und Wissen: Theoretisch-methodische Zugänge*, edited by Tilmann Köppe, 192–213. Berlin: De Gruyter, 2011.
Stieve, Barbara. *Der "Dritte Humanismus": Aspekte deutscher Griechenrezeption vom George-Kreis bis zum Nationalsozialismus*. Berlin: De Gruyter, 2011.
Stockhorst, Stefanie. "Geschichten der Menschheit: Zur Narrativität der historischen Kulturanthropologie in der Spätaufklärung." *Kultur-Poetik* 8, no. 1 (2008): 1–17.
Strohschneider-Kohrs, Ingrid. *Vernunft als Weisheit: Studien zum späten Lessing*. Tübingen: Niemeyer, 1991.
Süßmann, Johannes. *Geschichtsschreibung oder Roman? Zur Konstruktionslogik von Geschichtserzählungen zwischen Schiller und Ranke (1780–1824)*. Stuttgart: Frankfurter Historische Abhandlungen, 2000.
Swales, Martin. "Der Steppenwolf." In *A Companion to the Works of Hermann Hesse*, edited by Ingo Cornils, 171–86. Rochester, NY: Camden House, 2009.
Swift, Simon. "Kant, Herder, and the Question of Philosophical Anthropology." *Textual Practice* 19, no. 2 (2005): 219–38.
Szondi, Peter. *Versuch über das Tragische*. Frankfurt am Main: Insel, 1961.
———. *Die Theorie des bürgerlichen Trauerspiels im 18. Jahrhundert: Der Kaufmann, der Hausvater und der Hofmeister*. Frankfurt am Main: Suhrkamp, 1973.
———. *Theorie des Modernen Dramas*. Frankfurt am Main: Suhrkamp, 1986.
Taylor, Charles. *Hegel*. Cambridge: Cambridge UP, 1975.
Thielicke, Helmut. *Offenbarung, Vernunft und Existenz: Studien zur Religionsphilosophie Lessings*. Gütersloh: Bertelsmann, 1957.
Toellner, Richard, ed. *Aufklärung und Humanismus*. Heidelberg: Lambert & Schneider, 1980.
Toulmin, Stephen. *Cosmopolis: The Hidden Agenda of Modernity*. Chicago: U of Chicago P, 1990.
Trabant, Jürgen. "Language and the Ear: From Derrida to Herder." *Herder-Yearbook* 1 (1992): 1–22.
Troeltsch, Ernst. "The German Democracy." In *The Weimar Republic Sourcebook*, edited by Tony Kaes et al., 89–91. Berkeley: U of California P, 1994.
Unzer, Johann August. *Gedanken vom Schlafen und denen Träumen: Nebst einem Schreiben an N.N. daß man ohne Kopf empfinden könne*. St. Ingbert: Röhrig Universitätsverlag, 2004.
Vierhaus, Rudolf. "Moses Mendelssohn und die Popularphilosophie." In *Moses Mendelssohn und die Kreise seiner Wirksamkeit*, edited by Michael Albrecht et al., 25–42. Tübingen: Niemeyer, 1994.
Vormweg, Heinrich. "Prosa in der Bundesrepublik seit 1945." In *Die Literatur der Bundesrepublik Deutschand*, edited by Dieter Lattmann, 141–343. Munich: Kindler, 1973.

———. "Deutsche Literatur 1945–1960: Keine Stunde Null." In *Deutsche Gegenwartsliteratur*, edited by Manfred Durzak. Stuttgart: Reclam, 1981.
Wagner, Irmgard. *Critical Approaches to Goethe's Classical Dramas: Iphigenie, Torquato Tasso, Die natürliche Tochter*. Columbia, SC: Camden House, 1995.
Wahl, Daniel C. "'Zarte Empirie': Goethean Science as a Way of Knowing." *Janus Head* 8, no. 1 (2005): 58–76.
Waldby, Catherine. *The Visible Human Project: Informatic Bodies and Posthuman Medicine*. London: Routledge, 2000.
Waldmann, Walter. "Zur Gestaltung des klassisch-humanistischen Menschenbildes am Beispiel von Goethes Schauspiel 'Iphigenie auf Tauris.'" *Wissenschaftliche Zeitschrift der Universität Rostock* 22 (1973): 405–13.
Walser, Martin. "Imitation oder Realismus." In *Ansichten, Einsichten: Aufsätze zur Zeitgeschichte*, 116–43. Frankfurt am Main: Suhrkamp, 1997.
Wanberg, Kyle. "The Writer's Inadequate Response: Elizabeth Costello and the Influence of Kafka and Hofmannsthal." *European Journal of English Studies* 20, no. 2 (2016): 152–65.
Wedekind, Frank. *Prosa, Dramen, Verse*. 2 Vols. Munich: Langen & Müller, 1960.
Wegele, Franz X. von. "Schiller und die Geschichte." In *Geschichte der Deutschen Historiographie seit dem Auftreten des Humanismus*. Munich: Oldenbourg, 1885. [Reprint; New York: Johnson 1965].
Weimer, Klaus. "Der Effekt der Geschichte." In *Schiller als Historiker*, edited by Otto Dann et al., 191–204. Stuttgart: Metzler, 1995.
Weinstock, Heinrich. *Die Tragödie des Humanismus*. Heidelberg: Quelle and Meyer, 1953.
Wellbery, David E. *The Specular Moment: Goethe's Early Lyric and the Beginnings of Romanticism*. Stanford, CA: Stanford UP, 1996.
Wellmer, Albrecht. "Adorno, die Moderne und das Erhabene." In *Ästhetik im Widerstreit*, edited by Wolfgang Welsch and Christine Pries, 45–66. Weinheim: Acta humaniora, 1991.
Werber, Niels. "Das Politische des Unpolitischen: Paradoxien der Decision; Thomas Mann, Heinrich von Kleist, Carl Schmitt." *Athenäum: Jahrbuch der Friedrich-Schlegel-Gesellschaft* 20 (2010): 229–39.
———. "Das Politische des Unpolitischen: Thomas Manns Unterscheidungen zwischen Heinrich von Kleist und Carl Schmitt." In *Deconstructing Thomas Mann*, edited by Alexander Honold and Niels Werber, 65–86. Heidelberg: Winter, 2012.
Westling, Louise. *The Logos of the Western World: Merleau-Ponty, Animals, and Language*. New York: Fordham, 2014.
Whimster, Sam. "The Human Sciences." *Theory, Culture, and Society* 23, nos. 2–3 (2006): 174–76.
White, Hayden. *The Practical Past*. Evanston, IL: Northwestern UP, 2014.
———. "The Historical Text as Literary Artifact." *Clio* 3 (1974): 277–303.
Whitehead, Alfred North. *Process and Reality: An Essay in Cosmology; Gifford Lectures Delivered in the University of Edinburgh during the Session 1927–28*. New York: Macmillan, 1929.
Widdig, Bernd. "Mode und Moderne: Gottfried Kellers 'Kleider machen Leute.'" *Merkur* 48, no. 2 (1994): 109–23.
Wilson, Daniel, and Robert Holub, eds. *Impure Reason: Dialectic of Enlightenment in Germany*. Detroit: Wayne State UP, 1993.

Winter, Helga. *Naturwissenschaft und Ästhetik: Untersuchungen zum Frühwerk Heinrich Manns*. Würzburg: Königshausen & Neumann, 1994.
Wittkowski, W. *Friedrich Schiller: Kunst, Humanität und Politik der späten Aufklärung*. Tübingen: Niemeyer, 1982.
———. "Höfische Intrige für die gute Sache: Marquis Posa und Octavio Piccolomini." In *Schiller und die höfische Welt*, edited by Achim Aurnhammer et al., 378–97. Tübingen: Niemeyer, 1990.
Wölfel, Kurt. "Machiavellische Spuren in Schillers Dramatik." In *Schiller und die höfische Welt*, edited by Achim Aurnhammer et al., 318–40. Tübingen: Niemeyer, 1990.
Wolfe, Cary. *Animal Rites: American Culture, the Discourse of Species, and Posthumanist Theory*. Chicago: U of Chicago P, 2003.
———. *What Is Posthumanism?* Minneapolis: U of Minnesota P, 2010.
Wolin, Richard. "Jürgen Habermas and Post-Secular Societies." *Chronicle of Higher Education*, 23 September 2005, B16–17.
———. "Foucault the Neohumanist?" *Chronicle of Higher Education*, 1 September 2006, B12–14.
Wübben, Yvonne. "Moses als Staatsgründer: Schiller und Reinhold über die Arkanpolitik der Spätaufklärung." *Aufklärung* 15 (2003): 125–58.
Wysling, Hans, ed. *Thomas Mann: Briefwechsel mit Autoren*. Frankfurt am Main: Fischer, 1988.
Young, Robert J. C., ed. *Postcolonialism: An Historical Introduction*. Malden, MA: Blackwell. 2001.
Zammito, John. *Kant, Herder and the Birth of Anthropology*. Chicago: U of Chicago P, 2002.
———. *The Gestation of German Biology: Philosophy and Physiology from Stahl to Schelling*. Chicago: U of Chicago P, 2018.
Zaremba, Michael. *Johann Gottfried Herder: Prediger der Humanität*. Köln: Böhlau, 2002.
Zelle, Carsten. *Angenehmes Grauen: Literaturhistorische Beiträge zur Ästhetik des Schrecklichen im achtzehnten Jahrhundert*. Hamburg: Meiner, 1987.
———. "Sinnlichkeit und Therapie: Zur Gleichursprünglichkeit von Ästhetik und Anthropologie um 1750." In *Hallesche Psychomedizin im Spannungsfeld von Tradition und Moderne*, edited by Carsten Zelle, 5–24. Tübingen: Niemeyer, 2001.
Zeuch, Ulrike. "Kraft als Inbegriff menschlicher Seelentätigkeit in der Anthropologie der Spätaufklärung." In *Jahrbuch der deutschen Schillergesellschaft* 43 (1999): 99–122.
Zilcosky, John. *Uncanny Encounters: Literature, Psychoanalysis, and the End of Alterity*. Evanston, IL: Northwestern UP, 2016.
Ziolkowski, Theodore. "Vorwort." In *Hermann Hesse—Thomas Mann Briefwechsel*, edited by Anni Carlsson and Volker Michels, i–xvii. Frankfurt am Main: Suhrkamp, 1975.
Zweig, Stefan. *Die Welt von Gestern: Erinnerungen eines Europäers*. Frankfurt am Main: Fischer, 1985.
———. "The Monotonization of the World." In *The Weimar Republic Sourcebook*, edited by Tony Kaes et al., 397–400. Berkely: U of California P, 1994.

INDEX

Abel, Jacob Friedrich, 60, 77n27, 268
academic disciplines, 1–13
   freedom, 1, 4
Adler, Hans, 107, 114n2, 118n31, 268
Adorno, Theodor W., 19, 29n13, 30n17, 32n29, 35n51, 268
aesthetics, 26, 27, 51n8, 74, 79, 89, 91n4, 94, 112, 135, 138–141, 150–153, 158–59, 160n10, 168, 191, 192n1, 198, 200, 212, 214n13, 244
   classicist, 15, 79
   and education, 39–40, 42, 45–46, 49, 53n25, 53n28, 62, 74 (*see also* Lessing)
   of effect (*Wirkungsästhetik*) 62, 79
   modernist, 198
   neoclassical, 18, 121, 124, 129
   realist, 198
   and religion, 39–46, 64, 74
   subjectivist, 25, 80
Agamben, Giorgio, 35n51, 64, 74, 116n21, 267n4, 268
Age of Reason (*Aufklärung*), 37. See also Enlightenment
alienation, 26, 27, 61, 128, 164, 167, 173–176, 177n2
allegorical, allegory, 6, 24, 38–49, 53n28, 57, 61, 63, 74, 99, 117n23, 117n28, 171, 174, 179, 203, 207, 239, 252, 256n3, 259n24, 261, 265
Alt, Peter-André, 55, 56, 59, 69, 75n3, 77n6, 77–78n28, 193n5, 260n30, 268
Altenhofer, Norbert, 42, 44, 46, 52n19, 268
alter ego, 62, 130, 131, 209, 241, 243, 248
Althaus, Thomas, 43, 51n5, 52n17, 269
ambiguity, 46, 47, 66, 72, 116n21, 124, 155, 229, 248
anatomy, 38, 140, 161n14

animal, animalistic, 8, 21, 31n25, 32n26, 45, 52n16, 58–60, 67, 71, 74, 76n12, 77n24, 77n28, 99, 101, 104–106, 110, 116n20, 116n21, 120, 122, 154, 160n6, 167, 177n5, 184, 197–212, 212n1, 213n8, 214n11, 242, 244–255, 257n10, 257n14, 258n15, 258n17, 258n19, 258n21, 260n33, 264, 266, 267n4
anthropocentric, 24, 99, 100, 113, 139, 213n8
anthropological, anthropology, 6, 9, 10, 14, 23, 28, 30n18, 31n20, 32n28, 33n33, 36n58, 40, 53n28, 55, 59–61, 64, 75n7, 77n27, 90n1, 95, 98–107, 110, 113, 115n12, 116n19, 116n20, 117n25, 117n26, 117n28, 119, 122, 135n3, 136n8, 138, 141–143, 158, 160n9, 162n25, 167, 168, 178n9, 219, 229, 237n21, 250, 265
anthropomorphic, anthropomorphization, 22, 26, 36n57, 106, 139, 147, 148, 157–158, 163n27, 173
anti-humanism, anti-humanist, 11, 19, 27, 30n16, 218, 226, 231, 232, 242, 243, 257n12, 265
a priori, 101, 105, 121
Arendt, Hannah, 165–166, 175, 269
Arens, Katherine, 100, 116n17, 269
Ariosto, 129
aristocratic, aristocracy, 15, 30n14, 128, 130, 172, 194n14, 203, 218, 225
Aristotle, 22, 117n24, 257n10
art, artist, artistic, 15, 18, 35n53, 42, 48, 56, 59–61, 63, 79–80, 83, 84, 89, 91n4, 94, 101, 102, 123, 124, 128, 129–31, 133, 137n16, 138–40, 142–45, 148, 151, 153, 155, 157–59, 162n18, 162n21, 162n22, 165, 166,

171, 173, 174, 183, 185, 198, 218, 220, 222–23, 226, 227, 231, 233, 237n13, 242, 247, 251–54, 257, 260n31
arts and letters, arts and sciences, 1–2, 15, 26, 29n7, 57, 78n29, 79, 91n4, 94, 100, 138, 140, 143, 197
Assmann, Jan, 44, 45, 52n24, 52n25, 61, 76n10, 76n11, 76n14, 76n15, 269
Augustinus, 42, 44, 52n19
autonomous, autonomy, 4, 6, 7, 9, 10, 15, 16, 20, 21, 27, 31n21, 38, 41, 42, 45, 58, 60, 61, 72, 74, 80–84, 86–87, 97, 107–110, 112, 114n4, 117n28, 124, 129, 132–34, 136n11, 145, 148, 154–55, 157, 168, 177n3, 178n6, 178n8, 180, 183, 184–86, 191, 211–12, 220, 227, 231, 235, 241, 243, 261, 267n1. See also individual

Badiou, Alain, 4
Badmington, Neil, 3–4, 9, 241, 243, 269
Bandemer, Susanne von, 10, 33n35
Baumgarten, Alexander Gottlieb, 49, 52n11, 60, 269
Beiser, Frederick C., 122, 269
Benda, Oskar, 17, 269
Benjamin, Walter, 19
Benner, Dietrich, 15, 269
Bennett, Benjamin, 127, 269
Bible, biblical, 37, 38, 39–44, 47–48, 50n3, 51n9, 51n10, 60–63, 64, 66, 67, 72, 74, 92n12, 178n12, 262, 265
Biedermeier, 188, 191n1, 195n26
Bildung, 8, 18, 26, 27, 33n35, 34n44, 34n45, 38, 60, 128, 139, 140, 144–45, 147, 155, 157, 158, 161n15, 161–62n18, 203, 213n9, 259n27. See also education
Bildungsbürger, Bildungsbürgertum, 216, 217, 222, 232. See also bourgeois: citizen; bourgeosie
Bildungsroman, 10, 27, 174, 204, 212, 213n9, 214n13, 222, 235, 241, 244, 265
Bildungstrieb (life force), 114n1, 135n3, 144–45
biogenetics, 95

Blumenbach, Johann Friedrich, 75n7, 94, 114n1, 135n3, 145, 269
body, 3, 16, 25, 27, 54n35, 60, 63, 75n7, 77n27, 80, 84, 93–94, 96, 101–105, 109, 112, 117n25, 120–123, 135, 135n3, 136n8, 136n9, 143, 153, 155, 157, 159n1, 160n14, 161n18, 167–69, 171–72, 177n5, 180, 198, 202–204, 209, 211, 217, 222, 226, 228, 230, 242–43, 244–45, 247–48, 252, 254–55, 256n6, 257n10, 257n14, 259n24, 259n25, 261, 265, 232
Bölsche, Wilhelm, 197–98, 203, 213n2, 213n7, 270
Bohnen, Klaus, 51n6, 198, 270
Bonnet, Charles, 50n4, 51n6, 77n27, 135n3
Borchmeyer, Dieter, 64, 66, 76n17, 270
botany, 38, 138, 143
bourgeois
  artist, 124, 128, 129
  citizen, 7, 30n14, 171, 172, 216, 223, 226, 228, 244
  culture, 5, 165, 190, 191, 206–208, 211, 212, 223, 232–233, 242, 245, 247, 249, 258n20
  emancipation, 124, 132, 165
  ethics, 10, 26, 33n34, 80, 163n26, 168, 180, 183, 188, 194n12, 195n20, 212, 217, 222, 249, 261
  ideology, 124, 129–30, 132, 167, 168, 177n4, 178n6, 208, 211
  individual, subject, 4, 16, 27, 31, 37, 48, 80, 128, 130, 131, 133, 183, 191, 202, 203, 212, 214n14, 222–23, 242, 245, 253, 256n7
  tragedy, 180, 194n17
  values, 3, 27, 167, 168, 176, 178n6, 185, 190, 191, 194n12, 195n30, 206, 208, 211, 223, 241, 247, 261
bourgeoisie, bourgeois society, 5, 15, 26, 44, 128, 129, 136 n12, 155, 164, 167, 168, 170, 176, 178n6, 178n8, 194n14, 195n26, 207–208, 220–222, 223, 227, 232–233, 234–35, 243, 245, 253, 256n7, 258n16, 264, 266

292 ∽: Index

Braidotti, Rosi, 6, 7, 9, 20, 22, 29n10, 31n22, 35n52, 270
Brockmann, Stephen, 19, 35n50, 270
Buchwald, Reinhard, 35n50, 76n13, 270
Buffon, Comte de, 135n3, 154
Bürger, Christa, 15, 128, 136n12, 270
Butler, Judith, 7, 31n24, 36n60, 53n28, 54n31, 270

canon, canonical, canonized, 4, 8–12, 17, 25, 180, 192n1, 217, 263–5
capitalism, capitalist, 19, 20, 26, 164, 165, 168, 174, 176
Carlsson, Anni, 217, 227, 271, 289
Cartesian, 3, 21, 148, 207, 242, 243, 245, 256n6, 257n10. *See also* Descartes
Carus, Carl Gustav, 26, 31n20, 94, 114n1, 138–45, 150–59
  aesthetics, 141, 150–53, 271
  anatomy, 140
  Briefe über das Erdenleben (*Letters on Earthly Life*), 26, 141, 142, 144, 159n6
  Briefe über die Landschaftsmalerei (*Letters on Landscape Painting*), 141, 160n6
  gynecology, 140, 156
  landscape painting (*Landschaftsmalerei*), 141, 159
  philosophy of nature (*Naturphilosophie*), 139–45, 153–56, 159
  physiognomics, 141–42, 153–56, 159
  physiology, 140
  psychology, 140, 156–57
  science, 140, 141
  zoology, 140
Caruth, Cathy, 11, 33n36, 33n37, 271
Caucasian, 121, 142, 154, 162n25, 168
Césaire, Aimé, 7, 8, 31n22, 271
chauvinism, chauvinist, 30n18, 141, 154, 219, 230, 239
Christian, Christianity, 5, 14, 31n23, 35n50, 42, 44, 54n35, 80, 168, 188n12, 198, 212, 224, 226, 253, 259n27
civilization, 4, 5, 8, 14, 21, 31n20, 36, 37, 44, 46, 56, 58–59, 61, 72, 74, 119, 126, 127, 153, 154, 212, 219, 220, 234–35, 244, 246–47, 249–51, 252, 254, 258n18, 258n19, 258n20
classical, 2, 8, 9, 11, 13, 14, 15, 17, 28, 122, 124, 127, 133, 136n12, 137n15, 168, 194n15, 214n13, 230, 232, 262
classicism, 18, 126
classicist, 15, 16, 79, 81, 119, 122–35, 144, 153, 155. *See also* neoclassical
classics (classical works), 5, 11–14, 17, 18, 28, 33n37, 35n51, 53n28, 126, 264, 265, 266
Coetzee, J. M., 28, 262, 271, 212
compassion, 69, 95, 134
consciousness, 3, 8, 25, 27, 36n60, 59, 61, 96, 101, 104, 106, 108–112, 115n13, 142, 145, 155–57, 159n1, 165, 171, 223, 241, 244, 250, 257n11
conspiracy, 77n28, 127, 134
consumerism, consumerist, 19, 26, 164, 167, 168, 170–71, 174, 177
courtesy, 127, 132–33
courtly, 10, 30n14, 119–120, 122, 124, 127–31, 133, 163n26, 168, 183
cranioscopic, cranioscopy, 141, 159–160n6
Cudworth, Ralph, 76n11
Curtius, Ernst Robert, 18, 35, 271

Darwin, Charles, 16, 22, 246, 250, 266, 274, 286
Darwinism, 22, 36n57, 154, 197–98, 200, 202, 222, 257n14, 259n26, 282
Daston, Lorraine; Galison, Peter, 36n59, 89, 91, 200, 271
deceptive, deception, 62, 63, 66, 70, 72–73, 76n18, 108, 109, 119, 121, 122, 128, 132, 134–35, 155, 163n26, 168, 171, 181, 183, 195n19, 202, 207, 210, 230, 240, 253, 254
Declaration of Independence, 221
demagogue, demagoguery, 62, 66, 73
demystification, 150, 202, 211, 212, 228, 230
Dennis, John, 81, 272, 280
Derrida, Jacques, 4, 8, 251, 257n10
Descartes, René, 3, 21, 99, 148, 207, 242, 243, 245, 251, 256n6, 257n10, 272
Detering, Heinrich, 218, 272

Diamond, Cora, 8
Dilthey, Wilhelm, 89–90, 91n6, 272
discipline (academic, scientific), 1, 12, 13, 20, 24, 30n18, 33n39, 38–39, 57, 60, 91n5, 93, 94, 95, 97, 101, 113, 114n3, 117n28, 118n30, 138–40, 143, 153, 266
discourse
  academic, 13
  aesthetic, 103
  courtly, 122, 127
  humanist, 2, 5, 10, 19, 20, 31, 192n1, 263–64
  Enlightenment, 28, 32n29, 98
  literary, 40, 46, 97, 100 (*see also* poetic language)
  medical, 143
  philosophical, 93, 105, 136n11, 141, 240
  postcolonialist, 31n24
  posthumanist, 19–20, 108
  rational, 38, 46, 48, 49, 63, 202, 213n8, 261
  scientific, 96, 105, 107, 111–13, 150, 159
Dostoewsky, Fyodor, 217, 224
drama, 60, 116n16, 120–133, 136n5, 136n12, 180, 183, 192n1, 192n2, 193n6
Dülmen, Richard van, 44, 272

Eagleton, Terry, 1, 4, 167, 272
education, 1–2, 3–4, 8–10, 12, 14–15, 18, 19, 20, 21, 24, 26, 28n4, 29n7, 30n15, 33n32, 33n35, 37–40, 42, 44–50, 51n6, 53n28, 54n32, 54n35, 57, 60, 62, 67–69, 71, 74, 97–98, 121, 135, 139–40, 143, 145, 154, 158, 163n27, 167, 168, 175, 184, 192n1, 204, 207, 216, 217, 219, 220, 222, 224, 232, 241–43, 245–47, 249, 252, 254, 263, 265–66. *See also Erziehung*
Eibl, Karl, 41, 51n5, 52n13, 273
Einfühlung, 203
elegy, elegiac, 23, 146–47, 151
emotion, emotional, 6, 12, 15, 16, 22–23, 25, 31n24, 34n44, 38, 46, 48–49, 59–60, 68, 79, 81, 86, 89–90, 91n2, 91n3, 92n15, 96–98, 103–104, 106, 112–13, 119–21, 122–24, 129, 136n4, 136n7, 143, 147, 158, 159n1, 162n18, 163n27, 165, 170, 175–76, 183, 189, 194n14, 195n29, 197, 200, 224, 226, 229, 233, 245, 247, 261
empathy, 14, 16, 26, 48, 49, 52n25, 53n28, 98, 123, 148, 158, 174, 178n8, 181, 223, 229, 264
empirical, empiricism, empiricist, 17, 21, 23–24, 32n26, 38, 56, 57, 60, 67, 75n3, 79, 83, 89–90, 91n2, 93–94, 95, 96, 98–101, 103–104, 111, 113, 115n12, 115n13, 123, 124, 136n11, 138, 141–44, 146, 148, 150, 155, 156, 158, 159n1, 161, 168, 171, 178n6, 197, 198–99
Enlightenment, 1, 2, 4, 5, 7, 8–9, 10–11, 13, 14, 15, 21, 23, 24, 28n3, 30n14, 30n16, 30n17, 31n21, 32n27, 32n29, 34n42, 34n46, 36n58, 40–41, 44,v46–47, 49, 50n4, 54n35, 57–58, 64, 66–67, 73–74, 75n7, 76n17, 76n18, 77n23, 93, 98–99, 111, 112, 115n13, 120, 122–23, 126–27, 136n12, 141, 143, 158, 163n26, 165, 167, 177n3, 178n6, 213n8, 224, 225–27, 237n17, 238, 244, 259n27, 264, 267n3
Entsagung (abstinence), 121, 123
epigenesis, 121, 135n4
Epoptoi, 3, 72
Erziehung (education), 24, 37, 39, 40–50, 50n2, 50n4, 51n5, 51n7, 51n9, 51n11, 52n12, 52n25, 53n28, 54n31, 61, 62, 72, 74, 137n17, 227, 245, 250, 259n27, 265
essayistic, 27, 216–18, 231
ethical, ethics, 1, 2–6, 9–10, 14, 16, 18, 21–23, 25, 30n14, 32n26, 32n35, 33n39, 34n40, 42, 53n28, 57, 64, 70, 71, 72, 74, 75n2, 80, 81, 83, 84, 87, 89, 94–100, 110–11, 113, 114n4, 118n35, 120, 123, 129–30, 135, 168, 172, 178n6, 181, 183, 185–86, 187, 193n5, 194n12, 205, 213n8, 217, 226, 228, 229, 233, 240, 254, 262, 264–65, 266

ethnicity, 2, 6, 8, 9, 29n10, 36n58
Ette, Ottmar, 13, 29n7, 33n36, 273
Eurocentric, Eurocentrism, 1, 5, 6, 141, 157, 251, 261, 265
evolution, 3, 6, 16, 22, 24, 36n57, 37, 109, 110, 141, 145, 154–55, 198, 246, 250, 259

faculties (cognitive, intellectual, sensory), 14, 15, 22, 24, 38, 49, 56, 60, 63, 90, 92n11, 93–94, 100, 102, 111, 120–22, 154, 158, 211, 213n5
Fanon, Frantz, 7, 31n24
fascism, fascist, 7, 18, 19–20, 27, 30n17, 34–35n49, 35n50, 35n51, 95, 218, 232, 237n21, 240
Fechner, Gustav Theodor, 198–99, 203, 213n7, 273
feminism, feminist, 2, 6–7, 20, 29n10, 82, 95, 259n24
Feuerbach, Ludwig, 26, 164, 165, 167, 168, 172, 173, 178n9, 178n11, 179n13, 273
Fichte, Johann Gottlieb, 10, 31n20, 32n28
Fick, Monika, 198, 199, 273
Fiero, Petra S., 10, 33n32, 273
Fontane, Theodor, 217
Foucault, Michel, 7
Fracchia, Joseph, 177n5, 273
Fragmentenstreit, 41, 51n8, 52n14
Frank, Manfred, 98, 112, 115n10, 273
Frankfurt School (Frankfurter Schule), 5, 19, 177, 217
freedom, 1, 4, 15, 16, 21, 25, 34n45, 35n54, 53n28, 57–59, 61, 64, 71–72, 74, 80, 82, 87–88, 95, 96–98, 105–106, 114n4, 116n18, 116n21, 121, 122, 124, 131, 132, 155, 165, 168, 170, 177n5, 185, 188, 191, 193n5, 193n6, 200, 220, 221, 226, 228, 231
freemasonry (*Freimaurerei*), freemasons, 44–45, 52n22, 52n23, 61–62, 66, 76n11
French Revolution, 15, 122, 192n1, 219, 221, 224, 225, 237n14, 264
Freud, Sigmund, Freudian, 16, 25, 178n6, 250, 256n2, 258n19, 266, 274
Friedrich, Caspar David, 85, 140

Geist (spirit, mind, essence), 37, 56, 68, 107, 146, 175, 185, 220, 224, 232, 239, 254, 257n13
Geisteswissenschaften (humanities), 18, 33n39, 34n47, 90, 91n5, 200, 230
Gellert, Christian Fürchtegott, 67
gender, 1, 2, 6, 7, 10–12, 17, 20, 33n33, 33n35, 81, 86, 88, 121, 126, 155–56, 163n27, 193n11, 242, 259n24, 261, 265
genetic, genetics, 2, 95, 113, 155, 257n10, 264
Gilmore, Myron P., 14, 274
Gilroy, Paul, 3, 274
Girschner, Gabriele, 128, 27
Gleim, Betty, 10, 33n32, 33n35
Goethe, J. W., 5, 11, 15, 16, 18, 21, 22, 25–26, 30n19, 32n29, 35n50, 75n6, 76n11, 92n7, 94, 113, 113n1, 119–35, 135n1, 135n3, 136n6, 136n12, 137n13, 137n15, 137n16, 137n19, 138–45, 147–51, 157–59, 159n2, 152n6, 159n6, 160n8, 160n11, 161n15, 161n16, 161–62n18, 162n19, 163n27, 177n3, 195n22, 203, 213n10, 214n13, 217, 219–20, 226, 227, 229, 232, 237n15, 249, 253, 257n9, 257n12, 261, 263, 265, 274
"Dauer im Wechsel" ("Permanence in Transformation"), 144
Faust, 22, 37, 203
Goetz von Berlichingen, 177n3
Iphigenie auf Tauris, 5, 11, 16, 25, 30n19, 119–27, 133–35, 136n6, 136n12, 137n13, 137n14, 137n15, 232
Metamorphose der Pflanzen (*Metamorphosis of Plants*), 23, 26, 139, 144–50, 157, 158, 159n6, 161n17, 161n18, 163n27, 229, 265
"Natur und Kunst" ("Nature and Art"), 145
Torquato Tasso, 25, 92n7, 119–24, 127–33, 135, 136n6, 136n10, 136n12, 137n13, 212n1, 220, 265
Wahlverwandtschaften (*Elective Affinities*), 139
Gouges, Olympe de, 10

Grand Tour, 203, 204, 211, 215n17
Gray, Richard T, 135n2, 141, 155, 163n26, 230, 237n20, 274
Greek (antiquity, art, drama, mythology), 15, 18, 19, 28n4, 76n11, 92n12, 119, 120, 125, 127, 133, 162, 173
Grosche, Stefan, 141, 275
Guillory, John, 1, 4, 36n56, 275
Guthke, Karl, 187, 193n11, 194–95n19, 195n23, 275

Hadot, Pierre, 80, 275
Haeckel, Ernst, 199–201, 203, 246, 250, 275
Hahn, K. H., 76n13, 275
Haller, Albrecht von, 103–104, 117n25, 117n27, 135n3, 143, 275
Halliwell, Martin, 6, 275
Haraway, Donna, 3, 6, 8, 95, 275
Hartwich, W. D., 64, 66, 76n14, 76n19, 275
Hauff, Wilhelm, 180, 188
Hauptmann, Gerhart, 225
Hayden-Roy, Priscilla, 42, 51n8, 51n10, 51n11, 54n31, 275
Hayles, Katherine, 3, 6, 9, 29n9, 112, 275
Hebrew, 40, 61–62, 64, 67–73
Hegel, Georg Wilhelm Friedrich, 9, 10, 51n8, 61, 115n13, 165, 172, 256n6
Hegelian, 19, 39, 164, 179, 193n6, 229
Heidegger, Martin, 18, 107, 251, 257n10, 267n4, 275
Helmholtz, Hermann von, 200
Hen kai pan, 76n11
Herbrechter, Stefan, 3, 6, 9, 118n33, 276
Herder, Johann Gottfried, 9, 21, 25, 31n25, 36n58, 39, 50n2, 67, 76n11, 90n1, 93–113, 114n2, 114n3, 114n4, 115n9, 115n11, 115n12, 115n13, 115n14, 115n15, 116n16, 116n19, 116n20, 116n21, 116n22, 116n23, 117n24, 117n26, 117n28, 118n31, 118n32, 119–120, 122, 135n1, 135n3, 136n8, 138, 140, 143, 145, 147, 154, 158, 161n16, 162n18, 163n27, 168, 177n3, 179n14, 219, 251, 256n6, 259n27, 261, 265, 276
  Abhandlund über den Ursprung der Sprache (*Treatise on the Origin of Language*), 97, 101, 116n20
  "Auch eine Philosophie der Geschichte der Bildung der Menschheit" ("This Too a Philosophy of the History on the Formation of Humanity"), 50n2, 97, 98–101
  Ideen zur Philosophie der Geschichte der Menschheit (*Ideas on the Philosophy of the History of Mankind*), 50n2, 99–100, 105, 116–17n23, 161n16
  "Über das Erkennen und Empfinden der menschlichen Seele" ("On Cognition and Sensation of the Human Soul"), 25, 36n57, 97, 102, 103, 112, 113
hermeneutic, hermeneutics, 24, 39, 50, 50n3, 51n11, 52n25, 79–80, 90, 91n4, 155, 158, 255
Hesse, Hermann, 16, 17, 27, 216–17, 222, 227, 231, 235, 235n1, 236n4, 238–55, 255n1, 256n2, 256n8, 256n11, 256n12, 257n14, 258n16, 259n24, 260n32, 276
  Der Steppenwolf, 27, 235, 236n1, 238–60, 264, 266
Himma, Kenneth, Einar, 96, 114n7, 276
historian, 38–39, 50n2, 55–57, 61, 62, 64, 66, 67, 75n6, 76n13, 117n28, 177, 197, 224, 236n9
historical, 3, 6, 8, 11, 12, 13, 16, 17, 21, 24, 27, 28n3, 30n16, 36n58, 37–42, 48, 50n3, 51n8, 51n9, 55–58, 60, 64, 67, 68, 71, 75n3, 75n5, 75n6, 79, 80, 90, 91n5, 93, 98–101, 108, 110, 112, 115n9, 117n28, 117n29, 122–29, 135, 135n1, 141, 154, 161, 164, 168, 178n11, 239, 244, 250, 253, 256n3, 258n17, 262, 265, 266
historicity, 36n58, 112, 187
historiography, 37–61, 64, 75n3, 93, 102, 117n28
history, 13–20, 22, 24, 37–61, 75n3, 157, 262
Hofmann, Michael, 56, 57, 86, 126, 272, 276
Hofmannsthal, Hugo von, 27, 197–215, 266
  Andreas, 27, 197–215

Hölderlin, Friedrich, 15, 76n11
Holy Roman Empire, 221–22
Horkheimer, Max, 19, 29n13, 35n51, 267n3, 277
Humboldt, Alexander von, 94, 114n1, 162n20
Humboldt, Wilhelm von, 9, 10, 15, 21, 30n15, 31n20, 32n28, 75n7, 140, 158, 163n27, 163n28, 167, 256, 277
human/animal boundary, 8, 27, 197–215
humaniora, 15, 21
humanism, 1–9, 11–14, 17–20, 22, 25, 27, 28n3, 29n8, 29n11, 29n13, 30n16, 31n24, 34n47, 34–35n49, 35n50, 35n51, 93, 95–97, 107, 111, 113, 114n8, 120–21, 126, 135, 141, 142, 178n6, 216, 223, 224, 226, 232, 233, 235, 237n15, 238, 241, 242, 246, 253, 257n12, 261, 263–66, 267n1, 267n4
  humanist (ethics, ideals, ideology, scholars, tradition, values), 1–21, 24–28, 28n3, 28n4, 29n10, 29n12, 29n13, 30n16, 30n19, 31n23, 31n24, 32n26, 32n27, 33n32, 34n48, 34n49, 35n59, 35n51, 37, 38, 42, 44, 57, 60, 72, 84, 93, 95–98, 113, 119–22, 124, 126–27, 133–35, 138–141, 157–58, 165, 167–68, 176, 180, 181, 191–92, 203, 211–12, 213n9, 216–17, 218–222, 224, 226, 228, 231–35, 231, 241–44, 246, 247, 250, 254, 255, 256n6, 257n12, 261–66, 267n3
humanities, 1–2, 4, 6, 9, 11–14, 20–21, 24, 25, 28, 28n1, 28n2, 28n5, 28–29n6, 29n7, 30n16, 32n26, 33n38, 33–34n39, 35–36n36, 57, 79, 91n5, 93, 95, 97–98, 100, 107, 108, 113, 116n17, 135, 139, 143, 262–63, 266

Idealism, Idealist (philosophy), 16, 22, 25, 27, 32n26, 35n51, 35n54, 89, 93, 99, 114n1, 115n13, 116n21, 122, 134–35, 138, 140, 141, 144–45, 156, 159n2, 164–65, 167–69, 172, 176, 177n3, 178n6, 180, 181, 187, 192n1, 192n2, 197, 200, 202, 207, 212, 216, 217, 226, 241, 242, 244, 246, 249–51, 253, 254–55, 256n6, 257n10, 258n16, 259n26
idealization, 16, 26, 80, 134, 150, 164, 168, 170–72, 176, 180–81, 183, 194n14, 198, 205, 206–208, 212, 221, 254, 261, 267n3
identity, 5, 15, 29n10, 42, 61, 63, 68–70, 72, 112, 130, 132–33, 142, 158–59, 159n2, 160n11, 166, 168, 171, 173–74, 176, 195n28, 202, 214n11, 214n14, 214n15, 219, 223, 236n12, 237n16, 252, 254, 258n21
ideological, ideology, 3, 5–6, 7, 11, 13, 17, 19, 20, 24, 27, 29n10, 30n16, 30n18, 38, 66, 67, 73, 74, 77n27, 81, 95, 112, 117n27, 122, 124, 126, 129, 130, 132, 135, 136n12, 137n16, 155, 167, 168, 176, 177n4, 178n6, 191–92, 194n12, 212, 216–20, 224, 226–28, 232–35, 236n9, 239–41, 261, 262, 263, 265, 266
Illuminaten, Illuminatendebatte, Illuminati, 66, 74, 77n23
imagery, 6, 21, 22, 24, 25, 36, 38, 41, 42, 48, 49, 61, 72, 74, 97, 102, 113, 117n23, 117n28, 139, 147
individual, individual autonomy, individuality, 2, 4–5, 6, 7, 8, 9–10, 13–16, 17, 19, 20, 23, 25, 27, 28n3, 37–38, 40, 41, 44–48, 51n6, 57, 58, 60–61, 64, 66–67, 69, 70, 71, 72, 73, 74, 77n27, 80, 82–83, 86–88, 89, 95, 96, 97–98, 100–101, 106, 107, 110–13, 114n4, 115n9, 116n16, 116n18, 116n20, 120, 122, 124, 128, 129, 132–34, 136n11, 138, 140, 148, 153–55, 158–59, 160n14, 163n26, 165, 167, 168, 175–76, 177n3, 177n5, 178n6, 180, 183–88, 190–91, 198–200, 203, 211–212, 219–220, 221, 222, 224, 225–26, 228, 231, 235, 237n17, 240, 241–44, 245–46, 247, 250, 256n5, 258n14, 256n16, 259n27, 261, 265
industrial age, industrialization, 165, 168, 176, 181, 231
Innerlichkeit, 15, 219

instincts, instinctual, 5, 16, 26–27, 58–60, 64, 68, 69, 95, 98, 106, 116n20, 116n21, 120, 121, 132, 158, 168–69, 177n5, 178n6, 180, 183–84, 189, 191, 193n7, 196n30, 197–98, 200, 202–204, 207, 208, 210–212, 213n8, 214n13, 225, 227, 242, 243, 245–48, 251–53, 257n13, 261, 262, 264
intellectual, 3, 4, 5, 12, 15–16, 24, 33n35, 34n42, 37, 40, 44, 45, 48, 49, 56, 60, 64, 69, 71, 72, 73, 74, 76n11, 90, 93, 94, 120, 121, 122, 128, 135, 144, 154, 162n18, 163n27, 168, 178n6, 180, 183, 200, 202, 216, 217, 222–23, 226–27, 233, 238, 241, 245, 246–47, 248, 251, 259n22
Irmscher, Hans-Dietrich, 99, 101, 115n9, 118n32, 277
irony, ironic, 26, 89, 165, 167–71, 176, 181, 190, 206, 215n18, 217, 218, 220, 222–23, 227–28, 233–35, 241, 242, 246–47, 252, 254, 255, 257n12, 260n32, 265
irritation (*Reiz*), 102–106, 109
Israel, Jonathan, 8, 30n14, 31n21, 34n46, 277
Israelites, 45- 47, 53n30, 74

Jaeger, Werner, 17, 277
Jaspers, Karl, 18, 19, 277
Jay, Martin, 164, 177n2, 277
Johnson, Mark, 23–24, 25, 36n60, 93–94, 121, 135–36n4, 136n7, 136n9, 277, 279
Jung, Carl Gustav, 198, 244, 246, 250, 259n25, 259n26

Kafka, Franz, 16, 213n4, 213n10, 214n11, 214n15, 267n2
Kant, Immanuel, 8–10, 14, 21, 25, 30n16, 31n2, 32n28, 59, 64, 80, 82–84, 89, 90n1, 92n8, 92n11, 93–94, 100, 103, 105, 110, 115n12, 116n19, 116n22, 116–17n23, 117n26, 117n28, 118n3, 136n11, 154, 162n24, 164–65, 167, 172, 219, 221, 251, 256n6, 257n10, 278

Keller, Gottfried, 164, 167, 168, 170, 173, 174, 178n8, 178n9, 178n10, 217, 278
"Kleider machen Leute" ("Clothes Make People"), 26, 164–77
Klages, Ludwig, 141
Klimt, Gustav, 188–89, 195n26
Klinger, Cornelia, 83, 278
Knodt, Eva, 100, 117n24, 278
Koenen, Gerd, 20, 278
Koepke, Wulf, 114n3, 115n13, 117n28, 180, 268, 278–79
Kontje, Todd, 10, 11, 217, 236n5, 236n7, 236n9, 279
Kraushaar, Wolfgang, 20, 279, 280
Kurzke, Hermann, 219–20, 224, 236n6, 236n7

Lakoff, George, 23–24, 36n60, 136n9, 279
Lamarck, Jean-Baptiste, 22, 154
La Mettrie, Julien Offray de, 99
landscape painting (*Landschaftsmalerei*), 138, 140, 141, 150–51, 153, 157–58, 159
Lange, Sigrid, 10, 32n28, 279
language, 3, 11, 22, 24, 50n3, 101–107, 112–13, 115n9, 115n13, 116n20, 119–23, 126, 135–36n4, 142, 151, 192, 193n9, 200, 239, 265, 267n4
 artificial, 17, 136n7, 200, 239
 critical, 11, 135–36n4
 metaphoric, pictorial, 22, 23, 47, 54n31, 56, 62, 70, 72, 97, 112, 117n28, 136n7, 151
 poetic, 11, 21, 23, 24, 47, 97–98, 113, 151, 239, 265
 scientific, 90, 100, 200
 stylized, 119, 122–23, 126, 127–28
 theory of, 101–107, 112, 115n9, 115n13, 116n20, 136n7, 267n4
La Roche, Sophie von, 10, 33n35
Lauretis, Teresa de, 95
Lavater, Johann Kaspar, 30n18, 31n20, 154, 162n24, 237n20
Lehleiter, Christine, 121, 279
Lehnert, Herbert, 218, 220, 280
Leibniz, Gottfried Wilhelm, 50n4, 98, 99, 100, 117n26

Le Rider, Jacques, 205, 214n11, 215n21, 280
Lessing, Gotthold Ephraim, 5, 23, 24, 33n34, 39, 40–42, 44–46, 48, 49–50, 51n5, 51n8, 51n9, 51n10, 52n14, 52n15, 52n16, 52n18, 52n19, 52n22, 52n23, 52n25, 53n28, 53n29, 54n31, 54n34, 54n35, 56, 57, 58, 60, 61, 62, 63, 66, 67, 72, 74, 76n11, 121, 136n6, 140, 158, 162n18, 163n26, 179, 251, 261, 264, 265, 280
   Erziehung des Menschengeschlechts (Education of the Human Race), 24, 37, 39, 40–50, 50n2, 50n4, 51n6, 51n8, 52n12, 52n25, 53n27, 53n28, 61, 62, 63, 74, 76n11, 259n27
liberal arts (*die schönen Wissenschaften*), 1, 2, 28n4, 57, 79
life sciences, 13, 21, 27, 36n57, 38, 121, 138, 158, 159n1, 161n15, 178n6, 197, 198, 266, 267n1
Linnaeus, Carl, 116n21, 154
Lotze, Rudolph Hermann, 198–99
Lützeler, Paul Michael, 12, 280
Luther, Martin, 14, 15, 50n4, 82, 219, 221, 237n15

Mádl, Antal, 226
Maier, Hans Albert, 17–18, 280
Mann, Bonnie, 82, 83, 280
Mann, Heinrich, 221, 224, 236n10
Mann, Thomas, 216–235
   Adel des Geistes (Nobility of Spirit), 217, 236n3, 280
   Betrachtungen eines Unpolitischen (Reflections of an Unpolitical Man), 218, 220, 224, 231, 233–34
   Der Zauberberg (The Magic Mountain), 226–35
   Deutschland und die Demokratie (Germany and Democracy), 232, 234
   "Ein Appell an die Vernunft" ("An Appeal to Reason"), 233–34
   "Friederich und die Große Koalition" ("Frederic and the Great Coalition"), 218
   "Für das neue Deutschland" ("In Favor of the New Germany"), 225
   "Gedanken im Kriege" ("Thoughts during War"), 218
   "Gute Feldpost" ("Good News from the Trenches"), 218
   "Lübeck als geistige Lebensform" ("Lübeck as a Spiritual Way of Life"), 232–33
   Tonio Kröger, 222–26, 227
   "Von deutscher Republik" ("Concerning a German Republic"), 224–27, 229
   "Zuspruch" ("Encouragement"), 225
Marcuse, Herbert, 19, 267n3, 280
Marx, Karl, Marxism, 19, 26, 164–66, 167, 171, 173, 177n2, 177n4, 179n13, 243, 266, 281
materialism, materialist, 16, 21, 26, 104, 115n12, 117n26, 117n27, 164–65, 167–68, 172, 175, 176, 213n7
Mayer, Mathias, 204, 281
McCarthy, John A., 8, 28n3, 35n55, 50n1, 77n27, 281
McNeely, Ian, 9, 281
medical, medicine, 21, 60, 95, 103, 114n5, 140, 143, 161n14, 228, 230
Meinecke, Friedrich, 224
Menschlichkeit (humaneness), 114n8, 124, 134, 142, 198, 226, 232, 235
Merleau-Ponty, Maurice, 32n26, 35n56, 36n60, 53n28, 54n31, 281
metaphor, metaphorical, 6, 21–24, 25, 36n57, 36n60, 38, 40, 41–44, 47–49, 53n28, 54n31, 54n33, 57, 58, 60, 61–63, 74, 77n24, 79, 97, 100, 103, 105–106, 108–109, 112, 117n23, 127, 131, 136n7, 139, 148, 158, 179n14, 202, 207, 211, 215n17, 228, 242, 244, 248, 254, 265
metempsychosis, 40, 49, 54n32
Metzinger, Thomas, 25, 36n57, 96, 98, 107–112, 114n6, 114n7, 265, 281
Meyer, Conrad Ferdinand, 217
Middle Ages, 50n3, 221
middle class, 9, 15, 120, 155, 158, 165, 176, 177, 180, 181, 183, 186, 212, 222, 231, 246
Miles, David, 203, 204, 213n10, 214n13, 215n20, 282

mind, 21, 22, 43, 56, 58, 61, 71, 80, 89, 100, 109, 112, 115n13, 142, 145, 156, 185, 193n7, 199, 217, 229, 232, 246
mind-body dualism, 3, 27, 60, 63, 75n7, 77n27, 93–94, 96, 101, 103–104, 107, 109, 117n25, 120–22, 123, 135, 135n3, 136n8, 136n9, 157, 159n1, 167, 168, 171, 177n5, 180, 198, 202–204, 222, 230, 242–45, 247–48, 254–55, 256n6, 257n10, 257n14, 259n24, 261, 265
modernity, 29n12, 188, 216, 251
monism, monistic, 26, 157, 198–200, 203, 245–46, 250, 257n14
monotheism, monotheistic, 45, 47, 54n32, 61–64, 66–69, 71–74, 76n18, 173, 179n12
Moran, Dermot, 32, 282
Moritz, Karl Philipp, 90n1, 143, 193n10
morphology, morphological, 142–44, 148, 161n16, 161–62n18, 244, 257n11
Moses, 40, 61–74, 76n19, 77–78n28, 264
Mukherjee, Ankhi, 12, 33n37, 282
Müller-Seidel, Walter, 77n21, 282
Müller-Tamm, Jutta, 114n1, 138, 139, 141, 143, 159n2, 160n11, 282

narcissism, narcissist, 80–81, 83, 87, 88–89, 92n11, 178n6, 214n14
narrative, 23, 24, 27, 40, 44, 54n32, 55–57, 73, 104, 174–75, 197, 202, 205, 206–207, 211, 230, 235, 241, 242–44, 252, 254, 259n27, 263
nationalism, nationalist, 5, 18, 20, 27, 73, 170, 218, 225, 226, 227, 231, 233, 234, 237n16, 239, 256n2, 264, 265
National Socialism, National Socialists, Nazi, 5, 8, 17, 18, 19, 20, 126, 160n9, 227
natura naturans, 145, 150
nature, 10, 12, 17, 21, 23, 28n3, 49, 59, 61, 63, 71, 72, 81–84, 89–90, 91n5, 100, 102, 105, 106, 107–108, 110–111, 116n21, 118n31, 118n35, 119, 122, 123, 127, 130, 135n1, 136n8, 145–50, 154–57, 159, 160n12, 164–65, 185, 189, 193n7, 195–96n30, 198–99, 233, 253, 257–58n14, 265, 267n4
animal, 58, 60, 74, 116n21, 122, 202–203, 206–212, 242, 247, 249, 252
and art, 59, 82–83, 92n11, 94, 100, 145–53, 157–59, 162n21, 162n22, 163n28
human, 5, 6, 8, 14, 16, 21, 25, 26–27, 28n3, 32n27, 32n28, 35n50, 46, 56–57, 58, 59, 60, 64, 66, 73, 80, 83, 84, 92n11, 95, 97, 99, 100, 105, 107–108, 110–113, 120, 122, 123, 145–50, 156–57, 158, 167, 168, 178n11, 181, 184, 202–203, 206–212, 221, 228, 235, 237n15, 239, 240, 242, 245, 246, 251, 252, 253, 255, 262, 264–66
philosophy of (*Naturphilosophie*), 26, 94, 99, 102, 103, 105, 113–14n1, 122, 138–45, 154–59, 159n2, 160n11, 161n14, 162n20, 162n27, 177n3, 181, 184, 198–200, 217, 245, 258n18
representation of, 94, 99, 100, 106, 110, 150–53, 157–59, 160n10, 181, 184, 193n7, 195–96n30, 206–208
Naturwissenschaft (natural science), *naturwissenschaftlich*, 33n39, 89, 91n5, 142, 197–98, 230
Nayar, Pramod K., 7, 282
neoclassical, 15, 18, 59, 119–24, 126, 134–35, 153
neo-humanism (*Neuhumanismus*), 1, 9, 11, 13–14, 16, 21, 32n27, 33n32, 72, 126, 140, 167, 168, 212, 222, 228, 232, 256n6, 261–62, 265–66
neo-Marxism, neo-Marxist, 5, 7, 19, 177n2
neuroscience, neuroscientific, 25, 36n57, 95, 96–97, 108, 110–111, 121, 135n4, 136n9, 265
Niethammer, Friedrich Immanuel, 14–15
Nietzsche, Friedrich, 16, 25, 107, 216, 217, 218, 219, 226, 243, 244, 246, 248, 250, 256n2, 258n16, 258n17, 259n26, 260n33, 264, 266, 283

300 ⁓ Index

Nisbet, H. B., 42, 48, 51n6, 52n18, 52n22, 53n27, 54n31, 54n34, 283
nostalgia, 26, 164, 165, 266
Novalis, Georg Philipp Friedrich Freiherr von, 94, 214n15, 225, 226, 229, 237n17

Oakeshott, Michael, 39
objectification, 26, 91n2, 164, 170, 171, 173, 174, 179n30, 190, 230
objective, objectivity, 7, 12, 13, 23, 24, 25, 32n26, 36n59, 38, 41, 44, 56, 63, 78n28, 79–80, 83, 87, 89–90, 94, 97–98, 104, 112–13, 121, 132, 142, 157, 158–59, 163n27, 165, 178n11, 197, 200, 213n8, 230, 244, 254
Oken, Lorenz, 94, 138, 144, 160–61n14
ontogenesis, ontogeny, 51n6, 109–10, 116n19, 148, 150, 155, 161n15, 198, 250, 259n27
Ossar, Michael, 183, 194n17, 283

pantheism, pantheistic, 26, 44, 76n11, 99, 103, 113n1, 135n1, 136n8, 138, 145, 147, 160n11, 177n3, 199–200
parable, parabolic, 38, 42, 47, 53n28, 60, 108
pathos, 58, 85, 180–81, 183–84, 187–88, 192, 193n5, 193n6, 193n7, 193n9, 195n25
patriarchal, patriarchy, 5, 9, 10, 17, 20, 32n29, 33n34, 116n18
pedagogical, pedagogy, 23, 24, 37, 38, 41–42, 46, 49, 52n25, 53n58, 62, 70, 77n26, 123, 140, 151, 157, 256n3, 264, 265
perception, 22–24, 38, 40, 41, 49, 54n31, 63, 77n27, 81, 89–90, 92n12, 93, 102, 109, 110, 111, 118n31, 135n4, 144, 145, 151, 153, 197, 199, 200, 207, 210, 212, 230, 247, 250, 251, 265
phenomenal self-model (PSM), 96, 108–112
phenomenological, phenomenology, 32n26, 35n56, 36n60, 50, 96, 161n15
philosophical, 2, 9, 10, 13, 16, 18, 23, 25, 26, 27, 30n16, 33n33, 33n39, 37, 38, 39, 44, 56, 58, 60–61, 64, 67, 81, 91, 93, 94, 97, 98, 100, 105, 107, 108, 113n1, 117n26, 117n27, 117n29, 120, 121, 122, 124, 136n11, 139–41, 143, 145, 153, 155, 157, 158, 160, 160n9, 161n15, 162n20, 163n27, 164–65, 167, 168, 177n3, 178n3, 178n6, 198, 215n16, 216–217, 220, 221, 239, 240–41, 242, 244, 248, 251, 261, 262, 263, 265, 267n1
philosophische Ärzte, 60, 143
philosophy, 26, 35n54, 38, 59, 60, 77n27, 93, 98, 103, 107, 111, 115n13, 113n1, 117n29, 128, 164–65, 172, 177n3, 199–200, 203, 226, 227–28, 230, 246, 259n26
  of history, 32n28, 50n2, 50–51n4, 98–99, 101, 105, 110, 117n23, 179n14, 135n1
  of nature (*Naturphilosophie*), 26, 138–45, 153–157, 158, 160–61n14, 168, 213n7
physiognomic(s), physiognomy, 30n18, 141–42, 153–56, 159, 160n9, 162n24, 163n26, 219, 230–31, 237n20, 237n21
physiological, physiology, 38, 60, 94, 97, 103, 108, 112, 138, 140, 159n1, 161n14, 200, 230
Pietist, 15
Pikulik, Lothar, 236n10, 283
plant(s), 99, 104, 110, 147–49, 157–58
Plant, Sadie, 95–96, 284
Platner, Ernst, 99, 143, 284
Plato, (Neo)platonic, (Neo)platonism, 22, 80, 89, 108, 109–10, 120, 168, 213n10, 219, 229, 264
poet, 7, 35n50, 64, 92n14, 101, 128–29, 136n12, 192n2, 225, 229, 237n15, 237n17
poetic language, imagery, 6, 22, 23, 24, 25, 36n57, 38, 40, 41–44, 46–48, 57, 60, 61, 63, 66, 70, 96–98, 102, 105, 106–107, 109, 112–13, 115n9, 116–17n23, 143, 148, 150, 156, 162n23, 172, 249, 265–66
poetry, 22, 92n7, 117n24, 136n5, 162n23, 193n6, 213n2

polysemous, polysemy, 4, 11, 12, 38, 41, 47, 49, 54n31, 74, 81, 124, 126, 135
Popularphilosophie (empirical philosophy), 60, 93
postcolonial, postcolonialism, postcolonialist, 1, 2–3, 6, 7, 31n24, 126
posthuman, 7, 29n10, 112
posthumanism, posthumanist, 6–9, 11–12, 19, 25, 27–28, 28n2, 28n3, 29n8, 29n9, 29n10, 29n12, 30n16, 31n21, 32n26, 32n27, 34n42, 35n52, 40, 93, 95, 97, 107–108, 110, 112, 118n33, 134, 135, 235, 238, 241–44, 250, 255, 257n12, 261, 263–64, 267n1
post-Marxism, post-Marxist, 2, 19
postmodern, postmodernism, postmodernist, 2, 3, 6, 7, 35n56, 257n12
poststructuralism, poststructuralist, 2, 6
postwar, 18–20, 35n50, 35n51, 124–26, 134, 137n13, 239
preconscious, 36n60, 155, 156, 158, 200, 213n8
Protestant, 14, 82, 219, 246
psyche, 16, 60, 155–57, 159n1, 183, 190, 246, 247
psychoanalysis, 19, 211
psychological, psychology, 23, 68, 71, 73, 80, 90n1, 91n5, 95, 103, 106, 128, 129, 140, 141, 143, 240, 244

race, racial, racism, racist, 5, 6–8, 18, 26, 30n18, 36n58, 40, 46–47, 50n4, 51n6, 74, 95, 116n20, 120, 141–42, 153–56, 158, 160n9, 161n15, 162n25, 168, 219, 230, 237n21, 259n22, 261, 263, 265
rational, rationalism, rationalist, 5, 7, 14, 22, 24, 31n19, 31n20, 36n60, 38, 39, 40, 41, 48, 49, 54n31, 54n32, 57, 63, 68, 73, 80, 87, 92n11, 98, 99–100, 105, 111, 112–13, 120, 122–23, 141–42, 191, 197, 198, 202, 207, 211, 212, 213n5, 213n8, 218, 224, 226, 227–28, 231, 233–34, 241, 242–43, 244, 253, 256n3, 261, 266, 267n4

reason, 19, 21, 30n17, 30n19, 34n45, 37–49, 51n9, 52n25, 53n30, 54n32, 54n32, 57, 59, 60, 61, 63–64, 66, 67, 69–75, 82, 86, 89, 91n2, 95, 97, 100, 105, 107, 111, 114n4, 116n21, 118n31, 121–22, 126, 136n11, 160n10, 184, 190, 191, 212, 219, 228, 243, 252
Reill, Peter H., 75n7, 284
Reimarus, Johann Albert, 51n5, 52n18
Reimarus, Samuel, 41, 51n5, 51n8, 51n9, 51n10, 52n14
Reinhold, Karl Leonhard, 61, 64, 76n15, 284
Reiz (Irritation, stimulus, attraction, life energy), 102–105, 106, 109, 117n27
religion, religious, 1, 4, 5, 6, 13, 14, 16, 22, 38, 39, 41–46, 51n8, 51n10, 52n14, 52n21, 52n24, 53n28, 55, 61, 64–75, 76n18, 76n19, 91n5, 97, 107, 110, 117n27, 127, 133, 145, 150, 168, 173, 177n3, 178n11, 178–79n12, 187, 194n19, 195n23, 211, 213n6, 221, 230, 231, 233, 240, 263
Renaissance, 9, 13, 124, 128, 129, 262
res cogitans vs. *res extensa*, 200
revelation (*Offenbarung*), 39–40, 42, 43–49, 51n10, 52n25, 53n28, 53n30, 54n31, 63, 70, 82
Richter, Simon, 103, 117n27, 284
Riedel, Wolfgang, 60, 77n27, 117n25, 143, 198, 199, 200, 202, 213n4, 213n6, 284
Rigby, Kate, 145, 285
Ritter, Joachim, 150, 285
Roman, 5, 14, 28n4, 92n12, 116n18, 129, 221, 222, 264
Romantic, Romanticism, 5, 15–16, 26, 138, 141, 143, 144, 145, 154, 156, 157, 159, 159n2, 165–68, 170–72, 174–77, 180, 183, 185–88, 190–91, 194n19, 198, 210–12, 213n5, 213n7, 214n13, 214n15, 217, 218, 224–26, 227, 231, 237n17, 244, 251, 254n12
Rousseau, Jean Jacques, 34n42, 116n20, 224, 237n15, 258n18
Rychner, Max, 18

Safranski, Rüdiger, 77n27, 128, 285
Said, Edward, 1, 3–4, 7, 22, 28n2, 285
Salomé, Lou Andreas, 16
Sanders, Helke, 20, 285
Scaglione, Aldo, 14, 34n42, 285
Schelling, F. W. J, 76n11, 91n4, 94, 114n1, 138, 142, 143–45, 156, 158, 159n2, 160n11, 160–61n14, 213n7
Schiller, Fr., 8, 9, 14, 15, 21, 24, 25, 26, 31n20, 35n54, 55–75, 76n18, 76n20, 77n23, 77n26, 77n27, 80–81, 84, 86–90, 90n1, 92n13, 92n14, 92n15, 117n25, 120, 121, 124, 126, 133, 137n16, 137n17, 137n19, 140, 142, 143, 144, 153, 158, 163n26, 167, 168, 180, 183–85, 188, 192n1, 192n2, 193n5, 193n7, 193n9, 193n10, 194n16, 217, 224, 251, 253, 256n6, 261, 263, 285
Briefe über Don Carlos (*Letters on Don Carlos*), 66, 76n17, 81
Die Räuber (*The Robbers*), 72, 77n24, 81, 84–87
"Die Sendung Moses" ("Legation of Moses"), 61–75, 77n28
Die Verschwörung des Fiesco zu Genua (*Fiesco's Conspiracy at Genoa*), 77n28
Don Karlos, 16, 30n19, 81, 84, 87–88, 92n15, 136n6
Geschichte des Abfalls der vereinigten Niederlande on der spanischen Regierung (*History of the Revolt of the United Netherlands against Spanish Rule*), 66
Kabale und Liebe (*Intrigue and Love*), 77n24, 136n5, 136n6, 180–83, 185, 187, 192n3, 192n4, 193n11, 194n17, 195n23
"Philosophie der Physiologie" (Philosophy of Physiology), 77n27
"Über das Erhabene" ("On the Sublime"), 81
"Über das Pathetische" ("On the Melodramatic"), 181
"Über naïve und sentimentale Dichtung" ("On Naïve and Sentimental Poetry"), 183–85
Universalgeschichte (*Universal History*), 24, 36n58, 37, 39–40, 50n2, 55–61, 75n3, 76n13, 76n15, 76n16, 77n22, 77n24, 77n25
"Vom Erhabenen" ("Of the Sublime"), 81, 92n8
Schilson, Arno, 42, 44, 50n4, 52n17, 285
Schings, Hans-Jürgen, 66, 76n18, 77n23, 285
Schlözer, August Ludwig, 75n3, 117n28, 285
Schnitzler, Arthur, 16, 26, 183–91, 194n17, 212, 266, 286
Liebelei, 26, 180–81, 183–91, 192n4, 194n14, 194n17, 194n18, 196n29, 195–96n30, 212
Scholes, Robert, 4, 28n2, 36n56, 286
Schopenhauer, Arthur, 198, 200, 203, 213n4, 213n8, 217, 218
Schorske, Carl, 183, 195n26, 286
Schubert, Franz, 180, 188, 189, 195n26
Schulphilosophie, 105, 111, 117n29
Schulz, Karlheinz, 128, 286
science, sciences, scientific, 2, 5–6, 8–9, 12, 13, 15, 16, 20–28, 30n16, 30n18, 32n26, 33–34n39, 35n56, 36n57, 37–38, 39, 44, 56, 57, 60, 66, 75n7, 75n8, 79–80, 89–90, 91n5, 94–98, 99–100, 102, 104–105, 106, 107, 108, 110–113, 115n9, 116n17, 121–24, 135n4, 136n9, 138–45, 146–47, 150–51, 153–59, 159n1, 160n11, 160n12, 160n13, 161n15, 162n23, 168, 178n6, 197, 198–200, 213n2, 213n5, 213n6, 213n7, 229, 230, 232–33, 246–47, 250, 261, 265–66, 267n1
Scythian, 119
self, 21, 33n22, 52n19, 63, 79, 80, 81, 83, 90, 90n1, 91n6, 92n11, 96, 97, 106, 108–113, 132, 157, 172, 210–11, 240, 244, 248, 249, 258n16, 259n25
self-control, self-discipline, 59, 121, 123, 132, 183, 211, 219
self-determination, 9, 20, 37, 60, 70, 109, 121, 123–24, 134, 138, 155, 174, 177, 181, 185, 186, 200, 245, 265

self-improvement, 16, 43, 95, 155, 207, 211–12, 264
self-interrogation, self-examination, 14, 80, 107
self-model theory (SMT), 96, 108–13, 114n7, 118n34
self-perfection, 1, 9, 21, 27, 46, 48, 202, 224, 234, 241
self-reflection, 37, 48, 82, 176, 106, 110, 124, 126, 128, 132, 158–59, 242–43, 248, 257n12, 266
self-tutelage, 4, 49, 203, 264
sensate, sensations, 21–22, 49, 54n31, 74, 89, 90, 91n2, 94, 96, 102–103, 197, 200
senses, 46, 48, 56, 58, 61, 63, 64, 70–71, 74, 82, 84, 91n5, 92n9, 94, 99, 101–107, 111–12, 123, 145, 157, 162n22, 181, 199, 205, 247, 258n19, 261
sensibilities, 13, 38, 79, 81, 91n2, 91n3, 92n11, 103, 128, 143, 150, 157, 205, 213n10, 226, 264–65
sensorium, sensory, sensuous, 6, 22–23, 25, 36n57, 38, 39, 40, 47–49, 53n28, 54, 54n35, 56, 60, 62, 63, 66, 74, 77n27, 81, 82, 93–94, 96, 101–102, 104–107, 108, 110–112, 118n31, 121, 158, 160n10, 162n18, 172, 199–200, 203, 204, 222, 265
sensual, sensuality, 5, 25, 45, 60, 62, 63, 68, 71, 74, 77n26, 80, 83–84, 90, 97, 110–11, 138, 144, 179n13, 181, 184, 204, 246–50, 259n24
Shakespere, 35n50, 120, 177n3
Sieburg, Friedrich, 18, 286
sign, signification, signifier, 37, 43–44, 46, 62, 70–72, 74, 144, 155, 161n18, 170, 172, 173, 174, 178n9, 200, 230, 258n21
Sloterdijk, Peter, 28, 29n13, 35n51, 95, 156, 263–64, 286
Soper, Kate, 8, 286
specialization, 20–21, 39, 95, 140, 144, 178, 200, 263
Spranger, Eduard, 17–18, 34n47, 286
Sprengel, Peter, 198, 286
species, 37, 39, 46, 48, 49, 50n2, 51n6, 59, 64, 95, 99, 106, 108, 111, 116n21, 120–21, 153–55, 157, 161n15, 163n28, 167–68, 183, 198, 200, 246, 250, 253, 257n14, 258n17, 264
Stein, Charlotte von, 128
stimulus, stimuli, 47, 49, 53n28, 74, 77n27, 102–103, 108–110, 144, 155
Storm, Theodor, 214n15, 217
Sturm und Drang, 79, 119–20, 128, 136n5, 136n12, 163n26, 219
subconscious, 25, 38, 139, 156, 197, 198, 208, 213n5, 215n23, 228, 242–43
subject, 3, 6, 7–8, 14, 20, 23, 25, 30n19, 31n21, 31n22, 34n42, 35n54, 48, 79, 80, 82–83, 87, 89, 92n11, 95–96, 97, 98, 101, 105–106, 107–108, 109–110, 112–13, 116n16, 120, 121, 129, 132–33, 138–39, 142, 143, 145, 148, 150, 154, 155, 157, 159, 161n14, 161n15, 162n22, 163n26, 165, 166–67, 168, 170, 171, 173–75, 178n6, 183, 199, 202–203, 211–12, 214n15, 230, 242–43, 246, 250, 252, 253, 255, 259n24, 261, 265, 267n1
subjective, subjectivist, subjectivity, 7, 13, 21, 23, 24–25, 31n22, 34n42, 39, 43, 53n28, 56, 57, 63, 79- 81, 87, 89, 91n2, 91n4, 94, 96, 97, 98, 102, 104, 106, 108–110, 111–13, 115n9, 116n16, 121, 138, 143, 153, 157, 165, 178n11, 197, 199–200, 203, 215n22, 241
subject-object relations, 23, 132, 164, 168, 171, 173, 177n5
sublime, sublimity, 25, 79–90, 91n2, 92n9, 92n11, 150, 177n5, 181, 183–84, 193n11, 258n20, 264
Süßmann, Johannes, 76n13, 287

taxonomic, taxonomy, 26, 111, 116n21, 141, 144, 154, 159
Tolstoy, Leo, 217, 227, 237n15
Toulmin, Stephen, 22, 287
totality, 56–57, 63, 67, 94, 97, 102–103, 105, 107, 113n1, 143, 144, 150–51, 157
Trabant, Jürgen, 101, 287
tragedy, 88, 180, 183, 188, 191, 193n5, 193n6, 194n15, 194n17, 195n25

transcendental, 111, 115n13, 118n30, 133, 170, 187, 259n26
Trop, Gabriel, 29n8, 29n12, 31n21, 279

universal, universalism, 1, 2–3, 4–8, 13, 15, 17, 18, 20, 21, 23–24, 25, 31n21, 31n24, 56, 62, 64, 66, 67, 69, 70, 72, 75n3, 80, 83, 89, 94–95, 98, 99, 101, 102, 103, 105, 110, 112, 117n24, 118n30, 119, 121–124, 141, 143, 145, 153, 162n20, 163n27, 173, 177n3, 191, 200, 221, 231, 237n17, 240, 242, 253, 254
universal history (*Universalgeschichte*), 14, 21, 24, 36n58, 37–50, 50n2, 51n9, 55–75, 75n3, 76n16, 157, 259n27, 259n28, 265
Unzer, Johann August, 143, 287
Urpflanze (primordial plant), 147–48, 149

Venunftrepublikaner, 224
Vernunft. See reason
Vernunftreligion, 39, 41, 61, 64, 67, 70, 73
Vernunftwahrheiten, 49
Vienna (fin-de-siècle), 186, 189, 195n27, 214n11
Vienna Congress, 15
Virgil, 129
vitalist, 16, 75n7, 103, 117n26, 240

Wagner, Irmgard, 124, 125, 126, 128, 136n12, 137n13, 288
Waldby, Catherine, 95, 114n5, 288
Walser, Martin, 125–26, 137n15, 137n20, 288
Warburton, William, 44–45, 52n24, 52n25, 61–62, 76n10, 76n11
Weatherby, Leif, 29n8, 29n12, 31n21, 118n33, 279
Wedekind, Frank, 16, 192, 194n15, 288

Weimar classicism, 77n21, 124–26, 128, 137n13, 266
Weimar Republic, 18, 19, 27, 34n48, 160n9, 216, 223, 224, 226, 230–33
Wellbery, David, 136n5, 288
western, 3–9, 14, 18–20, 22, 26, 30n15, 31n20, 31n24, 34n42, 35n50, 36n58, 56, 74, 97, 112, 116n21, 154, 159, 164, 177n5, 178n6, 178n8, 219, 222, 224, 226, 231–35, 237n16, 263, 265
Westling, Louise, 32n26, 288
Whimster, Sam, 22, 288
White, Hayden, 38–39, 72n2, 271, 288
Whitman, Walt, 225, 226, 229
Widdig, Bernd, 168, 170, 176, 178n8, 288
Wiese, Benno von, 18
Wilhelminian, 216, 217
Winckelmann, Johann Joachim, 15, 193n7, 263
Winter, Helga, 198, 289
Wittkowski, Wolfgang, 76n20, 289
Wölfel, Kurt, 76n20, 289
Wolfe, Cary, 8, 9, 29n9, 250, 258n15, 258n19, 289
Wolff, Caspar Friedrich, 135n3
Wolff, Christian, 51–52n11, 98, 100, 117n29
Wübben, Yvonne, 64, 66, 76n14, 76n15, 76n18, 289

Young, Robert, J. C., 7, 289

Zammito, John, 38, 103, 115n12, 116n19, 117n26, 117n27, 117n29, 118n30, 289
Zelle, Carsten, 60, 79, 81, 90n1, 289
Zimmermann, Johann Georg, 143
Ziolkowski, Theodore, 216, 217, 289
zoological, zoology, 138, 140, 158, 161n16
Zweig, Stefan, 16, 236n3, 237n16, 289

www.ingramcontent.com/pod-product-compliance
Lightning Source LLC
Chambersburg PA
CBHW050207130526
44590CB00043B/3051